VIRTUES & PRACTICES IN THE CHRISTIAN TRADITION

VIRTUES & PRACTICES IN THE CHRISTIAN TRADITION

Christian Ethics after MacIntyre

EDITED BY

Nancey Murphy
Brad J. Kallenberg
Mark Thiessen Nation

UNIVERSITY OF NOTRE DAME PRESS
Notre Dame, Indiana

Reprinted in 2003 by University of Notre Dame Press
Notre Dame, Indiana 46556
http://www.undpress.nd.edu

Manufactured in the United States of America

Library of Congress Cataloging-in-Publication Data
Virtues & practices in the Christian tradition : Christian ethics after MacIntyre / edited by Nancey Murphy, Brad J. Kallenberg & Mark Thiessen Nation.
p. cm.
Originally published: Harrisburg, Pa. : Trinity Press International, 1997.
Includes bibliographical references and index.
ISBN 0-268-04360-4 (alk. paper)
1. Christian ethics. 2. MacIntyre, Alasdair C.
I. Title: Virtues and practices in the Christian tradition.
II. Murphy, Nancey C. III. Kallenberg, Brad J. IV. Nation, Mark.

BJ1251 .V57 2003
241—dc21
2002041254

∞ *This book is printed on acid-free paper.*

For our children
André
Daniel, Philip, and Stephen
Christina and Michael
with our prayers that they will grow up
to embody the Christian virtues

Contents

Part III
PERSPECTIVES ON CONTEMPORARY ISSUES

Preface and Acknowledgments

Long before salad bars became chic on the west coast, quaint towns in the nordic Midwest (towns with names like Upsala) had "smörgåsbord" restaurants (with names like "The Sweden House") whose proprietors (with names like Törvald and Lena) offered a staggering cornucopia of sumptuous fare. Of course, you couldn't trust the children. Children are notoriously ill-equipped to be discerning when given their druthers between Lutefisk (a "savory" dish of cod aged in lye water) and Krumkaka (a Christmas dessert). Habits of taste have to be properly formed before children could be trusted to serve themselves — by which time, incidentally, the children will have children of their own.

In many ways this book expresses our deep misgivings about the "smörgåsbord" approach taken by so many introductory courses in ethics: bewildered students are forced to decide whether a single welfare mother pregnant with her ninth, possibly retarded, child "ought" to abort, or whether a terminal cancer patient, whose treatment has exceeded insurance benefits, has the "right" to die. One reason we are suspicious of the casebook pedagogy is the fact that novices must become apprentices before they can become masters. This present book was occasioned by the problem we faced as instructors: who are the master practitioners of Christian ethics under whose tutelage we can be apprenticed?

Influenced by our teacher James Wm. McClendon, Jr., we each taught ethics persuaded that Christian convictions make a difference: Christians do ethics in a Christianly way. In the process of sorting out just what this Christianly way was we stumbled upon the conceptual resources that Alasdair MacIntyre provided in his book *After Virtue.* We were initially attracted to MacIntyre's work not primarily because of his role in the renaissance of virtue ethics but, more significantly, for his nuanced exegesis of our post-critical philosophical situation. We admit rather sheepishly that our enthusiasm for MacIntyre's thinking originally bewitched us to see a *theory* of Christian ethics lurking in his writings — as if Christian ethics needed yet another philosophical theory! Simply put (and therein lay the danger), MacIntyre seemed to be saying that moral oughts can be deduced in a straightforward manner from the answer(s) historical traditions give to the question "What is human life for?" However, this way of putting it overlooked MacIntyre's deeper insight, namely, that each member of any (and all) traditions required lifelong *training* in order to see rightly just what the given tradition maintained to be the *telos* of human life.

Because ethics necessarily involves the cultivation of moral vision, this present book has evolved into something of a training manual aiming to make apprentices out of novices. MacIntyre's work proved to be particularly useful as it provided the vocabulary for getting a handle on the family resemblance shared by the ethicists we have collected in this volume. The first few chapters provide an overview of MacIntyre's seminal work, *After Virtue,* and discusses his "fit" in the conversation within Christian ethics. Part II offers a collection of essays highlighting some of the practices and virtues that are constitutive of the Christian church. These chapters aim at helping us remember who is the "we" who claim to be doing Christian ethics. Part III swims against the complaint that an ethics which is blatantly "Christian" threatens to be too tribalistic, too fideistic, and too ethnocentric. On the contrary, we have found Christian ethicists have much to say about contemporary moral conundrums both to the church (in which case their words are a form of discipleship) and to the world (in which case their words are an instance of witness). However, since hearing them rightly presumes the sorts of skills that Parts I and II aim at cultivating, we have placed this collection of essays at the end. Part III is capped by a short essay that describes, in retrospect, why Christian ethics is more like aesthetics than calculus.

As authors we owe much to many. We are thankful for the many bright theological students who, as our guinea pigs, waded through insufferable volumes of sometimes obscure readings and without whose encouragement this book would have likely been longer than it already is! We are particularly indebted for conversations with Alasdair MacIntyre, which clarified his thinking to us. Along the way James McClendon has been an unfailing model of both the practice and the preaching of Christian ethics. Terry Larm's fluency in the grammar of the English language as well as in the grammar of computers proved indispensable for the final version of this text. In addition, we offer thanks to Trinity Press for publishing this book and especially to Laura Barrett, Barbara Hofmaier, and John Eagleson for their patient work on our behalf.

Finally, we are grateful to the following publishers both for their wisdom in publishing these essays in the first place and for permission to reproduce them here.

•

Several chapters of the present work appeared in slightly different versions in earlier publications and are reprinted here with permission:

Chapter 4: James Wm. McClendon, Jr., chap. 8 of *Ethics: Systematic Theology, Volume I* (Nashville: Abingdon Press, 1986), 209–39.

Chapter 5: Stephen E. Fowl and L. Gregory Jones, "Reading in the Communion of Disciples: Learning to Become Wise Readers of Scripture," in *Reading in Communion: Scripture and Ethics in Christian Life* (Grand Rapids, Mich.: Wm. B. Eerdmans, 1991), 29–55.

Chapter 6: John Howard Yoder, "Binding and Loosing," in *The Royal Priesthood: Essays Ecclesiological and Ecumenical,* ed. Michael G. Cartwright (Grand Rapids, Mich.: Wm. B. Eerdmans, 1994), 325–58.

Chapter 7: Craig Dykstra, "Reconceiving Practice," in *Shifting Boundaries,* ed. Barbara G. Wheeler and Edward Farley (Louisville: Westminster John Knox Press, 1991), 35–66.

Chapter 9: Richard B. Hays, "Awaiting the Redemption of Our Bodies," *Sojourners* 20, no. 6 (1991): 17–21; Luke Timothy Johnson, "Debate and Discernment, Scripture and the Spirit," *Commonweal,* 29 January 1994, 11–13.

Chapter 10: Stanley Hauerwas, "Abortion Theologically Understood," in *The Church and Abortion,* ed. Paul T. Stallsworth (Nashville: Abingdon Press, 1993), 44–66.

Chapter 11: Grady Scott Davis, "Pacifism as a Vocation," in *Warcraft and the Fragility of Virtue: An Essay in Aristotelian Ethics* (Moscow: University of Idaho Press, 1992), 27–51.

Chapter 14: Michael Goldberg, "Corporate Culture and the Corporate Cult," in *Against the Grain: New Approaches to Professional Ethics,* ed. Michael Goldberg (Valley Forge, Pa.: Trinity Press International, 1993), 13–36.

Chapter 15: William F. May, "Code, Covenant, Contract, or Philanthropy," *Hastings Center Report* 5 (1975): 29–38.

Introduction

Nancey Murphy

The editors of this volume are unabashed fans of Alasdair MacIntyre. He has accomplished three things of great value to Christian ethicists. First, he has revived the *virtue* tradition of moral inquiry, thus offering to contemporary thinkers a fresh version of a venerable moral language. This is a welcome addition to the resources of modernity, where the focus has been on rights, consequences, and the autonomy of the individual. We believe that this new vocabulary, along with MacIntyre's account of the *structure* of moral reasoning, is especially helpful for Christian ethicists. It allows us to say the things we need to say about the shape of the Christian moral life, and in a way more intelligible to ourselves and to outsiders than the language of modern philosophical ethics allows.

Second, there has recently been a sea change in *Christian* ethics, due largely but not exclusively to the prolific Stanley Hauerwas. Hauerwas tends to talk about Christian morality in terms of *narratives* and *community, virtue* and *character.* Although Hauerwas is not a disciple of MacIntyre, we perceive that MacIntyre's contribution to the understanding of moral discourse *in general* — his revival of the virtue tradition, his critique of Enlightenment theories of ethics — will serve to order and interpret this new movement in Christian ethics. We include essays by a variety of thinkers here: James Wm. McClendon, Jr., Stephen E. Fowl and L. Gregory Jones, John Howard Yoder, Craig Dykstra, Rodney Clapp, Richard B. Hays, Luke Timothy Johnson, Grady Scott Davis, Stanley Hauerwas, Tammy Williams, Mark Thiessen Nation, Michael Goldberg, William F. May, and D. Stephen Long. This list includes Protestants from a variety of traditions and Catholics; some identifiable as liberal, some conservative; and one Conservative Jew. What all have in common is that their works illustrate and apply MacIntyrean patterns of moral reasoning. Thus, we claim that MacIntyre's theory helps make clear the structure and rationale of each essay.

Third, a major controversy in meta-ethics, that is, in thinking about *how* to think about morality, involves the issue of particularity. It was an assumption of modern philosophy that moral prescriptions or judgments needed to be *universal.* So the very notion of *Christian* ethics — ethics especially for Christians — became oxymoronic. Modern "Christian ethicists" (if we may use the term) tended to accept this assumption and made it their task to show Christian moral teaching to be merely an instance of a universal moral code, or to show that Christian moral claims could be justified by means of patterns of moral justification universally accepted, whether this be utilitarian or Kantian or social contractarian.

Against the universalists, MacIntyre argues that all ethical thought is indebted to some *particular* moral tradition — even the Enlightenment tradition of "traditionless reason"! The danger inherent in such a recognition, however, is moral relativism, that is, that there will be no way to justify any community's or tradition's moral reasoning in the (alleged) public forum. MacIntyre has complex and ingenious arguments to show that, despite the tradition-dependence of all specific moral arguments, it is nonetheless possible to make respectable public claims, showing one tradition of moral reasoning to be superior to its rivals. So here is one case where it is possible to have one's cake (one's particularity as a Christian) and eat it too (justify one's claims in public).

It is important to know about this third accomplishment, but our business in this book will not be to review MacIntyre's meta-ethical arguments.[1] Rather, we concentrate here on making available to the reader MacIntyre's contribution to philosophical ethics — his critique of Enlightenment presuppositions and his revival of the virtue tradition — and on illustrating and applying his proposals within the sphere of Christian ethics.

The book is divided into three parts. In Part I we describe MacIntyre's approach to ethics as developed in *After Virtue* (Chapter 1). Next, we speak in general ways about how MacIntyre's moral vocabulary and his understanding of moral justification apply to Christian morality (Chapter 2). Finally, we pay some attention to how MacIntyre's work relates to and contrasts with other current options in Christian ethics (Chapter 3).

In Part II we include essays that reflect the sorts of moral issues that come to the fore when we view the Christian tradition from a MacIntyrean perspective. Our observation is that the very content of Christian ethics tends to get co-opted by culture. That is, current issues in society at large (abortion, homosexuality, and so on) tend to set the agenda for Christian ethicists. This is not all wrong (and we devote the latter part of the book to such issues). However, we believe that MacIntyre's account of the structure of a tradition, with its practices, institutions, formative texts, and exemplary life stories, helps us to answer the questions: What are the issues at the *heart* of Christian moral concerns? How must the Christian community live *in order to be the church?* The central topic of Part II, which we take to constitute a partial answer to these questions, is the practice of *community formation.* Community formation, in turn, is

1. See *Whose Justice? Which Rationality?* (Notre Dame: University of Notre Dame Press, 1988), especially chaps. 1, 10, 18; and *Three Rival Versions of Moral Enquiry: Encyclopaedia, Genealogy, and Tradition* (Notre Dame: University of Notre Dame Press, 1989). For a summary, see Nancey Murphy, *Beyond Liberalism and Fundamentalism: How Modern and Postmodern Philosophy Set the Theological Agenda* (Valley Forge, Pa.: Trinity Press International, 1996), chap. 4; and Nancey Murphy and George F. R. Ellis, *On the Moral Nature of the Universe: Cosmology, Theology, and Ethics* (Minneapolis: Fortress Press, 1996), chap. 1.

spelled out under the headings of exegesis of Scripture, discernment, theological education, reconciliation, and discipleship.

Part III turns to some of the hot issues in contemporary ethical debates. Here we selected essays on the family and sex, homosexuality, abortion, pacifism, racism, feminism, business ethics, medical ethics, and economic justice. In each case, we claim, moral description and ethical argument in line with MacIntyre's perspective shed greater light on the issue than do the (more common) treatments in terms of rights, duties, or consequences.

PART I

Appropriation of MacIntyrean Concepts for Christian Ethics

Chapter 1

The Master Argument of MacIntyre's *After Virtue*

Brad J. Kallenberg

What's All This Noise?

In September of 1995 the Associated Press released a wirephoto showing Russian lawmakers of both genders in a punching brawl during a session of the Duma, Russia's lower house of parliament.[1] Is this behavior an ethnic idiosyncrasy? Do only government officials duke it out over matters of great importance? Or have fisticuffs suddenly become politically correct? No, on all counts.

Pick a topic, any topic — abortion, euthanasia, welfare reform, military intervention in the Balkans — and initiate discussion with a group of reasonable, well-educated people and observe the outcome. Chaos ensues. Of course the volume of the debate may vary according to how "close to home" the issue hits the participants. But any moral discussion, given a group of sufficient diversity, has the potential of escalating into a shouting match . . . or worse.

An even more striking feature of moral debates is their tendency *never* to reach resolution. Lines are drawn early, and participants rush to take sides. But in taking sides they appear to render themselves incapable of hearing the other. Everyone feels the heat, but no one sees the light.

Many thinkers are inclined to see *shrillness* and *interminability* as part and parcel of the nature of moral debate. But Alasdair MacIntyre begs to differ. In *After Virtue* he offers the "disquieting suggestion" that the tenor of modern moral debate is the direct outcome of a catastrophe in our past, a catastrophe so great that moral inquiry was very nearly obliterated from our culture and its vocabulary exorcised from our language. What we possess today, he argues, are nothing more than fragments of an older tradition. As a result, our moral discourse, which uses terms like *good,* and *justice,* and *duty,* has been robbed of the context that makes it intelligible. To complicate matters, although university courses in ethics have been around for a long time, no ethics curriculum predates

1. Sergei Shargorodsky, "Russian Lawmakers Do Battle," *The Sun* (San Bernardino, Calif.), 12 September 1995, A5.

this catastrophe. Therefore, for anyone who has taken ethics courses, and especially for those who have studied ethics diligently, the disarray of modern moral discourse is not only invisible, it is considered normal. This conclusion has been lent apparent credibility by a theory called *emotivism.*

Emotivism, explains MacIntyre, "is the doctrine that all evaluative judgments and more specifically all moral judgments are *nothing but* expressions of preference, expressions of attitude or feeling. . . ."[2] On this account, the person who remarks "Kindness is good" is not making a truth claim but simply expressing a positive feeling, "Hurrah for kindness!" Similarly, the person who exclaims "Murder is wrong" can be understood to be actually saying "I disapprove of murder" or "Murder, yuck!"

If emotivism is a true picture of the way moral discourse works, then we easily see that moral disputes can never be *rationally* settled because, as the emotivist contends, all value judgments are nonrational. Reason can never compel a solution; we simply have to hunker down and decide. Moral discussion is at best rhetorical persuasion.

There are sound reasons for questioning the emotivist picture. In the first place, emotivism is self-defeating insofar as it makes a truth claim about the non-truth-claim status of all purported truth claims! To put it differently, if all truth claims in the sphere of ethics are simply expressions of preference, as emotivism maintains, then the theory of emotivism itself lacks truth value, and thus we are not constrained to believe it if we prefer not to. In addition, emotivism muddies some ordinarily clear waters. Any proficient language speaker will attest to the fact that the sense of "I prefer . . . " is vastly different from the sense of "You ought . . . " The distinct uses to which we put these phrases is enabled precisely because the sense of "You ought" cannot be reduced without remainder to "I prefer."

But MacIntyre is not content to offer first-order arguments against emotivism. Stopping there would have made his book simply another ethical theory — just the sort of thing that emotivism so convincingly dismisses. Instead, what MacIntyre is up to has been called *meta-ethics* — an exploration into the conditions (or conditioners) of human ethical thought. As a human enterprise, ethics must be shaped in the same way that language, culture, and history shape the rest of our thinking. By investigating the historical conditionedness of our moral life and discourse, MacIntyre undermines emotivism, making a strong case for its own historical conditionedness. Emotivism as a moral philosophy appears to explain why contemporary moral debates are irresolvable. But it cannot account for the oddity that rival positions within these debates all employ incommensurable concepts. Why cannot the Kantian ("The taking of human life is always and everywhere just plain wrong") concede even a modicum of legitimacy to the Lockean argument ("Abortion is the natural right of women") if

2. Alasdair MacIntyre, *After Virtue,* 2d ed. (Notre Dame: University of Notre Dame Press, 1984), 11–12. Hereafter, page numbers in parentheses in the text refer to this book.

both views boil down to "I don't/do approve of abortion"? Nor can emotivism explain the oddity that interminable moral debates are conducted with the expectation that such debates *can be* resolved and, in keeping with this optimism, are conducted in such a way that rival positions appeal to principles presumed to be ultimate. In other words, if all value judgments are expressive, how did this belief in ultimate principles arise? MacIntyre suggests that it makes more sense to look for a source of this optimism, and its belief in ultimates, in a tradition that predates emotivism.

In fact, if one looks closely at the modern moral self, it has the appearance of being dislocated, as if it were missing something. The moral self as conceived by the emotivist is "totally detached from all social particularity" and is, rather, "entirely set over against the social world" (32). This autonomous self has no given continuities, possesses no ultimate governing principles, and is guided by no *telos*. Instead it is aimless, having "a certain abstract and ghostly character" (33). If MacIntyre is correct in asserting that "the emotivist self, in acquiring sovereignty in its own realm lost its traditional boundaries provided by a social identity and a view of human life as ordered to a given end," then it comes as no surprise that such a self flounders helplessly and endlessly in moral quagmires (34). But how did this catastrophe come to pass, and what exactly are the social identity and *telos* that were lost?

The Failure of the Enlightenment Project

The catastrophe that left the modern moral world in such disarray was a series of failed attempts to provide *rational* justification of morality for a culture that had philosophy as its central social activity. This eighteenth-century culture was called the Enlightenment, and its misguided agenda MacIntyre dubs the Enlightenment Project.

Among the first attempts to justify morality were those of Denis Diderot (1713–84) and David Hume (1711–76). Diderot tried to make human desire the criterion of an action's rightness or wrongness but failed to answer how a conflict of desires, and hence a conflict between an action's rightness and wrongness, could be resolved. Like Diderot, Hume conceived human passion as the stuff of morality because it is passion, not reason, that ultimately moves the moral agent to act. Hume goes further than Diderot by specifying a ruling passion (he calls it "sympathy"), but he can provide sufficient explanation neither for why this passion ought to predominate nor for why his account of the moral life looks suspiciously like that of the English bourgeoisie he emulated.[3]

Provoked by the failures of Hume and Diderot to ground morality in human passion, Immanuel Kant (1724–1804) strove to ground morality in reason alone. He argued that if morality was rational, its form would be identical for all ra-

3. Alasdair MacIntyre, *Whose Justice? Which Rationality?* (Notre Dame: University of Notre Dame Press, 1988), 300–325.

tional beings. Therefore, the moral thing to do is to follow those principles that can be universalized, that is, to follow those principles that one could consistently wish for everyone to follow. This sounds suspiciously like the Golden Rule. What makes it different, however, is Kant's conviction that the principle of universalizability (also called the *categorical imperative*) gets its punch from the requirement that it be willed without falling into *rational* contradiction.[4] Unfortunately, Kant's system has several large flaws, not the least of which is its ability to "justify" immoral maxims such as "Persecute all those who hold false religious beliefs" as well as trivial ones such as "Always eat mussels on Mondays in March" (46).

Søren Kierkegaard (1813–55) heartily agreed with the content of the morality that Kant defended (middle-class German Lutheran piety), but he also perceived that Kant's *rational* vindication of morality had failed as miserably as its predecessors. According to Kierkegaard, all persons are free to choose the plane of their existence. But this leaves open the problem of how to decide which plane to inhabit, since the criteria for making the decision are internal to the plane under consideration. Shall I inhabit the plane of the pleasure-seeking aesthete or that of the ethical rule-follower? To choose according to passion is to be relegated to the plane of the aesthetic. To choose according to reason is to have already chosen the ethical plane. Hence, neither passion nor reason can be the criterion for making the choice. The choice is a criterionless leap. MacIntyre concludes:

> Just as Hume seeks to found morality on the passions because his arguments have excluded the possibility of founding it on reason, so Kant founds it on reason because *his* arguments have excluded the possibility of founding it on the passions, and Kierkegaard on criterionless fundamental choice because of what he takes to be the compelling nature of the considerations which exclude both reason and the passions. (49)

---

4. This can be understood by means of the following illustration. Consider first the case where lying is simply speaking the opposite of the truth. A person faced with the question of whether to lie on a given occasion should easily realize that lying cannot be universalized without rational contradiction. For if everyone lied, then lying would become the normal mode of communication. If everyone always lied, we would simply adjust our expectations and hence could navigate just fine. For example, one day my eight-year-old son declined my offer of a peanut butter sandwich but then reminded me with a grin that Tuesday was "opposite day." Once I knew the plan, we had no trouble communicating because I could bank on the opposite of what he said. ("Do you like it?" "No, it's awful. I hate it!") Similarly, in a world where lying was the universal practice, deception could not exist because lying, in effect, would have become the means of truth-telling. Of course, this would fly in the face of what we understand by the term *lying*. So we run headlong into a rational contradiction: *lying* cannot be universalized because when universalized, lying ceases to be lying. Therefore, the opposite of lying must be universalizable; or to put it differently, truth-telling is the categorical imperative.

Now imagine the case that lying is not simple opposite-saying but distortion of truth—a mixture of truth and error. It should be clear that the sort of confusion that would be produced by universalizing this brand of lying would be on the scale that disables all communication—*including deception*. In such a world "intent to deceive" has no meaning. So, once again, we run up against a rational contradiction: universalization of lying leads to the state of affairs in which what is universalized, i.e., lying, is logically impossible.

So by Hume's standards Kant is unjustified in his conclusions; by Kant's standards Hume is both unjustified and unintelligible. By Kierkegaard's, both Hume and Kant are intelligible, but neither is compelling. The proof of the Enlightenment Project's failure is the stubborn existence of rival conceptions of moral justification.

Why the Enlightenment Project Had to Fail

The important thing to realize is that the Enlightenment Project didn't simply happen to fail, it *had* to fail. What doomed the Enlightenment Project from its inception was its loss of the concept of *telos.* The word *telos* is borrowed from classical Greek and means "end" or "purpose." When applied to human morality the term signifies the answer to the question "What is human life for?" In Aristotle's day (fourth century B.C.), moral reasoning was an argument consisting of three terms. The first term was the notion of the untutored human nature, which so desperately needed moral guidance. The second term was human nature conceived in terms of having fulfilled its purpose or achieved its *telos.* Moral imperatives, the third term, was that set of instructions for moving from the untutored self toward the actualized *telos* (see fig. 1). In this way moral precepts weren't snatched out of thin air but got their "punch" or their "oughtness" from the concrete notion of what human life was for.[5]

The wristwatch is a good example of how this works. If we ask "what is the wristwatch for?" the usual answer is that watches are for timekeeping.[6] To put it more technically, we could say that the purpose or *telos* of the watch is timekeeping. Or, to put it in still other terms, we can say that the watch is *functionally defined* as a mechanism for keeping time. Knowledge of this *telos* enables us to render judgment against a grossly inaccurate watch as a "bad" watch. Furthermore, our functional definition also allows us to identify the functional imperative for watches: "Watches *ought* to keep time well."

Because the Enlightenment rejected the traditionally shared concept of what human life is for and started, as it were, from scratch by inventing the idea of humans as "autonomous individuals," the concept of *telos,* so very central to morality, was lost. Having rejected the received account of *telos,* the only remaining option upon which moral principles might be grounded was the *un*tutored human nature — the very thing in need of guidance and, by nature, at odds with those guiding principles! (see fig. 2).

The results of the failure of the Enlightenment Project were far-reaching. First, without the notion of *telos* serving as a means for moral triangulation,

5. Admittedly, the Aristotelian model of morality makes moral imperatives appear hypothetical — as means to socially conceded ends — but theistic morality has the same basic shape. The primary difference is that the theistic version contends that the human *telos* is divinely determined, a determination that has the effect of bestowing a categorical status on moral imperatives.

6. Of course, it could also be argued that watches make fashion statements, have sentimental value, and so forth. But for sake of the illustration, let us imagine that watches are useful only for timekeeping.

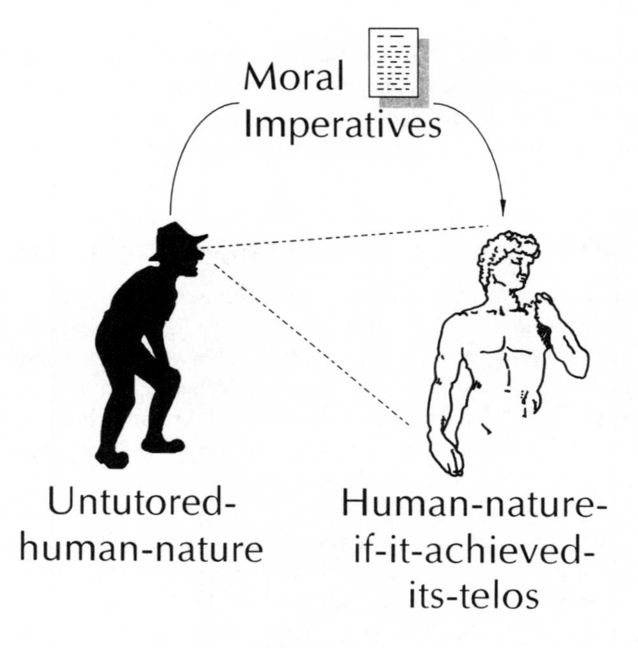

Figure 1

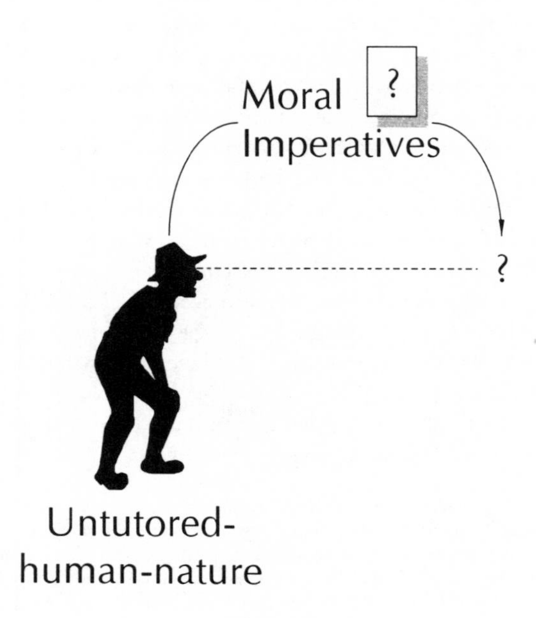

Figure 2

moral value judgments lost their factual character. And, of course, if values are "factless," then no appeal to facts can ever settle disagreements over values. It is in this state of affairs that emotivism, with its claim that moral values were nothing but matters of preference, flourishes as a theory. Second, impostors stepped in to fill the vacuum created by the absence of *telos* in moral reasoning. For example, utilitarianism can be seen to offer a ghostly substitute when it asserts that morality operates according to the principle of *greatest good for greatest number.* But this principle is vacuous because the utilitarians who assert it cannot adequately define what "good" means.[7] Similarly, Kant tried to rescue the (newly) autonomous moral agent from the loss of authority in his or her moral statements by attempting to provide "rational" justification for statements deprived of their former teleological status. Not only did Kant fail but later analytic philosophy cannot advance Kantian arguments without smuggling in undefined terms such as *rights* and *justice.* MacIntyre's point is that tradition alone provides the sense of terms like *good* and *justice* and *telos.* The presence of this moral vocabulary in debates today only goes to show that "modern moral utterance and practice can only be understood as a series of fragmented survivals from an older past and that the insoluble problems which they have generated for modern moral theories will remain insoluble until this is well understood" (110–11). In the absence of traditions, moral debate is out of joint and becomes a theater of illusions in which simple indignation and mere protest occupy center stage:

> But protest is now almost entirely that negative phenomenon which characteristically occurs as a reaction to the alleged invasion of someone's *rights* in the name of someone else's *utility.* The self-assertive shrillness of protest arises because the facts of incommensurability ensure that protesters can never win an argument; the indignant self-righteousness of protest arises because the facts of incommensurability ensure equally that the protesters can never lose an argument either. (71; cf. 77)

7. Please note, however, that the situation in the wake of the Enlightenment Project's failure is far worse than merely a state of being unable to settle disagreements. MacIntyre argues that the disagreements themselves are wrongheaded in the first place. Seventeenth-century empiricists thought themselves adequate to the task of dealing with *brute* facts, when the truth of the matter is that facts cannot be perceived apart from a conceptual framework that recognizes, sorts, prioritizes, and evaluates the facts. Value-laden theory is required to support observation as much as vice-versa. This insight was overlooked when, in the transition to the world of "modern" science, the medieval notion of final cause (i.e., causes that proceed according to *teloi*) was rejected in favor of making efficient causes the whole ball of wax. When this scientistic view becomes adopted by ethicists, what emerges is a mechanistic account of human action framed in terms of "laws of human behavior" with all reference to intentions, purposes, and reasons for action omitted. The "facts" of human behavior are thus construed free from value concepts (such as "good"), and human action is thereafter presumed to be predictable and manipulable like all other physical bodies. This presumption is embodied in the central character of the emotivist era: the bureaucratic manager. Unfortunately for the manager we do not possess lawlike generalizations for human behavior. In fact, human behavior is systematically unpredictable for a number of reasons. Both the expert manager and the attending virtue of "effectiveness" are fictions which expose the poverty of the Enlightenment Project. Cf. *After Virtue,* 93–99.

Nietzsche or Aristotle?

MacIntyre concludes that we are faced with a momentous choice. The present emotivist world cannot be sustained much longer. Nietzsche saw this clearly. He argued convincingly that every time a person made an appeal to "objectivity," it was none other than a thinly disguised expression of the person's subjective will. When we look at post-Enlightenment ethics through Nietzsche's eyes, we can see that insofar as the Enlightenment Project offers putative moral principles (that is, ones that are devoid of the background context that gives them their clout), it creates a moral vacuum which will inevitably be filled by headstrong people asserting their individual will-to-power; and to the victor go the spoils. To put it differently, the emotivist world is neither stable nor self-sustaining. Rather, it is a battleground of competing wills awaiting the emergence of a conqueror. Once the Aristotelian model of morality was rejected and the Enlightenment Project had failed, the danger of an imminent *Übermensch* (who resembles Hitler more than Superman) must be conceded. The only stopper to this danger is the possibility of recognizing that the Aristotelian model ought not to have been rejected in the first place. We are faced, then, with a momentous choice between Nietzsche and Aristotle. "There is no third alternative" (118).

In Praise of Aristotle

In order for MacIntyre to make a case that the Aristotelian morality ought never to have been discarded, he must first demonstrate the strength of this moral tradition from its origin in Homeric literature to its full-blown Aristotelian-Thomistic form of the late Middle Ages.

Heroic Society

Storytelling was the primary tool for moral education in classical Greece. It was for this reason that Homer's epic poems reflect the moral structure of their times. Not only does art reflect life, but literature in particular is the repository for moral stories, stories that have the peculiar ability of becoming embodied in the life of the community that cherishes them. This fact, that human life has the same shape as that of a story, will come up again in our discussion.

The moral structure of heroic society has two other outstanding features. First, morality has a social dimension. The social mobility that typifies our age was entirely absent in Homer's time. Then, one was born into a social structure that was fixed: "Every individual has a given role and status within the well-defined and highly determinate system of roles and statuses" (122). One's social place determined both the responsibility to render certain services to others (for example, it was incumbent on the head of the clan to defend and protect the clan) and the privileges one could expect from others in return. What one lacked in "upward mobility" was compensated by greater security. To know one's role and status in this small social system was to have settled forever the question "Who am I?" In fact, no one ever thought of asking such existential questions in heroic society because who one was was indistinguishable from what one did. Within this social framework the word *virtue* (*aretē*) describes any quality that is required for discharging one's role. As the clan's warrior-defender, the head of the clan needed courage as well as physical strength and battle savvy. Courage is also intimately linked to another virtue, fidelity. Fidelity and courage become obligatory because the community can survive only if kinsmen can be relied upon to fight valiantly on each other's behalf should the need arise.

This highlights a third feature of the moral structure of heroic societies. Since morality is bound up with the social structure of the clan, questions about moral value are *questions of fact.* Just as what qualifies as a "right" move in the game of chess is predetermined by the agreed-upon object of the game, so, too, the morally acceptable "move" was easily identified for those who participated in the "game." However, there was no way for a person in heroic society to step outside the moral "game" to evaluate it, as is possible with chess. "All questions of choice arise within the framework; the framework itself therefore cannot be chosen" precisely because the person who does try to step outside his or her given social position "would be engaged in the enterprise of trying to make himself [or herself] disappear" (126).

Athenian Society

Life in Athens illustrates an important moment in the life of a moral tradition: growth comes through crisis. In large measure, morality was a subject that received a great deal of attention from the Athenians because of a perceived discrepancy between their moral "scriptures" (the Homeric literature) and life as they knew it. No Athenian could conceive of living like an Achilles or an Agamemnon. This does not illustrate that the heroic society had been mistaken about morality's *social* dimension, but rather, that the social structure since the days of Homer had undergone such a drastic change (with the emergence of the city-state, or *polis*) that morality had necessarily changed shape too. The changes in the social world had the effect of broadening the range of application of the concept of virtue. The term no longer denoted excellence in the performance of one's well-defined social roles (where excellence could be understood only from within such a role), but rather *virtues* signified qualities that were applicable to *human life in general* (or, at least, human life in Athens, which in their minds *was* human life *par excellence!*). While the Athenians inherited the vocabulary of the virtues from heroic society, the content of these terms was up for grabs.

For example, the Sophists were inclined to see *virtue* as the generic name for those qualities that ensure successful living, and what counts for success was relative to each different city-state. When in Sparta, do as the Spartans do — treasure physical prowess and warcraft — but when in Athens do as the Athenians do and hanker after beauty and truth. In response to their appalling relativism, Plato charged the Sophists with failing to discern the difference between mundane virtues and "true" virtue. Plato is willing to grant that the virtues are the means to a happy life, but getting clear about the nature of "true" happiness (and "true" virtue) requires shifting one's focus from the earthly *polis* to contemplate instead the "ideal" world. Plato was convinced that this exercise in contemplation would show that true happiness is the satisfaction of having lived in accordance with one's true nature. Human nature, according to Plato, was composed of three parts. The highest part — that which participates most fully in the realm of the Ideal — is the intellect and is assisted in its function by the virtue of wisdom. The lowest part — that which is shared with the beasts — is the desiring part and is to be constrained by the virtue of prudence. Between lay a motivational well-spring, or high-spirited part, which is assisted by the virtue of courage. A fourth virtue, justice, refers to the state of affairs when all three are in proper order with respect to each other. This set of four virtues is called *cardinal* (from the Latin *cardo* which means "door hinge") because they are the qualities upon which the truly happy life hangs.[8]

It is important to remember that these two contemporaneous but varying conceptions of the virtues were attempts to align the concept of virtue with the purpose of life as understood in the newly broadened context — that of the *polis*. This broadening was the first movement toward the belief in a universal moral order, which finds clearer expression in Aristotle.

But Plato did not have the last word even in his own day. His package of virtues, together with the moral order it depicted, was all too neat. The tragic dramatists, such as Sophocles, explored the kinds of real conflicts that might arise *between* virtues or *between* goods. To put it differently, the moral order sometimes makes rival and incompatible claims on a person which can force him or her into a tragic situation of having to make a choice between two or more socially incumbent duties, each of which entails dire consequences. In grappling with this conflict, the Sophoclean protagonist is forced to transcend his or her society while remaining inescapably accountable to the higher moral order.

Here, then, is not simply an argument over which of two lists of virtues is better (Achilles' courage or Oedipus's wisdom) but rather an argument over which narrative form (Homer's epic poetry or a Sophoclean tragedy) best depicts the form of human living. MacIntyre suggests a general lesson to be learned: "to adopt a stance on the virtues will be to adopt a stance on the narrative character of human life" precisely because narrative and virtues are mutually supporting and "internally connected" concepts (144).

---

8. Plato goes on to argue that society is, or ought to be, arranged along the same lines. The bronze class of society are those working folk whose citizenship is assisted by the virtue of prudence. The silver class comprises the warriors in whom the high-spirited part of the soul dominates. The quality they need above all is courage. The gold class, of course, is made up of the philosopher-kings, whose role in society is not merely to rule but to contemplate truth with the aid of the virtue of wisdom. Social justice, in Plato's view, signified keeping the classes in the proper order, which amounted to maintaining the status quo. In this way Plato's system is by nature conservative: change (including progress) was bad; stability was good.

Aristotle's Model

To defend Aristotle as the apex of virtue theory, MacIntyre must make a characteristically un-Aristotelian move. He must show that Aristotle lies along the historical trajectory that begins with Homeric literature and is, therefore, indebted to and dependent upon his predecessors.[9] Furthermore, MacIntyre must show that Aristotle's formulation of moral philosophy has advanced beyond his predecessors while retaining characteristic features of the overall tradition. To do this MacIntyre focuses on four features in Aristotle's thought.

First, the concept of a moral order, which began to emerge in Plato's thinking, becomes more explicit in Aristotle. However, unlike Plato's conception of moral order, which ruled as it were from above, Aristotle sees this moral order as internal to what it means to be human. Humans are *teleological* beings, which is to say, human living aims at an end, or *telos*. Some ends are intermediate rather than terminal. The ship at which shipbuilding aims may in turn be means for the practice of warcraft, which itself may be a means to a yet more distant end. Aristotle reasons that human action consists of means-end chains, which converge on one ultimate end called the Good. The extent to which humans achieve their *telos* is the extent to which they participate in the Good. In Aristotle's mind, the *telos* can be conceived only in terms of a thing's natural function. Similarly, virtues are function-specific, or more precisely, excellency of function.[10] To illustrate, if the function of a horse is to run, then the *telos* of a horse is racing, and its virtue is its speed. Virtues, therefore, are qualities that assist achievement of the *telos*, and the *telos* of a thing is bound up in the nature of the thing.

The nature of human beings, upon which the notion of the human *telos* depends, is bound up in the metaphysical structure of the soul. According to Aristotle, while we may share the vegetative (growth) and locomotive (movement) soul-stuff with the animals, humans are distinguished in the chain of being by their rational souls. The end of human life, therefore, is rationality, and the virtues are (1) *virtues of character* which assist living according *to* reason and (2) *virtues of thought* which enable proper exercise *of* reason itself.

The notion of a function-specific *telos* represents an advance over earlier formulations of the tradition by providing a clearer account of moral imperatives. As noted earlier in the wristwatch illustration, it is the concept of *telos* that provides human beings with moral imperatives. If the function of a watch is

9. Frederick Copleston notes that Aristotle, like Hegel, saw himself to be systematizing and improving upon previous philosophy. See *A History of Philosophy*, 9 vols. (New York: Doubleday, 1985), 1:371–78. Yet while Aristotle appreciated his platonic heritage, he conceived his own work in terms of "getting it right" in those places Plato "got it wrong." What is un-Aristotelian, therefore, is MacIntyre's historicist claim that Aristotle's work lies along a trajectory that stretches from Plato to the Middle Ages and beyond; a claim that necessarily relativizes Aristotle's contribution to the conceptual framework he shared with his predecessors. Thus the "new ground" Aristotle broke must be seen as nothing more than *intrasystematic* improvements.

10. In *Nicomachean Ethics*, Aristotle writes, "every virtue causes its possessors to be in a good state and to perform their functions well." *Nicomachean Ethics*, trans. Terence Irwin (Indianapolis: Hackett Publishing, 1985), 1106a16.

timekeeping, then it *ought* to keep time well. If the function of human beings is rationality, then humans *ought* to live in accordance with, and in right exercise of, reason.

The second feature of Aristotle's moral philosophy is *eudaimonia.* A difficult word to translate — blessedness, happiness, prosperity — it seems to connote "the state of being well and doing well in being well, of man's being well-favored himself and in relation to the divine" (148). *Eudaimonia* names that *telos* toward which humans move. Virtues, then, assist the movement toward *eudaimonia,* but *eudaimonia* cannot be defined apart from these same virtues:

> But the exercise of the virtues is not in this sense a means to the end of the good for man. For what constitutes the good for man is a complete human life lived at its best, and the exercise of the virtues a necessary and central part of such a life, not a mere preparatory exercise to secure such a life. We thus cannot characterize the good for man without already having made reference to the virtues. (149)

The apparent circularity of the relation between *telos, eudaimonia,* and *virtue* is not a mark against Aristotle's system but, rather, an advance over Plato's. For Plato, "reality" not only denoted the world of rocks and doorknobs, it also included the world of intangibles such as "love" and "17" — things whose existence in the realm of Form is every bit as real as the middle-sized dry goods that clutter our sensible world. As Plato saw it, "true virtue" belonged to the realm of Form, and particular human qualities were deemed "virtuous" to the extent that they resembled the "true virtue" of which they were copies. Thus, there could be no inherent conflict or disunity between particular virtuous qualities; any tragic conflict was simply a function of imperfection in copying universal virtue into particular living. In this way, morality was thought to be objective and moral reasoning an exercise of the intellect according to which the mind grasped the Form of "true virtue." Ironically, Plato's doctrine failed even to overcome the relativist claims of the Sophists and tragic dramatists of his own day. Although MacIntyre does not think that Aristotle himself explicitly conquered the problem of what to do when virtues conflict, his model, which defines *telos, eudaimonia,* and *virtue* in terms of each other, does point the way toward conceiving moral reasoning as a *skill* rather than as an exercise of intellect (as Plato and the later Enlightenment thinkers imagined). Such skill could be attained and cultivated only *from within* the form of life in which these concepts were at home.

The third feature of Aristotle's system is the distinction between theoretical reasoning and practical reasoning. Practical reasoning begins with a want, or goal, or desire and always terminates in action. Suppose you are thirsty after a long day of shopping. The major premise of your reasoning process is your (obvious) belief that anyone who is thirsty is well advised to find a drinking fountain. The minor premise of this line of thought is your knowledge that a drinking fountain exists in the northwest corner of this particular department store. Your practical reasoning terminates in your act of walking to the northwest corner of the store and quenching your thirst.

In Aristotle's way of looking at things, moral reasoning is an instance of practical reasoning. It is assisted by virtues of character (which temper, guide, and shape initial desires) and virtues of thought (such as *phronēsis,* which enables the perception of practical reasoning's major premises).[11]

Perhaps the most important use of practical reason is its employment in the balancing of human activities. I cannot spend all my time in theoretical contemplation, the highest faculty of reason and thus the highest human good (158), because I would soon starve to death. In order to maximize the amount of time I can engage in contemplation, I must balance this activity with work, civic duty, and the like. This mental balancing act is the domain of practical reason. This explanation also sheds light on why virtuous persons make the best civic leaders, since skill in practical reasoning is also what it takes to run the *polis.*

The fourth feature of Aristotle's moral philosophy that MacIntyre emphasizes is friendship. Friendship, of course, involves mutual affection, but for Aristotle, "that affection arises within a relationship defined in terms of common allegiance to and a common pursuit of goods" (156). This is to say that Aristotle's notion on friendship presupposes, first, the existence of the *polis,* which renders common good possible, and second, that this good itself is the health of the *polis:* "We are to think then of friendship as being the sharing of all in the common project of creating and sustaining the life of the city, a sharing incorporated in the immediacy of an individual's particular friendships" (156).

The emphasis on friendship in Aristotle illustrates one aspect of continuity in this historic tradition, namely, that the moral structure is intimately linked with social relationships.

Obstacles to Be Hurdled

Aristotle is definitely the hero of MacIntyre's account. And at the time *After Virtue* was written (1981, revised 1984) MacIntyre saw Aristotle as the apex of the virtue tradition.[12] However, if MacIntyre is to succeed in rejuvenating the Aristotelian tradition, he must overcome three difficulties in Aristotle's account that threaten to topple the whole project. First, Aristotle's notion of *telos* rests on his distinctive "metaphysical biology." In Aristotle's view, the form guarantees that all humans share a common essence. The essence of humanness is rationality. Rationality is of two sorts, theoretical and practical. The *telos* of human

11. Since right action follows in straightforward fashion from the initial desire and major premise, and since differences in initial desires as well as differences in major premises boil down to variations in the exercise of the respective virtues, moral quandaries are nonexistent for Aristotle. When in a bind, he can always defer to the maxim "the morally right action is that taken by the virtuous person."

12. In later works, MacIntyre becomes convinced that Aquinas had succeeded in surpassing Aristotle on several points. See Alasdair MacIntyre, *Whose Justice? Which Rationality?* and *Three Rival Versions of Moral Enquiry: Encyclopaedia, Genealogy, and Tradition* (Notre Dame: University of Notre Dame Press, 1990).

life, then, is actualization of both forms of reason. The goal of theoretical reason is contemplation; the goal of practical reason is life in the *polis.* Aristotle's problem was to give an account of how pursuit of these two forms of rationality could be reconciled. MacIntyre's problem is to provide a replacement for Aristotle's concept of form that will enlighten us as to the *telos* of human life. Traditions provide answers to this question. Second, the virtue tradition sees morality as inextricably enmeshed in the life of the *polis.* What does this do for the applicability of the Aristotelian model today, in view of the extinction of the *polis?* Third, Aristotle retains Plato's belief in the unity of the virtues, which implies that every putative case of tragedy reduces to an instance that is "simply the result of flaws of character in individuals or of unintelligent political arrangements" (157). As Sophocles dramatized, instances of tragic evil were not inconceivable. Can such real conflicts be interpreted as contributing to the moral life rather than confusing it?

In addition to the three problems internal to Aristotle's account, MacIntyre notes one problem external to it. To identify the trajectory from Homer to Aristotle to Aquinas to the present as a single tradition, something must be done to reconcile the diversity in the lists of virtues taken from every age. Not only have the *lists* changed with each successive formulation of the tradition,[13] but *how* virtue is defined at one point in history is at odds with the definition explicated in another age.[14] Thus, the fourth problem MacIntyre must overcome is the challenge of demonstrating the kind of continuity between these formulations that makes these disparate accounts a single, unified tradition.

We now turn to MacIntyre's own "metanarrative" to see if he is successful in his endeavors.

Ethics à la MacIntyre

The disparity between virtue lists and even between the definitions of the term can be reconciled, says MacIntyre, by bringing to light the particular backdrop that each formulation presupposes. The tricky part of his analysis is that each of the central concepts — *virtue, practice, narrative,* and *tradition* — can be defined only, finally, in terms of the other concepts. This does not make the MacIntyrean version guilty of circularity. It simply means that getting a handle on his explanation is not like building a house (which progresses incrementally, brick by brick) but like watching the sun rise — the light dawns gradually over the whole.[15]

13. E.g., the early church fathers champion humility as a virtue, while Aristotle repudiates it as a vice (182)!

14. E.g., Aristotle sees virtues as the means to internal ends, while Benjamin Franklin sees virtues as means to external, even utilitarian, ends (184).

15. This illustration comes from Ludwig Wittgenstein, *On Certainty,* ed. G. E. M. Anscombe and G. H. von Wright, trans. Denis Paul and G. E. M. Anscombe (New York: Harper Torchbooks, 1969, 1972), §141.

Practices

The cornerstone of this backdrop is the idea of practices. MacIntyre defines a *practice* somewhat tortuously as

> any coherent and complex form of socially established cooperative human activity through which goods internal to that form of activity are realized in the course of trying to achieve those standards of excellence which are appropriate to, and partially definitive of, that form of activity, with the result that human powers to achieve excellence, and human conceptions of the ends and goods involved, are systematically extended. (187)

Attention to the grammar of this sentence reveals four central concepts. First, practices are human activities. However, these are not activities of isolated individuals but socially established and cooperative activities. Such activities cannot be executed alone but require participation by like-minded others. In addition to being social, these activities are also complex enough to be challenging, and coherent enough to aim at some goal in a unified fashion. Building a house is a practice, while taking long showers is not. The game of tennis is a practice, but hitting a backhand is not. Medicine is a practice, while gargling mouthwash is not.[16]

Second, practices have goods that are internal to the activity. Some practices, for example, jurisprudence, have external goods — money, fame, power — which come as by-products of the practice. But true practices are marked by *internal* goods — those rewards that can be recognized and appreciated only by participants.[17] For example, I can bribe my son with pieces of candy to learn the game of chess. But at some point he may begin to enjoy the game of chess for itself. At this point he has become a practitioner and member of the greater community of chess players. He has, furthermore, become hooked on its internal reward — the joy of chess — something to which all players have access.

Third, practices have standards of excellence without which internal goods cannot be fully achieved. The joy of chess is in having played *well.* And what counts for excellence has been determined by the historical community of practitioners. The practitioners have recognized that stalemate is not as desirable an endgame as checkmate. And to execute a queen-rook fork is more satisfying than simple *en passant.*

Fourth, practices are systematically extended. As practitioners have striven for excellence day in and day out over the years, the standards of the practice, along with practitioners' abilities to achieve these standards, have slowly risen. Perhaps no field better illustrates this than medicine. Doctors were no doubt sincere when they once treated fevers with leeches, but contemporary physicians possess skills that far surpass those of their predecessors. Yet the dependence of contemporary practitioners upon their predecessors is unquestionable: it is

16. For an extended discussion of practices see Chapter 7 in this volume.

17. It is often, but not always, the case that internal rewards are shared among all practitioners without diminution.

precisely because previous doctors strove for excellence that the specific advances in medicine that have been made *have* been made. But increase in technical skill does not quite capture what is meant by the notion of systematic extension. It also includes the way technically proficient doctors have come to appreciate how the health of a patient is a function of a larger system. Thus, the practice of medicine is slowly being extended to encompass care for the whole patient in all his or her psychosocial complexity.[18]

Against the backdrop of practices, virtue can be defined as "an acquired human quality the possession and exercise of which tends to enable us to achieve those goods which are internal to practices and the lack of which effectively prevents us from achieving any such goods" (191). The clan leader who *practices* warcraft and the church father who *practices* evangelism are assisted by the qualities of courage and humility respectively. Against this backdrop many of the discrepancies between virtue lists can be reconciled as a matter of differences of practice.

In our smörgåsbord era it is tempting to think of practices as self-contained exercises. In fact, many practices are so complex that they have become an entire tradition in themselves. Medicine, science, and warcraft all have attending epistemologies, authoritative texts, structured communities and institutions, and histories of development. Other practices are parts of clusters that contribute to the identity of a tradition. For example, the Christian tradition defines itself as a socially expanding movement called "the kingdom of God." At its core, therefore, Christianity seems to consist primarily of the practice of community formation. Subpractices that contribute to community formation can be categorized under the rubrics of *witness, worship, works of mercy, discernment,* and *discipleship.*[19] Other schemes can be imagined of course, but my point is that Christianity cannot be explained or understood without reference to a distinctive cluster of practices. In order to participate in the tradition called Christianity one must necessarily participate in these practices. To put it another way, to participate in the community is to participate in practices because communal life is the point at which the practices intersect. Furthermore, knowing the constitutive practices of Christianity tells us a great deal about how Christians ought to live. If virtues are cultivated by striving for excellence in the practice of practices, then we are unable to grow in Christlikeness unless we participate in Christianity's practices.

Narrative

A second crucial concept that serves as a backdrop to our understanding of the virtues is *narrative.* MacIntyre explains narrative this way. Imagine that a woman

18. The changing mode of physician-patient relationships is detailed by William F. May in *The Physician's Covenant* (Philadelphia: Westminster, 1983) and in Chapter 15 of this volume.

19. See Chapter 2. For an alternate list of constitutive Christian practices see Craig R. Dykstra, "No Longer Strangers: The Church and Its Educational Ministry," *Princeton Seminary Bulletin* 6, no. 3 (1985): 188–200, as well as Chapter 7 in the present volume.

approaches you at a bus stop and says "The name of the common wild duck is *histrionicus histrionicus histrionicus.*" Now, what would you make of this person? Truth is, you can't make anything of her, or of her action, without more information. Her act is completely unintelligible. But now suppose it becomes known that this woman is a librarian, and she has mistaken you for the person who earlier had asked for the Latin name of the common wild duck. We can now understand her action because it has been put into a context. The contexts that make sense out of human action are *stories* or *narratives.* To explain an action is simply to provide the story that gives the act its context. We can imagine any number of stories that might make sense out of the bus stop incident (for example, perhaps she is a Russian spy whose password is the sentence in question). But we will also say that the explanation of her action is rendered more fully if we can tell the story that takes her longer- and longest-term intentions into account and shows how her shorter-term intentions relate to the longer-term ones. So we might discover that she has rushed out of the library in search of a particular patron because she has been put on a standard of performance under threat of losing her job. Her longer-term intention is to save her job. Her longest-term intention might be uncovered in telling the story of how she is the sole provider for her paraplegic son. MacIntyre reasons that if human actions are intelligible only with respect to stories that contextualize intentions, then that which unifies actions into sequences and sequences into a continuous whole is the story of one's life. My life as a whole makes sense when my story is told.

This has important consequences for the problem of Aristotle's "metaphysical biology." Imagine we had the opportunity to ask Aristotle "How can I know that I am the same person as the me of ten years ago?" He would likely reply, "Though your body changes through growth and decay, your form, or essence, is immutable." But this answer is not likely to fly very far for a modern audience. In contrast, MacIntyre suggests that *narrative* provides a better explanation for the unity of a human life. The self has continuity because it has played the single and central character in a particular story — the narrative of a person's life. MacIntyre puts it this way: the unity of the self "resides in the unity of a narrative which links birth to life to death as a narrative beginning to middle to end" (205).

Just as practices have a characteristically social dimension, so also do narratives. Humorist Garrison Keillor reminisces about the distinctive characters who populated the Lake Wobegon, Minnesota, of his childhood. But notice how in identifying themselves as "Norwegian bachelor farmers" such folk have immediately linked who they are with others who share these ethnic, gender, and occupational features. I cannot explain who I am without utilizing some social placemarkers which identify me with certain strata of my community. If pressed to go beyond this first-level answer to "Who am I?" where can one go but to say that I am also someone's neighbor, child, sibling, student, mate, friend, constituent, or employee? In occupying these roles we simultaneously become subplots in the stories of others' lives just as they have become subplots in ours. In this way, the life stories of members of a community are enmeshed and intertwined. This entanglement of our stories is the fabric of communal life: "For the story of my life is always embedded in the story of those communities from which I derive my identity" (221). Our stories are concretely embedded, or our stories intersect, in those practices in which we are co-participants. For example, the role of ethics professor links the instructor with the rest of the faculty in general and one group of students in particular, within the wider practice of graduate education.

This construction overcomes the fear that the Aristotelian account of the virtues cannot be sustained after the extinction of the *polis.* In MacIntyre's construction, virtues are those qualities that assist one in the extension of his or her story, and, by extrapolation, the extension of the story of his or her community or communities. The question "What ought I to do?" is not a question of one's political duty as it was in Aristotle's day, but it *is* a question whose answer must be preceded by the logically prior question: "Of which stories am I a part?"

Although none of us will ever have the clear moral parameters that were to be had in the well-defined social framework of Aristotle's *polis,* the concept of narrative embeddedness still explains the presence of natural boundaries and moral momentum. In 1994 a U.S. postal worker lost his job and retaliated by going on a killing spree. Our responses to his actions were telling. People reacted by saying he "flipped out," "snapped," "went berserk," or "had gone insane." Our expectation is that postal workers (even unemployed ones) aren't killers, and once a postal worker type, always a postal worker type.[20] This illustrates our deeper belief that *rational* human behavior is action that stays within the boundaries of "character." To step outside these boundaries is not merely to act irrationally but to lose one's sanity. This is because the narrative shape of human life carries with it a certain degree of moral momentum. For example, my wife can bank on the fact that I won't wake up tomorrow morning and say "Today I think I'll become an ax murderer!" There is a certain momentum in who I am; I will generally stay "in character." The transition from who I was yesterday to who I am today will be a smooth one, marked only by minor changes. A drastic change in character — whether for the better or for the worse — is always taken to be the result of a long-term, preexistent (though perhaps not publicly visible) process.

Tradition

The third term that forms the backdrop to all the various accounts of virtue is the notion of *tradition.* MacIntyre defines tradition as "an historically extended, socially embodied argument, and an argument precisely in part about the goods which constitute the tradition" (222). This definition has three components. First, MacIntyre's understanding of tradition is really the logical extension of his treatment of narrative. To be "historically extended" is to be narratively ex-

20. We would even say that someone who sincerely harbors paranoia that the mail carrier is a killer is mentally maladjusted.

tended. Just as the self has the unity of playing a single character in a lifelong story, so too the community has its own continuity — despite loss and gain of members — because the community itself is a character of sorts in a narrative that is longer than the span of a single human life. For example, Christians in the Reformed tradition feel kinship with John Calvin because they can tell the story (recount the history) of the Reformed Church from Calvin's Geneva to their present church community.

Second, a tradition is "socially embodied" because traditions are lived in community. A tradition has its inception in the formation of the community that is defined by those who have pledged corporate allegiance to the tradition's authoritative voice or text.[21] In that this prophetic word shapes the practices of communal life, the community is said to "embody" the tradition's persona in that age. For example, early Christians prayed because their scriptures exemplify, illustrate, and command the practice of prayer. Outsiders, who have no access to the authoritative text, can still read the nature of the Christian tradition off the lives and practices of the community's members. Should the community die off or disband, the tradition passes out of existence (at least until another group rallies in the same way around the same text). In this way the tradition has the quality of being "socially embodied." However, because the application of the authoritative text or voice is done afresh in every successive generation, the tradition remains a live option only so long as the discussion about the text's relevance and meaning is sustained. Hence, third, traditions are necessarily long-standing arguments. But let's get clearer on the notion of historical extension because this will help us evaluate the current status of the virtue tradition.

Just as selves and communities are characters in their respective stories, so too traditions are also characters in an even wider narrative. When we recount Christian, Jewish, or Muslim history, we are telling the story of just such a character. The viability of any one tradition is not merely its historical survival, however, but its *historical extension.* MacIntyre uses this term to describe the growth a tradition undergoes through time as it overcomes obstacles raised against it. In his sequel to *After Virtue* called *Whose Justice? Which Rationality?* he defines a tradition as

> an argument extended through time in which certain fundamental agreements are defined and redefined in terms of two kinds of conflict: those with critics and enemies external to the tradition . . . and those internal, interpretive debates through which the meaning and rationale of the fundamental agreements come to be expressed and by whose progress a tradition is constituted.[22]

For example, early Christians faced a crisis when they tried to reconcile three seemingly inconsistent beliefs: God is one, Jesus is divine, and Jesus is not the Father. The well-known "solution" to this quandary came when the Cappadocian

21. For an extended account of how traditions are born and develop see chap. 18 of MacIntyre's *Whose Justice? Which Rationality?*

22. *Whose Justice? Which Rationality?* 12.

fathers borrowed Platonic resources to frame the doctrine of the Trinity. This enabled Christians to believe all three propositions without logical contradiction. The universal adoption of their formulation as orthodoxy at Constantinople (381 A.D.) freed the Christian tradition to move on to tackle the next obstacle in its path.[23] We don't know how long the trinitarian problem might have been sustained had the Cappadocian fathers not entered the debate. We *do* know that by 325 A.D. the stakes were very high — unacceptable proposals were deemed heretical, and their authors were banished from the community (or worse). Were it not for belief in God's sovereignty over history, it would be tempting to wonder how long Christianity might have lasted had not the trinitarian problem been overcome.

If virtue theory is itself a tradition in the sense just described then we can see that its viability depends upon overcoming the obstacles that threaten the Aristotelian version. We have already seen how *narrative* overcomes the problem of Aristotle's metaphysical biology and how *practices* overcome the problem of discrepancies in the virtue lists. The extinction of the *polis* is a third crisis that must be overcome. For Aristotle, the *telos* of life, together with the attending virtues, can be expressed only in terms of life in the *polis.* One reason the virtuous person was identical to the virtuous citizen was that without the prosperity and leisure engendered by the shared life of the city-state, the highest *telos* (for Aristotle, metaphysical contemplation) was an impractical and impossible ideal. But by exercise of practical reason the *polis* flourished in such a way that contemplation could be maximized (at least by the elite). However, a more fundamental reason virtue was tied to the *polis* was that the Good, at which human life aims, was thought to be a *corporate* good that could not be possessed by isolated individuals but only jointly in community. The *polis* was the by-product of pursuing this corporate Good together. To put it differently, the Good *was* this corporate life. But now the *polis* is no more. Therefore, in order for the virtue tradition to be extended, there must be an alternative way to understand the social dimension of virtue. Of course, this is ground we have already covered. The narrative shape of human existence — that is, that human sociality is identical to the embeddedness of our respective narratives — shows the way to preserve the sociality of virtue theory even in the absence of the *polis.*

Narrative extends the Aristotelian tradition in another way as well. MacIntyre credits the high medieval age with conceptualizing the genre of our narrativity to be akin to the quest for the Holy Grail: "In the high medieval scheme a central genre is the tale of a quest or journey. Man is essentially *in via.* The end which he seeks is something which if gained can redeem all that was wrong with his life up to that point" (174–75). MacIntyre goes on to say that this move was *un*-Aristotelian in at least two ways. First, it placed the *telos* of life beyond life, in contrast to Aristotle, who imagined the *telos* of life to be "a certain kind of

23. The next major debate was the doctrine of Christ: if Christ was God the Son, how are we to understand the relation of his divine and human natures while preserving the unity of his person?

life." Second, it allowed for the possibility of positive evil in contrast to the Aristotelian scheme, which understood evil as always the privation of good. These two features gave the medieval view an advantage over Aristotle in dealing with the problem of tragic evil. In the eyes of the medieval person, the achievement of the human *telos* counterbalanced all evil, even evils of the tragic sort envisioned by Sophocles. Thus, the fourth objection that threatened *Aristotle* (that is, tragic evil) has been overcome by the Aristotelian *tradition:*

> The narrative therefore in which human life is embodied has a form in which the subject ... is set a task in the completion of which lies their peculiar appropriation of the human good; the way toward which the completion of that task is barred by a variety of inward and outward evils. The virtues are those qualities which enable evils to be overcome, the task to be accomplished, the journey to be completed. (175)

MacIntyre concludes, therefore, that tragic choices are real but that the inevitability of such choice does not render morality unintelligible or criterionless (as the emotivist claims, thereby concluding that moral choices boil down to matters of preference). Rather such choice plays a central role in the development of character by providing an occasion for moral agents to exercise and build virtue when they sustain the quest for good precisely at the time it is most costly to do so. If "the good life for man is the life spent in seeking for the good life for man, and the virtues necessary for the seeking are those which will enable us to understand what more and what else the good life for man is," then tragic evil is overcome because evil, even evil of the tragic sort, cannot diminish this kind of good (219). Instead of detracting from this kind of goodness, tragic evil can even be thought to *contribute* to the moral fiber of the life so lived. This solution to the problem of tragic evil employs a view of life that has come out of a particular historical cross-section of the tradition. Because the medieval period provides them with the resources for overcoming this obstacle, adherents to this tradition are warranted in retaining this feature from their corporate past. So then, not only are practices and narratives sources for understanding the human *telos,* but tradition itself contributes to this understanding.

Identifying the genre of a tradition's narrative also makes sense out of the fractal symmetry that can be seen when we look at the way in which the narrative unity of (1) a life, (2) a community, and (3) a tradition are mutually nested. Individual, community, and tradition, while telling different parts of the master story, nevertheless share equally in the genre of that story. Thus, if the genre of the tradition is that of a quest, the genre of a human life is also that of a quest. And if human life is a quest, then human virtues are those qualities that assist it:

> The virtues therefore are to be understood as those dispositions which will not only sustain practices and enable us to achieve the goods internal to practices, but which will also sustain us in the relevant kind of quest for the good, by enabling us to overcome the harms, dangers, temptations and distractions which we encounter, and which will furnish us with increasing self-knowledge and increasing knowledge of the good. (219)

Retrospect

Looking back, we can see not only that the virtue tradition that MacIntyre has recounted fits MacIntyre's definition of tradition but that it is one in which MacIntyre represents the most recent advance! He has succeeded in overcoming four important obstacles to the Aristotelian model by elucidating the story about stories, or what has been called the metanarrative about the narrative quality of human life. In so doing he has clarified how the notions of *telos, virtue, practice, narrative,* and *tradition* form a mutually supporting and interlocking web of concepts.

Let us recall now the master argument of *After Virtue.* MacIntyre challenged us to reconsider the emotivist conclusion (namely, that morality is by nature nothing more than matters of preference) by arguing that the Enlightenment Project's move to repudiate all things social (that is, virtues and practices) and all things historical (that is, narrative and tradition) was a major misstep. He argued further that moral imperatives can be derived from an answer to the question "What is human life for?" In the same way the functional definition of a watch ("A watch is for timekeeping") entails its virtue (accuracy), its functional imperative ("A watch *ought* to keep time well"), and its ground for being evaluated ("This grossly inaccurate watch is a *bad* watch"). To have a grasp on the human *telos* affords us with moral virtues, moral imperatives, and sufficient grounds for moral judgment. Furthermore, because narratives intersect at social practices, and practices constitute traditions, and traditions are historically (that is, narratively) extended, to understand virtue adequately as those qualities that assist pursuit of *telos* at all three levels, virtue itself must be given a threefold definition:

> The virtues find their point and purpose not only in sustaining those relationships necessary if the variety of goods internal to practices are to be achieved and not only in sustaining the form of an individual life in which that individual may seek out his or her good as the good of his or her whole life, but also in sustaining those traditions which provide the practices and individual lives with their necessary historical context. (223)

This relationship might be diagrammed as in Figure 3.

Aristotle's notion of virtue as "excellency of function" has thus been expanded. Human virtues are learned qualities that assist us in achieving the human *telos,* which can be understood by considering (1) the functional definition of the human person, which is provided by the master story of the tradition, (2) the internal goods of those practices that constitute the tradition, and (3) those roles that arise at the intersection of our life stories. To put it differently, moral imperatives arise from that understanding of the human *telos* that arises within the context of those practices, narratives, and tradition in which we locate ourselves.

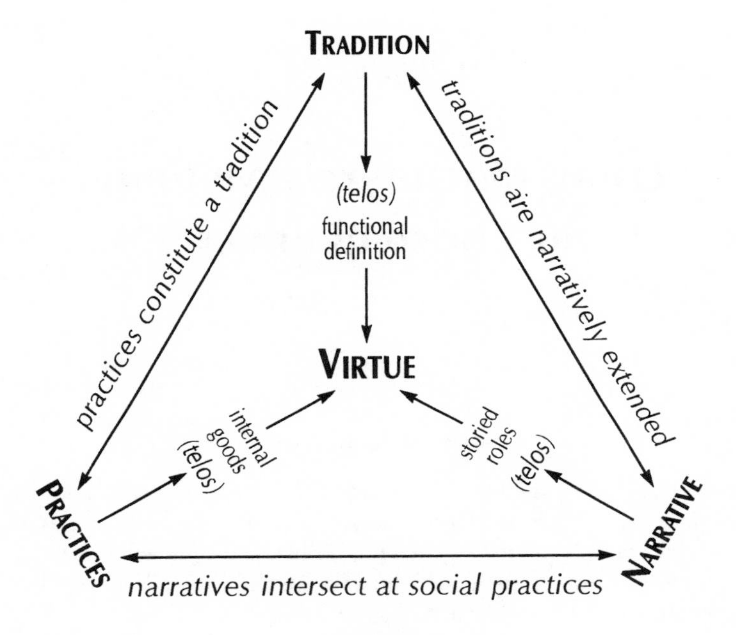

Figure 3

Conclusion

In the end there is much unfinished business. MacIntyre himself bemoans the marked absence of moral communities in the modern world. But this is not the only problem that must be addressed in the wake of *After Virtue.* For example, if the answer to "What is human life for?" is supplied to each of us by our respective practices, narratives, and traditions, doesn't this still leave us with an incurable problem of moral pluralism if not one of downright relativism? Are there some criteria for adjudicating multiple traditions? Further, if MacIntyre's project succeeds, are we in the Western world not faced with the dilemma of being inheritors of at least two conflicting traditions (namely, Aristotelianism and political liberalism)? Or can MacIntyre's thesis possibly succeed if, in fact, the Aristotelian tradition *died* with the Enlightenment? With what resources can it be exhumed and resuscitated?

MacIntyre is not unaware of these perplexities. Some of the objections earned responses in the second edition of *After Virtue* while others he has made the central concern of later books. But the mere presence of these objections does not count against his system because they become the fodder for enlivening the debate by which the tradition is extended. The question "Is MacIntyre's moral philosophy the *final* word?" is wrongheaded. The better question is "Is it the best one so far?"

Chapter 2

Using MacIntyre's Method in Christian Ethics

Nancey Murphy

Why MacIntyre?

What is the *substance* of the Christian moral life? There are heroic and paradigmatic instances. My childhood imagination was stocked with stories of the saints: martyrs who persevered to the end, monks and nuns who devoted their days to prayer, servants of the poor who gave all their worldly possessions and bodily strength to alleviate the sufferings of others.

We teach Christian morality in two ways: one is by example, and most important here is the life of Jesus; the other is by means of theoretical accounts that attempt to sum up what is good about the good lives, to give reasons for counting some lives as exemplary and others not. Both kinds of teaching are essential, and they cannot be unrelated to one another. Without the lives lived, there is nothing for the theory to be *about,* but without the theory our choice of exemplars can go awry — for instance, taking Jesus' long hair and itinerant lifestyle, rather than the cross, as relevant.[1]

There are levels of discourse in ethics. We call some judgments "first order"; for example, "It is good to care for the poor," or "Christians must cultivate the virtue of hope." Second-order discourse has to do with the right sort of *categories* or *concepts* to use in making first-order judgments and the right sort of *reasoning* or *warrants* to use in justifying them. Our claim in this book is that MacIntyre's work, surveyed in Chapter 1, offers Christians an extremely valuable second-order, or meta-ethical account. That is, MacIntyre's set of concepts (*virtue, practice, narrative, tradition*) and his account of the relations among them offer the best available resources for making and justifying first-order Christian ethical claims.

There are two ways to understand the relation of meta-ethical theory to the moral life. One way gives moral theory priority in determining what is right; the other gives theory the humbler role of attempting to summarize and regu-

1. Note the inseparability of Christian ethics and Christian doctrine: What is it about Jesus that makes *his* life normative? What is it *about* his life that is normative?

larize prior moral thought and practice. We take the latter position. To put it in Wittgensteinian terms, moral theory ought to display the "grammar" of moral discourse.[2] So it will be the task of this chapter to present an overview of the *fit* between Christian moral thinking and MacIntyre's second-order, meta-ethical theory. Chapters in Parts II and III will fill in more of the substance.

Briefly, we shall identify Christianity as a *tradition* (or set of related traditions) with its *formative texts.* We shall begin to identify the *practices* and *virtues* constitutive of the community formed by those texts. We also need to see how the Christian tradition conceives of the *telos* of human life and history and how all of this relates both to the day-to-day life of the church and to the pressing moral issues confronting us in the contemporary world. We shall suggest that MacIntyre's concept of a *practice* is an especially illuminating contribution to understanding the Christian moral life. Thus, a central question will be, What practices must the Christian community sustain in order for the church to be the church? This will serve as a point of reference for further questions concerning the virtues Christians must acquire, the shape of the communal life of the church and its relation to the wider world, and, finally, responses to current issues such as abortion, economic justice, violence.

The Bible and Ethics in the Christian Tradition

It is common to speak of the Christian *tradition,* so it should come as no surprise to find that Christianity fits MacIntyre's more technical understanding of the term. Traditions are historically extended and socially embodied. MacIntyre speaks of them as *arguments.* The arguments concern refinement of the community's concept of the good for humankind, as well as a continuing discussion about how best to interpret and apply the community's formative texts.

It is important to notice that traditions admit of containment relations. So, for instance, Lutheranism is a subtradition within Christianity. Liberal Protestantism is another kind of subtradition within Christianity, and some, but not all, liberal Protestants are Lutherans. Thomas Aquinas's moral theology contributes both to the Christian tradition and to the tradition of moral philosophy that focuses on the virtues. So the containment relations are not simple ones as with a set of Russian dolls.

The focus on Christianity as a tradition in this sense has an important consequence for Christian ethics. Prior to the Enlightenment, it could be taken for granted that the Bible was authoritative (in some degree, at least) for Christian ethics. However, during the modern period the life and teachings of Jesus became for many merely an illustration of universal moral principles available to any rational person. MacIntyre has been one of the leaders in recognizing the untenability of this notion of universal moral reasoning. All reasoning, ethics

2. Ludwig Wittgenstein, *Philosophical Investigations,* trans. G. E. M. Anscombe (New York: Macmillan, 1953), esp. sections 54, 217–42, 373.

included, is dependent upon some tradition: "To be outside of all traditions is to be a stranger to enquiry; it is to be in a state of intellectual and moral destitution. . . ."[3] Traditions themselves begin with an authority of some sort, usually a text or set of texts. This is as true of scientific traditions[4] and secular traditions of moral enquiry as it is of Christian ethics. So Christians can return unselfconsciously to the claim that the Bible is authoritative for Christian ethics. Our resort to our own *particular* texts is but an instance of a *universal* characteristic of all moral reasoning.

The vexing question, though, is *how* to use the Bible in Christian moral reasoning. Most agree that "proof-texting" is not the way (although we probably all resort to it upon occasion). Most agree that the texts need to be handled with the same critical care by the Christian ethicist as by anyone else engaged in Christian scholarship. We expect as well that even after recognizing the historical distance between one text and another, and the different theologies of authors and redactors, it is still in some sense the *whole* of the biblical witness that we want to bring to bear on our reasoning about each moral issue.

MacIntyre reckons with the fact that much of the argument within a tradition will be just this sort of wrestling with the question of how to interpret and use its formative texts. We claim that MacIntyre's own account of the relations among traditions, practices, and virtues provides new insight about how to read our own Christian texts for the purposes of ethics. Briefly, we can ask, in light of the entire canon, what is the *telos* of the church — what is God's ultimate goal for the creation, and what is the church's role in that plan? And what are the *practices* essential to the church in light of that plan?

An adequate formulation of God's purposes for the church in the space of this short chapter requires more theological and literary skill than this author possesses. Catechism answers come readily to mind: to know, love, and serve God in this life and to be happy with him in the next. However, some authors of the chapters that follow would see an answer such as this to be too individualistic. Stanley Hauerwas and John Howard Yoder focus instead on the *telos* of the church. The purpose of the church now is to prefigure the will of God for human sociality as a whole. It is to show the world how all people will live in the kingdom of God.

---

3. *Whose Justice? Which Rationality?* (Notre Dame: University of Notre Dame Press, 1988), 367. See also *Three Rival Versions of Moral Enquiry: Encyclopaedia, Genealogy, and Tradition* (Notre Dame: University of Notre Dame Press, 1989), 59–60: "What this alternative conceals from view is a third possibility, the possibility that reason can only move towards being genuinely universal and impersonal insofar as it is neither neutral nor disinterested, that membership in a particular type of moral community . . . is a condition for genuinely rational enquiry and more especially for moral and theological enquiry. . . . What emerged from Socrates' confrontation with Callicles in the *Gorgias* was that it is a precondition of engaging in rational enquiry through the method of the dialectic that one should already possess and recognize certain moral virtues without which the cooperative progress of dialectic will be impossible."

4. See Thomas Kuhn, *The Structure of Scientific Revolutions*, 2d ed. (Chicago: University of Chicago Press, 1970).

An important aspect of MacIntyre's work for understanding the role of Scripture in Christian ethics is his emphasis on the necessity of acquiring virtue in order to be able to read one's formative texts aright. Thus, reading the Scriptures in community involves an ongoing dialectic of formation and information.[5]

The Practices of the Church

We find the concept of a *practice* particularly illuminating. In an individualistic culture like our own it is difficult to take account of social realities. We recognize the role of institutions and of such clearly defined social groups as families and political parties. MacIntyre's concept of a practice, though, helps us to recognize a level of social reality that might well have gone entirely unnoticed, except perhaps for a few instances such as organized sports and some of the professions such as law and medicine.

In this section I hope to bring into view some of the (overlooked) practices of the church. In so doing, I intend to give a large part of the answer to the question, What must the church do to be the church? Such practices, in turn, will provide starting points for consideration of other issues that more often come to mind when we ask about the substance of Christian morality.

Worship

The praise and worship of God have been central to the life of God's people beginning in ancient Israel. The Book of Acts describes the first days of the church: "Day by day, as they spent much time together in the temple, they broke bread at home and ate their food with glad and generous hearts, praising God and having the good will of all the people" (Acts 2:46–47). Today it is difficult to think what would remain of church life if Sunday worship services were canceled.

So worship is central to the life of the church. Let us see what light can be shed on it *and what relevance it has for Christian ethics* if we consider it to be a practice in MacIntyre's sense. Recall that a practice is defined as

> any coherent and complex form of socially established cooperative human activity through which goods internal to that form of activity are realized in the course of trying to achieve those standards of excellence which are appropriate to, and partially definitive of, that form of activity, with the result that human powers to achieve excellence, and the human conceptions of the ends and good involved, are systematically extended.[6]

If we distinguish between public worship and saying a prayer in private, it is clear that the former requires social cooperation. Denominational require-

5. See Chapter 5 below.
6. Alasdair MacIntyre, *After Virtue,* 2d ed. (Notre Dame: University of Notre Dame Press, 1984), 187.

ments or patterns, and now ecumenical cooperation such as shared hymnals or lectionaries, provide a great deal of coherence.

Public worship indeed manifests the complexity of a MacIntyrean practice, more so in some denominations than others — consider the range from meeting-house Quakers to Russian Orthodox. In most Christian communities it includes public prayer of various kinds, ordinances or sacraments, reading of Scripture, and preaching.

We can take Jesus' teaching to be a warning against exchanging internal for external goods in worship: "do not be like the hypocrites; for they love to stand and pray in the synagogues and at the street corners, so that they may be seen by others. Truly I tell you, they have received their reward" (Matt. 6:5). James McClendon recognizes three conceptions of worship: the affective, the magical, and the dialogic. Only the last, he believes, reflects an adequate conception of the goods internal to the practice:

> Affective worship supposes its goal to be *changing the worshiper* by way of the worshiper's feelings. Services are acclaimed when they are "impressive" or "inspirational." Prayer is auto-suggestion (or other-suggestion); preaching manipulates audiences; singing arouses enthusiasm. So common worship becomes not response to God but corporate self-arousal or mutual entertainment. . . . Who can deny that there is some truth in all this? Yet there is a profound moral argument against this subjective interpretation of worship. . . . For true Christian prayer addresses not oneself nor one's fellows but the heavenly Father and present Lord. . . .
>
> The other distorted view, magical worship, may not seem so tempting, but its long history suggests that it, too, appeals to something deeply embedded in human nature. The following distinction between magic and religion is assumed here: in religion, creatures submit themselves to their God to discover and pursue God's way for them; in magic, the magicians gain power over the gods (or over God!) for their own ends. Magic means manipulation; it follows prescribed rites in order to achieve supernatural control. . . . As with the subjective theory of worship, it is right to acknowledge the truth of the magical theory: there is a "magic" in worship, an element beyond all earthly calculation. God does answer prayer. . . . Yet God never surrenders the initiative to earthly magicians of any stripe.[7]

McClendon bases his dialogic account of proper worship on the biblical narrative in which God takes the initiative and human response consists in worship (service). This, he says, is the narrative plot throughout all the Scriptures:

> God *summons* Abraham and *fulfills* Sarah; God *frees* Israel; God *anoints* David; God *punishes* but *restores* a rebellious nation; God *sends* Jesus, *accepts* his death, and *raises* him from the dead; God *pours forth* as Spirit; in the end the risen Christ *returns*. Each of these divine-action initiatives both requires and (in the happy case) enables a human response which is taken up into the divine action: Abraham (with a sometimes amused Sarah) *obeys* the call; Israel *crosses* the Reed Sea; David *rules* his people; the people, chastised, *renew* their covenant faithfulness; Jesus at

7. James Wm. McClendon, Jr., *Doctrine: Systematic Theology, Volume II* (Nashville: Abingdon Press, 1994), 374–75.

> Jordan and again in Gethsemane *accepts* his ministry; Spirit-filled believers *speak* in new tongues; the faithful church *expects* the coming of Christ in his kingdom at the end. In such, God acts and enabled people answer; in the broadest sense this elicited answer is their reasonable worship (Rom. 12:1).[8]

Much more could be said about the internal goods toward which the practice of Christian worship aims; such reflection is itself a part of the practice, the progressive refinement of Christians' concept of those standards of excellence that are partially definitive of this form of activity.

It may seem peculiar to treat worship as a central topic of Christian ethics. However, I suggest that we consider the question, What are the acquired human characteristics the possession and exercise of which tend to enable worshipers to achieve the goods internal to this practice? If so, we shall find ourselves drawn to reflect on many of the virtues considered central to Christian life.

The humility that features in Christian lists of the virtues is in the first instance to be understood as submission to God — it is the virtue that prevents worship from turning into magic. True worship requires penitence and the ability to forgive others: "And forgive us our debts, as we also have forgiven our debtors" (Matt. 6:12).

If Galatians 3:28 — "There is no longer Jew or Greek, there is no longer slave or free, there is no longer male and female; for all of you are one in Christ Jesus" — was indeed an early baptismal formula, then proper participation in this normative part of public worship requires the overcoming of ethnic, class, and gender discrimination.

Along with these (and other) well-recognized Christian virtues there are requirements for proper worship for which we have no names. What is that characteristic in virtue of which some are able to recognize their Lord "in the breaking of the bread"? to sense the movement of the Spirit in the midst of the gathered community? to tremble in awe at the majesty of God? These acquired human characteristics may well be gifts rather than skills taught and learned, but it is equally part of the ethical business of the church to ask what kind of formation will leave the door open to such transformation.

The Practice of Witness

A second activity central to the life and survival of the church is its witness or evangelism. Witness to Christ, to his resurrection, to his kingdom, is commanded again and again throughout the New Testament and, practically speaking, it is the means by which the church community is maintained — ideally by witnessing to all the world, but as a start in our own neighborhoods and to those who live under our own roofs.

Here, again, it may be useful to think of this collection of activities — evangelistic preaching, door-to-door visitation, revivals at the home church, mission

---

8. Ibid., 376.

work in all its forms abroad — as a MacIntyrean practice or set of such practices. As is to be expected, people debate about the internal goods involved in these practices, about their aims or *teloi.* For instance, some ask whether individual conversion and church growth are the central goals or whether the witness to Christ is best accomplished by carrying on his work among the economically poor and oppressed. Answers to this question are necessary in order to recognize the goods internal to the practice(s).

That the proper ends of evangelism and the virtues required for its sustenance are indeed moral issues can be seen in the sad history of the distortion of missions to serve the goals of empire and cultural imperialism but also in the simple ineffectiveness of witnesses who do not live the life they try to promote.

James McClendon in his *Ethics* describes the virtue of *presence* as an acquired human characteristic necessary to achieve the goods internal to the practice of witness:

> Presence is being one's self for someone else; it is refusing the temptation to withdraw mentally and emotionally, but it is also on occasion putting our own body's weight and shape alongside the neighbor, the friend, the lover in need.
>
> But is presence, even in this extended sense, really a virtue, or is it like left-handedness or curiosity, merely somebody's quality or distinguishing feature? Earlier in this chapter [of *Ethics*] the black church was set forth as displaying the quality of presence. When black slaves had no other earthly resource, they knew how to be present to and for one another, and knew that Another was present for them as well. . . . To characterize this presence as a virtue is to say that it is a strength or skill, developed by training and practice, which is a substantive part of (the Christian) life. . . .[9]

Presence is necessary for witness. As examples McClendon cites, among others, the seventeenth-century followers of George Fox:

> . . . we see that the appeal to truth and to witness required the full *presence* of the witnesses to that truth — even their presence to and for the churches and denominations and civil authorities that sought to eject them. They could not, *could* not just go away and leave the others alone as they were asked to do and still be true to this virtue. Presence is one of the profound forms of Christian witness. There is a Catholic religious order whose members live inside South American prisons and jails in order to be present to and for the prisoners — the ministry of presence.[10]

Works of Mercy

Another set of activities central to the life of the church are those that carry on Jesus' ministry to the poor, the sick, and the outcast, activities often housed now in para-church institutions. Here, again, we find cooperative and complex social activity. Here again we find ongoing debate about the goods internal to

9. James Wm. McClendon, Jr., *Ethics: Systematic Theology,* vol. 1 (Nashville: Abingdon Press, 1986), 106–7.
10. Ibid., 108.

the practice. One central aim is certainly to alleviate the suffering of others, but there are also goods that accrue to the givers rather than to their recipients. For instance, Jesus asks the rich young man to sell all and give to the poor so that *he* might be free to follow Jesus. At least as important is the value of these practices for witnessing to the character of God, so this practice is intimately related to the practice of evangelism.

If we recognize as an internal good the transformation of the giver as well as assistance to the recipient, this sheds light on the question of how charitable work ought to be organized. Even if it is more efficient, say, for church members to contribute to national or international agencies to feed the hungry, it is nonetheless essential for them to have more involvement than mere check-writing.

Essential Practices?

These three practices, works of mercy,[11] witness, and worship, provide one answer to the question, What is the church *for;* what must the church do to be the church? Readers may not agree that these (or only these) are *the* practices constitutive of the church's mission and identity. We will be happy if this proposal provokes thought, especially if it provokes discussion and controversy, because we believe that just such questions should be at the very heart of Christian ethical discourse. This is one way of phrasing the question that ought to precede any attempt to tackle the ethical issues that our wider context provides. First let the church be the church; then let the church speak to the world on moral issues.

We add two more practices to the list of essentials — discipling and discernment — because they are essential for maintaining and guiding the church itself in its community formation.

We use the term *discipling* to refer to the church's teaching and formation of its members. The institutions of Sunday school and seminary house relevant practices. But we also include here practices of church discipline, what John Howard Yoder refers to in Chapter 6 below as the Rule of Christ. This means following the instructions in Matthew 18 for reproof of errant members and (when successful) their reconciliation with the body.

Communal discernment is a complex social practice used by the church to "test the spirits to see whether they are from God" (1 John 4:1). It may also be called the rule of Paul, since the Reformers found instructions for this practice in Paul's letter to the church at Corinth (1 Cor. 14:26–33).[12] The sorts of judgments involved vary. In the New Testament we see discernment involved in recognizing genuine prophets (1 Cor. 14:29; 1 Thess. 5:20–21), in receiving guidance from the Spirit for mission work (Acts 13:2), and for determining church policies (Acts 15:28).

---

11. We choose the no-longer-stylish term *works of mercy* for alliterative reasons, not to endorse particular forms of such practices (like giving alms instead of working for economic justice).

12. See John Howard Yoder, *Body Politics: Five Practices of the Christian Community before the Watching World* (Nashville: Discipleship Resources, 1992), chap. 5.

The Reformers used the practice to settle questions of doctrine and scriptural interpretation. Ignatius of Loyola promoted a form of discernment for recognizing one's vocation. During the Great Awakening Jonathan Edwards provided public criteria for distinguishing between the work of the Spirit of God and merely psychological phenomena. Contemporary Quakers use the practice to make decisions in matters of teaching and to guide their social action.

The practice varies somewhat from one era and group to another. However, in most cases most of the following elements are involved: prayer, study of Scripture, and open discussion leading to consensus. The discussion involves application of criteria, which usually include consistency with the apostolic witness; fruits, such as moral improvement, unification of the church, and the fruits of the Spirit (Gal. 5:22); and circumstances — "open doors."[13]

So we have here a complex and relatively coherent, socially established, and cooperative form of human activity. The chief good internal to this practice is recognition of the activity of God in the world, especially perceiving God's directions for the mission of the church and the reform of its other practices. This practice itself is capable of development, as participants grow in knowledge of the ways of God's working, in the humility required to submit to God's will and to accept that others speak a part of the truth, in patience to wait upon God and for the group consensus that is a sign of the Spirit's leading.

We suggest that the communal practice of discernment plays a role in Christian ethics comparable to that of the virtue of *phronēsis* (practical wisdom) in Aristotle's system. *Phronēsis* is the ability to exercise judgment in particular cases and thus is a virtue without which none of the other virtues can be properly exercised. In Aristotle's system, each person needs the ability to prioritize goods and to know when to exercise each virtue. For Christians, the practice of discernment draws upon a variety of gifts and virtues within the community, with the goal not of finding the best human wisdom but rather of being led by Divine Wisdom.[14]

As mentioned above, there may be arguments about whether these five are the essential practices of the church. The last two are likely to be more controversial than the others. However these arguments come out, our central claim is that the first questions to ask with regard to Christian ethics are these: Are we as a community doing all of these things well? And are we forming in our members the virtues necessary to sustain these practices? As a sampling of the issues thus raised, chapters in the second part of this volume consider the practices of community formation and the relation between worship at the Lord's Table and the practice of reconciliation (McClendon), discernment (Fowl and Jones), discipling (Yoder), and theological education (Dykstra).

13. For a more detailed account see Nancey Murphy, *Theology in the Age of Scientific Reasoning* (Ithaca, N.Y: Cornell University Press, 1990), chap. 5.

14. See John Howard Yoder, "The Hermeneutics of Peoplehood: A Protestant Perspective," in *The Priestly Kingdom: Social Ethics as Gospel* (Notre Dame: University of Notre Dame Press, 1984), 15–45.

Rules

There is an old conundrum: does God command things because they are good, or is what God commands good because God commands it? This question cannot be evaded forever, but it can certainly be put off by showing that God commands what is necessary for the flourishing of the practices constitutive of the church.

Despite MacIntyre's primary emphasis on the virtues, rules find their place in his scheme in that certain acts must be prescribed or proscribed in order for a practice to be possible at all. For example, in chess the rules specifying the moves of each piece are partially constitutive of the game. The (unstated) negative rule "no cheating" rules out behavior that would defeat the whole purpose of playing.

We believe that a systematic analysis of the commandments in Scripture would show God's commands to be rules essential for the constitution or preservation of practices essential to the identity of Israel or the church. McClendon argues in his *Ethics* that the Ten Commandments begin as rules constitutive of the practices of the new nation of Israel. For example, the command to keep holy the Sabbath sets up the community's system of time-keeping and holy-day observances:

> Here we meet a principle vital to interpreting all the commandments. Exactly because the Ten Words condense all biblical law, each must be read as implying whatever expansion its provenance requires. Thus with the Sabbath the whole calendar of Jewish festivals around the year is brought to mind. . . . The Sabbath was said to be for remembering and for rest. In Exodus, this memory looks back to creation (God rested on creation's seventh day); in Deuteronomy it looks to Israel's Egyptian slavery (in which there had been no rest day) and to the divine deliverance from that ceaseless toil. So the people who keep this commandment will celebrate their liberation and their creaturehood as they remember God the Creator who is also God the Liberator. Doing so, they will show that time is for Israel no bare succession, but means recapitulation as well.[15]

For a New Testament example, consider the following: "no adultery" is a rule constitutive of the practice of marriage — any marriage practice. However, marriage for Christians is significantly different from what it is for non-Christians. New Testament teaching links it with witness to the faithfulness of God. Marriage is thus a subpractice within the broader constitutive Christian practice of witness. So the rule "no adultery" takes on a deeper significance for Christians. Infidelity within marriage essentially destroys the value of the practice in testifying to the fidelity of God — it prevents participants from attaining what Scripture teaches is a primary internal good toward which the practice itself aims.

Another function of rules is to provide guidance for beginners. To stay with our chess analogy, we might teach children learning to play chess a few rules for good strategy. But no such set of rules can ever fully capture the strategies of the masters. Similarly, "Love your neighbor as yourself" is a very simple rule, yet developing a sense of the breadth and depth of this requirement is a lifelong task; its corollaries could be listed in no book.

---

15. *Ethics,* 179.

To attempt systematically to relate each New Testament injunction to the practices of the church would require a book quite different from this one. However, we hope to show in the chapters that follow (and in the analyses provided in the editors' introductions to the chapters) that such an effort is a powerful tool for understanding why God's commands are what they are and not otherwise.

Virtues

In the course of describing what we take to be essential practices of the church, I have mentioned some of the virtues needed to sustain those practices; others are discussed in chapters that follow. In this section we consider several theoretical issues regarding the virtues in relation to the Christian life.

In a class of Protestant seminary students, someone can always be counted on to raise the question whether a virtue ethic is not a subtle endorsement of some form of "works righteousness." It is important to note that a virtue is here defined as an acquired human characteristic, but there is no specification of *how* it is acquired. A long-standing debate in Western culture is reflected in the difference between Aristotle's assumption that virtue is in an unproblematic way teachable and Augustine's conclusion that the human will is perverted in such a way that a person, unassisted by grace, can form only bad habits. So it is important to note that the requirement that virtuous behavior be practiced does not imply that no grace is involved. It may well be that divine assistance is required to make practice of any virtue possible. Yet this does not mean that a virtue could be acquired without practice, since a virtue is manifest only in its exercise — it is an excellence in performance.

The ancient claim that exercise of the virtues (or vices) makes lasting changes in the person such that it becomes easier to continue that pattern of behavior has found recent scientific confirmation. G. Simon Harak has collected scientific accounts of the physiological foundations of habit, changes in biochemical, neurological, and hormonal responses.[16]

Paul M. Churchland has proposed to explain learning of all types by means of a model that relies on the notion of neural "prototypes"; that is, neural networks are formed by a learning process in such a way that receptors are set to fire in response to particular patterns of stimulation. This understanding of brain function suggests that both moral behavior and application of moral concepts depend on building up specific sets of neuronal connections. He concludes that neurologically we are much better endowed to think in terms of virtues than rules:

> The alternative [to a rule-based account of moral capacities] is a hierarchy of learned prototypes, for both moral perception and moral behavior, prototypes embodied in the well-tuned configuration of a neural network's synaptic weights [that is, tendencies to fire as a result of degrees and kinds of stimulation]. We may find

16. *Virtuous Passions: The Formation of Christian Character* (New York: Paulist Press, 1993).

> here a more fruitful path to understanding the nature of moral learning, moral insight, moral disagreements, moral failings, moral pathologies, and moral growth at the level of entire societies....
>
> On these ... assumptions, moral learning will be a matter of slowly generating a hierarchy of moral prototypes, presumably from a substantial number of relevant *examples* of the moral kinds at issue. Hence the relevance of stories and fables, and above all the ongoing relevance of the parental example of interpersonal behavior, and parental commentary on and consistent guidance of childhood behavior.[17]

So there is some evidence that however virtues come to be exercised, whether by human initiative alone or aided by divine impulse, the exercise brings about lasting changes in the person, realized physiologically.

Churchland even offers a neurological account of the virtue Aristotle called *phronēsis:*

> People with unusually penetrating moral insight will be those who can see a problematic moral situation in more than one way, and who can evaluate the relative accuracy and relevance of those competing interpretations. Such people will be those with unusual moral *imagination,* and a critical capacity to match. The former virtue will require a rich library of moral prototypes from which to draw, and especial skills in the recurrent manipulation of one's moral perception. The latter virtue will require a keen eye for local divergences from any presumptive prototype, and a willingness to take them seriously as grounds for finding some alternative understanding. Such people will by definition be rare, although all of us have some moral imagination, and all of us some capacity for criticism.[18]

Life Stories, the Church's Story, and God's Story

Narrative has an important role in MacIntyre's ethics. The acquired characteristics needed for participation in practices are merely *candidates* for virtues until we see how they contribute to the whole of a human life from birth to death. So prudent choice of the practices in which one engages depends on the particularities of one's life story: debts to a particular set of parents, responsibilities to a particular community, and so on. A life story is judged according to the good at which it aims and its success in attaining that good.

One person's life story is embedded within the stories of others, as well as in the histories of the practices in which that one participates and in the traditions of which one is a part. So virtues are those characteristics needed to sustain communities and traditions as well as practices. "I can only answer the question 'What am I to do?' if I can answer the prior question 'Of what story or stories do I find myself a part?'"[19]

---

17. *The Engine of Reason, the Seat of the Soul: A Philosophical Journey into the Brain* (Cambridge: MIT Press, 1995), 144, 146.

18. Ibid., 146–47.

19. MacIntyre, *After Virtue,* 216.

Notice how this emphasis on story makes sense of the attention Christians regularly pay to their own history. For Christians recognize three important narratives: their own life stories, the story of the church, and God's story. The church gets its purpose from the role it plays in God's larger purposes. The individual's life story gets its *telos* from the role she or he plays in the church and in God's greater purposes.

I have already noted that a judgment regarding the practices essential to the church depends on what one takes the mission or purpose of the church to be. We can understand the practice of witness as telling the story of God and of God's involvement with us, especially in the life of Jesus. Worship involves ritual reenactment of the story. Works of mercy are a major part of living out the story of God in Jesus.

The concept of *vocation* has been important in Christian thought. MacIntyre's discussion of life stories, with their unity and *telos,* provides resources for sorting out various conceptions of vocation. In the New Testament one's calling was to the Christian life itself, or to salvation. In the Middle Ages, *vocation* was used only of one's calling to the religious life. In contrast, Luther claimed that all stations in life in which it is possible to live honestly — including both marital state and job — are divine vocations.

In keeping with the New Testament we can maintain that there is in fact one central calling for all Christians — to be a part of the people of God. Yet the particularities of our roles and responsibilities differ. Some are married, some are single. Some are called to one ministry within the church, some to others; but all are called to participate in some way in the work of the church. So the concept of calling cannot rightly be restricted to the unmarried or to clergy. Neither, however, can it be used of just any family relationship or of any job or career choice, because not all marriages or all walks of life are suited to contribute to the achievement of the *telos* of one's Christian life.

Reading Scripture

Christians have become accustomed to reading Scripture more for insight about what they are to *do* (or not do) than insight about what kind of people they are to *be.* Our claim in this book is that the linguistic categories provided by MacIntyre's virtue ethics provide better resources not only for theoretical ethicists but also for those who appreciate and wish to appropriate the moral teaching of Scripture. That is, his approach to ethics is highly congruent with the New Testament's way of thinking.

Let us see what comes to light when we ask of a text (here, Ephesians) what *virtues* are expected of Christians, what *practices* they are to engage in, and how the *story* of God and God's *purposes* for the church explains why these virtues and these practices are required.

In light of MacIntyre's analysis, we can read the letter as an exhortation to practice the Christian virtues (and avoid Gentile vices) because the Ephesians (and we) are the community whose tradition is founded on the remembrance of what God has done for us in the past and the community that knows the true destiny (*telos*) of human life. We have practices suited for achieving that goal, and each follower has a role to play in those practices.

The virtues are hope, which involves awareness of our *telos* (1:18), humility, gentleness, patience, love, kindness, tenderheartedness, forgiveness (4:1–3). The latter seven are necessary because the central practice of the church is community formation—building up the body of Christ (4:12), including especially the making of one new people out of what used to be two (2:11–22). Subpractices intended to achieve that goal are evangelism, teaching, and pastoring (4:11–12). The rules needed to protect the practice of community formation are no lying, no stealing, no evil talk, and always to reconcile within a day (4:25–29). This practice of preserving the unity of the body is appropriately the highest goal for Christians because of God's ultimate goal, the adoption of this new people as children through Jesus Christ (1:5).

The Christian's life story is generally the story of one who formerly lived under the rules of this world, following desires of the flesh, but then was made alive together with Christ, according to God's prior plan (2:1–10). Each Christian's calling is conditioned by the roles and relationships in which he or she is involved (5:21–6:9).

We might add that Paul's own vocation, to bring the good news to the Gentiles, fits the larger pattern of salvation by grace and also gets its point from its contribution to God's plan to incorporate the Gentiles into his adopted people.

Current Issues

The current social context continually presents its own issues for the Christian ethicist's agenda. We take these up last in this volume because we believe that the issues pertaining most directly to the life of the church itself provide a necessary vantage point for a Christian approach to such issues as abortion, homosexuality, medical and business ethics. That is, these issues are not central to the New Testament's agenda. How, then, do we bridge the gap between those early concerns and the moral questions raised by our culture? The essays collected in the last part of this book all illustrate the ways current issues can be addressed by considering their relation to the central practices of the church and to the virtues there involved, or to the story of God and God's purposes for the church and for humankind as a whole.

For example, Stanley Hauerwas has argued that Christians cannot rightly understand their own opposition to abortion unless they can first answer the question, Why have children? His answer is that our willingness to bring another generation of children into the world is a form of witness to our hope for the future and to our confidence that our own tradition is worth handing on. Our hope is based on the story of God's faithfulness in the past. Thus, the practice of bearing and raising children is an instance of the central Christian practice of *witness.* A central virtue needed to sustain the practice is hope.

Meta-ethics, or, How Can Christians Defend Their Particularity in Public?

Hauerwas has argued that Christians will get nowhere attempting to influence public debate on issues like abortion if they limit themselves to the language of secular society. Instead, they ought to make their arguments — in public — in the language of their own tradition. Hauerwas has been much criticized for this "sectarian" move. However, MacIntyre's analysis of the nature of moral reasoning makes it clear that Hauerwas's strategy is in no way sectarian (or at least, no more so than anyone else's). All moral reasoning, if it is to be cogent, must draw upon the resources of some tradition, without which one lacks the virtues necessary for having a moral outlook.[20] Public discourse in terms of "rights" is just as particular as Christian discourse; social contract theory places its own story of an original state and the development of society alongside that of Genesis. No rational argument has been advanced for why the Enlightenment tradition should be privileged over all others.

In response to the charge that such a clash of narratives is sure to foster moral relativism, a MacIntyrean reply would be that the relativism is already a fact of life in our society, and the interesting question is whether awareness of the traditions out of which we speak will not in fact help us find ways of overcoming disagreements. MacIntyre's defense of the virtue tradition over against the Enlightenment tradition provides a model that Christian apologists might use for a public defense of the Christian tradition and its resources for ethics.

Conclusion

This chapter has been intentionally brief, lest it attempt to do the work of the rest of the book. Its purpose is simply to begin a process of redescription — of bringing to light the congruity between scriptural patterns of moral thought and MacIntyre's set of moral concepts. Or, rather, it is to make clear the MacIntyrean features of the writings of a variety of ethicists, whose work, we believe, more accurately interprets and applies scriptural teaching than has the "mainline" of Christian ethics in the recent past.

However, before pursuing these issues further, it is important to take a look at the competition. What are some of the other patterns that have been proposed for structuring Christian moral thought, and how does this MacIntyrean system compare?

---

20. See note 3 above.

Chapter 3

Positioning MacIntyre within Christian Ethics

Brad J. Kallenberg

The seventeenth-century Protestant scholastic Abraham Calovius has been credited with the prayer, "Lord, fill me with the hatred of heretics!" His prayer epitomizes the long-standing and widespread religious conviction that dialogue with alternative points of view is, at best, unfruitful and, at worst, downright dangerous. But if religious believers are perpetually suspicious of other points of view, where does this leave our hope for fruitful appropriation of Alasdair MacIntyre's thinking within the field of *Christian* ethics? Do we seriously think that MacIntyre can do any better than merely talk past, rather than with, Christian ethicists? In this chapter we will examine the work of a number of religious ethicists in order to explore whether MacIntyre can speak with others on their terms of discussion and do so in a way that is mutually enriching. Once we have shown that MacIntyre's work is germane for Christian ethics, the remaining essays in this volume can then demonstrate the "Christianness" of our project both by showing how churchly life can be richly described in MacIntyrean terms (practices, virtues, and so on) and by showing how ethical conclusions that fully fit with our Christian story, concerning specific contemporary issues, can be generated in MacIntyrean fashion. But our first task is to answer the more basic question: "What is *Christian* ethics anyway?"[1]

What Is *Christian* Ethics?

Broadly speaking, *ethics* denotes rational reflection on the problems of human morality. On the contemporary scene this usually amounts to providing rational defense of some course of action taken in response to a given quandary: "Should she pull the plug?" "Should he pull the trigger?" And so on. The justification is supposed to be arrived at by employing a *theory* of justification. But, as we have

1. See, e.g., Stanley Hauerwas and D. Stephen Long, "Ethics, Christian," in *A New Handbook of Christian Theology*, ed. Donald W. Musser and Joseph L. Price (Nashville: Abingdon Press, 1992), 160–67.

seen already in Chapter 1, where theories abound, a clear criterion for deciding among theories is entirely lacking.

How can *Christian* ethics be distinguished in this fray? If ethics is identified with rational reflection upon philosophical, scientific, and experiential sources, then perhaps Christian ethics is, as James Gustafson has suggested, nothing more than reflection that additionally takes Christian *sources* into account.[2] However, one is always entitled to ask whether the *mode* of reflection itself possesses a theological component. In other words, perhaps ethics is not Christian simply because we reflect on Christian sources (such as the Scriptures or the churchly tradition) but because we reflect in a *Christian* way. This way of looking at things brings the character of the person(s) engaged in ethical reflection to the center of the discussion. It *matters* what kind of people we are while we are doing ethics. Yet, oddly, this point is given a wide berth in many approaches to ethics today. So, before we can sample different "Christian" ethical approaches and measure MacIntyre's compatibility with each, I must first sketch the history of Christian ethics by drawing attention to the three watershed events that help to explain why there is such a diversity within the field.

The *Christian* character of ethics is most recognizable in the first three centuries after Christ. During this period, the term *Christian ethics* refers to the crazy way Christians actually lived. Clement of Rome reports that some Christians actually sold themselves into slavery in order to use that money to ransom others (apparently with worse owners) and to feed the poor.[3] Athenagoras describes those first Christians this way:

> But among us you will find uneducated persons and artisans, and old women who, if they are unable in words to prove the benefit of our doctrine, yet by their deeds exhibit the benefit arising from their persuasion of its truth: they do not rehearse speeches, but exhibit good works; when struck, they do not strike again; when robbed, they do not go to law; they give to those who ask of them, and love their neighbors as themselves.[4]

This sort of countercultural behavior meant that these early Christians were frequently misunderstood, persecuted, and even killed for living against the grain. But they were willing to tolerate this misunderstanding because their peculiar behavior pointed to the particular character of their God. Because Christian ethics in this age involved a description of the way a particular group of people behaved, we can say that the concept is marked by *particularity* and *praxis* (practice).

---

2. James M. Gustafson, "Christian Ethics," in *Westminster Dictionary of Christian Ethics,* ed. James F. Childress and John Macquarrie (Philadelphia: Westminster Press, 1967), 87–90. For Gustafson, the most important Christian source for doing Christian ethics is Christology.

3. 1 Clement 55:2. See S. Scott Bartchy, "Slavery, Greco-Roman and New Testament," in *Anchor Bible Dictionary* (New York: Doubleday, 1990).

4. Athenagoras, "A Plea for Christians," in *Classical Readings in Christian Apologetics, A.D. 100–1800,* ed. L. Russ Bush (Grand Rapids, Mich.: Zondervan, 1983), 44.

The first watershed event that changed the flavor of ethics was the universalization of Christianity by the emperor Constantine early in the fourth century. In one fell swoop the church found itself not only married to culture but apparently stuck with the task of managing culture as well. Although perpetual religious persecution prior to the Edict of Milan (315 A.D.) had virtually guaranteed a basic consensus regarding what beliefs Christians considered worth dying for, once the danger and stigma of following Christ were removed, it became politically and socially advantageous to "convert." As a result, virtually all of the rest of the empire's population swarmed into the church. The Christian church and the secular kingdom merged, giving birth to the new Christian kingdom, or "Christendom."

This mass conversion left historians scratching their heads regarding which group deserved the title "Christian" or "church." On the one hand, it seemed fitting to reserve the terms for that small remnant of religious primitivists for their authentic religious faith. But on the other hand, their numbers were so disproportionately small that they, in effect, seemed to be irrelevant to the rest of culture. The overall scope of the merger was so colossal that theologian and philosopher Ernst Troeltsch didn't think twice about simply dismissing the purist minority with the pejorative label "sectarian" and reserving the term *Church* to describe everyone else.

Ethics or morality was "Christian" after Constantine, therefore, in the sense that it applied to everyone in the "Church." What was previously a uniform standard of practical holiness for a particular religious group became, by default, a moral "sliding scale." It is easy to imagine why this might happen. Church leaders, who took seriously their "divinely appointed" job of managing culture, found themselves ranking the morality of behaviors to help *nominal* Christians, who couldn't identify with "saintly" behavior (such as loving one's enemies), to understand what moral improvement might look like *in their case.* So the particular and practical character of early Christian ethics was lost. Nevertheless, ethics after Constantine retained an explicitly theological flavor. This meant three things. First, the "oughtness," or obligatory character, of ethical prescriptions was understood to be an aspect of the authority God holds over creation. Just as the world was called into existence by divine fiat, so too God calls human beings to moral behavior by *divine command.*

Second, because ethics was understood as linked to the will of God, and this God was believed to be God over all creation, all creation was seen as bearing the imprint of divine intention. This premise had the advantage of making ethical reasoning a matter of *natural law,* which is to say, universally accessible to all rational creatures. For example, in the Middle Ages it was claimed that the sexual perversion of bestiality was plainly sinful because it was plainly *unnatural,* that is, obviously contrary to God's design for same-species copulation, in a way that anyone could see.

Third, despite the assumption that laypersons could read the moral laws written in nature, in practice moral reasoning lay in the hands of the clergy, who alone had the education and leisure to argue among themselves how natural law should be applied in each of a virtually limitless number of cases. *Casuistry,* as it became known, was a communal practice in the full sense of the term used in Chapter 1 and bore a striking resemblance to modern jurisprudence; its practitioners were even sometimes called "natural lawyers."

A second watershed moment was the Protestant Reformation. By drawing attention to the moral self which stands naked and accountable to its Creator, such thinkers as Luther and Calvin managed to effect a nearly total disjunction between the public and private spheres in human life. In other words, communal ethical reasoning (casuistry) was one thing, but the onus of moral responsibility rested squarely on the shoulders of the *lone individual* faced with the question: "What ought I do?" The Protestant Reformers' turn to the individual human subject may very well have contributed to the Enlightenment, but it also seems to have virtually guaranteed preoccupation with "decisionism" over the past nearly five hundred years of moral reflection.[5] The term *decisionism* refers to the assumption that ethics has to do with nothing other than *deciding* what is *the* moral thing to *do.*

Thus, "Christian ethics" after 1500 took two distinct shapes. Roman Catholic moral theology retained the medieval character of Christian ethics as *communal* (with respect to the practice of casuistry within the clerical community) and *juridical* (with respect to natural law). Ethics in the Protestant vein lost the communal and, for the most part, the juridical aspects and, with the discarding of the practice of casuistry, came to be thought of exclusively as *deontological* (with respect to the *binding* character of divine commands). This emphasis can be seen in the central role that sin played in the theology of the Reformation (Calvin, Luther, and so on) and the Radical Reformation (for example, the Anabaptists). Whether one spoke of commission, omission, or corruption, Reformers viewed sin as *sin* because it missed the mark of what had been divinely commanded.

The third watershed movement was the mid-seventeenth-century shift known as the Enlightenment. This shift amounted to the divorce of reason and faith — and for that matter, the divorce of reason from history, language, culture, and tradition. The hope was that Reason, once freed from these "restraints," might provide the means for definitive resolution of all moral quandaries by discovering genuinely objective and universal moral principles. But because ethics in this vein sought *a priori* principles — that is, moral principles *abstracted* from human living — morality took on the flavor of something alien, antithetical, and even inhuman. Not only was the role of theology for ethics entirely lost (after the Enlightenment, the question of sin was thought to be irrelevant to moral perspicacity and the divine command an insufficient basis for the deontological

5. See Alasdair MacIntyre, *A Short History of Ethics* (New York: Collier Books, 1966); Edmund Pincoffs, "Quandary Ethics," in *Revisions: Changing Perspectives in Moral Philosophy,* ed. Alasdair MacIntyre and Stanley Hauerwas (Notre Dame: University of Notre Dame Press, 1983), 92–112.

character of moral imperatives), but the importance of personal character and point of view for moral reasoning was discarded as well.

In summary, there have been three watershed events — Constantine, the Reformation, and the Enlightenment — that drastically altered the shape of Christian ethics. In each case, a former aspect of ethics was lost. The *particular* and *practical* character of original Christian ethics was lost with Constantine; the *communal* and *juridical* nature of medieval ethical reasoning was lost with the Protestant Reformation, which retained only the *deontological* character of moral reasoning; the *theological* and *anthropological* aspects of ethics were lost with the Enlightenment. This way of telling the story of Christian ethics helps us see that what we call ethics today has been the product of a long process of "stripping down." Does this mean that we've finally gotten to the heart of the matter? No more than divesting an artichoke of its leaves reveals its essence! Naturally, with every reduction, voices have been raised in opposition. Today we hear a cacophony of voices, each calling us to attend to an aspect of ethics formerly lost. Because Alasdair MacIntyre's work resonates strongly with these voices, he is able to earn a place in Christian ethics.

What follows is a parade of spokespersons, each hearkening us to a different feature that has been lost to the practice of ethics over time. We will work backward through the watershed events, listening to voices that remind us to attend to the *anthropological, theological, communal, juridical, deontological,* and *practical* and *particular* aspects of Christian ethics. Since the most recent watershed event, the Enlightenment, resulted in the bifurcation of theology and philosophy, the first two thinkers we shall consider have virtually no theological sympathies to speak of. Nevertheless, the advice they give is a fitting reminder of what Christian ethics can and should be.

Carol Gilligan and Bernard Williams: Attending to Human Existence

Carol Gilligan urges us to attend to the *anthropological* dimension of ethics by reminding us that human existence is not everywhere uniform. Thus, her answer to the question, "Why be moral?" is colored by the answer to a different question: "Whose account is in view?" The title of her book *In a Different Voice* reflects her conviction that the explanation of what morality amounts to depends on which gender is telling the story. Females have been typically classified, by such notables as Piaget and Kohlberg, as morally *under*-developed simply because the criteria for moral development have historically been based on data gathered exclusively from male subjects![6] Given the possibility that women have a unique moral development, a different set of criteria may be required to evaluate their moral maturity.

6. Carol Gilligan, *In a Different Voice* (Cambridge: Harvard University Press, 1982, 1993), 11–17.

It turns out that the way one views the world is a by-product of gender identity. Very early on the male begins to identify who he is in terms of *separation* and *difference* from "Mom," his opposite-sexed primary caregiver. Separation and difference thus become the fundamental interpretive categories for a male view of the world. In contrast, self-identity for the female is based on the perception "I'm the *same* as Mom." Hence, *connection* and *relation* become primary categories for a female perception of self and the world.

Gilligan's chief contribution to the discussion of morality is that *perception* itself is profoundly moral. What usually pass for moral *facts* are nothing other than *evaluative* judgments spoken with a particular moral "voice." Male voice differs from female voice in the same ways that male self-identity differs from female self-identity. So, if a male views the world through the lenses of separation and difference, then his moral outlook will likely be concerned for things like objectivity, logic, principles, rights, justice, equality, highest good, and contest. On the other hand, if a female perceives the world in terms of connection, then her moral perception is bound to be concerned with things like contextuality, relationships, actual consequence, responsibility, care, equity, lesser evil, and peacemaking.

Gilligan's research demands that significant changes be made in the standard textbook account of morality. First, if the way one sees a moral quandary influences the verdict, then *objectivity* (a form of separation) can no longer be maintained as the *sine qua non* (that is, the absolutely essential ingredient) of moral development. There is no *morality-as-such* but either *morality-as-perceived-from-a-male-point-of-view* or *morality-as-perceived-from-a-female-point-of-view.* This suggests, second, that a complete account of morality requires *both* male and female voices. The developmental directions of men and women are complementary. Men emerge from childhood assuming separation and objectification and are plagued forever after with the problem of connection; men don't readily hear others.[7] Women, on the other hand, emerge from adolescence assuming connection and therefore have perennial problems with separation; women don't readily hear their own selves.[8] Third, the way the field of ethics typically assumes masculine criteria (objectivity, principles, rights, and so on) is not only one-sided; it is shortsighted as well. The differences between men and women suggest that the end of moral development lies *beyond both.* Men need to move past "equality" to see that equality blinds justice to seeing real difference, and women need to move past "equity" to see that any account that treats difference as real is inherently violent.[9]

To summarize, Gilligan brings out clearly the dangers implicit in ignoring the "humanness" of moral reasoners. Too often it is presumed that ethical discourse glides smoothly on the currents of *a priori* (that is, self-evidently reasonable)

---

7. Ibid., 38, 161.
8. Ibid., 51, 160.
9. Ibid., 100.

moral principles. In fact, moral reasoning is irreducibly turbulent because none of us is immune to the way certain aspects of our humanity — such as gender — shape our moral vision. *Ethical* is an adjective that applies to the way real people describe life and live out these descriptions with each other. Gilligan's point is that in overlooking the difference that gender makes for moral reasoning, moral reasoning itself becomes immoral for denying other voices a chance to speak.

Another thinker who highlights the importance of the anthropological for ethics is the British moral philosopher Bernard Williams. Like Gilligan, Williams insists that it is impossible to conjure up "an a priori nonrelative principle" for adjudicating moral positions.[10] But where there are no *a priori* principles, Williams continues, there are *conditions* for morality, called *a posteriori* (literally, "from that which is after") because they can be read off the way people actually live with each other. The fact that these conditions are contingent upon the human form of life prevents us from discounting all cross-cultural moral outcry as mere parochial emoting. For example, when Westerners decry genocide in Rwanda, it is not simply a case of one group finding another's practices "distasteful." Westerners are saying something stronger because they consider both Hutus and Tutsis to be genuinely human. To regard the other as genuinely human is essential to moral systems.

What Williams arrives at is an account in which morality is equated with being human. Not human in the brute biological sense but human in the sense of being socially and culturally conditioned. Williams concedes that motivation to follow social mores is entirely a product of social conditioning. But then so is everything else that makes us human. Take these away and one is left less than human. Thus, the amoralist (that is, one who claims that all morality boils down to matters of preference) is *sub*human. Now, Williams expects that an amoralist will object vehemently to this. However, if in the defense of his or her humanity the amoralist claims to *care* about other persons, then, despite claims to the contrary, he or she would be conceding what Williams takes to be the basic starting place for morality — the ability to think in terms of others' needs and interests:

> [My] model is meant to suggest just one thing: that if we grant a man with even a minimal concern for others, then we do not have to ascribe to him any fundamentally new kind of thought or experience to include him in the world of morality, but only what is an extension of what he already has.[11]

Like Gilligan, Williams's method is an *a posteriori* one: the present human condition can be exegeted to discover what morality amounts to. Williams contends that when we do our exegetical homework, we will discover that in every

10. Bernard Williams, *Morality,* Canto ed. (New York: Harper and Row, 1972; reprint, Cambridge: Cambridge University Press, 1993), 23, xviii (pages referred to are from the 1993 edition).
11. Ibid., 12.

case, humans tend to regard the general disposition of selflessness as the *bona fide* moral standard.[12]

It appears, then, that both Gilligan and Williams have something important to say about attending to the human character of ethical life. But insofar as each attempts to *identify* morality with an aspect of humanity, then it seems to me that Gilligan and Williams struggle to rise above the level of what Kant labeled the "hypothetical imperative," namely: if one wants *X* then one is "obligated" to do *Y*. Or, in this case, if one wants to be human in this particular way, then one must discover, trust, and risk one's socially conditioned impulse to "do things of the non-self-interested sort."[13] Does this take the punch out of moral prescriptions? Williams doesn't think so. He claims that, the question of God aside, morality still has *transcendent* leverage, even though it appeals to something *within* the scope of human existence.[14] Yet I am confused by this. How can human existence generate a conviction about how human nature *ought* to be? If, further, we hold the Christian conviction that humanity is depraved, then how can we, by beginning with human nature, ever rise above the level of our current condition?

MacIntyre attacks this problem head-on and makes it a central theme in *After Virtue*.[15] MacIntyre argues that ever since the writings of David Hume (1711–1776), moral thinkers have been under the illusion that there is no justifiable connection between *is* and *ought*. MacIntyre dissents, pointing out that Hume's mistake was to seek moral imperatives as *ends* in and of themselves rather than as the *means* for attaining a greater end. What human life is all about and aims for is called the human *telos*. The best way to understand moral imperatives, therefore, is to see them as the means of getting from the *untutored human nature* to *human-nature-if-it-achieved-its-telos*. Unfortunately, the Enlightenment project discarded all positive accounts of the human *telos*. Thus left without clear knowledge of our *telos*, we face the impossible task of elevating our moral condition by tugging at the bootstraps of the untutored self. MacIntyre insists that our moral chaos will not end until we reclaim the knowledge of our *telos*. So, then, we *can* move from *is* to *ought* so long as the *is* contains an account of the *telos*. In a now famous example, if the *telos* of a watch is time-keeping, then clearly it *ought* to keep time well.[16] The first step in ethics, therefore, is to identify the *telos* of human life.

---

12. Williams takes pains to show that morality has to do with one's relationship to others. Therefore, insofar as relationships include at least two parties, selfishness is not completely outlawed because selfishness does not necessarily exclude other-interest. This finds resonance with Gilligan's "ethics of care."

13. Williams, *Morality*, 69–70.

14. Ibid., 78–79.

15. Alasdair MacIntyre, *After Virtue*, 2d ed. (Notre Dame: University of Notre Dame Press, 1984), 51–61. This is what some have called the "master argument" of *After Virtue*. See James R. Horne, "Two Ethical Modes and MacIntyre's Narrative Ideal," *Scottish Journal of Religious Studies* 14, no. 1 (1993): 89–101, esp. 92.

16. MacIntyre, *After Virtue*, 219.

What is human life for? One must be careful not to confuse MacIntyre's metanarrative (that is, his story about religious-ethical traditions) for a particular first-order answer (for example, how the Christian tradition answers the question, "What is human life for?"). Although MacIntyre himself is aligned most closely with the answer given by Thomas Aquinas (d. 1274), his philosophical writings aim at uncovering the way all moral traditions work, and not just that of the Thomistic Roman Catholic one. Thus, he highlights two features shared by all particular descriptions of the human *telos*. First, all tradition-derived accounts of what human life is for can be characterized as *quests for the human good*. Second, according to these accounts, the ability of community members to see the *telos* requires of them a lifetime of seeking: "the good life for man is the life spent in seeking for the good life for man, and the virtues necessary for the seeking are those which will enable us to understand what more and what else the good life for man is."[17] However, apart from these general considerations, MacIntyre insists that no universal answer can be given to "What is human life for?" Only specific answers from within particular traditions can be given to this question.

MacIntyre's description lends itself nicely to Christian appropriation. There is a human dimension to moral reasoning: Christian believers are particular human beings who live out a particular moral outlook. MacIntyre does not simply give Christians permission to retain aspects of their particularity but insists that ethics in the Christian community, if it is to be *ethics* at all, retain *all* the distinctively Christian elements. The Christian *telos*, whether formulated by Augustine, Aquinas, Pascal, Calvin, or Luther, is uniquely Christian. And the virtues necessary to sustain successfully the Christian practices, the Christian quest, and the Christian tradition are distinctively Christian virtues as well.[18]

Paul Ramsey: Attending to Sin

One of the premier Christian ethicists of the late twentieth century was Paul Ramsey.[19] Ramsey saw morality as the stuff of human relationships, and ethics as the fight to get a clear and realistic picture about just what kind of moral world human beings inhabit. Ramsey drew attention to the explicitly *theological* character of ethics by showing the ways in which both the perception and the

17. Ibid.

18. Much of MacIntyre's energies early on in *After Virtue* are directed toward dissolving the objection that virtue theory is incoherent because of its inability to produce a standard, uniform list of the virtues. A favorite example from the side of objectors is to note that humility, while virtuous for Christians, was listed among the *vices* for citizens of ancient Athens.

19. There is perhaps no issue for which consideration of human depravity plays a more central role than that of war. Ramsey's final written work, published posthumously as *Speak Up for Just War or Pacifism: A Critique of the United Methodist Bishops' Pastoral Letter "In Defense of Creation"* (University Park and London: Pennsylvania State University Press, 1988), is therefore not only a good reflection of his mature thinking but a clear example of the centrality of theological convictions (such as human depravity) for his ethical model.

realization of moral justice are hampered by the sinful character of the present world. This character shows itself in three ways.

First, the sinfulness of the world implies that moral justice can be only *roughly approximated*.[20] The real and lasting effects of the Fall mean that human beings are stuck in a world where "will to power" describes every human interaction and institution. Because "power can finally be limited only by further power," a tenuous balance of power yielding a barely endurable peace is the best that can be expected for human society.[21] Furthermore, sin turns moral decisions into *quandaries* because unintended evil consequences threaten every moral decision. Every moral decision is a cause for anguish because, as fallen creatures, human beings can never, on his view, do better than to choose the lesser of two or more evils.[22]

Second, the world is characterized by "not yet." As Ramsey saw it, Christ is present for the church "already," but only in the Eucharist. To counter the utopianism of liberal theologians, for whom "not yet" simply means "some day," Ramsey insisted on an "aeonic slash" between "already/not yet."[23] Christ's presence is a *trans-historical* reality — that is, one that can never be fully realized within human history but only beyond it.[24] This has the effect of limiting the present applicability of Christ's life for Christians. Ramsey argued that both the diversity of the Christologies that litter our theological textbooks and the failure in analogy between Christ's life and ours suggest that the rule of thumb "What would Jesus do?" can never see us through our morally perplexing world.[25] Rather, additional principles are needed for moral navigation in a "not yet" world.

Ramsey found Augustine's realism much more applicable. Sin is the present reality that renders eschaton-by-evolution impossible. Therefore, sin must be endured and seen as the necessity that will occasion Christ's eventual return. But in the meantime this realistic view of the human condition carries with it the implication that Augustine's "two cities" are inextricable. Christian moral agents are simultaneously members in *both* the kingdom of God *and* the kingdom of the world. On the one hand there is "an enduring tension between loyalty to Christ and our responsibilities in a less than ideal world."[26] But on the other hand, only a single ethic can speak to our *dual* existence as Christians and cosmopolitans; there is but one ethic.

Third, Ramsey saw that our dual existence in this fallen world required moral guidance because sin has rendered our moral vision myopic. The only guides suitable for the task are *reason* and the *church*. These two are in a power balance

20. Ibid., 89, 129.
21. Ibid., 4, 187.
22. Ibid., 72–73.
23. Ibid., 37.
24. Ibid., 43.
25. Ibid., 113.
26. Ibid., 142.

of their own. Reason prevents the church from offering *illogical* guidance, and the church prevents reason from advocating *unchristian* ends and means.[27]

It is very easy to see that theological presuppositions saturate Ramsey's outlook. Yet this theology creates a tension for the role that reason plays in Ramsey's scheme. Ramsey nurtures a practical view of human reason which has intention (the good will) at its center.[28] Why be moral? Because principled living is the most reasonable way to be. Yet for Ramsey, the good will could never be *fully* good. On one level, the presence of rival and power-hungry wills renders principled living, at best, a tenuous approximation to moral justice: "No calls for clarity, forthrightness, and faithfulness to a structured or determinate set of principles for ethico-political decision-making can remove the uncertainty and contingency from specific or particular policies."[29] Therefore, the morally perfect public policy is always just out of reach. And not only is it impossible to *realize* morality in any given policy, but at a more basic level, speaking of each human will as twisted is tantamount to saying that even the *perception* of morality is universally hampered. Ramsey framed the problem of *perception* as one of a distortion that forever lay between us, the justice-seeking individuals, and the transcendent moral principles we are trying to get a grip on.[30] He saw a divisive pluralism to be the inevitable result: "in a fallen world there is no 'universal view' of justice, only 'views of universal justice.'"[31]

This poses a serious problem for Ramsey's ethics. Ramsey's theological account of human nature as depraved entails an invincible barrier to the kind of mental clarity required by his approach. For if human nature is sinful, fallen, and depraved, then each individual's account (including Ramsey's own) of how human beings ought to be will be inevitably twisted by her or his own will-to-power.

The impotence of fallen human reason is a long-standing Protestant problem. If human beings are unable to see God's standards clearly, how can they be certain that these standards are unitary rather than conflicted, and transcendent rather than imaginary? Ramsey's response to this objection was mixed. On the one hand, he seemed to hold that there were absolute moral norms that transcend the human situation and could be accessed by rigorous regenerate thinkers who have divine revelation at their disposal. Yet, on the other hand, Ramsey very nearly conceded the force of this objection with his insistence that a balance of power was the best we could do to prevent from running amok the real

---

27. On the one hand, Ramsey chided the Methodist bishops' pastoral letter (titled *In Defense of Creation: The Nuclear Crisis and a Just Peace* [Nashville: Graded Press, 1986]) for proposing a logically impossible mixture of just warfare and pacifism. On the other hand, he takes the bishops to task for confusing questions of secondary ends (e.g., "What will be the social consequences of going to war?") with questions of primary ends (namely, "How are injustices to be rectified?"). Ibid., 57.

28. Ramsey, *Speak Up,* 104.

29. Ibid., 106.

30. Ibid., 91.

31. Ibid.

and present danger of subjectivism (the view that morality is whatever you or I take it to be).

In Ramsey's defense, it is not necessary to conclude that the specter of subjectivism defeats moral inquiry altogether. For example, Bernard Williams suggested that while there may be an objective solution to *factual* questions (namely, "Look at the facts"), there is no such eliminatory procedure for *moral* hypotheses. But such lack is not problematic. In fact, as we have seen, Williams viewed this as essential to morality:

> For the vital difference is that the disagreement in morality involves what should be done, and involves, on each side, caring about what happens; and once you see this difference, you see equally that it could not possibly be a requirement of rationality that you should stop caring about these things because someone else disagrees with you.[32]

Williams concluded that there are no objective moral norms to which we can compare moral situations and beliefs, as there might be in science. In matters of fact, dispassion is a virtue, but in matters of morality, by contrast, caring deeply is a virtue.[33] To cease caring is to cease from *moral* inquiry. Of course, it is possible that Williams's conclusion would afford Ramsey no comfort, for, as Ramsey might point out, "caring deeply" may, in fact, turn out to be the will-to-power in disguise!

MacIntyre's "tradition-constituted enquiry" offers another way out of this impasse. MacIntyre shares with Ramsey a concern for understanding the sources of discrepancy between various conceptions of morality. However, MacIntyre will not be contented with an explanation of perceptual distortion that stops at the level of the individual human volition as Ramsey's account of will-to-power has done. Rather, perceptual "distortion" is characteristic of the fact that all moral inquiry is tradition-bound.

In *After Virtue,* MacIntyre worked backward from the shrill and interminable character of modern moral debates in an attempt to discover where philosophy had gone wrong. According to the now three-hundred-year-old Enlightenment project, objectivity was supposed to be obtained by jettisoning all things historical, social, and religious. As we saw in Chapter 1, this project backfired. Instead of generating one timelessly true, reason-based account of morality, the Enlightenment project precipitated *multiple* answers to the question "Why be moral?" Not only has no clear winner emerged from the plethora of options available today (for example, utilitarianism, social contract theory, Kant's categorical imperative) but, further, no single system can even be understood on its own terms — each theory is parasitic on the moral vocabulary of former history-laden traditions. For example, how can we tell whether the term *good* signifies pleasure (utilitarianism), peace (social contractarianism), or duty (Kant's deontological ethics) when, in fact, all three theories borrowed the term from Aristotle,

32. Williams, *Morality,* 34.
33. Ibid., 35.

who could not define goodness without first answering the question "What is human life for?"[34]

Does our failure to find a universal account of morality imply that morality is simply a matter of taste? On the contrary, MacIntyre suggested that the move to jettison all things historical was the wrong move. To recap the discussion of Chapter 1, moral inquiry, argued MacIntyre, is *tradition-constitutive* and *tradition-constituted.* By the first term he meant that moral inquiry is done *within* a tradition because traditions are "the repositories of standards of rationality . . . which are crucial to moral deliberation and action."[35] At a basic level, a tradition requires a shared language. To share a language is to share a form of life. To share a form of life is to be a community. To be a community is to be concerned over the meaning of the story that explains the group's joint history. Thus, tradition, for MacIntyre, is defined as "historically extended, socially embodied argument."[36] Apart from the shared life within some particular tradition, "There is no standing ground, no place for enquiry, no way to engage in the practices of advancing, evaluating, accepting, and rejecting reasoned argument."[37]

By the second term, *tradition-constituted inquiry,* MacIntyre signified that the tradition itself is a part *of* the argument. In *Whose Justice? Which Rationality?*— the sequel to *After Virtue*—MacIntyre expanded his definition of *tradition:*

> an argument extended through time in which certain fundamental agreements are defined and redefined in terms of two kinds of conflict: those with critics and enemies external to the tradition . . . and those internal, interpretive debates through which the meaning and rationale of the fundamental agreements come to be expressed and by whose progress a tradition is constituted.[38]

An example of an external challenge to the Christian tradition was the requirement (under penalty of death) placed upon all citizens by Roman emperor

---

34. The danger of equivocation in moral vocabulary disables the most rigorous moral systems. For example, Jeffrey Stout takes John Rawls's *A Theory of Justice* (Cambridge: Harvard University Press, 1971) to task in his book called *Flight from Authority,* Revisions Series, ed. Stanley Hauerwas and Alasdair MacIntyre (Notre Dame: University of Notre Dame Press, 1981). Rawls argued that the only fair way to write policy governing, say, an institution, would be to pretend that all the framers of the policy stood behind "a veil of ignorance," where each had an equal chance of being janitor or CEO. Stout torpedoed the workability of Rawls's theory in a single sentence: "What language is spoken behind the veil of ignorance?" (220). It is for ignoring linguistic archaeology— for failing to see the multifarious ways a moral concept is actually used in disregard of its history— that participants in modern moral debates fail to communicate with each other. Apparently Rawls subsequently abandoned the claim that his meta-ethical system possessed an ahistorical validity. Cf. Richard Rorty, "Solidarity or Objectivity?" in *Objectivity, Relativism, and Truth: Philosophical Papers, Vol. 1* (Cambridge: Cambridge University Press, 1991), 30, n. 12; and in the same volume, "The Priority of Democracy to Philosophy," 175–96.

35. John Horton and Susan Mendus, "Alasdair MacIntyre: After Virtue and After," in *After MacIntyre: Critical Perspectives on the Work of Alasdair MacIntyre,* ed. John Horton and Susan Mendus (Notre Dame: University of Notre Dame Press, 1994), 11.

36. MacIntyre, *After Virtue,* 222. Cf. MacIntyre, *Whose Justice? Which Rationality?* (Notre Dame: University of Notre Dame Press, 1988), 12, 354–55.

37. MacIntyre, *Whose Justice?* 350.

38. Ibid., 12.

Decius to provide written proof that they had offered sacrifice to Caesar. An example of an internal challenge to the same tradition was the dilemma that Arian Christians posed to the rest of the church when they asserted that the Son was subordinate to the Father. Locating moral inquiry within a narrative tradition is not tantamount to succumbing to relativism because rival traditions are able to compete for viability in a battle of "survival of the fittest" where justification entails overcoming external challenges and internal crises. The tradition that fails to vindicate itself in such a "historical process of dialectical justification" will, and ought to, die, and in dying will no longer be a rival.

We have seen that Ramsey's account makes a central place for theology in ethics. Unfortunately, his construal of sin, in effect, jeopardizes the ethical normativeness of Jesus' life and places just out of reach the very objectivity Ramsey insisted was required for moral reasoning. In contrast, MacIntyre's treatment enables Christian believers to retain both a robust doctrine of sin and a Christology that is not superfluous to ethics by showing that moral inquiry is done from within communities made up of those who share just these sorts of convictions. MacIntyre's treatment of traditions gives us good leverage for claiming that ethics must be qualified by some adjective. As Christians we do *Christian* ethics.

Stanley Hauerwas: Attending to Community

Since mid-century there has been a growing awareness that human existence cannot be fully explicated without reference to social realities that must be accounted for on their own terms. For example, Ludwig Wittgenstein and J. L. Austin have opened up our realization that language is inextricably tied to the social life of its speakers. More recently, Jeffrey Stout used "conceptual archaeology" to argue that no account of a community's language is complete without reference to its history.

The interplay of language, community, and history as a character-shaping reality is the basis for a communitarian ethics.[39] Acknowledging the communal dimension in ethics draws attention away from those philosophies that "have sought to make episodes of decision the whole of morality."[40] In contrast, communitarian ethics brings into focus the narrative context in which decisions are framed. As James McClendon explains:

> For narrative ethics (as I have construed it) never wanted to deny that people decide, or that their decisions are sometimes morally significant, or that those significant decisions might be framed by rules or principles of so high a degree of abstraction that they would no longer have the appearance of narrative summaries. It only wanted to insist that the principles . . . have a context, as do the decisions

39. James Wm. McClendon, Jr., *Ethics: Systematic Theology, Volume I* (Nashville: Abingdon Press, 1986), 158–86.
40. Ibid., 171.

> they are meant to guide, only to insist that that context is a narrative one, and that the meaning of both the propositional principles adopted and the decisions these are meant to guide is to be found in the terms of their narrative setting.[41]

According to Stanley Hauerwas, questions receive answers and actions receive explanations only by reference to a narrative that provides the background against which answers and explanations make any sense at all. Since communities embody these interpretive stories, Hauerwas must add to the clarifying questions of Gilligan, "Which voice?" and of Ramsey, "Which world?" a question of his own: "Which community?" The centrality of community in Hauerwas's account of the moral life shows itself in at least three ways.

First, moral agents never exist in isolation. Modern political liberalism teaches that the authentic human self is realized in direct proportion to how thoroughly its historical and communal ties are broken. In stark contrast, Hauerwas observes that if a person could ever be successfully "freed" from his or her historical and communal ties, the person's identity would be *lost,* not gained. In more technical terms, the human self is not monadic — a generic and interchangeable political atom — but dyadic, which is to say, having only the identity that derives from occupying a place in *others'* lives! Furthermore, Hauerwas maintains that only a narrative understanding of the self provides a community — the network of people occupying a place in each other's lives — with a real common good apart from which justice is unintelligible.[42]

Second, there is no objective vantage point from which the moral life can be described. Before we can answer "Why be moral?" we must talk about a set of skills, called virtues, which an individual must possess in order to understand rightly what morality is. These skills can be learned only through participation in the communal life. It takes a community successfully to pass on moral skills from one generation to the next through the training of the youth by recognized moral guides (clergy, teachers, parents, and so on). Notice how this differs from Williams's view. Bernard Williams contended that ethical discourse is possible only if it makes sense to speak intelligibly about a God who guarantees ethics as "objective." And, unfortunately for the atheist Williams, there is no way to talk coherently about God.[43] Hauerwas counters with the observation that the difficulty with moral discourse is not the intelligibility of our beliefs about God's reality but the assumption that ethics must be "objective" in order to be ethical. Hauerwas insists that it makes better sense to think in terms of a "communal

41. James Wm. McClendon, Jr., "Narrative Ethics and Christian Ethics," *Faith and Philosophy* 3, no. 4 (1986): 392.

42. Arne Rasmusson, *The Church as Polis: From Political Theology to Theological Politics as Exemplified by Jürgen Moltmann and Stanley Hauerwas,* vol. 49, *Studia Theologica Lundensia* (Lund, Sweden: Lund University Press, 1994), 290–91.

43. "If God existed, there might be special, and acceptable, reasons for subscribing to morality. The trouble is that the attempt to formulate those reasons in better than the crudest outline runs into the impossibility of thinking coherently about God. The trouble with religious morality comes not from morality's being inescapably pure, but from religion's being incurably unintelligible." Williams, *Morality,* 72.

form of ethical rationality"[44] and concurs with Gilligan's observation that perception itself has an ethical dimension.[45] Ethics must always be qualified by an adjective (for example, *Christian* ethics). Morality is therefore, by necessity, relative to particular accounts of history, theology, politics, and so on, owned by particular communities.

Third, Hauerwas argues that right perception is not the product of natural human development but the product of historical and communal forces reproduced in individuals under the tutelage of the community's expert practitioners. Such character formation occurs within community because of the relation between the community and its core narrative(s). For example, Hauerwas argues that Augustine embraced the Christian story because it made sense out of his life. What was formerly a random series of diversions for Augustine became a unified whole when seen through the lens of the gospel. Each period in his life — licentiousness, Manichaeism, Platonism, and so on — could be seen as an episode in a single larger story. And it was the gospel that told him where this story was headed — he was on a quest for God. By embracing this interpretive framework Augustine himself joined the story line. In other words, once Augustine had found his rest in God, his life became an exemplar of the gospel's point that we are *all* questing for God. In this way Augustine "lived out" the gospel's message and became another character in the cast whose lives together were an extension of their master story.[46] In the absence of a community that embodies and extends the master story, moral life could not be navigated because the map would remain hidden.

In this light, the differences between the respective stories of the modern liberal tradition and the Christian tradition are paramount for Hauerwas. The liberal story has at its root the Promethean myth that humans control the future of society by making policy decisions that can be implemented "from above" with relative ease.[47] In addition, liberals see society as monolithic and on an evolutionary trajectory that consists of the progressive liberation of authentic human existence from all restraints. Freedom thus is defined in terms of autonomy and liberation (from which we get the terms *liberal* and *liberalism*).[48]

In contrast, the Christian story sees freedom as the power to live faithful to our master story.[49] Autonomy, leading to individualism, is not primary. Rather, subordination to community (through which the skills to live morally are gained) is of utmost importance. The truths about morality are not mediated to generic individuals by means of a universal theory. Rather, moral life is embodied in a

44. Rasmusson, *Church as Polis,* 262.

45. Ibid., 176, 215.

46. Stanley Hauerwas and David Burrell, "From System to Story: An Alternative Pattern for Rationality in Ethics," in *Why Narrative?* ed. Stanley Hauerwas and L. Gregory Jones (Grand Rapids, Mich.: Wm. B. Eerdmans, 1989), 158–90.

47. Rasmusson, *Church as Polis,* 367.

48. Ibid., 281.

49. The Vulgate translates δύναμις (power) as *virtus* (virtue) in 1 Thess. 1:5.

particular people.[50] Sustaining and forming the community becomes then the chief end of human existence[51] and the truth value of a master story is found in its ability to shape characters who will be adequate to the task of living out that story.[52]

Why then be moral? Utility is out. Kant is mistaken. Social contract is irrelevant. Reasons to be moral must be *Christian* reasons. Morality amounts to living the gospel faithfully on three planes. First, actions form character. Moral (virtuous) actions form our ability to describe, understand, and live the moral life.[53] Second, moral living enables us to tell adequately the story that we have embraced as our interpretive framework. Living unfaithfully is evidence that one has lost (or abandoned) the interpretive power of the story. For example, let's say that after his "conversion," rather than becoming pastor of a North African church, Augustine traveled to a distant land where he became a soldier of fortune in a Teutonic army and learned to rape, pillage, and kill with the best of them. Something is wrong with this picture, isn't it? We would wonder, "What in the world was he after?" Fame? Fortune? Pleasure? And this is exactly the right question to ask. If Augustine had sought something other than God, he would have been tacitly admitting that the gospel told him neither who he was nor what life was about. Therefore, immorality (that is, unfaithfulness to the master story) results in the loss of identity. Third, "the original creation is aimed at a new creation, the creation of a community... that glorifies God."[54] That's why Augustine became a pastor instead of Rambo, so that he could nurture this community, which is the kingdom of God on earth. Morality is the "happy" (what Aristotle called, *eudaimonistic*) state of living in fulfillment of this purpose.

If MacIntyre's own distinctive position is seen more clearly in the contrast between his views and those of the first three thinkers we have examined in this chapter, then he is rendered almost invisible when set against the background of communitarian thinkers such as Hauerwas. Not that this should be surprising, since MacIntyre and Hauerwas are mutually indebted to the other's contribution in their joint labor to explicate the "narrative shape" of ethics.[55]

The communal dimension of MacIntyre's ethics is revealed in his sevenfold use of *narrative* to describe the character of human existence.[56] First, knowledge is narrative-shaped in the sense that no action performed, no sentence spoken,

50. Rasmusson, *Church as Polis,* 187, 208, 216–17.

51. Ibid., 181.

52. Stanley Hauerwas, *A Community of Character* (Notre Dame: University of Notre Dame Press, 1981), 10, 36, 51, 62, 93, 95.

53. Rasmusson, *Church as Polis,* 265.

54. Ibid., 181.

55. As an example of their collaboration, see Stanley Hauerwas and Alasdair MacIntyre, eds., *Revisions: Changing Perspectives in Moral Philosophy* (Notre Dame: University of Notre Dame Press, 1983).

56. L. Gregory Jones, "Alasdair MacIntyre on Narrative, Community, and the Moral Life," *Modern Theology* 4 (October 1987): 53–69.

is intelligible apart from a greater context that gives it its sense. Stories are the means by which we learn. Even in the "objective" sciences a statement such as "f = ma" is simply a shorthand way to recall a whole host of "story problems" that have shaped one's ability to identify correctly the relevant terms of the equation. We learn ethics by means of stories too. The stories that constitute the interpretive tools for moral navigation are the stockpile of the community's moral values, and without them newcomers (for example, the children) are left "unscripted, anxious stutterers in their actions and in their words."[57] (This fact gives basis for sociologists' fear concerning the future of a generation that has no heroes to champion.)

Second, human life can be rightly called narrative because of the *historical* character of its morality. There is no such thing as morality-as-such but only plural moralities "embodied in the historical lives of particular social groups and so possessing the distinctive characteristics of social existence."[58] Just as human action requires a story to make it intelligible, so too human morality needs a story — the story embodied in the life of the community — to make it intelligible: "I can only answer the question 'What am I to do?' if I can answer the prior question 'Of what story or stories do I find myself a part?' "[59] Even a recluse has neighbors and therefore ought to behave in a "neighborly" fashion.

Third, to speak of the narrative unity of the self is to say that the continuity of my life today with my life of a decade ago is found in the fact that I play the same character in the story of my life. Fourth, our lives intersect (or, to use MacIntyre's phrase, are mutually "embedded") in such a way that we can never be more than co-authors of those stories. Whether I like it or not, the crooks who steal my car, or burgle my house, become significant characters in the story of my life. Our lives cannot ever be completely told without reference to others.

Finally, the last three of MacIntyre's uses of narrative display a fractal symmetry.[60] The human self plays an enduring character in the story of that community in which he or she is embedded. The community also plays a character in the story of the historic tradition in which it is embedded. And finally, the tradition also plays a character (and, therefore, can be said to have character) in the greater story of human history.[61]

In addition to agreeing with Hauerwas regarding the communal dimension of human existence in general, MacIntyre also sees ethics in particular as inextricable from human sociality. Recall that the master argument of *After Virtue* involved the claim that ethical imperatives derive their force solely from the relationship between *man-as-he-is-in-his-untutored-self* and *man-as-he-would-*

57. MacIntyre, *After Virtue,* 216.

58. Ibid., 265.

59. Ibid., 216.

60. The term *fractal* denotes a pattern that is repeated at different levels of complexity. A snowflake is a good example. The geometry of the largest branch is congruent (isomorphic) with the crystalline design of each of the subbranches, and sub-subbranches, etc.

61. This upper-level story is the theme of MacIntyre's volume *Whose Justice? Which Rationality?*

be-if-he-realized-his-telos. In that the *telos* of human beings, as discussed above, cannot be formulated apart from specific narrative traditions in which people are situated, MacIntyre sees three classes of ethical imperatives rooted in the social life of human persons.[62]

First, we are obligated to extend the tradition in which we find ourselves. This means that we are to live in a way that is faithful to those narratives around which our tradition was, and continues to be, formed. Second, as traditions are constituted by practices, we are obligated to sustain those practices. For Christians this involves participation in practices such as worship, witness, and works of mercy. Third, this participation must be of a certain sort: the kind of participation that strives for excellence. This kind of participation demands, therefore, that we acquire those virtues necessary for excellence and, somewhat paradoxically, that are achieved by means of participation in those practices.[63]

Yet, oddly, MacIntyre himself declares "I am not a communitarian."[64] To this one might object that if MacIntyre is correct in the major theses of *After Virtue,* then mustn't he concede allegiance to *some* community? Perhaps by his confession MacIntyre is simply trying to identify himself as a political philosopher rather than as a moral theologian. But as James Horne notes,

> MacIntyre is in an interesting philosophical position, which is all the more interesting because it approximates the predicament of many intellectuals in his time. He is critical of contemporary culture...while at the same time respecting the accomplishments of some of its disciplines....[65]

However, the problem runs deeper than this. What MacIntyre seems to mean by his admission is that the account offered in *After Virtue* is not meant to be a defense of a particular communal tradition (unlike Aristotle's account) but a *meta*-narrative — a story about stories. Nevertheless, as Gregory Jones points out, "MacIntyre's claim about the narrative quality of human life is dependent upon a specific description of a telos-oriented historicity which he believes is fundamental to an adequate understanding of human life (i.e., he is presupposing a normative tradition)."[66] In other words, if MacIntyre is correct to claim that the problem with all modern ethical theories is their divorce from moral

62. MacIntyre, *After Virtue,* 273.

63. Another way of stating this threesome is to describe moral life in terms of virtues: "My account of the virtues proceeds through three stages: a first which concerns virtues as qualities necessary to achieve the goods internal to practices; a second which considers them as qualities contributing to the good of a whole life; and a third which relates them to the pursuit of a good for human beings the conception of which can only be elaborated and possessed within an ongoing social tradition." Ibid.

64. Giovanna Borradori, *The American Philosopher: Conversations with Quine, Davidson, Putnam, Nozick, Danto, Rorty, Cavell, MacIntyre, and Kuhn,* trans. Rosanna Crocitto (Chicago and London: University of Chicago Press, 1994), 151. Cf. Alasdair MacIntyre, "I'm Not a Communitarian, But...," *The Responsive Community* 1, no. 3 (1991): 91–92, in which MacIntyre states his opinion that "the political, economic, and moral structures of advanced modernity...exclude the possibility of realizing any of the worthwhile types of political community...."

65. Horne, "Two Ethical Modes," 99.

66. Jones, "Alasdair MacIntyre on Narrative," 59.

traditions (because only by participating in these traditions does one gain the skills needed for moral reflection), then he himself must be drawing on some tradition, *lest his thesis be self-defeating.* Now, to his credit, MacIntyre has since forged stronger ties with Roman Catholicism. But at the time of this essay, Jones rightly concluded that MacIntyre's account would be fortified by a stronger and more determinate account of "community" precisely because a community is the bearer, interpreter, and concrete expression of its tradition. Now, because Christians *can* offer such an account, instances of Christian moral reflection that resonate with MacIntyrean themes simultaneously exemplify a stronger account of the moral life precisely because of their close ties with a particular community — something MacIntyre lacks. Insofar as the Christian community is a radical alternative, both to the now-extinct Aristotelian city-state and to the society of modern political liberalism, we must next examine the source of this radical difference.

Thus far we have examined the ways in which MacIntyre's analysis corroborates the witness of those moral philosophers and ethicists who urge that practitioners of moral reasoning recover the losses due to the Enlightenment, namely the anthropological, theological, and communal aspects of the practice of ethics. The next four thinkers we examine attest to the need to recover aspects of ethics lost after the Reformation and Constantine. The first of these is the voice of Pope John Paul II, who recalls the *juridical* character of moral reasoning.

Veritatis Splendor: Attending to Natural Law

The view of ethics most frequently associated with Roman Catholic theology is called natural law ethics. Ethics from this angle resembles jurisprudence and reminds us to attend to the *juridical* nature of ethical reasoning. Because the legal profession is an easy example of a MacIntyrean practice, we might expect to find many points of congruence between natural law ethics and MacIntyrean practices. But there is one curious feature of natural law ethics that must be harmonized with MacIntyre's account before other similarities can be fully appreciated.

I have previously discussed how the upshot of a MacIntyrean approach to ethics is the conception of moral principles as relativized both to specific understandings of the human *telos* and to tradition-based standards of rationality. How then might MacIntyre respond to the apparent claims of *universal* (contextless? traditionless?) morality from within his own recently adopted Roman Catholicism? This universal ethic is called natural law and is the basis for *Veritatis Splendor,* the recent document Pope John Paul II wrote for Catholic bishops.

The central concern of the *Veritatis* is to expunge moral theology of two philosophical wrong turns. The first of these is liberalism's misconception of freedom as unqualified autonomy. This misstep led secular philosophy to elevate human freedom to a position outside the confines of God's law. In particular, this view means that human freedom can be defined apart from any reference to God's law. In contrast, the official Roman Catholic position is that no aspect of human life, including that of human freedom, can be understood apart from the fundamental question of how human beings stand in relation to God. God granted human beings freedom as a means toward an end, that they "might seek after [their] Creator and freely attain perfection."[67] True human freedom is therefore not freedom *from* constraint but freedom *for* attaining God's purposes. Because people were designed by God, when freedom lacks obedience (that is, conformity to God's law), it ceases to be human.[68] Freedom is not thereby diminished by demands for obedience. Rather, human freedom and God's law intersect compatibly. What results is better described as *theonomy* than *heteronomy*.[69]

Thus, theonomy — the intersection of human freedom and divine law which constitutes the internal rule of God — is the participation of human beings in natural law. Natural law is so termed not because it "refers to the nature of irrational beings, but because the reason which promulgates it is proper to human nature."[70] For nonhuman creatures natural law is expressed in the natural order and its external laws. Yet for humans, natural law is an internal compass and the means by which humans participate in divine governance. This position implies that human reason is rational and free only insofar as it is subordinate to, or, better, participates in, divine wisdom: "The rightful autonomy of the practical reason means that man possesses in himself his own law, received from the Creator."[71]

The papal encyclical obviously differs greatly from, say, the views of Bernard Williams. Although both give human nature a central role in ethical reflection, human nature is construed differently in each. Williams thinks that the set of all socially conditioned features exhausts what we mean by "human nature." But the *Veritatis* asserts that there is something of human nature that endures all cultural changes.[72] This permanent and transcendent feature, to which each human subject is morally accountable, is none other than God's immutable intentions, which are embossed on each individual's heart like an image upon a wax seal.[73]

> [Natural law] refers to man's proper and primordial nature . . . which is the person himself in the unity of soul and body, in the unity of his spiritual and biological inclinations and of all the other specific characteristics necessary for the pursuit

67. John Paul II, *Veritatis Splendor, Origins, CNS Documentary Service* 23, no. 18 (1993): §39.

68. Ibid., §42.

69. *Theonomy* literally means "the law of God." The phrase connotes the transformation of the inner disposition into that of willing compliance by means of the internalization of the rule of God. The term *heteronomy* might literally be rendered "the law of another." The phrase is somewhat pejorative since it implies the loss of autonomy in the act of subordination to an external authority.

70. *Veritatis*, §42.

71. Ibid., §40.

72. Ibid., §53.

73. Ibid., §51.

> of his end. "The natural moral law expresses and lays down the purposes, rights and duties which are based upon the bodily and spiritual nature of the human person."[74]

What is necessary for each person to be able to read this image rightly is a properly functioning conscience — that internal faculty that makes judgments regarding which acts accord or fail to accord with natural law.

The second theme of the *Veritatis* is its pronouncement against the modern bifurcation of morality into the (lesser) realm of concrete choices and the (greater) realm of overall life-orientation or "fundamental choice."[75] The separation of morality into these two spheres has led some moral theologians to reduce concrete choices to the level of mere physical (and hence amoral) processes which, they reason, ought to be governed by consequentialist considerations. For example, a doctor may feel constrained to recommend an abortion procedure, or even to assist a suicide, for purely pragmatic reasons. But this two-tiered morality judges the concrete decision of the doctor not to be a moral matter *per se,* so long as it is insignificant to the overall trajectory of the doctor's life. It is this overall direction of one's life, the *fundamental option,* which is the strongest, if not the sole, measure of one's morality. Thus, this view tends to see the full weight of morality as residing in the sphere of the "fundamental option." But the *Veritatis* insists that while there *is* a fundamental choice spoken of in Scripture, such a choice is contained within, and inseparable from, concrete moral decisions such as assisting an abortion procedure.[76] While there may be a general teleological character to the moral life (that is, it *does* matter what overall direction my life takes),[77] nevertheless, one's *intention* to order one's actions to God, taken together with the *consequences* of each act, still does not get to the root of moral culpability. Acts themselves can be classified, ranked, and judged by their *intrinsic* quality. This intrinsic character has nothing to do with intention or outcome but has everything to do with the object of the choice.[78]

Veritatis Splendor, then, has raised two important challenges to the MacIntyrean view. Rather than understand moral precepts as means to achieving the *telos-as-it-is-perceived-within-a-particular-tradition,* the *Veritatis* appears to

74. Ibid., §50. Internal citation taken from *Acta Apostolicae Sedis* 80 (1988): 74.

75. Josef Fuchs attributes the origin of this notion to Jacques Maritain and Joseph Maréchal via Karl Rahner. Josef Fuchs, "Good Acts and Good Persons," in *Considering Veritatis Splendor,* ed. John Wilkins (Cleveland: Pilgrim Press, 1994), 22. Cf. also McClendon, *Ethics,* 52–55, for a discussion of Timothy E. O'Connell, Fuchs, and Bernard Häring on the issue of "fundamental option."

76. *Veritatis,* §66–67.

77. "Acting is morally good when the choices of freedom are in conformity with man's true good and thus express the voluntary ordering of the person toward his ultimate end: God himself, the supreme good in whom man finds his full and perfect happiness. . . . Consequently the moral life has an essential 'teleological' character, since it consists in the deliberate ordering of human acts to God. . . ." Ibid., §72–73. However, notice that the *Veritatis* uses the term *teleological* as descriptive of human ordering and not descriptive of the quality of life in general as aiming toward a *telos.* This is not a trivial point; the author of *Veritatis* fears that the latter use might be misconstrued as supporting the understanding of the fundamental option that *Veritatis* is intended to repudiate.

78. Ibid., §73, 76–78.

construe natural law in *trans*-traditional terms as independent, immutable, and universally binding. Second, by disallowing the fundamental-option approach, the *Veritatis* seems to deny what MacIntyre calls the "narrative unity of the self"[79] in favor of an account of human agency that bifurcates one's intentions from his or her discreet, unrelated, and self-contained (external) actions.

Both these challenges have in common an apparent disregard for the concept of *telos*. To predict MacIntyre's own response has been made easier by his own paper on the subject.[80]

He begins by noting that the *Veritatis* can be read in more than one way. It can, and should, be read as an occasional document, namely, as a papal encyclical addressed to Catholic bishops. This observation alone puts into perspective the "traditionless" and oracular tone of the letter. But the *Veritatis* also makes a contribution to the ongoing discussion about the relationship of Christian teaching to secular moral philosophy. Nevertheless, even to read it in this second way, as a philosophical treatise, does not require that it be read ahistorically. Like all philosophy, the *Veritatis* cannot escape the need to answer how culture, religion, and training affect the way that each reader reads it (not to mention the manner in which the *Veritatis* itself was written). This implies that those who find the arguments of the *Veritatis* compelling surely *already* share with the author a prior commitment to do philosophy "in the light afforded by the Christian gospel."[81] In the same vein, just as neither author nor reader possesses an objective vantage point, neither can the response that MacIntyre himself gives be an "objective" one, but only that of a North American Thomistic-Aristotelian Catholic moral philosopher. With this introduction MacIntyre makes three moves to reconcile the *Veritatis* with his own Thomistic-Aristotelian teleology (that is, *telos*-ology).

MacIntyre's first move is to show that natural law, as conceived by the *Veritatis*, names the set of prerequisites for achieving the Christian *telos*. "So the human good can be achieved only through a form of life in which the positive and negative precepts of the natural law are the norms governing our relationships."[82] And again,

> The natural law teaches us what kinds of actions we need to perform, what kind of actions we need to refrain from performing, and what kinds of person we need to become, if we are to achieve our own final end and good and to share with others in achieving our final end and good.[83]

In other words, natural law is universal in the sense of describing the preconditions for the flourishing of traditions in general, and of the Christian tradition in particular. But the recognition and explication of natural law could have been made from within the (Christian) community for whom these precepts already

79. MacIntyre, *After Virtue*, 218.
80. Alasdair MacIntyre, "How Can We Learn What *Veritatis Splendor* Has to Teach?" *The Thomist* 58, no. 2 (1994): 171–95.
81. Ibid., 172.
82. Ibid., 173.
83. Ibid., 178.

have been found to hold, and apart from which community such recognition could not have taken place.

Because Karol Wojtyla was trained in Thomistic philosophy before he became Pope John Paul II, it is not difficult for MacIntyre to tease out the Thomistic-Aristotelian teleology just below the surface of the pages of the *Veritatis.* Thus, borrowing the language of the *Veritatis,* MacIntyre shows the affinities between his notion of the human *telos* and the papal conception of "our final end and good,"[84] authentic freedom,[85] God,[86] and the achievement of a proper moral character befitting the moral quest.[87] But, in addition, it is the relationship of natural law to our *telos* which makes sense of the *Veritatis's* claim that natural law is universal.[88] On the one hand, the Christian conviction about what human life is for cannot be adequately expressed without casting it in universal terms:

> We cannot adequately characterize — adequately, that is, for practical life, let alone for theory — that good towards the achievement of which we are directed by our natures and by providence, except in terms which already presuppose the binding character of the exceptionless negative precepts of the natural law.[89]

An authentic Christian cannot say "These principles are right and true for me but may not be right and true for others" without being untrue to his or her own Christian faith! To say the same thing differently, the Christian tradition's concept of God as the final good toward whom human living aims implies that Christian believers conceive their *telos* to possess infinite value. In this case, the notion of "outweighing" has no use: if the negative precepts of natural law name the prerequisites of the quest for an infinitely valuable prize, then no utilitarian calculation can be performed. In sum, the Christian conceptual scheme prevents believers from understanding the demands of natural law as anything less than "exceptionless" demands.

On the other hand, saying that natural law is universal in scope is appropriate because natural law expresses the *ground rules* without which every human quest for the human *telos* would self-destruct. True freedom is the unencumbered pursuit of the *telos* by means of possessing the necessary virtues for overcoming hindrances along the way:

---

84. Ibid.

85. Freedom is construed both by the *Veritatis* and MacIntyre as the exercise, development, and actualization of telos-oriented capacities rather than mere autonomy or free choice. Ibid., 183.

86. Ibid., 178.

87. Ibid., 183–84.

88. MacIntyre does not deny that universal claims can be made. He insists only that such claims are always made from within a specific tradition. Therefore, speaking as one standing in the Thomistic-Aristotelian Roman Catholic tradition, MacIntyre is able to invoke a realist concept of truth, one in which truth is construed as objective, universal, and culture-transcending. Ibid., 186–87. Why then do members of rival traditions fail to perceive the "universal" truths of natural law? Because these truths are perceivable only by those whose minds are working properly, which is to say, working in accordance to Catholic epistemology and religious commitments. In this way MacIntyre can affirm a unity between natural law and reason. The universality of natural law is that it is universally accessible to all who take the narrow path of becoming an insider to this tradition.

89. Ibid., 177.

> To have become free is to have been able to overcome or avoid those distractions and obstacles which frustrate or inhibit the development of a capacity for judgment . . . and for action in accordance with such judgment.[90]

MacIntyre goes on to point out that this development of our capacities itself requires the virtue of prudence (*phronēsis*). But the acquisition of prudence is impossible without the precepts of natural law[91] because those practices, by which virtues are cultivated, are cooperative social enterprises that will self-destruct without the ground rules of natural law:

> Those universal and invariant requirements specify the preconditions for the kind of responsiveness by one human being to others which makes it possible for each to learn from the others' questioning. . . . And they are in fact the requirements imposed by the precepts of the natural law.[92]

We've seen that MacIntyre's first move to reconcile his writing with the *Veritatis* lies in his interpretation of natural law as the necessary prerequisite for pursuing the human *telos*. The second reconciliatory move MacIntyre makes concerns the threat that defining morality solely in terms of the objects of discrete moral decisions (with little or no reference to a fundamental option) poses to the unity of the moral self. A cursory reading might allow one to conclude that the *Veritatis* hews the moral life into isolated acts each of which is unrelated to the acts that precede and follow. But MacIntyre denies that Pope John Paul II could ever view the moral life in this way because he knows as well as any that each concrete decision requires a very complicated interplay between knowledge of relevant concepts, one's character, one's social situation, and so on. For example, according to natural law, it's wrong to steal. But this prohibition presupposes a right understanding of the concept of property.[93] But how I understand "property" is a function of my character and of my community. Where some of our country's forefathers viewed possession of property as an inalienable right,[94] the Christian story trains me to understand property in terms of a stewardship of goods on loan from God. One's ability to own the Christian story is the upper limit on the extent to which the concrete acts of his or her life are, in fact, knit together into a single tapestry.

---

90. Ibid., 183.

91. Ibid.

92. Ibid., 184. To summarize MacIntyre's earlier works, traditions are constituted by practices, and participation in these practices cultivates those virtues necessary for sustaining practices, the community, the tradition, and the narrative quest for the good. MacIntyre, *After Virtue,* 204–25. Also helpful is Horton and Mendus, "Alasdair MacIntyre," 1–15.

93. This illustration is MacIntyre's. Cf. MacIntyre, "How Can We Learn?" 180–81.

94. My strong contrast between property rights and Christian views of stewardship is not entirely fair since the right to property was thought to be inalienable because it was given by God to protect the individual against misuse of power by government. See Carl J. Friedrich, *Transcendent Justice: The Religious Dimension of Constitutionalism* (Durham, N.C.: Published for the Lilly Endowment Research Program in Christianity and Politics by Duke University Press, 1964), 93–94. For a better description of Christian stewardship see D. Stephen Long, "Christian Economy," in the present volume.

The third move MacIntyre makes to reconcile his teleology with the natural law approach of the *Veritatis* is to answer his essay's title question: "How can we learn what *Veritatis Splendor* has to teach?" This closing discussion picks up a thread with which the essay began, namely, the assertion that philosophy cannot be done in the rarefied ionosphere of putative objectivity but only in the denser atmosphere of cultural, religious, and philosophical commitments. The *Veritatis* does more than merely explicate the philosophical presuppositions of Roman Catholic Christianity. It also presents "what is in effect a theology of moral philosophy embedded in a theology of the moral life."[95] In other words, the genius of the *Veritatis* lies in its tacit presupposition that ethics is informed by one's convictions. How then can we learn from the *Veritatis?* By becoming insiders to the tradition and the form of life that conditioned the writing of the *Veritatis* in the first place! Insiders to this tradition have already settled the question regarding their ultimate *telos*. Furthermore, without this self-involving commitment it will be difficult, if not impossible, to understand and heed the admonitions of the *Veritatis*. MacIntyre concludes: "Unless, unlike the rich young man, we respond to God's offer of grace by accepting it, we too shall be unable to fully understand and to obey the law in such a way as to achieve that ultimate good [*telos*] which gives to such understanding and obedience its point and purpose."[96]

The argument of the *Veritatis* is not that of one philosophy against another but that of instruction for insiders concerning the danger of secular (that is, outsider) obstacles that block *our* way toward *our telos*. Because the *Veritatis* recognizes itself as the product of a tradition (something that philosophy and secular moral deliberation either overlooks or denies), it can classify philosophical errors as moral ones for hindering achievement of the *telos:*

> Each of these . . . kinds of error turns out to be an attachment to something which in the end deprives us not only of our good, that is of God, but also of something crucial in ourselves, something without which we will become incapable of achieving that which alone in the end gives point and purpose to our activities. One central moral and theological lesson of the encyclical is that, without understanding of and obedience to God's law, we become self-frustrating beings.[97]

In effect, MacIntyre has succeeded not only in reconciling his description of ethics with the natural law views of contemporary Roman Catholic moral theology but in clarifying ways in which ethics is *juridical*. That is to say, the adjective *juridical* does not invoke simply the legal metaphor behind morality as the laws of God inscribed on nature, but also the *forensic* character that the practice of

95. MacIntyre, "How Can We Learn?" 189. N.B. The responses of Roman Catholic theologians, as collected and edited by John Wilkins in the volume entitled *Considering Veritatis Splendor,* reveals that the *Veritatis* does not speak for Roman Catholicism as a whole but, rather, is itself a partisan voice in a wider debate. Here MacIntyre's broad understanding of the notion of tradition has led him to be more inclusive (more "catholic") than the Pope.

96. Ibid., 190.

97. Ibid., 194.

moral reasoning exhibits. Remember, in MacIntyre's view, traditions are historically extended arguments. Not only is MacIntyre's response to the *Veritatis* the translation of the Roman Catholic views into his nomenclature, it also resembles, in its form, an "appeal" to the "verdict" of *Veritatis*. This shows MacIntyre to be an exemplar of the long-standing communal practice of formally debating ways in which the "legal" community (that is, the Roman Catholic clergy) may properly interpret papal decisions.

Robert Adams: Attending to Divine Command

If Roman Catholic moral theology reminds us, in general, that ethics has a juridical face, then Protestant ethics strives to remind us, in particular, of the *binding* (deontological) character of morality. For the Protestant Reformers, the obligatory nature of moral maxims stems from their being expressions of God's commands. As we shall see, the project of precisely specifying God's commands requires employment of three concepts central to MacIntyre's account.

First, divine command ethics depends upon there being a rich enough narrative to identify who is the God who commands. Unless the identity of God can be pinned down, there is no way to escape the famous puzzle posed by Plato.

The dilemma, as it appears in Plato's record of Socrates' dialogue with Euthyphro, runs something like the following. If the good act is that which corresponds to what God commands, we are left wondering *why* God commands one thing rather than another. Does God command something because it is good, or is something good simply because God commands it? If God commands something because it is good, then there is some quality of goodness that exists independently of God's commands and that even God is not free to ignore. Goodness, so conceived, puts claims of God's sovereignty in question. How can God be fully God and necessarily knuckle under to something external to God's free will? On the other hand, if something receives its goodness from its being commanded by God, what stops God from being entirely capricious? Imagine a scenario in which God commands human beings to do something morally unacceptable. For example, what if God were to command us to be cruel for no good reason, but for cruelty's sake alone? Our reflex would be to insist that God will never command us to do something morally wrong. But if rightness and wrongness are tied to nothing but God's command, and God has so commanded, then cruelty for cruelty's sake would be morally imperative. Now our response can only be one of horror!

In his landmark essay "A Modified Divine Command Theory of Ethical Wrongness," Robert Adams points out that the confusion inherent in this problem lies in the limits of language.[98] Adams argues that more than knowledge of God's commands is required for us to know the meaning of the term *wrong*. We

98. Robert Adams, "A Modified Divine Command Theory of Ethical Wrongness," in *The Virtue of Faith and Other Essays in Philosophical Theology* (Oxford: Oxford University Press, 1987), 97–122.

learn what words mean in the context of a communally shared form of life.[99] For example, we learn what *chair* means by participating in certain activities in which we encounter chairs — we sit in chairs, fetch chairs, stub our toes on chairs, upholster chairs, and so on. Similarly, we learn what the word *God* means by engaging in the form of life in which the word *God* is at home: we pray to God, confess our sins to God, worship God, witness to God, and so on. Without these activities our concept of God is vacuous. It is in this manner that our understanding of what the word *wrong* means is intimately tied to life in our moral community. And the fundamental formative presupposition of *this* Christian moral community is the conviction that *God loves us.*[100] Without belief in a loving God, not only would there be no activities (such as prayer and witness) to ground the meaning of the word *God,* there would be no community at all — around which idea would they rally? No community means no shared concept of wrong either. Euthyphro's dilemma gives us brain cramps because when we are asked to imagine the case in which God commands what we, *as a convictional community,* discern to be cruel acts, *our* language goes haywire. We want to say that the command to cruelty is wrong but are prevented from saying this because we take wrong to be synonymous with "contrary to God's commands," and, in this imaginary case, the command to cruel action is *not* contrary to God's explicit command. But rather than conclude that it is wrong *both* to obey *and* to disobey the command, we need only to point out that for our convictional community the word *God* names Someone in particular. Because we take God to be the One who immutably loves us and wills our good, the divine command theory is better rendered this way: "If *X* is wrong, it is contrary to the commands of a *loving* God." Following this modification, believers see themselves bound to divine command precisely because our conviction is that God has the right sort of character — namely, because God is *good* (where the word *good* is shorthand for a huge list of attributes such as kind, faithful, and so on). It is this prior belief — belief that God loves us — that allows the notion of divine command to get off the ground. To put it differently, without prior belief in a God describable in these terms, there would never be a community of religious believers who have pledged loyalty to *this* God, and therefore, no talk about how *this* God's commands are binding on them. So Adams ultimately points in the direction of *community* to solve the Euthyphro dilemma. But the questions facing divine command theorists do not end there. Since the Christian moral community identifies the character of God by the scriptural stories they hold as

99. Adams admits his own indebtedness to Wittgenstein in a later paper entitled "Divine Command Metaethics Modified Again," in *The Virtue of Faith and Other Essays in Philosophical Theology* (Oxford: Oxford University Press, 1987), 128–43. Cf. Ludwig Wittgenstein, *Philosophical Investigations,* trans. G. E. M. Anscombe (New York: Macmillan, 1958), §§19, 23.

100. For an account of convictional communities which is similar to, but earlier than, MacIntyre's see James Wm. McClendon, Jr., and James M. Smith, *Convictions: Defusing Religious Relativism,* rev. ed. (Valley Forge, Pa.: Trinity Press International, 1994; originally published as *Understanding Religious Convictions* [Notre Dame: University of Notre Dame Press, 1975]).

canonical, we can see how a divine command ethics requires other aspects of a "narrative" assist.[101]

A second concept central to MacIntyre's account which contributes to the divine command model is "tradition-constitutive practices." Consider the difficulties the following questions pose for divine command ethicists:

- By what *criteria* should the source(s) of divine commands be determined? Which source(s) manifests the divine command(s)?
- Can God's command be read from the *natural* world?
- Do *human institutions* embody the divine command(s)?
- Which *written texts* (if any) reflect the divine command(s)? What does it mean for God to authorize a text?
- In what sense do the Christian *Scriptures* communicate the divine commands?
- What *aspect(s)* of the biblical text express the divine command(s)? (Imperative verb structures only? Some narratives?)

The list of questions could be extended, but this list is long enough to show that the divine command theory is feasible only if there is already in place a group of master exegetes whose answers, however provisional, stand firm for the community members. That the community recognizes such "expert practitioners" is evidence of the way, in MacIntyrean terms, practices constitute traditions.

The third conceptual assist MacIntyre provides for understanding why divine command ethics has persisted in some Protestant circles is that of tradition-dependent teleology. Every text-based ethic is plagued with the hermeneutical version of the chicken and the egg: how can one insist that the Scriptures *ought* to be interpreted in such-and-such a manner when knowledge of moral imperatives (the "oughts") is derived from the text by means of the very exegetical and hermeneutical principles in question? It seems that the most promising way to escape this problem is to affirm that a community conditions its incoming members to read the canonical texts in light of the joint conviction (a conviction that is logically prior to the reading of texts) about what human life is for.[102]

101. MacIntyre himself accuses Adams of not going far enough in specifying the identity and nature of God, for "unless that god is just and is justly owed obedience by us, such obedience cannot be justly required of us." Alasdair MacIntyre, "Which God Ought We to Obey and Why?" *Faith and Philosophy* 3, no. 4 (1986): 359.

102. This is simply an acknowledgment of the fact that communities are historically extended, and thus it may not make sense to speak of a *first* member's *initial* encounter with *the* canonical text. Rather, community and text emerge dialectically, and this emergence manifests the way the community's most central convictions have converged on a particular stance toward what human life is all about. In the case of the Christian tradition, the answer to the question "What is human life for?" is recorded repeatedly in the community's written history. For example, Augustine speaks of life as a quest to find rest in God, and the Westminster Catechism describes the chief end of human living as glorifying and enjoying God forever. In the mature community, this central conviction can be found in the text that has emerged as canonical and can be defended by appeals to the canon,

In sum, the voice of Protestant divine command ethics calls us to attend to the deontological character of morality; moral maxims are binding because they express the will of God. However, the divine command theory is in need of what Richard Mouw has called a narrative assist.[103] The work of Alasdair MacIntyre is useful for explicating what this assist amounts to. If divine command ethics is to make sense at all, it must presuppose a narrative (including both a set of stories and the community that lives out these stories) rich enough to identify God as of the "good" sort. Second, divine command ethics depends upon the perpetual presence, in the community, of skillful practitioners in the art of reading the text rightly. Third, divine command theory hinges on a prior conviction about what human life is for.

Gustavo Gutiérrez and John Howard Yoder: Attending to Praxis and Particularity

The last two thinkers whom I bring into conversation with MacIntyre represent voices that remind us that ethics must attend to *praxis* and *particularity*. The massive influx of nominal Christians into the church after 315 A.D. dramatically changed the character of the church as a whole. As a result, the actual practice of the church could not be relied upon to be the starting point for ethical reflection. In this milieu, theory came to dominate practice in matters of ethics. However, throughout church history there have been persistent witnesses (for example, St. Francis, Philip Jacob Spener, Søren Kierkegaard) to the view that right living (praxis) is logically prior to right thinking. Voices like these remind us of the ways in which ethics is rooted in practice. This reminder comes out very strongly in the contemporary liberation theology of Gustavo Gutiérrez.

Earlier in our own century, Walter Rauschenbusch argued that changes in the social consciousness and practices of Christians (namely, the social gospel movement, which took seriously the care of the poor) may reasonably occasion readjusting points of doctrine because God is involved with all human history and hence could reveal himself through changes in social practices.[104] The belief that the pattern of historical change was evidence of something very important is reminiscent of Karl Marx (who agreed that history progressed dialectically, but insisted that this was a purely material process). Although neo-Hegelian thinkers like Marx have largely fallen into disrepute in the northern half of the western hemisphere, the Central and South American Christian communities have retained many of their valuable insights in the form of liberation theol-

---

but because this conviction also expresses how these texts are to be taken (e.g., Christians take the biblical text as a means toward knowing God who is our final end), there may be no way to get behind this conviction to answer the question, "Which came first, the community or the canon?"

103. Richard J. Mouw, *The God Who Commands* (Notre Dame: University of Notre Dame Press, 1990), 116–49.

104. Walter Rauschenbusch, *A Theology for the Social Gospel* (New York: Macmillan, 1918). See also McClendon, *Ethics*, 244–47.

ogy. Chief among their spokespersons is Gustavo Gutiérrez. For Gutiérrez the church witnesses to Christ's resurrection as the sign that "life and not death has the final say about history" because God indwells human history as his temple.[105] The conviction that history's progress manifests the presence of a God who is tirelessly at work precipitates four conclusions.

First, to do theology (and by implication, ethics) is to exegete the actions of God as they are manifested in the Christian community. Therefore, theology is nothing but "a critical reflection on Christian praxis in light of the word of God."[106] Yet if God is at work in all of human history, then the recent emergence of a new class of people — the formerly invisible poor — as a distinctive and transcultural social reality indicates *their* preferential status in God's eyes as well.[107]

Second, the conviction that the Spirit has formed *this* new people implies that theological work must especially consist in reflection upon, and analysis of, Christian praxis *in the impoverished* context.

> What we see here is an authentic spirituality — that is, a way of being Christian. It is from this rich experience of the following of Jesus that liberation theology emerges; the following constitutes the practice — at once commitment and prayer — on which liberation theology reflects.[108]

Third, God's ultimate intention — read from the direction that his liberating work is taking — is the creation of a new humanity.[109] Gutiérrez criticizes secular models that conceive history in terms of steady development because they invariably overlook the fact that development is a zero-sum game: development in one sector of society always comes at the expense of another.[110] Gutiérrez also shrugs off the traditionally Christian "two-planes" model that recounts history in terms of the coexistence of an entirely worldly world and an otherworldly church.[111] He asserts that there is but one "single convocation to salvation" by which "all persons are in Christ efficaciously called to communion with God."[112] Thus, in Gutiérrez's eyes, God intends the construction of a single just society in which there is total communion with God and the fullest possible fellowship with others.[113]

---

105. Gustavo Gutiérrez, *A Theology of Liberation: History, Politics, and Salvation,* trans. Sister Caridad Inda and John Eagleson, rev. ed. of the original English translation of *Teología de la liberación* (Maryknoll, N.Y.: Orbis Books, 1988), xxxvi, 115; also 106.

106. Ibid., xxix. Here the "word" referred to is not merely the Christian Scriptures but God's call to all people to a salvation that consists in "the progression of the awareness of freedom" (19, paraphrasing Hegel).

107. Poverty is both a scandalous human condition which begs for salvation and the blessed state of spiritual childhood. Ibid., 164–69.

108. Ibid., xxxii.

109. Ibid., 81.

110. Ibid., 49–57.

111. Ibid., 38, 41, 46, 86.

112. Ibid., 45.

113. Ibid., 66, 113.

Fourth, salvation can be construed only as the removal of those obstacles that hinder the realization of the kingdom of God within history. Because salvation and creation are theologically linked, salvation is not only for *all* persons but also for the *whole* person.[114] Thus salvation is liberation on three levels:[115] (1) liberation from "social situations of oppression and marginalization which force many (and, indeed, all in one or another way) to live in conditions contrary to God's will for their life";[116] (2) liberation from internalized patterns of servitude to oppressive powers through personal conscientization and transformation;[117] and (3) liberation from sin through reconciliation with God.

Morality in this schema becomes *cooperation with God's work in history.* Since change-by-reform fails, along with the entire developmental model, change can be thought of only as the product of forceful, even violent, revolution against those "developers" who hold the reins of power.[118] To cooperate with God means participation in the breaking down of those human structures that prevent freedom: "To place oneself in the perspective of the Kingdom means to participate in the struggle for the liberation of those oppressed by others."[119] To do this with integrity requires workers who imitate the *kenōsis* (emptying) of Christ[120] in forming their own solidarity with the poor.[121]

To affirm God's action in history is to insist that the old has passed away and that the new must come. This newness is seen in both the emergence of a preferred class of people and the emergence of liberation theology itself:

> Theology as critical reflection on historical praxis is a liberating theology, a theology of the liberating transformation of the history of humankind and also therefore that part of humankind — gathered into *ecclesia* — which openly confesses Christ. This is a theology that does not stop with reflecting on the world, but rather tries to be part of the process through which the world is transformed. It is a theology that is open — in the protest against trampled human dignity, in the struggle against the plunder of the vast majority of humankind, in liberating love, and in the building of a new, just, and comradely society — to the gift of the Kingdom of God.[122]

John Howard Yoder concurs with Gutiérrez that God intervenes in history and that, therefore, ethics must pay attention to the presence of God in the "eschatological" community. But what makes Christian ethics *Christian,* in Yoder's eyes, is not simply that Christians behave distinctively, or that this distinctiveness can simultaneously be described in Aristides' words as "something Divine

114. Ibid., 83–91, 143.
115. Ibid., 25, 103, and elsewhere.
116. Ibid., xxxviii.
117. Ibid., 52.
118. Ibid., 30–31, 54. On violence, see, e.g., 160.
119. Ibid., 116. Cf. also 148.
120. Phil. 2:7.
121. Gutiérrez, *A Theology of Liberation,* 63, 151, 172, and elsewhere.
122. Ibid., 12.

in the midst of them." What makes Christian ethics Christian is the way the resurrection of Jesus forms the eschatological community.

The resurrection makes all the difference for Christian ethics.[123] First, it is taken to be the vindication of the manner in which Jesus lived and died, a manner that is normative for those who would be his followers. Second, it constitutes a new way of looking at the world because the resurrection subordinates all other claims to human allegiance under the single lordship of Christ. Third, the resurrection offers transformation of human life here and now. Yoder's fellow "baptist," McClendon, aptly summarizes:

> It is not only that the resurrection of Jesus Christ from the dead is the vindication of the justice of God and hence our "acquittal by resurrection"...; it is not only that *and* the consequent re-vision of the social structures, seen now in resurrection light...; it is both of the above and another still — the transformation of life in the body itself, here and now....[124]

John Howard Yoder agrees with Gutiérrez that eschatology is of central importance to ethics. Yet while *eschatological* describes for Gutiérrez the hope of a future just society, the same term names for Yoder the present reality of a community that endeavors to live in imitation of Jesus. Thus, Yoder disagrees with Gutiérrez in three important ways. First, because he understands politics as necessarily conflictual, Gutiérrez concludes that increasingly radical social praxis, even to the point of violent revolution, is divinely warranted.[125] In contrast, Yoder contends that Christ's rejection of worldly means (namely, coercion and violence) to accomplish divine ends is the true revolutionary revelation. If God be God, and has revealed himself in Christ, then it is God's job, not ours, to control history's outcome. Christians' responsibility is to conform to the paradigmatic exemplar they have in Jesus,[126] whose passive nonresistance at Calvary broke the backs of the "principalities and powers" by exposing their true colors: fallen, violent, contingent, inimical to God, and possessing only the illusion of power.[127]

The resurrection proclaimed the complete defeat of all the principalities and powers (whether religious institutions like the Mosaic law or socially embodied evils like racism) because the resurrection established a new community (a genuinely new world order) of those set free by the truth in Jesus.[128] For this community, pacifism is not an arcane or eccentric theory but *the way in*

123. McClendon, *Ethics,* 247–55.

124. Ibid., 253.

125. Gutiérrez, *A Theology of Liberation,* 31. Rather than see the failure of violent revolution to bring about just societies as a failure of *means,* Gutiérrez concludes that most revolutions fail in *scope:* "Moreover, it is becoming more obvious that the revolutionary process ought to embrace the whole continent [!]. There is little chance of success for attempts limited to a national scope" (55).

126. John Howard Yoder, "Radical Reformation Ethics in Ecumenical Perspective," in *The Priestly Kingdom* (Notre Dame: University of Notre Dame Press, 1984), 105–22.

127. John Howard Yoder, *The Politics of Jesus,* 2d ed. (Grand Rapids, Mich., and Carlisle, England: Wm. B. Eerdmans and Paternoster Press, 1994), 134–61, 228–47.

128. For a helpful introduction to the notion of "social evil" as analogous to the Pauline phrase

which its members relate to one another. Thus, for Yoder, eschatology is central because Christ's resurrection is evidence that the eschaton has begun already and is embodied in the eschatological community.

The second objection Yoder might raise to Gutiérrez concerns the place the church occupies on history's stage. Because Gutiérrez locates the significance of the gospel in the *future* realization of the kingdom of God,[129] he deems the church's claim to history's spotlight to be something of an obstacle. The church must get off center stage to make room for the *humanity-wide* kingdom of God.[130]

In contrast, Yoder argues that the church is the corporate "new man" which Scripture declares to have been God's intention from the beginning.[131] Though not yet completely, the church already embodies the eschatological kingdom. But *this* church is not to be confused with the powerful institution of the post-Constantinian age. Instead, the true church is that community of believers which conforms to the pattern of Jesus' life and operates from a position of weakness in this present age by the principle of revolutionary subordination.[132] Yoder notes that the Anabaptists have preserved this view better than most. But what Yoder purports to do is not call the church to some other age, or to some denomination within Christianity, but to call the church to its true identity as revealed in the Gospels. This is not a call for withdrawal *from* society but a summons to authentically Christian living *within* society.[133] Therefore, the best social ethic Christians have to offer to the world is merely, though not easily, that the church be the church.

Finally, Yoder would object that by making praxis the locus of theology, Gutiérrez has unintentionally left a theoretical vacuum which will inevitably be filled by some secular social theory or other. The obvious favorite of Gutiérrez is Marxist socialism.[134] But Yoder wants no theory to govern Christian theology.

"principalities and powers" see Walter Wink, *Unmasking the Powers: The Invisible Powers That Determine Human Existence* (Philadelphia: Fortress Press, 1986).

129. Gutiérrez, *A Theology of Liberation,* 155.

130. Ibid., 143–44. The church's penchant for occupying center stage is what Gutiérrez labels as "constantinianism." In contrast, Yoder reserves this term for describing the tendency of the Christians, when they wield collective power, to use that power to attempt to coerce the outcome of history.

131. See Eph. 1:3–14, 2:11–22, esp. 2:15, where the phrase καινός ανθρωπος ("new man") names the new corporate person formed by God out of the two social groupings of the Jews and the Gentiles. See also Col. 3:5–11. Paul also contrasts the present reality of the Body of Christ with the diaphaneity of pre-Christ religion in Col. 2:17. On this reading of Col. 2:17 see Petr Pokorny, *Colossians: A Commentary,* trans. Siegfried S. Schatzmann (Peabody, Mass.: Hendrickson Publishers, 1991), 144–45.

132. Yoder, *Politics,* 162–92.

133. John Howard Yoder, "The Kingdom as Social Ethic," in *The Priestly Kingdom* (Notre Dame: University of Notre Dame Press, 1984), 80–101.

134. Gutiérrez, *A Theology of Liberation,* 65–66. Yoder discusses this and five other adaptive strategies open to Christians who are faced with rival truth claims from the "wider world." Yoder notes that these strategies all fall prey to the fallacy of assuming "the priority in truth and value of the meaning system of the world claiming to be wider." John Howard Yoder, "'But We Do See Jesus':

Rather, the meaning system of the wider world — its concepts, theories, language — is to be transformed in such a way that no scheme is treated as ultimate but rather subordinated to the lordship of Christ.[135] So then, for Gutiérrez, theology is reflection on Christian praxis governed by a secular social theory, while for Yoder, theology retains its integrity by being governed by the "hermeneutic community":

> The free church alternative ... recognizes the inadequacies of the text of Scripture standing alone uninterpreted, and appropriates the promise of the guidance of the Spirit throughout the ages, but locates the fulfillment of that promise in the assembly of those who gather around Scripture in the face of a given real moral challenge.[136]

In sum, Yoder insists that the eschatological reality of the kingdom of God is proleptically present in Christ's resurrection, is partially embodied in the new order of human existence called the church, and is the *telos* toward which all history is moving under God's sovereign direction. The proper role of the church is not to change the world but to witness to it by living faithfully to the form of Jesus' life and proclaiming him in all his particularity.[137]

One could trace many parallels between MacIntyre and these two thinkers. It is easy to spot the way Gutiérrez derives the liberation imperative from his understanding of the *telos* of humanity. The way Yoder sees theology as constrained by the hermeneutic community comes exceedingly close to MacIntyre's technical explanation of "practices."[138] Furthermore, despite the radical differences between Yoder and Gutiérrez, their dispute has the flavor of a "family argument" because both views coexist in what MacIntyre calls a single "historically extended, socially embodied argument" known to us as the Christian tradition.[139]

For MacIntyre, traditions cycle through three stages of *formation, epistemological crisis,* and *resolution.*[140] Inherent in MacIntyre's concept of tradition is the

---

The Particularity of Incarnation and the Universality of Truth," in *The Priestly Kingdom* (Notre Dame: University of Notre Dame Press, 1984), 46–62.

135. Yoder offers first-century Christology as an example: "A handful of messianic Jews ... refused to contextualize their message by clothing it in the categories the world held ready. Instead, they seized the categories, hammered them into other shapes, and turned the cosmology [of classical Greece] on its head, with Jesus both at the bottom, crucified as a common criminal, and at the top, preexistent Son and creator. ..." Yoder, "'But We Do See Jesus,'" 54.

136. Yoder, "Radical Reformation Ethics," 117.

137. See John Howard Yoder, *The Christian Witness to the State* (Newton, Kan.: Faith and Life Press, 1964). Yoder argues further in "'But We Do See Jesus'" that we have a universal message not because we have access to universal criteria of rationality but because of the universal ordinariness of Jesus' humanity. If the cosmic Christology was appropriate in the New Testament context because of resident secular cosmologies which Christians seized and transformed, then in our pluralistic and relativistic age Christ can again be heard if we seize the contemporary language of pluralism but transform it to proclaim Christ as Lord in a particularistic way.

138. See MacIntyre, *After Virtue,* 187.

139. Ibid., 222.

140. See MacIntyre, *Whose Justice?* 349–69.

notion that history has a direction, a notion that is essential to both developmentalism (for example, of the sort that Gutiérrez repudiates) and Christian eschatology (as espoused by both Yoder and Gutiérrez, albeit with important differences between them). But in construing history as the dialectical process of justification, MacIntyre's view resembles more the evolutionary thought of such philosophers of science as Imre Lakatos than it does views of history based on Christian eschatology.[141] For MacIntyre (and Lakatos) there is no ultimate tradition (or research program) toward which a tradition (or a research program) converges. Nevertheless, progress is real. Feeble traditions die and strong traditions get stronger because former ways of looking at the world are discarded as "false."[142]

However, although Christianity can be construed as a MacIntyrean tradition, in which both Yoder and Gutiérrez can be understood to have a voice, it is ironic that Yoder and Gutiérrez agree on a serious flaw in MacIntyre's paradigm, namely, his own reticence to affirm that a given tradition progresses toward some particular *telos*.[143] If the narrative of the individual, the community, and the tradition displays a fractal symmetry, and if *After Virtue*'s master argument is teleological, then it makes sense to ask, "What is the *telos* toward which the tradition *itself* quests?" Hauerwas, Yoder, and Jones describe this *telos* as the formation of the eschatological community.[144] Political theologians such as Gutiérrez and Jürgen Moltmann borrow Paul Tillich's metaphor of history questing for the kingdom of God.[145] But on this point MacIntyre himself is strangely silent.

Conclusion

Alasdair MacIntyre does not come to the roundtable as a Christian ethicist. Nevertheless, his contribution is fruitful because he makes sense out of a cacophony of contemporary Christian voices which together challenge the inadequacies of the contemporary received explanation of ethics. These voices urge us to attend to the *particular* and *practical, communal, juridical, deontological,*

141. For comparison of MacIntyre and Lakatos see Nancey Murphy, "Postmodern Antirelativism," in *Anglo-American Postmodernity: Philosophical Perspectives on Science, Religion, and Ethics* (Boulder, Colo.: Westview Press, 1997), 49–62.

142. MacIntyre, *Whose Justice?* 356.

143. The notion that the *telos* is unattainable has two likely sources. First, it has roots in MacIntyre's own Aristotelian heritage. Cf. *Nicomachean Ethics,* trans. Terence Irwin (Indianapolis: Hackett Publishing, 1985) 1096b30–35. Second, the idea follows from the nature of traditions as socially embodied inquiry; it is their nature to remain open-ended lest they die. Cf. Alasdair MacIntyre, *Three Rival Versions of Moral Enquiry: Encyclopaedia, Genealogy, and Tradition* (Notre Dame: University of Notre Dame Press, 1990), 124–25.

144. Jones, "Alasdair MacIntyre on Narrative," 65.

145. Gutiérrez, *A Theology of Liberation,* 81–97. Moltmann's view of progressive history has led him to identify with each new social movement (e.g., the new left, feminism, liberation theology), and by showing how Christianity is relevant to them, he justifies both these movements and Christianity itself. For an excellent discussion of Moltmann's journey see Rasmusson, *Church as Polis,* 42–172.

theological, and *anthropological* aspects of moral reasoning. While these voices may bicker among themselves and disagree dramatically on specifics, MacIntyre's central concepts enable us to see these disparate voices as bearing a family resemblance. Although this essay in no sense constitutes a *Christian* justification of MacIntyre's nomenclature, it does illustrate that he makes for a welcome and fruitful dialogue partner in the historically extended family argument we call Christian ethics.

PART II

Virtues and Practices of the Christian Tradition

Chapter 4

The Practice of Community Formation

James Wm. McClendon, Jr.

Editor's Introduction

It may be good to remind the reader at this point of the purposes of this book. Our goal is to bring together the work of Alasdair MacIntyre in philosophical ethics with the writings of a variety of Christian ethicists in such a way that the latter *exemplify* the patterns of moral description and moral reasoning defended by MacIntyre, while allowing MacIntyre's philosophical concepts to shed light on the shape and justification of the theological positions. To this end, we introduce each of the following chapters with a brief essay that summarizes its MacIntyrean features.

The goal in this part of the book is to highlight themes that appear central to the Christian moral life when it is viewed through a MacIntyrean lens. Thus, we begin this part with a chapter from James Wm. McClendon, Jr.'s, *Ethics* in which he argues that *community formation* is the central *practice* of the Christian church *(Ethics: Systematic Theology, Volume I* [Nashville: Abingdon Press, 1986]).

McClendon writes from the perspective of the "little 'b' baptist tradition." By this he means to refer to a broad spectrum of Christian life that has been influenced by (or simply happens to be like) the churches of the Radical Reformation. McClendon argues that Christian ethics must take account of a threefold complexity: (1) Christians are (along with others) *embodied,* a part of nature; (2) Christians participate in the social structures of society but also develop their own social structures; and (3) the ongoing life of the church is open to the continuing activity of God in its midst. Thus, there are three interwoven strands of thought, all needed in order to give a complete account of the Christian moral life: the body strand, the social strand, and the resurrection strand. This chapter by McClendon focuses on the social strand of Christian ethics and makes effective use of a concept of *practice* comparable to MacIntyre's.

In short, the formation of a community of disciples is the sum and substance of Christian social ethics. McClendon reflects on two subpractices that effect community formation. One is sharing in the covenant meal. "At the fundament of missionary, Gentile Christianity, there is a rite not magical, nor even (in many usual senses of the term) *sacramental* — but moral and ethical first of all; that is, aimed at the shaping of the common life of Christian community.... The meal is part and parcel of a practice...which we might roughly name the practice of *establishing and maintaining Christian community.*" The rules for the meal are constitutive of the life of the church. They are linked to the life story of Jesus: to follow, to witness, to remain faithful until death.

McClendon describes a second practice constitutive of community formation: reconciliation. How was it to be possible for the Christian community to take the costly way of Jesus? How was it to be kept on track? "In terms of technique, the answer lay in a never-ending congregational *conversation* – a conversation that may now engage only two or three, but again will involve the gathered *ekklēsia* itself." McClendon points out that the rules for communal discipline in Matthew 18 are wisely calculated to result, in the happy case, not in the expulsion of offenders but in forgiveness and reconciliation.

Finally, McClendon finds the concept of social practice useful for exploring the question of the church's relation to the world. It is not helpful to set up the question, as H. Richard Niebuhr did, in terms of Christ and *culture,* for culture itself is not one global unity. Better, says McClendon, to recognize in it an indefinite congeries of powerful practices, toward which Christian witness will necessarily take a variety of forms, ranging from conscious engagement to complete withdrawal.

So McClendon's work illustrates the rich use that can be made in Christian ethics of the MacIntyrean concept of a practice. In MacIntyre's work we find a theoretical account displaying the relations between practices and the traditions they help to constitute, and between practices and the virtues that make them possible. We also find in MacIntyre's work a justification for employing an analysis in these terms, in contrast to the analyses in terms of rights and duties and utility that have become so common in modern ethical discourse.

NANCEY MURPHY

The Nature of Christian Social Ethics

The account of social ethics to be offered here depends on a "three-stranded" analysis of Christian ethics. The moral life of the Christian community, I argue, can be understood only by recognizing the complex interplay of factors concerning our embodied existence (strand one), our communal structures (strand two), and the ongoing engagement of God in our individual and social lives (strand three).[1]

Christian social ethics is ethics engaged by the structures of social or political life — its practices and institutions — but also by its mass movements and migrations, its wars and upheavals. It responds, in one way or another, to these drumbeats of social or political destiny. Such engagement involves for the

1. See James Wm. McClendon, Jr., *Ethics: Systematic Theology, Volume I* (Nashville: Abingdon Press, 1986).

participant an intense inner journey that must display its own distinctive moral features. Our theoretical account must provide a way of thinking about social ethics (strand two) as well as a way of thinking about the inwardness of the moral life (aspects of strand one). In addition, it must show how these two are to be connected. If it cannot, the theory still requires work.

This would seem, however, to be a predicament all too common in contemporary Christian life. On the one hand, many Christians are aware of some inner dynamic of blame, shame, and guilt, and their churches may provide religious therapy or "counseling" to minister to such symptoms of the soul. On the other hand, the same Christians are often offered by their churches a social ethic that takes no account of the embodied selfhood of each of us, with its drives, needs, and capacities. Instead, it offers prescriptions for social ills grandly defined — idealistic remedies for "racism and sexism" (or, in another current version of social morality, nostalgic remedies for "weak-kneed churches" confronting a "godless society"). Yet these diagnoses and these remedies seem alike untouched by any awareness of the needs of our souls, just as the pastoral remedies churches offer seem to be untouched by any sense of societal structure and its bearing on our lives.[2]

The life of Dietrich Bonhoeffer well reflects the difficulties in bringing together the needs of the soul and the needs of society in a single life. The pathos of his story, I have shown, lay in the fact that the instrument he so unerringly grasped in response, and then so helplessly relinquished, was the political life of church and congregation.[3] That instrument must become the key to the present essay.

An interesting project, though not one to be carried out here, might be to go back to the roots of our current theologies in seventeenth-century England (the time of the Caroline divines and the rise of the Puritan movement within the Church of England; the time, also, when the English language began to replace Latin in theological writing there and in America). At that time, it would appear, this schism between the ethics of interiority and the ethics of society first appears.[4] Here, also, might be found the circumstances in which Christian morality became more and more preoccupied with a mission to the individual that concentrated upon solitary conscience and its problems, accompanied by a mission to society concentrated upon public and legal rights, with no organic links between the two.

My claim is that for Christians the connecting link between body ethics and social ethics, between the moral self and the morals of society, is to be found in the body of Christ that is the gathered church. The place where conscience comes to light in a baptist ethic is not in solitary or Kierkegaardian introspec-

2. Archie Smith, *The Relational Self* (Nashville: Abingdon Press, 1982).

3. See McClendon, *Ethics*, chap. 7.

4. Thomas Wood, *English Casuistical Divinity during the Seventeenth Century* (London: SPCK, 1952); and "Caroline Moral Theology," in *Dictionary of Christian Ethics*, ed. John Macquarrie (Philadelphia: Fortress, 1967).

tion, nor is it in the social concerns of individual private citizens who happen to be Christian as well (not even in their widely held and in that sense "common" concerns). Rather the link is found in congregational reflection, discernment, discipline, and action, whose model is nearer to the Wesleyan class meeting or the Anabaptist *Gemeinde* than to the denominational social action lobby agency or the mass membership churches of today's suburban society. It is such gathered sharing (so goes my thesis) that issues in directives for the pilgrimage of each *and* issues in a shared witness to the outside world. This explains why, although conscience and judgment could be described along with guilt and blame and shame as strand-one *phenomena* of the moral life, these could not be adequately discussed in these terms. Their functioning in the moral life requires for Christians also strand two, where conscience and judgment can be evoked in the communal setting of the faithful congregation and its common life.

The task of this essay, then, will be to explore the shape of the gathered church as the integral and necessary form of the moral life of Christians. A convenient beginning can be made by considering the community for whom the Gospel of Matthew was first written. This Gospel's author or redactor deliberately sought to relate Christian community to the community of the Law, to Israel and Torah. Perhaps partly for this reason Matthew, with its Sermon on the Mount (chaps. 5–7) and its account of the discipline of forgiveness (chap. 18), has played a large role in the baptist movement that is our touchstone.[5] Matthew is no mere partisan traditional choice, however. For it is "a well-known fact," says Krister Stendahl, "that the spiritual and religious atmosphere of this gospel is most nearly akin to post-apostolic Christianity" generally.[6] Thus, to understand Matthew is to get a handhold upon the social morality of early Christianity. Lest anyone nevertheless believe that this Gospel is in some important way atypical of the primitive Jesus movement, I will sometimes substantiate my main points by reference to the Pauline communities, about which there is even more abundant evidence.[7]

The arrangement of the essay will be threefold. First, I present the Matthean (and in general, the early Christian) concepts of *discipleship* and *community*, showing their relation to one another and to the community for which Matthew was written, and their bearing on our communities. Second, I show how the understanding of *law* and *forgiveness* in these sources occupied a place in the disciple community, and will explore the concept of forgiveness as a crucial element of the social life of Christians. Third, I treat the Christian understanding of *the church in the world*, showing that it is no afterthought or mere contingency that puts the church in relation to its wider environment. Rather, Christian conduct, guided by the Great Commission, must be distinctively engaged in such

5. This is the movement typified by Radical Reformation sources and others. My use of *baptist* is an equivalent of the (earlier) use of *Täufer*.

6. Krister Stendahl, *The School of Matthew*, new ed. (Philadelphia: Fortress Press, 1968).

7. Wayne Meeks, *The First Urban Christians* (New Haven: Yale University Press, 1983).

worldly presence — a point as vital to the risen Jesus Christ of Matthew's Gospel (cf. Matt. 28:19–20) as to any present-day social activist.

An Ethics for Disciples in Community

Who Were the Disciples?

Who, really, were "the disciples" Matthew's Gospel tells about? Preeminently, this Gospel portrays the men and women Jesus summoned to follow him in the days of his flesh. In another sense, though, "the disciples" were the readers for whom the Gospel was written.[8] I am following the informed guess that these first readers were in fact members of a mixed, but increasingly non-Jewish, Christian community in Syria, perhaps in Antioch, about 80–85 A.D.[9] So while the *setting* of the Gospel is early first-century Palestine, with Jesus and Peter, James, John, and company as its chief actors, readers would realize that the stories Matthew told were also their own later stories: The call to fishermen to leave their nets perhaps called into question the occupations of these later Syrian disciples; Simon's "You are the Christ" made him also the spokesman for these second- and third-generation Christians; the debates with Pharisees, the question about temple tax, the temptations to greed and lust and violence that the Master encountered along the way — all these corresponded to later Syrian debates, Syrian questions, Syrian temptations. The setting was bygone Galilee and Judea, but the *impact* was contemporary Syrian, here and now. In our terms, the "baptist vision" was at work; "this" was "that"; and it was this doubleness that gave these tales their power. Matthew the writer had turned the telescope around, put its large end to his reader's eye, made the immediacy of Christian life in Syria seem as distant as Palestine in the first days of Christ's ministry, and, by replacing their own story with the true story of Jesus and Peter and Judas and Herod, had given the readers perspective from which to judge both stories aright. Our own task is to turn the telescope back again for a moment, so that, from what is said to them in their Gospel, we can form an idea of these Syrian Christians and their church.

These readers, then, knew themselves to be *disciples* (*mathêtai*). "Come, follow me" (19:21) is the Matthean Jesus' characteristic phrase. Jack Dean Kingsbury has shown how Matthew uses "with" (*meta*) as a term of art to distinguish those who in this sense follow Jesus: it is just the inner circle, the twelve or eleven, Mary, tax-collectors, and sinners who are said to be "with Jesus." The crowds, even when they surround Jesus, are not in this way of speaking "with" him. Thus it is Matthew who has Jesus saying, "He who is not *with me* is against me" (12:30).[10]

8. I develop this dual identification further in *Ethics,* chap. 12.

9. See Robert Hamerton-Kelly, "Matthew, Gospel of," in *Interpreter's Dictionary of the Bible,* Supplementary Volume (Nashville: Abingdon Press, 1976).

10. Jack Dean Kingsbury, *Matthew,* Proclamation Commentaries (Philadelphia: Fortress, 1977), 80.

At the very least, then, Matthean discipleship implies the willing participation of each follower. Matthew recalls a community, and addresses a church, of intentional or voluntary participants. His is not, like the "Christian" faction in modern Lebanon, a hereditary or ethnic community, nor is it, like some current American religiosity, a civil religion. Wayne A. Meeks has picked up the threads of an old discussion by noting that the household (*oikia*) was often a basic unit in the narration of the story of the earlier, Pauline missionary developments. Whole households were converted (Acts 10, 16), baptized (see also 1 Cor. 1:16), and sometimes as households commended for Christian service (1 Cor. 16:15f.). Meeks notes that in such group conversions, "not everyone who went along with the new practices would do so with the *same* understanding or inner participation."[11] It is a case of modern practice shaping exegesis, however, if we extrapolate from Meeks's cautious inference to the unwarranted conclusion that some members perhaps had no faith at all, and were helpless infants or hapless slaves. For as Meeks correctly notes, Paul's letter to Philemon makes it clear that "not every member of a household always became a Christian when its head did," in Paul's understanding of the matter.[12] Whatever lapses may have occurred then or later, Paul's doctrine was in this regard consonant with Matthew's. Discipleship meant following Jesus, each disciple a follower, each follower "with Jesus," if and only if a disciple. In the strict Troeltschian sense, then, the church Matthew addresses is sectarian, composed of men and women of whatever age who have freely obeyed the "follow me" of Christ. Some are Jews, more, we think, Gentiles; all are united by their shared solidarity with Jesus: "For where two or three meet together in my name, I am among them" (18:20 REB).

Solidarity is expressed in *obedience*. Whenever in the Gospel Jesus' calls to follow are met with a willing response, Jack Suggs has pointed out, there ensues a fresh commissioning. Those who will follow are then blessed, given a new name or a new role or a new task, and finally are empowered by Jesus to fulfill that task (see 5:1–20; 16:17–19; 28:18–20).[13] Of great interest for us here are the typical tasks disciples are given in chapters 5, 16, and 28: (1) to fulfill (with Jesus) the law (every jot and tittle of it!); (2) to administer discipline and forgiveness; (3) to carry this "teaching" to all the Gentiles so that they, too, may become disciples. These three are logically related: the disciples in community are to be the "treasurers," the wise stewards, of the law (5:20; cf. 13:52); therefore their practice of discipline must undergird this stewardship (16:17–19; cf. 18:15–20); finally, their full mission is to share this same stewardship with all, everywhere — thus becoming the church in the world (28:18–20).

Discipleship meant such obedience; it also meant *solidarity with one another*. Matthew would have his Syrian readers understand that by voluntarily linking their lives to Jesus, they have linked them to each other as well. These ties

11. Meeks, *First Urban Christians*, 77; emphasis added.

12. Ibid., 76.

13. Jack M. Suggs, *Wisdom, Christology, and Law in Matthew's Gospel* (Cambridge: Harvard University Press, 1970).

override the existing links of kinship and of household (12:46–50; 10:34–39). Members are not ranked as "fathers" or "rabbis" — such titles are actually forbidden (20:25–28; 23:8–12), and the Matthean church seems to know nothing of the prestigious hierarchy that would spring up later and elsewhere. They are brothers and sisters, or they are one another's servants. All this is eloquently expressed in their simple meal of recollection, in which they "significantly" share the body of their Master. As they do so, they renew their own unity, acknowledging the forgiveness of each, and they renew their common hope, eating bread and sharing a cup "until that day" (26:26–29).

The Covenant Meal

Perhaps it is inevitable that any rite that has come to be so widely used by such diverse communities, pre-Christian, Christian, and post-Christian, should have amalgamated to itself various meanings and purposes. Already this was true of the Passover meal that (according to Matthew 26) formed the basis of the Last Supper. It may be helpful, then, to note afresh the elegant simplicity of the First Gospel, which devotes (in the Aland Greek text) a scant ninety-five words (26:26–30) to the account of that foundation. Central to the rite Matthew describes are two acts of sharing by Jesus: one of bread, the other of a cup (of wine). The principal words are simply these performative acts of sharing: "Take, eat . . . Drink from it, all of you" (vs. 27). For each act a single interpretation is furnished: for the bread, "this is my body"; for the cup, "this is my blood of the covenant, which is poured out for many for the forgiveness of sins" (vs. 28). Thereby two notes are sounded, *solidarity* ("my body," "my blood," "covenant") and *redemption* ("unto forgiveness of sins").

It is the first, the solidaristic, that is uppermost for us here, so let us consider its three governing images. Theological doctrine has concentrated on the first and second of these, body and blood, understood mystically, or philosophically, or in some combination of these, but never to the satisfaction of all interpreters. Perhaps theological ethics does well, then, if it concentrates on covenant, reading it not "this is my *blood* (of the covenant)," but with a better exegesis: "This is *my* blood-of-the-*covenant*"; that is, "This rite we share tonight in the upper room is *my* reaffirmation of the LORD God's ancient pledge, linking us to it and thereby to the ancient solidarity of God-and-Israel, and [as the reader knows with foreboding] linking it also to the ultimate blood-sacrifice, that of the Servant who will witness to God's truth, even on a Roman cross, on the morrow." In that case, the new union expressed in this passage is the solidarity of Master and disciples, who are linked by this very meal to their wider Jewish tradition.

In this light, what of the other images? What will "this is my body" mean? Our best exegesis is found in the New Testament, in the very place where we find the oldest account of the Thanksgiving Meal itself, 1 Corinthians 10–12. Here the widespread perception of the ancient world, that sharing a meal is communion (*koinōnia*) with the one who either as host or as *numen* presides over the meal, is linked (1 Cor. 10:16) with the powerful metaphor of the gathered church identified as the body of Christ (chap. 12). Set between these two pictures (in sociological style we might call them respectively the contaminative and the organic) is Paul's recounting of the Lord's Supper tradition he had received and delivered to the Corinthians, including the words of Jesus over the (already broken) bread: "This is my body, which is for you" (11:24 REB). In such a context, the ideas to which we are led are those of group solidarity, of an identity that includes rather than excludes, that inclusion being the incorporation of the lives of the gathered disciples not only into their crucified and risen Lord, but also into one another.

Now if we permit "body" in 1 Corinthians 10 and 12 to shape our understanding of that image as it is used in the intervening Lord's Supper account in chapter 11; if, that is, we allow the notions of communion and sharing and organic oneness in the gathered disciple band to form our understanding of "this is my body" in 11:26, what follows? This, I think: At the fundament of missionary, Gentile Christianity, there is a rite, not magical or even (in many usual senses of the term) "sacramental" — but moral and ethical first of all; a rite aimed at the shaping of the common life of Christian community. This is the rite, and the emphasis, that Matthew's church also has found, a generation or so later, in its own passion narrative, Matthew 26.

Here we see an exact way in which the "religious" life of Christians is inseparable from their moral formation. It is a way that totally escapes the sweep of standard modern ethical theory. For it is not that the act of communion in the Lord's Supper provides the church with motives for good behavior as emotivists might concede, or that this act changes the balance of utilitarian goods for its communicants. Rather the meal is part and parcel of a *practice*, which we might roughly name *the practice of establishing and maintaining Christian community*. The "rules" for the meal are included among the constitutive rules for that practice. Among those rules are ones that link the conduct of participants to their participation in the meal. In Matthew, this is presented in narrative form. Jesus, the presiding communicant, goes out to the Mount of Olives, leading his followers on a *via crucis* they must follow if they are to follow him. In the long run, they will, but in the short run, he alone takes that path of witness, faithfulness, and death. By the thread of the larger story we see the consonance between what he does and what at the meal he enacted.

This comes clearest if we imagine the contrary — Jesus slips out of town after the meal, escapes, becomes a well-known intellectual leader in another country, and lives to a ripe old age. In that case, though, it is not only the longer story that is changed; the meal is different, too. Now for Jesus to say, "this is *my* shed-blood-of-the-covenant," must be read as ironic, or merely empty. Paul makes this point not by narrative but by argument: If when you assemble, you ignore one another, each going ahead with his own meal, some hungry, others overindulging, then the meal you have just eaten is not the Lord's Supper after all (1 Cor. 11:20f.). For the point of that meal is solidarity in the Kingdom;

those who ignore that have missed the first lesson of Christian social ethics; they have lost sight of the meaning of the rite. If this meaning has to do with the conduct of Christians at the meal itself, it also has to do with their conduct in the daily fellowship, and in their relation to the wider society as well, as the surrounding chapters (10 and 12) of 1 Corinthians bring out.

In giving the Matthean and Pauline interpretations of the Supper, I have said nothing about two further elements of its significance.[14] There is for one *its thrust into the future.* "I tell you," says Jesus, "I will never again drink of this fruit of the vine until that day when I drink it new with you in my Father's kingdom" (Matt. 26:29). Thus Matthew allots nearly a fourth of his account to this eschatological saying. And Paul's spare account concludes, "For as often as you eat this bread and drink the cup, you proclaim the Lord's death *until he comes*" (1 Cor. 11:26). Its omission here parallels my omission so far of the third, eschatological strand of Christian ethics. It brings out the demand to press on to strand three.[15]

The other element is one inherited from the Jewish Passover — *the eucharistic or thanksgiving note.* While I have emphasized the quality of remembrance (explicit in Paul, implicit in the Matthean narrative structure), I have passed over the central note of awed gratitude in that remembrance.[16] As the other future note, when supplied, points on to strand three, thanksgiving looks back to strand one, where embodied selfhood with its affective focus gives shape to the moral life of Christians. The more general lesson to be learned from these two further (but central) elements of the supper is that, though privatistic understandings of communion might focus exclusively on gratitude or other attitudes, and though a liberation-oriented sacramental meal might focus exclusively on God's coming kingdom and its demands, each would thereby fall short of the supper itself, just as a Lord's Supper that focused exclusively on solidarity or redemption would be untrue to full-sphered Christian morality.

Community Formation as Powerful Practice

To speak of one-sided or false versions of the ritual meal brings us to the *power* of the practice of Christian community-formation and maintenance, and hence of its embedded practice of the memorial meal. It may be helpful at this point to recall "the powers."[17] These are linked with religion and politics; their standing with respect to the one God JHWH is ambiguous; they are in conflict with Jesus, yet victory over them is decisive; they are identified not only with pagan empires and persecutors of the faithful but also with the sacred structures of Jewish and Christian life; and, finally, Christians are called to exercise discerning

14. See further, James Wm. McClendon, Jr., *Doctrine: Systematic Theology, Volume II* (Nashville: Abingdon Press, 1994), 400–406.

15. See McClendon, *Ethics,* chaps. 9–11.

16. See James Wm. McClendon, Jr., and James M. Smith, *Convictions: Defusing Religious Relativism* (Valley Forge, Pa.: Trinity Press International, 1994), 70–74.

17. See McClendon, *Ethics,* chap. 6.

selectivity toward particular powers. Too much emphasis can hardly be laid on this theme of discrimination. Governments are not all as wicked as they can be, though all exercise power. Not all churches, nor all religious rites, are beneficent, and they are powers, too. If we discard the mythical (and unbiblical) idea that all the powers "fell" in some timeless prehistoric catastrophe, then we are free to inquire, instead, about the actual history of a particular power: the degree to which its politics and claims are functions of the creative and redemptive power of God in Christ, and the degree to which these are corruptions of that power. This analysis of the powers is a necessary biblical corrective to Alasdair MacIntyre's overly positive evaluation of practices.

What then of the powerful practice of Christian community, with its embedded practices of baptism and Lord's Supper? So far we have seen a practice as a way of giving social shape to Christian life. As a practice, we know it must have its end and its lawlike means, and it must exist only by way of the intentional participation of "the players," its members. Their goal-directed participation will evoke the excellences of the practice itself and enhance its progress. But in keeping with what has just been said, we must also understand our churchly practice as an existing *power.* To do so will remind us, not merely that practices as powers may undergo "sequences of decline as well as progress"[18] (a qualifier allowing unblemished optimism about any human practice!), but also that this powerful practice, like others, may rebel, "fall," lash out at the reign of the Lamb, and persecute the saints. To think of the church as a practice reminds us of all the inspiring things the New Testament says about it: built on rock (Matt. 16:18), the body of Christ (1 Cor. 12:12f. and parallels), temple of the Spirit (1 Cor. 6:19), God's own assembly (1 Cor. 1:2), destined to be holy and without blemish (Eph. 5:27). Yet to think of it as a power should also remind us of other (inspired, though less inspiring) utterances also in our New Testament: the church Christ died for is, alas, one he may spew out of his mouth (Rev. 3:16). To see the church as a set of *powerful practices* is to turn from dogmatic blindness to the empirical reality of church. Not every "church" is a font of Christian practice and faith, nor is every liturgy life-breathing, though it be called Lord's Supper or Eucharist most holy. That nevertheless many are, even in sparse spiritual times, is a matter of divine gift and promise (Matt. 16:18). This brings us to a final point: Even corrupted powers *may* be redeemed. Telling the difference between what is and is not redeemable will concern us in the next section.

The Politics of Forgiveness

Forgiveness and Law

Forgiveness is our theme, but there can be no forgiveness unless there is something to forgive, some offense against some requirement or rule or law. So we

18. Alasdair MacIntyre, *After Virtue: A Study in Moral Theory* (Notre Dame: University of Notre Dame Press, 1981), 177.

must first seek some clarity about the sense in which the Christians of the New Testament, and particularly those of the Matthean church, were a community of lawkeepers. The inquiry here goes against the widespread, if unspoken, understanding that Jesus abolished the law and that early Christianity, led by Paul, opposed it, for this *cannot* literally be the case in a community of shared practices. Every practice is according to a rule, even when rules are never made explicit.[19] Since many Christians today suppose they have come to terms with the Pauline injunctions, we will concentrate upon the apparently more alien Matthean community.

For Matthew's church the lawlike pattern was tied closely to an understanding of Jewish law. Yet even this must be qualified. Since they did not reside in the land of Israel, where alone, according to traditional understanding, the law had been fully in effect, and since Jerusalem and its temple had been destroyed, there was disagreement at this time among non-Christian Jews about how the law was to be kept in the new situation. Moreover, the Syrian church's understanding of Jesus, transmitted in their own Gospel, represented the Master in a complex way: On the one hand, not a jot or tittle would pass from the law, he had said, "until all is accomplished" (5:18), and his behavior in the narrative shows him respecting the legally flexible Pharisaic tradition (23:23) while challenging its current representatives. Yet on the other hand Jesus shows a surprisingly cavalier freedom with respect to some Pharisaic regulations (see 15:1–20). And, hardest of all to grasp, in the very context where the law is reinforced in his teaching, there appear a set of six "antitheses" that sometimes merely amend, but sometimes seem even to abrogate or cancel Mosaic legislation. Sorting out these complicated, not to say paradoxical, moral signals must indeed have produced "kingdom scribes" in the Matthean community! (see 13:51).

We can reduce the problems Matthew raises for us here to four: (1) How is the strong affirmation of the law to be reconciled with its paradoxical "repeal" in some cases (5:18, 31f., and so on)? (2) More generally, how is the authority of Jesus to be reconciled with the authority of Torah? (3) What is the role, in a lawkeeping community, of such ideas as the higher righteousness, the law of love, the gospel of the kingdom, the will of God, or, in Matthew's term, being perfect, "as your heavenly Father is"? (4) What agency is to adjudicate and administer the law to the congregation? Recovering Matthew's answer to these questions should disclose the moral structure of the Syrian church he wrote for, and begin to disclose the politics of forgiveness in Christian community. The role of forgiveness is the goal of our inquiry, but to see it in context, we must find how it worked for a community shaped, as any community is, by law.

The second of our four questions, about authority, provides the best approach to all. In an elegant analysis of the First Gospel's teaching, Jack Suggs has shown that its deep rooting in Israel's wisdom tradition made it inevitable for Matthew to interpret Jesus in terms of the divine Wisdom. In brief, God's Son, Jesus, *was*

19. See McClendon, *Ethics,* chap. 6.

Sophia, Wisdom, and since Wisdom was the source of Torah itself, when Jesus spoke, it was Wisdom-Torah speaking. Hence the authority of Jesus and that of Torah need not be further reconciled, for they are at bottom one authority.[20] To see this, however, is to see the answer to our first question as well. The antitheses of the Sermon on the Mount are of two sorts:[21] Some of them deepen or intensify the law's demand; others change or correct it. Broadening the Sixth Commandment to forbid murderous hate as well as hateful murder is the first sort of antithesis; not only the awful deed, but its crescendo of angry preparation, is forbidden to disciples (Matt. 5:21f.). Abolishing the provisions that the law had made for retribution (see Exod. 21:23–25) is of the second sort: Nonresistance, not the vendetta, is to be the law of the kingdom (5:38–42). Each of the antitheses can be understood in one or the other of these ways, though opinions may differ on which is which. Is love to enemies (5:44) simply the radical restatement of Leviticus 19:18 ("love your neighbor as yourself"), or does it go beyond its bounds altogether? Or what about divorce? Mosaic legislation had restrained but in the end permitted it — for males at least (Deut. 24:1–4). With one exception, Jesus here forbids it. But Jesus (in 19:8) explains that the Mosaic permission was "because you were so hard-hearted," thus arguing that his new law regarding marriage is more in line with the original *practice* as that practice coheres with the Mosaic story.

And this is our clue to the whole. Where the typical or Matthean first-century community of Christians continues a practice of the Mosaic community, albeit with revised goals or directions (for example, new understandings of kinship and of marriage), the Messianic law is revisionary. Where the community must take up a radically different stance with regard to a former practice (for example, full abandonment of violence) the legal revision may amount to abolition of the relevant law — by the authoritative Lawgiver. Where laws are understood as the rules for practices, and practices are the substance of an ongoing story, the necessity for their firmness *and* their flexibility are alike evident.

This brings us to our third question. How are we to understand having "righteousness greater than . . . ," or "doing the will of God," being "perfect," that is, "wholehearted," keeping the "love commandment," and the like, in this Christian community? To answer this, we need to recall that the central function of Matthew is to tell a true story, the story of God's own Son who preaches and demonstrates a Way so costly that it issues in his suffering and death and resurrection. If we compare this Way and story with the Way and story of Torah as epitomized in the Ten Commandments, we find not so much contrast as continuity. As the biblical story becomes (for Jesus' followers) the Christian story, some practices (and hence some rules or laws) must change, but the reason is that Jesus sees where the story must go, and therefore gives new overall direction of the Way. This is most clearly expressed in his own beginning and life

20. Suggs, *Wisdom, Christology, and Law in Matthew's Gospel,* 114f., and chap. 2.
21. Kingsbury, *Matthew,* 82–86.

and mysterious end. So there is a need for signals to the reader not to read the familiar commandments only in the light of what they had known of the old story. Rather, the reader must look for *a new sense of where the story is going* and must find that sense in Jesus' own way, which the reader is now summoned to live out afresh.[22]

That defines the role of "will of God," and "perfect," and the others. These are not meant to abrogate the law with its cases and qualifications and nuances. Rather they are meant to show the direction — the re-defined direction — of the law. To be "perfect" is not to be flawless; it is rather to take Jesus' way, the way of the ripe or full-grown kingdom now at hand. The best illustrations of this are the summing up of all the law in terms of love to God and neighbor (22:36–40), or the Golden Rule (7:12). As a *substitute* for law or rules, such summaries are pitifully inadequate. (The Golden Rule, for example, *if taken alone,* would work as well for a band of sado-masochists as it would for a community of disciples.) But as showing how to take all the rest — the direction of Torah — these summaries have an important role. Certainly that role is not to set up an impossible standard for disciples, for in that case all else that Matthew says with rabbinic care would be wasted.

How, then (our fourth question), *was* such a way practically possible? How, in a "sectarian" community that was distinct from the state and its powers of enforcement, as well as from previous Jewish legal procedures, could an entire community, even of committed disciples, be kept on the track? In terms of technique, the answer lay in a never-ending congregational *conversation* — a conversation that may now engage only two or three, but again will involve the gathered *ecclêsia* itself. When a brother or sister believes another is sinning, a procedure is invoked that at its simplest involves a private rebuke, confession, and forgiveness (18:15, 21f.), and at its most elaborate, a full-scale congregational review of the matter in the presence of the offender (18:17). This procedure is not to be seen as equivalent to the excluding or shunning practiced by some modern sectarians. Its genius lies rather in the confidence it places in the church's ongoing conversation as a means of pastoral guidance. There is, to be sure, a bottom line of expulsion when the church must for the time being admit its failure. But that expulsion puts the offender in the class of those whom Jesus especially befriended — Gentiles and tax collectors. Such a process will, of course, make law in the same sense that civil courts make law — by its decisions. So it is here that the often abused notion of "decision" at last comes into its own in ethics, not as the private willful optings of moral individuals, but as the guiding limits set from time to time by the brothers and sisters in the course of their ongoing conversation. It is the dynamics of that conversation that protect discipleship from legalism.

The word *conversation* rightly points to the informal, almost casual nature of

22. See Michael Goldberg, *Jews and Christians: Getting Our Stories Straight* (Nashville: Abingdon Press, 1985).

congregational interchange. Yet there underlies the ongoing community conversation something akin to judicial process. It is important to examine this underlying structural element, for only with it will we understand how Christian community is a *politics* of forgiveness. Note first that forgiveness and punishment have something in common. What is it to punish (as opposed to merely mistreating, assaulting, or injuring) another? Among many widely held theories of punishment, the formulation of the distinguished legal philosopher Herbert Morris commends itself. Imagine, says Morris, a community bound together by common goods (such as individual freedom and safety) in which each member assumes certain burdens (such as not infringing on the freedom and safety of the others). In such a community, what is to be done in the case of one who does discard his own burden by stealing, breaking the peace, or otherwise taking others' goods away from them? Morris's answer is that he be punished according to a rule that will both specify the punishment and limit its extent. For a rule-breaker is one who unbalances the community, threatens its existence, while just deprivation laid upon such a one constitutes the restoration of the disturbed balance and threatened existence, achieving this by taking away some limited good or privilege that the offender had enjoyed. Thus he has a burden (the punishment) to take the place of the burden he had unfairly discarded, and the community balance is thereby righted.[23] However, Morris makes an important qualification. The equilibrium of a society may be restored in yet another way.

Forgiveness — with its legal analogue of a pardon — while not the righting of an unfair distribution by making one pay his debt is, nevertheless, a restoring of the equilibrium by forgiving the debt.[24] It is usually the belief that its frequent use will increase violations that disqualifies pardon as the regular remedy for offenses. While we must remember this danger, my suggestion is that *Christian community is exactly one in which forgiveness, not punishment, is the norm.* Such forgiveness has as its goal, exactly as would a just practice of punishment, the restoration of a rupture in the community. Forgiveness is the healing of a broken church. As such, it is intimately linked with salvation itself — with atonement, with Christ's presence, with the goal of the common life in the body of Christ. Its great beauty is that, unlike most systems of punishment in the world we know, forgiveness really works, realistically achieves its goals.

The Anatomy of Forgiveness

To see why this is so, it will be necessary to think a little more carefully about the nature of forgiveness itself. To forgive, says a common definition, is to grant pardon without harboring resentment. This points to two elements, one formal,

23. Herbert Morris, *On Guilt and Innocence* (Berkeley: University of California Press, 1976), 31–45. Morris further claims that offenders have a "right to punishment," that is, a right to be treated according to the rules of such a system, and that this right is part and parcel of a fundamental right to be treated as a person in society rather than as a mere manipulable object or a candidate for "therapy" (46–57).

24. Ibid., 34.

socially structured, judicial — the granting of pardon; the other affective, attitudinal, inward — the relinquishing of ongoing resentment by establishing new ties with the one forgiven. The *act* of forgiveness is at home in strand two; it is a transaction; the *attitude* belongs to strand one. Forgiveness, to be itself, requires both.

Consider first the inward, strand-one element, for it will show us well why the other must exist also. Joseph Butler, in his sermon "Upon Resentment," has shown how natural and appropriate the feeling of resentment is upon our receiving any real (or supposed) injury.[25] Resentment, Butler says, is God's good gift, protecting us in an injurious world from greater harms and inciting us to secure a justice we might otherwise be too placid or too compassionate to enforce. But like any of God's gifts, resentment is subject to abuse; thus Butler immediately follows his discussion of it with his sermon on forgiveness. We are meant to resent mistreatment of others or of ourselves, but resentment must come to an end, and how that will happen is the present question. For most of us, there is nothing that sticks more persistently in memory than rankling resentment of old wrongs. Forgiveness is never easy.

This brings up the recurrent belief that forgiving means forgetting. And indeed, Scripture says that God tells Israel, "I . . . remember your sins no more" (Isaiah 43:25 REB). Yet this forgetting cannot be understood with literal simplicity, for in the following verses (26–28) the forgiving God recounts those very forgiven sins Israel has committed. In this passage, then, to forget must mean to cease to harbor resentment, must mean *to hold their sins against them* no longer. Indeed, it might be more truly said of forgiveness that it is not forgetting but a special kind of remembrance. One who forgives knows the other's offense to be offense; forgiveness takes its rise, begins, as Butler has shown, from natural resentment, else there is nothing to forgive. Then the forgiving one takes that offense up into his or her own life, makes the other's story part of his or her own story, and by owning it destroys its power to divide forgiver and forgiven. In this sense, to forgive is truly to love one's offending neighbor *as oneself.* Forgiving is not forgetting, for we can repress the memory and still be at enmity with one another; for Christians, forgiving is rather remembering under the aspect of membership in the body of Christ: it is knowing that he who is our body and we, forgiven and forgiver, are all one.

In this sense, to forgive is to learn a new and truer story about myself by discovering how fully my life is bound up with those whose sins are also sins against myself. Horace Bushnell, pastor to a congregation of New England business folk, tells of an older man who took in a partner, befriended, aided, and trusted him. Then the younger betrayed that trust, used the partnership for crooked schemes, nearly ruined it and both the partners. So the generous one lost his business and all that he had. Yet with Yankee industry (we may suppose) he re-

25. Joseph Butler, *Butler's Fifteen Sermons Preached at Rolls Chapel and a Dissertation on the Nature of Virtue* (London: SPCK, [1729] 1970), 72–79.

covered, and after some time was again prospering. The other, however, went his way from disaster to disaster. The older certainly did not forget his betrayer — the very name brought up bitter memories, and he would cross the street rather than meet him face to face. Yet this honest man believed he should forgive, and said he did forgive. Then there came a time when it was said the younger was destitute, and his family suffering. The first saw it as an opportunity to express forgiveness — anonymously, he sent money. Next the child of the younger was in trouble with the law, and the older went to intercede; forgiveness seemed to require it. Finally, dangerous illness struck the other's home. There was no one else, and the first, remembering he said he forgave, went and built the fire, washed the dishes, laundered, nursed, risking infection, while his former partner sat helpless by and wept. But now, Bushnell asks, where is the reluctance, the enmity, that made the other's name hateful? All gone, melted in the caring work of forgiveness. "You have taken his sin upon you in the cost you have borne for his sake. . . ."[26]

This may or may not be a true story (I suspect it is a disguised account of events in Bushnell's own life). But in any event it rings true. Do we not know cases where two whose lives are intertwined have hurt and been hurt, and yet the injured one has taken the hurt in such a way that atonement, at-one-ment, has been achieved between them, and their lives are made closer than if there had been no offense and no costly work of forgiveness? Attitudinally speaking, forgiveness is this: one takes another's life up into one's own, making the offender a part of one's own story in such a way that the cost of doing so overcomes the power of the injury, healing it in a new bond of union between them.

Here, though, we must pass from attitude to act — and not just the acts of reconciliation and mercy Bushnell has told us about, but (in that story) the older partner's act of forgiveness that preceded all of these, his "I do forgive him." In the happy case, this act is two-sided, the one saying in effect "I forgive"; the other in effect, "I accept forgiveness." But even where the response from the one forgiven is muted or absent, the act of forgiveness, by reaching out as in a transaction to the other, is yet a real act if real consequences flow from it. This is the act that is formalized in the Disciples' Prayer taught in the Sermon on the Mount. "Forgive us our debts *as we forgive*" (Matt. 6:12) — the "as we forgive" is not the report of some prior state of mind in the worshipper; it is not an attitude avowed; it is the performative act of the disciple *granting* pardon to those who have offended. And this is done in the very moment of seeking pardon for one's own unpayable debts owed to God. When Matthew's church prayed this prayer, they would know themselves to be granting forgiveness, whether of uncollectable debts, or of untruthful words, or of injury at the hands of family members long gone, or of enmity from a world acknowledged to be against them. In saying the words, these disciples did not merely tell about pardon, they extended it to their

26. Horace Bushnell, *Forgiveness and Law,* in *Horace Bushnell,* ed. H. Shelton Smith (New York: Oxford University Press, [1874] 1965), 317–19.

debtors, in the eyes and under the authority of God, and were bound thereafter to live accordingly.

With these perhaps familiar but often neglected points about forgiveness as act and attitude before us, we may read with fresh eyes the process of Matthew 18. The crucial paragraph (vss. 15–20) is set in a wider context of Jesus' teaching about sin, temptation, and forgiveness in community. The preceding passages in Matthew deal with relations with those struggling with temptation, and with the joy in recovering the one stray sheep in a flock of a hundred, while those that follow give the saying about how often to forgive (seventy times seven) and relate the parable of the fate of the *un*merciful servant. In such a setting, we may expect that a paragraph beginning "If another member of the church sins . . ." (vs. 15) will certainly have something to do with forgiveness. In fact, the first instruction is "go and point out the fault when the two are alone"—a procedure whose happy outcome would be reconciliation: "you have regained that one." We remember that if there is no resentment, forgiveness is meaningless. Clearly the Matthean process respects this fact. A private conference can bring out whatever resentment there is on either side; it can also resolve misunderstanding and achieve harmony. Perhaps there will turn out to have been nothing to forgive. If on the other hand the resentment is merited, such a conference provides maximal privacy for acknowledgment of the offender's fault and the crucial assurance of forgiveness by the other.

If, however, the resolution is not so easily achieved in private meeting, the process points to a step-by-step enlargement of the number of those involved. Conflict management in the Matthean church was at once rule governed and creative, since the "one or two others along with you" (v. 16) may have their own insight into the fresh formation of discipleship that the situation requires. And finally, as we have noted, the task may need to involve the entire fellowship, and even a formal meeting for its resolution. Even here, the goal is that each shall "hear" all, and the dynamic of the meeting is still toward forgiveness, as the question of verse 21 brings out. Even the refusal to "listen to the church" at this last stage is not without recourse: the erring one is now reckoned in the outsider state again, but that is the very state in which the traditional author of our Gospel had been when he first heard the good news (Matt. 9:9). So it is a hopeful state.

So far, our evocation of a New Testament politics of forgiveness has been confined to the Matthean model, so that some may wonder if the picture of community social structure we have called up can also pass the Pauline checkpoint. Turning back a generation or so to the mission churches established by Paul the Missionary, what sort of common life and social control do we find there? Were the Pauline communities informed by "law," and did that law shape itself around a focus of forgiveness? While there have been many approaches to Pauline ethics, a good beginning for us may be the conclusions of Wayne Meeks's discussion of these churches' "governance." "In the letters," Meeks summarizes, "the norms of the Pauline communities are only rarely stated as rules."

We may surmise the reason: Paul was too busy defending his churches (for example, in Galatia) against the arbitrary imposition of old rules to find rhetorical space to acknowledge the new. But Meeks then goes on to say that nevertheless, "there were rules," though some of them were quite general (for example, no *porneia*), and though all were qualified by Paul's free interpretation and by the flexibility of decision required in applying them.

> The impression is one of great fluidity, of a complex, multipolar, open-ended process of mutual discipline. Perhaps this fluid structure... marked the end of the time when "the Law" shaped the limits of God's people and the beginning of the new age that would yield to his Kingdom.[27]

Yet as we have just seen, it was a combination of fluidity (or complexity) of structure and a Messianic awareness that marked the Matthean community as well. And (disregarding for the moment the Messianic consciousness) *"fluidity" must be the mark of any community with living law* — that is, law that is interpreted, applied, and adjudicated case by case in a community where some kind of ongoing reconciliation is a communal goal.

Summary

For our purposes, two lessons arise here. The first is that the practice of community establishment and maintenance was at the center of the social ethic of earliest Christianity; if its Apostolic Writings speak authoritatively to us, it is such community practice that they require of us. This practice was for them no mere social convenience; the risen Christ was at the center of their meetings; their assemblies were his "body"; their nourishment was his proffered selfhood. Just such a practice of community is the social norm for Christian existence. So the second lesson is part of the first: For us too a central skill for this community maintenance is forgiveness of one another, based upon and empowered by our own forgiveness from God through Jesus Christ. *"As a community"* (we might paraphrase, struggling to retain in English the lost force of the New Testament's plural imperatives) "*be merciful,* with tender hearts *forgiving* one another as God in Christ forgave you" (Eph. 4:32). This central skill at forgiveness sets the character of Christian community, just as the imperatives of the Decalogue had pointed a direction with regard to Israel's community practices. It is exactly this skill of forgiveness that is the divine gift enabling disciple communities to cope with the looming power of their own practice of community, otherwise so oppressive, so centripetally destructive. Without forgiveness, the social power of a closed circle will crush its members, ruin itself, and sour its social world. Examples of such soured communitarianism soil the pages of every honest church history. But with forgiveness controlling everything, the closed circle is opened, the forgiven forgivers' practice of community is redeemed and becomes positively redemptive; thus this powerful practice offers obedience to the law of the Lord Jesus.

---

27. Meeks, *First Urban Christians,* 138f.

The Church in the World

If we explore here the relation of such a church to the world in which it lives, it is not likely that much that is genuinely new will appear, for the theme has been opened from the earliest New Testament writings (1 Thessalonians?) to the most recent pronouncements of church and ecumenical agencies. Indeed, the church-world relation is intrinsic to Christian existence: The line between the church and the world still passes through the heart of every believer, and we may now add, through the heart of every churchly practice as well. What we can hope to do is to remind ourselves of the old arguments and add to them present evidence and in their light see afresh the relation between these two.

Three Models: Niebuhr, Barth, Hauerwas

In the social strand, three models or paradigms for understanding church-world relations dominate most discussion, at least implicitly: We may for convenience call these the (H. R.) Niebuhrian, the Barthian, and the Hauerwasian; all others can be seen as some adaptation or combination of these three. In brief, the paradigm offered by the younger Niebuhr brother may be called *interactional:* "Christ" is one entity in the world, represented by all that is truly his; "culture" is another entity, represented by all else, and the question to be answered is, what has the one to do with the other — Christ with Caesar, Athens with Jerusalem? The Niebuhrian answer is found in an Aristotelian golden mean, where extremes are the rejection of "culture" by "Christ" (minimal interaction, an extreme imputed by Niebuhr to our own baptist heritage!) and identification ("the Christ *of* culture," attributed to liberal culture-Protestantism), and where the happiest form of the happy mean is an interaction called "transformation": "Christ" transforms "culture," not vice versa. Niebuhr presented his argument via a sociological typology, using these three and two further intermediate types to display the full range of historic Christian possibilities.[28]

But the typology, by its definitions and its choice of examples, is rigged so as to *make* the Aristotelian answer emerge at the end! Thus, the overall Niebuhrian picture of Christ and culture captivates us too easily. But to display the radical heritage as "withdrawn" over against Catholics or Protestants as "responsible" (besides begging many questions of historical fact) fails to reckon with the character of either the world or the church as these have been revealed here. The world (or "culture") is not one smooth global unity but an indefinite congeries of powerful practices, spread over time and space, so that any number of these practices may impinge upon believers in a variety of ways, while our witness to them will necessarily take a corresponding variety of forms. Conscientious withdrawal from the practice of warfare may be coupled with conscientious engagement in practices of peacemaking or education, economics or the arts. "Culture" is not (as H. R. Niebuhr would too often have it) monolithic; "the

28. H. Richard Niebuhr, *Christ and Culture* (New Haven: Yale University Press, 1951).

world" is itself divided. Meanwhile, "the church" is exactly the realm in which responsibility to Jesus Christ is the hallmark of discipleship, so in it the call to be "responsible" can only be defined in terms of his Lordship over all, not by some worldly measurement. The greater temptation for today's disciples may be to feel "responsible" to the world as worldlings perceive it while "withdrawing" from the absolute claim of Jesus Christ's Lordship.

The Barthian and Hauerwasian theses display variations on the theme of interaction. For Barth, the key term is *exemplarity.* The task of Christian community is to be an example and foretaste of what God in Christ intends for all human community. By shaping its law (the rules that structure its liturgy, service, and common life) according to the "christologico-ecclesiological concept," that is, the principle of Christ's headship, the church provides this model for the world, and even though the world and its law are evil, by their very nature unable to acknowledge Christ as King, the church's witness will be effectual, for the world is not wholly evil: "They also are in the hand of God and have not escaped his judgment and grace."[29] Barth goes on in the fine print to show some of the gifts church community may have to offer civil community: its order or structure based upon service, its foundation in mutual trust, its involvement of *all* members, its emphasis upon absolute brotherhood, its fluidity as "living" (flexible) law. We might say that on this paradigm the church's role in society's transformation is primarily the social example of its common (internal) life — a city set on a hill.

Still different is the Hauerwasian theme of *interpretation.* "The world," he rightly notes, is not just there, available for observation; that there *is* a world, a realm that knows not God and is disobedient to him, is a truth discernible only from the standpoint of church — that is, the standpoint from which "people faithfully carry out the task of being a witness to the reality of God's Kingdom."[30] That this is so evokes in Hauerwas thoughts of relativism, the theoretical impossibility of finding any truth really true. But Hauerwas believes there is no theoretical defeating of relativism; instead, it is just the church that is the community that will enable us to comprehend the "splintered and tribal existence" of the world we live in.[31] In other words, the standpoint of church community and only that enables Christians to see the world for what it is and thus to make their moral way through its disorder. Certainly there is more to Hauerwas's understanding of church-world relations than this interpretive theme, just as there is more to Barth's than exemplarity. I have introduced these, however, with Niebuhr's more comprehensive (but more vague) category of interaction, because the three together pretty well cover the bases of current

29. Karl Barth, *Church Dogmatics* IV/2, trans. G. W. Bromiley (Edinburgh: T. & T. Clark, 1958), 724.

30. Stanley Hauerwas, *A Community of Character* (Notre Dame: University of Notre Dame Press, 1981), 109.

31. Ibid., 92.

strand-two thinking. Now let us compare them to our touchstone Matthean community understood as a community of shared powerful practices.

The Matthean Model

One thing that leaps out, in our inspection of the church for whom the Gospel according to Matthew was written, is that it was so fully a church *in* the world. None of the early Christian communities followed the well-known example of the Essenes, who had withdrawn to the Dead Sea and lived a separated existence; none took the route of later monasticism. Instead, these Christians selectively but deliberately remained a part of the wider world, both on Jewish and on Gentile soil. Therefore, the practices in which their lives were engaged were often enough the practices of the older world that surrounded them. In Syria, these would have been the practices of a polyglot and pluralistic Near East, overlaid with dominant Hellenism and (by this time) with Roman law and culture. Therefore the form taken by the gospel as "new law" was set by an encounter with an alien but very present world. Laws, by our account, are rules guiding a community's engagement in practices, and for Syrian Christians (as for earlier Palestinian ones) the practices that involved them included those of a government and an economic structure in a society at odds with the kingdom of Christ. Here lay the point of turning the other cheek, of refusing any kind of oath, of settling lawsuits by reckless generosity, and of being a generous, even an imprudent, lender (5:33–42). Here, too, lay the root of total refusal to engage in ways of violence — the pacifism of Matthew's Gospel. Behind these refusals and selective ways of participating (no to war and all violence, a yes and a no to some economic practices, yes both to marriage and to single chastity) lay a deeper motive — the Christians' engagement in *evangelism* or witness, the overriding practice that shaped participation in all other social practices. For Matthew, the central task of this witness was *discipling* (*mathēteusate*), forming lives in accordance with the gospel story, whose elements were *going* (hence, withdrawal was impossible), *baptizing* (entailing full communal commitment by each to the Way), and *teaching* (and thus the formation of a church culture that would stand creatively over against the world's culture by imparting its own) (28:19f.). So engagement with the world was not optional or accidental but lay at the heart of obedient Christian witness.

On this communal journey, two sorts of foes confronted disciples. One was external, the other inner. The external foe (in Pauline terms, the "principalities and powers") is given narrative shape in the Gospel story of a confrontation that leads to a public execution. The powers of the land exact the cross, and Jesus' and the disciples' responses to it are presented intertwined. In bearing the cross alone, he redeems the disciples' lives from their own failure; only thus do they become followers of the Way; the power of outmoded institutions and their practices is symbolically torn only by the event of Calvary (27:51).[32] Thus

32. See McClendon, *Doctrine,* chap. 5, sec. 3.

readers, identifying with the disciples, know that they, too, will confront the powers afresh (16:24) but with Christ's help will overcome them.

Alongside this external foe lurks an inner one. Syrian readers would perhaps find themselves, like their Gospel proxies, understanding but failing to act (25:45), succumbing to the seduction of wealth (13:22), despising other brothers and sisters (18:10), becoming status-seekers (23:8–12), unwilling to forgive (18:21–35), nourishing inward, evil thoughts (15:19).[33] Their very "powerful practice" of community formation, in other words, threatened to make (stereotypical) Pharisees. Yet they could know also the forgiveness of Christ's blood-of-the-covenant and could use the process of Matthew 18 to guide one another's conduct in a different way. Matthean Christianity, we might conclude, was not "perfectionist" if that meant lacking a sense of their own shortcomings, but they knew themselves summoned to a mature way of life and to wholehearted sharing in it.

Today's Church in the World

What does all this add to our modern Niebuhr-Barth-Hauerwas summary of church-world interaction? Perhaps a stronger sense than they provided of the dynamic *clash* of Christ and power, of disciples and their adversary world, and of Christ's assured final victory. For some, that may suggest turning to the insights of today's liberation theology. But that will be to look on to the resurrection strand, where this account can be completed. Perhaps, for present purposes, a clearer vision of the way the concrete practices overflow into engagement with society is our best goal.

Our example must still be the Christian practice of community building. Those who have learned to deal with brothers and sisters within the community will not find it difficult to adapt both the forgiveness process and the sort of action that wipes clean the slate to new contexts outside the community. Indeed "forgive us our debts as we also have forgiven" (Matt. 6:12) seems already unrestricted in range. And had not Jesus on the cross, by one tradition, been praying forgiveness for his executioners even as they did the deed (Luke 23:24)? So both the process of life together and its guiding theme of forgiveness seem suited to be means of community witness. Disciples will share in the common life and practices of the church. They will also share other commonalities with other neighbors, and in those settings Christian ways can overflow into the wider society. Taken to the full, the analogy will be both to individuals within a society, and to the relation of communities, nations even, to one another, modeled upon Christian interchurch or ecumenical relations.

Here is an opportunity some heirs of the baptist vision have yet to take with full seriousness. Captured by a confessionalism more appropriate to the seventeenth than to a later century, they persist in a kind of vicious sectarianism that draws ever more tightly the lines of "fellowship," ever more narrowly the

---

33. Kingsbury, *Matthew,* 91ff.

lines of cooperation, and therefore ever more pitiably the lines of influence upon their fellow Christians and upon the world. Happily that is not true of all. For the strong evidence of the New Testament is that the conversation guiding life within the meeting congregation was carried on also beyond its borders. Letters and visits engaged the church at Corinth, about which we happen to know most, and visitors were by no means screened for uniformity of teaching (1 Cor. 1:12f.; 3:1–9). Yet there was indeed among the churches a concern for concert and unity, and the chief means for resolving outstanding conflict was the familiar one of meeting and talking things over[34] — compare the technique of Acts 15, for example, and the Pauline parallels, with that of Matthew 18.

These are for today's Christians, East and West, in rich lands and poor ones, vital issues now, for our capacity to be reconciled one to another as the people of God may be the best foretaste we can offer a divided and struggling world of the overcoming of its own deadly divisions. For those who believe that world empire and imperial church structure are now alike inadequate to the reconciling of these differences, there is hope in the less rigid, more pluriform, and yet not impotent unities that Christian fellowship via correspondence, visits, and conferences across party lines may offer in our day. Finally, the real ecumenism takes place at the grass roots of neighbor congregations, not in world-class councils.

This does not rule out the role of Christian appeals to the environing societies themselves. While I find no reason to believe in any "natural law," standing outside the law of Christ, as a universal basis for such appeals,[35] and while no single social model (capitalist, Marxist, or other) has any claim upon Christian thought save in terms of the powerful practices it sponsors or inhibits, some of the features Christians may need to urge upon any social order, East or West, are worth noting down. Christians know that their own life engages body, mind, and spirit, and thus they will seek an environment consonant with the health of all three: Bodily life requires some minimal *stability,* that is, an economic, political, and social order sufficiently stable to foster life in a family setting, decent health for ourselves as well as our neighbors, enough prosperity to permit all of these. Synonyms for stability are justice, well-being, and peace. The life of the mind needs an order possessing some measure of *integrity.* This means society not propped chiefly upon lies; it means opportunity for education that nurtures openness of mind, critical examination of current beliefs, coherent or integral ways of thought for each consistent with the item next to follow, full spiritual liberty. The life of the spirit requires *liberty.* This will be preeminently what we have come to call "religious" liberty. It is the acknowledgment that society and its practices, though they are paraded as gods, are not God; for God alone is God, and social structures must retain a corresponding modesty about their writ and competence. To these three one other feature must be added: *plurality.* For Christians this demand is a function of the biblical doctrine of election and the

34. Meeks, *First Urban Christians,* 113.
35. See McClendon, *Ethics,* chap. 2.

knowledge of the world's dividedness, but it may be advocated in terms outsiders will accept as due to the variety in human life within every social boundary. Within the human race, the varieties of racial grouping, national entities, tribes, clans, families, classes, trade and work groups, religions, cities, countrysides, all facing one another in diversity, may serve to determine policies of acceptance, freedom, inclusiveness, and cooperation for common ends in contrast to that Babel-like drive to towering unity which has marked the great empires and the totalitarianisms of our era. Our social impulses to unity are strongly rooted in human nature; the Christian concern must be that neither these impulses nor the drives to conquest, both blighted by sin, shall overturn the contingent stabilities, integrities, liberties, and pluralities human history has so far achieved.

Our only care must be that such appeals by lobbying, education, and the like not be allowed to erode the distinctive Christian social witness conveyed by example more than precept. The disciples who join in a witness of public protest and who thereby show that reproach is the first step toward forgiveness; the disciple who investigates, criticizes, proposes reconstruction of the current penal system, guided by the forgiveness model learned in Christian community; the disciples who, victims as Jesus was a victim, bear the long weight of political prison camps and transform their punishment into redemption by the alchemy of forgiveness — these vivify the application of Christian common life to social structure. Perhaps a single example can now focus and interpret these reflections.

Will Campbell, in his evocative biographical-autobiographical story of a life with his older brother, *Brother to a Dragonfly,* tells how he grew up in south Mississippi, the son of poor dirt farmers, but always aimed toward the "preacher" image they perceived as fitting. So his maturing was a growing to discover the length and breadth and depth of that imposed yet elusive ideal. He went with family encouragement to the "best" religious schools, ending at Yale Divinity School, and took up the career of a Baptist Southern liberal — as he envisioned it, a kind of prophetic chaplain to church and society. Called to Ole Miss as university chaplain, he espoused integration in the fifties; employed next by the National Council of Churches, he aided civil rights work and workers. God and national law were handily allied for him in this struggle, though curiously, Will's own white Southern "redneck" people had now become the enemy.

The turning point came when one Jonathan Daniels, a gentle white divinity student working for the summer at black voter registration in Lowndes County, Alabama, was shotgunned to death by an enraged white deputy sheriff named Thomas Coleman. The news flash of this outrage drove preacher Will to frustrating phone calls to the Department of Justice, the American Civil Liberties Union, and a concerned lawyer friend.

> I had talked of the death of my friend as being a travesty of justice, as a complete breakdown of law and order, as a violation of Federal and State law. I had used words like redneck, backwoods, woolhat, cracker, Kluxer, ignoramus, and many

> others. I had studied sociology, psychology, and social ethics and was speaking and thinking in these concepts. I had also studied New Testament theology.[36]

That last ironic sentence sets the stage for the scene that followed. Will's Christian assessment of the slaying was challenged by a highly skeptical but theologically acute friend, P. D. East. In the course of a long and somewhat boozy evening, East demanded to know whether Christian teaching held that God regarded both slayer and victim as sinners (as they put it, whether both were "bastards"), and whether on Will's view God now loved one of those "bastards" more than the other.

> He leaned his face closer to mine, patting first his own knee and then mine, holding the other hand aloft in oath-taking fashion.
>
> "Which one of these two bastards does God love the most? Does he love that little dead bastard Jonathan the most? Or does He love that living bastard Thomas the most?"
>
> Suddenly everything became clear....

The transformation Will Campbell then experienced in that summer night was nothing less than the discovery of the overflow of the gospel of forgiveness and its application to his own situation. Perversely, P. D. East was right. Forgiven, one could forgive even Thomas Coleman.

> Loved. And if loved, forgiven. And if forgiven, reconciled. Yet sitting there in his own jail cell, the blood of two of his and my brothers on his hands.[37]

Will Campbell found his ministry wrenched around toward reconciling mission to his own Southern white outcasts — the "Kluxers, woolhats, rednecks" he had been seeing only as the enemy. In the sequel, he became something of a legend among socially concerned Southern Christians, a kind of saint in a wool hat, himself.

But when my own seminary students in Berkeley were asked to read this story, some of them regarded it as a story of Campbell's loss of vision. "Once a racist, always a racist," was the reaction of one South African of color to the passage just quoted. They wished that Will, like themselves, was willing simply to condemn whites for racism and fight on for black victory. There is here, I think, a fundamental juncture in Christian understanding. Certainly (as Will Campbell knows well enough) my South African student and his kin had deep reason for intransigence. Certainly forgiveness that is not preceded by resentment and reproach is empty forgiveness. And certainly the world's wrongs (and my Christian brother's wronging me) remain grievous sins.

Yet I think Will Campbell, without denying any of those truths, has found a deeper one, nearer the gospel, nearer the disciples' Way. If that is a depth gained only at personal cost and by way of conversion, does that make it any stranger to the gospel? But if it comes in so costly a way even into the Christian

36. Will Campbell, *Brother to a Dragonfly* (New York: Seabury Press, 1979), 221.
37. Ibid., 221f.

camp, how will it fare among the Gentiles and the tax-gatherers? If this is our social ethic, must we not ask with the disciples (though in another context than theirs) "Who can be saved then?" Though then, also, we must hear Jesus' answer: "By human resources, he told them, this is impossible; for God everything is possible" (Matt. 19:25f. NJB).

We have in this essay sought a connecting link between body ethics (strand one) and social ethics (strand two) for Christians, and have found that link in the self-involving common practices that draw the disciples of Jesus Christ into solidarity in their obedient following of him. One main practice is establishing and maintaining Christian community, with its embedded symbolic meal, the Lord's Supper. Community maintenance presumes rules, that is, laws spoken or unspoken by which the practices function, and these in turn give rise to the ongoing process of community guidance, focused upon Christ's forgiveness of us and our forgiveness of one another. This process is necessarily internal to the Christian community. But the call to evangelize and the demand for public Christian witness point to the overflow of the Christian Way into action toward and with and for the outside neighbor as well. The church is in the world, not as an added requirement of Christian duty, but by the very nature of what church and world mean in gospel perspective. Very simply put, Christian ethics makes central the cross that the world will be sure to provide for members of Jesus' community. The question for Christian ethics is not whether there is such a cross but rather how the spirit and deeds of forgiveness shall engage those other spirits, still in prison. Yet the full account of this engagement would require the introduction of a third strand, the resurrection strand.[38]

Suggestions for Further Reading

Hauerwas, Stanley. "Constancy and Forgiveness: The Novel as a School for Virtue." In *Dispatches from the Front: Theological Engagements with the Secular,* 31–57. Durham, N.C.: Duke University Press, 1994.

Jones, L. Gregory. "The Craft of Forgiveness." *Theology Today* 50 (October 1993): 345–57.

———. *Embodying Forgiveness: A Theological Analysis.* Grand Rapids, Mich.: Wm. B. Eerdmans, 1995.

Roberts, Robert C. "Therapies and the Grammar of a Virtue." In *The Grammar of the Heart,* ed. Richard H. Bell, 149–70. San Francisco: Harper and Row, 1988.

38. See McClendon, *Ethics,* chaps. 9–11.

Chapter 5

Scripture, Exegesis, and Discernment in Christian Ethics

Stephen E. Fowl and L. Gregory Jones

Editor's Introduction

Fowl and Jones claim that "Scripture is the primary source and norm for Christian ethics." However, the interpretation of Scripture is not a straightforward procedure but "an open-ended and controversial activity requiring the virtue of practical wisdom." Interpretation is an arduous endeavor to gain the right sort of character, one that is adequate for the task of interpreting "rightly." This chapter explores a cluster of interrelated ways in which we can become wise readers.

First, interpretive skills are cultivated in *community* because a text (such as the Bible) becomes "scriptural" only for the community composed of all those who willingly accede to its authority. Outsiders can read the *Bible* but cannot read the Scriptures because the term *Scripture* epitomizes the stance one takes toward the moral authority of the canonical text. Using Scripture as the lens through which life is viewed, one becomes capable of learning to see in a whole new way. Assuming this stance is identical to becoming an insider to the believing community.

At the core, this stance is one of humility, one that relinquishes claims on the possibility of uncovering *the* correct interpretation of a passage. But this doesn't mean that everything is up for grabs. On the contrary, there must be substantial areas of agreement in order for community members to sustain a life together. So this humility suggests, second, that proper character is cultivated by *conversation.*

On the one hand, we read in conversation with other community members. Some of these are our tutors who, within the safety or "hidden space" of community life, guide our first steps in right reading. (Ethical formation thus precedes, as well as follows, right reading of Scripture.) Others are biblical scholars who help us read Scripture "over-against ourselves" by reminding us of our (that is, the church's) long history, lest we become enamored with our own prejudices and fail to let Scripture interrogate us while we interrogate Scripture.

On the other hand, we read in conversation with our larger social context. In part, this is necessary because we can never overcome our hermeneutical blind spots unless we understand the impact our social location has on the manner in which we interpret. Thus, a reading of our world will inform our reading of Scripture. But, furthermore, the world has a reading of us which, if appropriated wisely, will assist us in living more faithfully.

So scriptural interpretation is not a cut-and-dried exercise performed by isolated individuals upon a neutral text that mirrors the voice of God without distortion. Rather, scriptural interpretation is a communal practice whose practitioners steadily acquire the skills necessary to read rightly and, thereby, to live faithfully.

Fowl and Jones have done us the service of providing an extended illustration of a MacIntyrean practice. First, as for MacIntyre, *practice, character, virtue, practical wisdom,* and *skills* are interrelated to such an extent as to make definition of any one of these impossible except in terms of the others. Second, the practitioners of scriptural interpretation constitute a "narrative" community both in the sense that their corporate life is formed by the story of Jesus they uncover in their reading of Scripture, and in the sense that each practitioner is "embedded" in the lives of the others. These mutually dependent relationships assist members in the common use of language, sound judgment, and faithful living. Third, Fowl and Jones's conception of the exegetical practice as standing in dialogue with its own history fits MacIntyre's contention that a living tradition is an "ongoing argument" whose vitality depends, in part, in the richness of its conversations with both insiders and outsiders in the course of overcoming obstacles that each kind of conversation poses.

BRAD J. KALLENBERG

Becoming Wise Readers of Scripture

For Christians, interpreting Scripture is a difficult task. But it is difficult *not* because one has to be a specialist in the archaeology of the ancient Near East, an expert in linguistics, or a scholar of the literature of the Greco-Roman world. Though we argue in this chapter that Christians can learn important things about the Bible from the investigations pursued by people who do have such expertise, they are not necessary for wise readings of Scripture. Rather, the interpretation of Scripture (which is different from interpreting the Bible) is a difficult task because it involves a lifelong process of learning to become a wise reader of Scripture, who is capable of embodying that reading in life.

Learning to embody Scripture in our lives, both corporately and personally, requires that we develop specific patterns of acting, feeling, and thinking well. An exercise in practical reasoning, it depends on our ability to judge a certain situation as being similar in some respect to another situation, moral maxim, or canonical text. The presence of such insight, however, presupposes a prior and ongoing formation and transformation in moral judgment.[1]

Some of the contexts of that formation and transformation occur in and through specific friendships and practices of Christian communities. At this point, however, it is important to indicate the link between Scripture and Christian ethics as it relates to the *necessity* of such formation and transformation.

Practical Wisdom and Interpretation

There are several reasons that the interpretation of Scripture is an open-ended and controversial activity requiring the virtue of practical wisdom.[2] The first reason is that interpretation in general is always open-ended. We are never completely sure that we have interpreted someone's thoughts, feelings, or actions (including our own) accurately. Thus we always need to check our interpretations over-against those of others, including our own earlier interpretations.

Second, the interpretation of Scripture is open-ended because Christian Scripture itself is a diverse, multistranded witness reflecting diverse social and historical circumstances. The scope of Scripture includes, for example, preexilic Israel and first-century Rome. Even Paul's letters address a wide variety of circumstances. Thus, as we argue in more detail later in this chapter, discerning the larger sense of Scripture and developing strategies for reading difficult texts in the light of that larger sense are complex and ongoing tasks.

Third, the persistence of temporal and cultural change ensures that the interpretation of Scripture will remain indeterminate. If our readings are simply to remain faithful, they will need to change. Nicholas Lash makes this point in a lighthearted way in regard to ecclesiastical dress:

> If, in thirteenth-century Italy, you wandered around in a coarse brown gown, with a cord round your middle, your "social location" was clear: your dress said that you were one of the poor. If, in twentieth-century Cambridge, you wander around in a coarse brown gown, with a cord round your middle, your social location is curious: your dress now says, not that you are one of the poor, but that you are some kind of oddity in the business of "religion." Your dress now declares, not your solidarity with the poor, but your amiable eccentricity.[3]

Lash's point is not an attack on the Franciscans but a logical argument about how temporal and cultural change necessitates ongoing interpretation. The manner of dress needed to identify with the poor in contemporary Britain or

1. For a more extended discussion of the importance of formation and transformation in moral judgment, and a discussion from which we have drawn considerably in what follows, see L. Gregory Jones, *Transformed Judgment: Toward a Trinitarian Account of the Moral Life* (Notre Dame: University of Notre Dame Press, 1990), particularly chap. 3.

2. Practical wisdom, a notion that goes back to Aristotle, is the virtue of knowing how appropriately to discern a situation and to enact that discernment. The need for practical wisdom arises with questions that do not admit of demonstration. Ethics is one of those areas, and so is interpretation.

3. Nicholas Lash, *Theology on the Way to Emmaus* (London: SCM, 1986), 54.

America would be markedly different from what it was in thirteenth-century Italy. Hence two different types of dress would be needed to continue identifying with the poor. As Lash incisively suggests, "Fidelity to tradition, in action and speech, is a risky business because it entails active engagement in a process of continual change."[4]

But fourth, and most decisively, the interpretation of Scripture is indeterminate and requires the moral formation and transformation of people's lives because of the manifold ways in which people do not judge wisely. More precisely, our complicity in sin leaves us captive to destructive patterns of life. Such captivity undermines our ability to read Scripture well. Liberation from our captivity requires an ongoing process of being formed and transformed by God's grace in and through the friendships and practices of Christian communities.

It is true that becoming a Christian involves living in a "new" world. Indeed some have gone so far as to suggest that Scripture "creates" a world,[5] or that Scripture creates a community as the bearer of that world.[6] But that is in itself an insufficient characterization. Scripture does not create anything *de novo;* in the encounter with Scripture, believers' "old" selves and perceptions of reality are confronted with that new world. Hence the emphasis must be placed on *learning* to live in that world, for it involves not only discerning the "new" world but also diagnosing what is wrong and corrupting about the "old" one. Such learning is a lifelong process requiring as a necessary correlative, at least in most social settings, a rather extensive unlearning of believers' old habits, dispositions, and judgments. Thus the interpretation of Scripture is an ongoing task because appropriate discernment is a task that must be achieved in communities guided by the Spirit; it cannot be assumed, nor is it simply created.

Both character and interpretive skill are formed in relation to each other over time, particularly as we engage in the process of learning to read Scripture wisely and unlearning the ways in which our lives have been corrupted. This cultivation of practical wisdom sometimes requires us to separate ourselves from day-to-day activities and concerns.

We see an important example of this need in one of the Servant Songs of Isaiah (see Isa. 49:1 ff.). The Servant is appointed to a task before birth (49:1, 5). Yahweh entrusts the Servant with a message to proclaim, making the Servant's tongue a sharp sword and making the Servant a polished arrow (49:2a, c). Such formation, however, takes place in secret, out of the way: "in the shadow of his hand he hid me; . . . in his quiver he hid me away" (49:2b, d). The Servant's mission is to recall and restore the people of Yahweh and, ultimately, to be a light unto the nations (49:6). In spite of the apparent failure of this mission, the Servant proves his character by recalling Yahweh's formative work in his

4. Ibid., 55.

5. See George Lindbeck, *The Nature of Doctrine* (London: SPCK; Philadelphia: Westminster, 1984), 117–18.

6. This is Stanley Hauerwas's suggested revision of the claim that Scripture "creates" a world in his *A Community of Character* (Notre Dame: University of Notre Dame Press, 1981), 57.

life. The Servant ultimately rests in the knowledge that Yahweh is the one who has formed him for his mission and who ultimately ensures the success of that mission (49:5).

The formation that takes place in the Servant's life is carried out in hidden places: the womb, the shadow of God's hand, and as a polished arrow hidden in God's quiver. Such imagery is significant, for it suggests both the ways in which God forms and transforms our character for particular vocations and the importance of discovering "hidden places" in which such formation and transformation can occur. These hidden places can include such possibilities as the Wesleyan class meetings of early Methodism, patterns of regular retreats, and disciplined prayer. Even such acts as working in a soup kitchen can provide a "hidden space" where Christians begin to discern more clearly what God is calling us to be and do.

There are at least two reasons that, as Christians, we should establish separate spaces where we can instruct and form each other to be disciples and wise readers. The first reason is pragmatic. That is, the formation needed to develop the character of disciples requires commitment and concentration that can best be achieved apart from the routines of everyday life.

The second reason is conceptual and is related to the fact that Christians are not called to manifest just any sort of character. Their lives are to be a faithful reflection of God's character. Ironically, the need for the type of separate space we are talking about is particularly urgent in those places where most people claim to believe in God. This is because of the heightened danger of that belief becoming acculturated or trivialized. When Christians are the only ones around who proclaim allegiance to the God of Jesus Christ, there is little chance of their knowledge of God becoming profaned through exposure to a non-Christian culture. The earliest Christians found themselves in this situation.

But if and when Christians find themselves in a context in which people both claim to know the God of Jesus Christ and attempt to reduce knowledge of God to a series of platitudes ranging from the inane to the incoherent, they must struggle to create a separate space in which they can teach each other about God away from the reductionistic practices and profaning tendencies that otherwise dominate their lives.[7] We think that the church in Britain and the United States finds itself in this latter situation. But we are also convinced that too few churches have recognized the need for a separate space devoted to forming people's character to be disciples of the Triune God.

When the early Christians found themselves in situations in which their talk about God was becoming less distinct from what their neighbors said about their god(s), they developed patterns of worship and life that would provide hidden spaces for the formation of disciples. Such a "discipline of the secret" was a part of the early church's life devoted to nurturing the knowledge of God and Chris-

7. This is a lesson that Dietrich Bonhoeffer learned and reflected on in the midst of Nazi Germany.

tian character in committed disciples.[8] Such discipling was arcane or mysterious because it was not open to the merely curious or the general inquirer. This was because the early Christians recognized that discipleship can be distorted and misdirected by those who are not disciples; they understood that true discipleship is too important to the ongoing life of the church to risk this possibility.

Recovering and developing such disciplines are important for forming people to become wise readers of Scripture. In particular, such disciplines are important because we need to learn how closely our character and our witness are linked to our use of language. After all, Scripture tells the story of God calling forth a world, through the Word, where both humanity and God would dwell. As people who seek to structure our lives in accordance with this narrative of God's Word, we ought to place a very high value on the disciplined use of words in forming our lives and our witness. As Lash has suggested,

> Commissioned as ministers of God's redemptive Word, we are required, in politics and private life, in work and play, in commerce and scholarship, to practice and foster that philology, that word-caring, that meticulous and conscientious concern for the quality of conversation and the truthfulness of memory, which is the first casualty of sin. The Church, accordingly, is or should be a school of philology, an academy of word-care.[9]

Learning to become wise readers of Scripture requires, then, that we have the kind of character that enables us to be disciplined in our use of words.

Becoming disciplined in our use of words, however, also requires us to become wise readers of Scripture. As Augustine suggested, a person "speaks more or less wisely to the extent that he has become more or less proficient in the Holy Scriptures."[10] And, as Augustine further notes, we seek to read and speak not only wisely but also eloquently. We not only want to instruct ourselves and others in wise readings of Scripture, we also want to persuade ourselves and others so that the words we use may move us to more faithful living before God.[11]

Because our lives are to be patterned in relation to the One confessed in Scripture to be the Word incarnate, we need to be more than simply disciplined in our use of words; we need also to be disciplined by the Word made flesh. Being disciplined by the Word entails allowing our lives to be patterned in Christ. As such, we are to have a character that reflects neither that egocentric reading

---

8. We take the phrase "discipline of the secret" from Dietrich Bonhoeffer. In his *Letters and Papers from Prison,* Bonhoeffer reflected, albeit briefly and somewhat cryptically, on the importance of recovering the early church's *disciplina arcana* for contemporary Christian life and witness. We think Bonhoeffer's judgment is important.

9. Nicholas Lash, "Ministry of the Word or Comedy and Philology," *New Blackfriars* 68 (1987): 476–77.

10. Augustine, *On Christian Doctrine,* trans. D. W. Robertson, Jr. (New York: Macmillan, 1958), 122.

11. For an extended discussion of the rhetorical character of Christian theology in general and the interpretation of Scripture in particular, see David S. Cunningham, "Faithful Persuasion: Prolegomena to a Rhetoric of Christian Theology" (Ph.D. diss., Duke University, 1990).

and witness in which God gets (at best) second billing nor that faceless reading and witness in which it is presumed that the messenger is irrelevant to the message. Rather, it involves a willingness to have our lives formed and transformed in and through particular Christian communities so that the words we use become means of pointing to the Word whom we follow.

Thus we need to participate in the friendships and practices of Christian communities in order to become wise readers of Scripture who can link the words we use with the Word whom we follow. As we have already suggested, this is not simply a general claim about the importance of community. We are called into such communities by the Triune God to whom the scriptural texts bear witness. Hence Christian communities provide the contexts whereby we learn—as the body of Christ through the power of the Holy Spirit—to interpret, and to have our lives interrogated by, the scriptural texts such that we are formed and transformed in the moral judgment necessary for us to live faithfully before God.

Making this case requires that we indicate more fully how and why the formation and transformation of our character is intimately connected to readings of Scripture in Christian communities that have been called into being by the Triune God.

God, Christian Communities, and Scripture

As we have already noted, Christians' complicity in sin prevents us from being disciplined in our language, judging righteously, and living well. Upon entering the body of Christ, we are to rely on our brothers and sisters to help us recognize and overcome those features of our lives that undermine and frustrate our use of language, our judgment, and our desire to live faithfully before God. Christian communities provide the occasions in which, in the context of the "dangerous" remembrance of Christ's passion, believers are enabled by Christ's resurrection to converse about how faithfully to live before the Triune God.[12]

The conversations and practices of Christian communities help to liberate us from our sin, enabling us to judge righteously. Nevertheless, we should not be surprised to find that Christian communities will often be puzzled about how best to understand their own existence and character in relation to the Triune God. Such puzzlements are found in the Scriptures themselves. After all, Paul reminds us that this side of the Kingdom we see in a mirror, dimly; only in the Kingdom will we see face to face (1 Cor. 13:12). More generally, the biblical narrative both tells the story of the Triune God, focused in the life, death, and resurrection of Jesus of Nazareth, and displays the puzzlement of particular communities seeking to discern the significance of that story for their own existence and character.

12. The notion of the "dangerous" memory of Jesus Christ is taken from Johann Baptist Metz, *Faith in History and Society: Toward a Practical Fundamental Theology*, trans. David Smith (New York: Crossroad, 1980).

The claims made on our lives by the Triune God are closely linked to the shape of the particular communities in which we seek to become wise readers of Scripture. The interpretation of Scripture as an activity of communal discernment — the conversation in the good which is both formative and transformative and involves both destruction and construction of identities — is enabled by the Holy Spirit through Christ's resurrection. Communal discernment also provides the contexts for learning the judgments and rules by which Christians ascertain how we ought to live and what we ought to do.

Thus Christian communities are central for the ongoing task of enabling people to become wise readers of Scripture. To become wise readers of Scripture, we need to acquire a range of skills and virtues manifested in Christian discipleship. These skills and virtues are given their shape and form under the guidance of the Holy Spirit in and through the particular friendships and practices of Christian communities. They are both the prerequisite for, and the result of, wise readings of Scripture. These skills and virtues enable not only wise reading but faithful practice. They show forth a witness to God's ways with the world.

Even so, it may be objected that despite our criticisms of other writers on the Bible and ethics, our own account is truncated. After all, we have not discussed either how we should learn to read Scripture in Christian communities or the relationship between our readings of Scripture in the church and other people's readings of the Bible (particularly in the academy). Moreover, we have not discussed what role Scripture ought to have in relation to other possible sources of ethical insight and wisdom.

We have not done so because there is no way to formulate these questions, much less answer them, outside of the particular contexts and situations in which Christians find themselves. Even so, we can indicate some of the ways in which we think such issues ought to be addressed.

Readings of the Texts

We have argued that Christian communities are constituted and reconstituted politically by Scripture, because Scripture provides the primary context for understanding what it means to live faithfully before God. Thus Christian communities must engage in "readings of the texts." By that we mean not only that we should provide readings of the texts that make up the Scriptures but also that we need to allow these texts to provide readings of our lives.[13]

However, we have not yet adequately explicated our understanding of these texts. As Scripture the Bible provides the church with a canon, a normative standard for the faith, practice, and worship of Christian communities. We dis-

13. For this idea of phrasing our readings in a systematically ambiguous way, we are indebted to Rowan Williams's argument with reference to the "judgment of the world" in his "Postmodern Theology and the Judgment of the World," in *Postmodern Theology*, ed. Frederic B. Burnham (New York: Harper and Row, 1989), 92–112.

tinguish between the Bible and the church's Scripture, and we need to explicate this difference and its relevance to learning to become wise readers of Scripture.

Part of the ethos of academic exegesis is the presumption that the Bible is simply one text that a scholar may study. Within the academy one scholar's comments about a biblical text are of the same logical status as another scholar's comments about a Shakespearean sonnet. To be admitted to the guild of professional biblical scholars one need not (some would say should not) have any particular predisposition toward the Bible other than the conviction that it is a text about which one can say numerous interesting things.

When the church, however, calls that same Bible its Scripture, or recognizes the Bible as its canon, it immediately places itself in a relationship to the Bible that is different from the academy's. When the church calls the Bible its Scripture, it not only assumes that the Bible is a text about which Christians can say many interesting things, it also claims that this text has provided and still provides the basis for Christian communities' ongoing struggle to live faithfully before God. When the church recognizes the Old and New Testaments as its canon, it means that these texts are the norm or rule to which we will conform our faith, practice, and worship.[14] The Bible, then, as Scripture or canon forms the life of Christian communities in ways far different from and more comprehensive than the ways that the Bible (as a text around which interested interpreters congregate) forms the academy of professional exegetes.

To emphasize the Bible's significance as the church's Scripture or canon, however, invites misunderstanding because of the rather acrimonious debates in recent years over "canonical criticism" and the "canonical approach."[15] Clearly, we cannot adjudicate all of these debates. We can, however, try to explain and to qualify our use of the term *canon* in ways that will limit misunderstanding if not disagreement.

First, it is quite common to use *canon* to refer to a fixed list of books. Accord-

14. It seems that Christians are almost always in the dangerous position of forgetting the significance of the presence of the Old Testament in the Christian canon. If the church is to see itself as the people of the God of Abraham, Deborah, Moses, and Jesus (as it should), then the Old Testament will always be of abiding importance for faithful living. How any particular Christian community will manifest the importance of the Old Testament in any particular situation is an open question. This is particularly true in regard to the Old Testament's relationship to the New Testament. There is no context-independent way to specify the relationship between the Old and New Testaments.

15. The term *canonical criticism* is most closely associated with the work of James A. Sanders. See particularly *Torah and Canon* (Philadelphia: Fortress, 1972) and *Canon and Community: A Guide to Canonical Criticism* (Philadelphia: Fortress, 1984). The term *canonical approach* is often used to describe the somewhat different proposals of Brevard Childs. Childs has been developing his position over the last thirty-five years. The best examples of his views are presented in *Introduction to the Old Testament as Scripture* (London: SCM, 1979); *The New Testament as Canon: An Introduction* (London: SCM, 1984); and *Old Testament Theology in a Canonical Context* (London: SCM, 1985). Childs's most persistent if not perspicacious critic has been James Barr. See particularly *Holy Scripture: Canon, Authority, Criticism* (Oxford: Oxford University Press, 1983). The most sympathetic reconstruction of Childs's position can be found in Mark Brett's book *Biblical Criticism in Crisis?* (Cambridge: Cambridge University Press, 1991).

ing to this usage, the Christian canon is a list of books that was largely in place by the end of the second century and was finalized by the middle of the fourth century. We think, however, that the significance of the canon for understanding Scripture in Christian ethics is as a norm, a standard of judgment. *Canon* can correctly refer to either list or norm, but it is important to be precise about how one is using the term.

For example, using *canon* to refer to a fixed list, one would have to admit that the earliest Christians did not have a canon. The fixing of a list was a later historical development. According to our use of *canon,* however, one would have to say that the earliest Christian communities recognized some texts and traditions as the norm to which their faith, practice, and worship were to conform. We cannot completely specify the contours of that canon. Neither is it likely that all the earliest Christian communities agreed on the precise contours of the canon.[16] Without doubt, however, the Old Testament (probably in Greek) and a host of more or less formalized traditions about the life, death, and resurrection of Jesus would have been the basis for the standard to which the earliest Christian communities sought to conform their common life. This, at least, is what Paul seems to have presupposed in his own writings to these communities.

All communities that seek to form faithful lives must have at least relatively formalized standards against which to judge what is faithful and what is not. It is not at all problematic to call that standard a canon. That standard for Christian communities is Scripture. To sustain this claim Christians need not believe that God dictated the text of the Bible to faithful scribes in ancient times. We do, however, need to have a view of Providence. Christian convictions about the canonical status of Scripture are sustained by a faith that the God who has called us to be the church would not leave us bereft of the resources we need to follow that call faithfully.

Neither do Christians need to be surprised that those preceding them in the faith revised the shape and content of their canon in the light of their changing circumstances. Even if we cannot trace the rationale for, or the exact shape of, these changes, critical biblical scholarship has persuasively shown that such processes were at work in earlier communities of believers. Those who seek to be wise readers of Scripture may well benefit from knowing about these various stages of the reception of the texts of the Bible. Christian communities must

16. Even today, the contours of the Christian canon vary to some degree depending on whether one is Roman Catholic, Orthodox, or Protestant. It is not clear to us, however, that this is a major problem. Without doubt there are large differences between these Christian groups. Some of these differences are due to interpretive disputes. Nevertheless, these differences (with a few possible exceptions) do not seem to depend on the shape of any particular group's canon. Important issues do need to be addressed within ecumenical contexts about how we ought to construe "Scripture" in these various traditions.

Even in ecumenical discussions, however, we ought not overemphasize the differences. One would need to show how a concrete dispute hinges on differences over the shape of the Christian canon before we allow these differences to become too prominent in discussions of Scripture's place in Christian ethics. When such a case arises, such as the reference to purgatory in 2 Maccabees, it will have to be resolved in conversation among the various parties (as with all ecumenical disputes).

remember, though, that it is the present form of the text of the Bible that is canonical for them.[17] Christian communities conform their life and practice to the present form of their Scripture and not to J or E or to L or Q.[18]

Such convictions, however, need not limit the types of readings of Scripture which Christian communities might provide. Long before the rise of critical scholarship Christians gave a rich variety of faithful readings and embodiments of Scripture without the benefit of source, form, or redaction criticism. They used the diversity within the canon to their advantage, reading various texts in the light of others.[19]

There are manifold ways in which this has been and can be legitimately done. For example, difficult passages in Scripture about the place of women might be read in the light of Jesus' ministries to women and their ministries to him or in the light of Galatians 3:27–29.[20] Likewise, passages in the Old Testament may well be read "directionally" through Jesus and Paul.[21] But there is no a priori way of knowing which texts can or should be used in any particular situations or interpretations. Practical wisdom, learned in and through particular Christian communities, is the means by which the appropriate texts and their interpretations are discerned.[22]

---

17. This does not eliminate the issues raised by textual criticism about how we discern what is the "final form" of the text. To take a well-known example, does the Gospel of Mark properly end at 16:8 or 16:20? Such questions are important, but they do not undermine the notion of reading the final form of the text. Rather, as we suggest below, these questions point to the importance of developing critical virtues that will enable us to discern wisely how to construe the final form.

18. See also the comments of Charles Wood: "It is, for example, the book of Exodus or the Gospel of Matthew which is canonically decisive, and not the various strands, strata, and sources of tradition which may lie behind either and which might be reconstructed as oral or written 'works' in their own right. This does not mean that historical considerations are irrelevant to a canonical reading of the texts. Historical awareness of the ways in which a given writing was perceived and read at the time of the formation of the Christian canon may provide crucial insight into its canonical significance, while the history of its subsequent interpretation may well be relevant to one's own attempts at canonical exegesis." *The Formation of Christian Understanding* (Philadelphia: Westminster, 1981), 92.

19. For examples of how this was done in early Christianity, see Rowan Greer's discussion in James L. Kugel and Rowan A. Greer, *Early Biblical Interpretation* (Philadelphia: Westminster, 1986), 107–203; for examples from medieval Christianity, see Beryl Smalley, *Study of the Bible in the Middle Ages* (Oxford: Basil Blackwell; Notre Dame: University of Notre Dame Press, 1964).

20. See, for example, Letty Russell, *Household of Freeman* (Philadelphia: Westminster, 1987).

21. See the comment by John Howard Yoder on the heritage of "the believers' church": "Instead of a timeless collection of parabolic anecdotes for allegorical exposition, the Bible is a story of promise and fulfillment which must be read directionally. The New Testament, by affirming the Hebrew Scriptures which Christians have come to call the Old Testament, also interprets them. Abraham and Moses are read through Jesus and Paul." *The Priestly Kingdom* (Notre Dame: University of Notre Dame Press, 1984), 9.

22. Some might object that this practice sets up a canon within a canon, ultimately failing to take seriously the canon as it stands now. Within a canon as diverse as the one Christians recognize, there is no reason to think that all of its texts will be equally relevant all of the time. Some texts will be more appropriate than others in any given situation. This sets up a *functional* canon within the canon. But a functional canon within the canon, discerned in the particular contexts of Christian communities, is considerably different from a *normative* canon within the canon which *a priori* excludes some texts from consideration. We reject the notion of a normative canon within the canon. A functional one, however, is not a problem as long as Christians recognize that in a different context

Our claims about the canonical shape of Scripture should not lead Christians to forsake critical biblical scholarship as it is carried out in the academy. Clearly, not all critical interests and activities are at all times equally relevant to any particular community. Nor do all people need to become critical biblical scholars. Yet the exercise of "critical virtues" as nurtured in university departments and professional societies is important to the church for a variety of reasons. First, as we have already suggested, such critical virtues enable us to analyze textual traditions in order to discern the final form of the text. They enable linguistic skills for discerning how best to translate particular texts.

Second, critical scholarship can remind contemporary Christian communities that they are not the first people to desire to walk faithfully with Yahweh. Communities today stand within a Christian tradition that extends back beyond the time when the contours of our present Scripture were stabilized. We cannot escape being situated in such a tradition, nor should we wish to escape. Our predecessors in the faith, both Jewish and Christian, have asked questions, found answers, formulated texts, and given readings of those texts which provide us with resources for our own lives. We cannot hope to become wise readers of Scripture in isolation from these resources in the tradition.

Further, critical scholarship can provide us with descriptions, analyses, and interpretations of these various stages and various conflicts in the Christian tradition.[23] This is so both in terms of sociohistorical awareness of the contexts in which particular writings were formed and received during the formation of the canon and in terms of the subsequent histories of how the texts have been interpreted by previous generations as well as other contemporaneous communities. The results of such critical practices serve as the long-term memory of contemporary Christian communities. A critic in the service of such communities will use that memory to help shape both the interests a community brings to the reading of its canonical texts and the results of such interested readings.

In general, the exercise of critical virtues can help Christian communities withstand their tendencies to self-deception in the reading of Scripture. Such self-deception takes many forms, but it is generally based on the presumption that we today are the only ones who have heard the word of the Lord, that ours is the only true interpretation.

Ironically, some contemporary critical biblical scholars fall into this trap by presuming that they can deliver to us the meaning of the text apart from and

---

different texts may provide the basis for a faithful response. No text — no matter how "difficult" — should be excluded from the ongoing processes of communal discernment in relation to the whole witness of Scripture.

23. The Christian tradition embodies continuities of conflict among different ecclesial groups (as well as within them) about how to construe the whole of Scripture as well as how to read particular texts of Scripture. Such conflicts have been and in many ways continue to be divisive. We are not convinced, however, that in many contemporary contexts differences in ecclesial traditions either are or ought to be predominant in understandings of the place of Scripture in Christian ethics. The fact that many people today participate in more than one community of Christians has significantly altered the ways in which those people read and understand Scripture.

despite thousands of years of interpretation and embodiment. Divested of any pretensions to deliver the meaning of the text, the practices of critical biblical scholarship are important to the ongoing life of Christian communities. Even so, by characterizing the importance of critical biblical scholarship in terms of critical virtues we want to emphasize that this task involves the interdependence of people with well-formed character in particular communities, not the dependence on experts that has so often rendered nonprofessional interpreters irrelevant.

There is at least one further reason why Christian communities committed to reading the final canonical form of their Scripture will always want to engage in critical biblical scholarship. While such communities believe God would not leave the people of God without the resources they need to live in a manner faithful to God's call, they also need to recognize that the Bible did not fall complete from the mouth of God. Individuals and communities over time performed the tasks needed to form the Scriptures. In this process of formation, which is itself an act of interpretation, various interests were brought to bear on the final shaping of this text. Those interests include not only serving the needs of the people of God but also preserving the status of one's own social group, class, or gender.

Recently, for example, the sociohistorical analyses of Norman Gottwald in regard to the Hebrew Bible and Elisabeth Schüssler Fiorenza's feminist reconstructions of early Christianity have brought this point home.[24] Although many scholars have questioned the actual details of either Gottwald's or Schüssler Fiorenza's accounts, their work has been important because they raise issues about the types of interests brought to bear on the formation and interpretation of the texts that the Christian canon comprises.

It would be a mistake, however, to suggest that the texts themselves are distorted. Such a claim presupposes that there is some undistorted, neutral text against which other forms are judged to be distorted. We need to recognize that whenever people engage in writing or reading texts, they do so from particular standpoints and with particular interests. However, those need not be the standpoints and interests that subsequent readers adopt.

Indeed, the recognition that we all write and read texts with particular interests in mind can help contemporary readers to adopt strategies for interpreting Scripture that will expose and challenge influential presumptions about such issues as power, class, and gender.[25] The history of scriptural interpretation shows that the canon provides a wealth of material for readings, particularly the narra-

24. See Norman K. Gottwald, *The Tribes of Yahweh* (London: SCM, 1979); and Elisabeth Schüssler Fiorenza, *In Memory of Her: A Feminist Theological Reconstruction of Christian Origins* (London and New York: Crossroad, 1986). See also Itumeleng J. Mosala, *Biblical Hermeneutics and Black Theology in South Africa* (Grand Rapids, Mich.: Wm. B. Eerdmans, 1989).

25. See, for examples, Phyllis Trible, *Texts of Terror* (Philadelphia: Fortress, 1984); Ched Myers, *Binding the Strong Man* (Maryknoll, N.Y.: Orbis, 1988).

tives of Jesus Christ in the Gospels, that can subvert any particular community's sedimented interpretations and performances.

Christian communities must be aware of the possibilities of interpreting Scripture in such a way that it supports rather than subverts corrupt and sinful practices. This means that we Christians will need to learn to read the Scriptures "over-against ourselves" rather than simply "for ourselves."[26] This is the sense in which our readings of the texts involve allowing the texts to provide readings of us.

Our ability or our failure to read Scripture over-against ourselves can have significant consequences for our day-to-day struggle to live faithfully before God. Nevertheless, no method guarantees that we will read Scripture in that way. At least two rules of thumb, however, can help us. First, we must be as willing to be interrogated by Scripture as we are to interrogate Scripture.[27] Of course, since Scripture does not actually talk, Scripture's interrogatory power will come to any community through the voices of interpreters with well-formed character within the community and concerned outsiders.

Scripture interrogates us in manifold ways. For example, as we have already noted, we come to Scripture with particular predispositions, ideologies, and theological presumptions. Left unchallenged, we will fail to recognize the corrupting power of these predispositions, ideologies, and theological presumptions. The interrogatory power of Scripture challenges us to be constantly reforming the preconceptions we inevitably bring to interpretation.[28] For example, the biblical identification "God is love" has yielded a popular picture in middle-class America that God is a "therapeutic nice-guy." This picture needs to be challenged by such texts as Amos, where God demands repentance and justice rather than prescribes therapy.

Further, allowing ourselves to be interrogated by Scripture entails a willingness to struggle with difficult and obscure texts. But of course there is no a priori way to know what texts we will find difficult or obscure. For example,

26. We borrow these terms from Dietrich Bonhoeffer, who develops them in his lecture "The Presentation of New Testament Texts," in *No Rusty Swords,* trans. E. H. Robertson et al. (London: Collins, 1970), 302–20.

27. See also J. D. G. Dunn and James P. Mackey, *New Testament Theology in Dialogue* (London: SPCK; Philadelphia: Westminster, 1979), 6, where they note: "At the same time we may well find that the New Testament writings do not merely answer back our questions. The New Testament may put *us* in question."

28. Many theological and political disputes within the church are interminable because we don't want Scripture to interrogate us. But as David Kelsey has noted, there are also theological disputes about how to construe Scripture. See *The Uses of Scripture in Recent Theology* (Philadelphia: Fortress, 1975). While it is important to recognize such theological disputes about how to construe Scripture, the focus ought to be not on the theological arguments but on how we ought to order our lives in relation to Scripture. Rowan Greer's comment about the early church is instructive: "For [the fathers of the early church], Scripture yielded a theological vision when rightly interpreted. And theological disputes in the early Church were largely arguments about how rightly to describe that vision and to define the hero of the story that comprised the vision. Nevertheless, the theological vision did not exist for its own sake. It was meant to be translated into renewed human lives" (in Kugel and Greer, *Early Biblical Interpretation,* 195).

middle-class British and North American Christians may find the story of the rich young ruler very difficult (Mark 10:17–22 and parallels), and followers of Rudolf Bultmann may find particular miracle stories or apocalyptic texts difficult unless they are demythologized. In the context of South African oppression, Allan Boesak has found the injunction of Jesus to forgive others not seven times but seventy times seven (Matt. 18:21–22 and parallel) — a passage many middle-class people in Britain and North America seemingly take for granted — to be an extraordinarily difficult passage. And yet, even though this passage is not particularly suited to his own desires, he allows the text to interrogate him.

Boesak asks, "Is it possible to transcend our present situation in South Africa? Can it still happen? I do not know. I do not know how to tell the Blacks in South Africa to forgive seventy times seven times — those who have seen their own children shot and killed in the streets. I do not know how to tell them this." He insists that in such a context people ought not speak too hastily about forgiveness and such matters. "And yet," he continues, "we read these words of the Lord, words that we cannot avoid. Ought we to believe that what is impossible for us is possible for God? With God all things are possible, including forgiveness welling up out of the hearts of suffering and oppressed Black South Africans. That too. Precisely that."[29] Boesak provides an important example of how and why we not only should interrogate texts but also ought to allow texts that we find difficult (for one reason or another) to interrogate us.[30]

A second rule of thumb for learning to read "over-against ourselves" is that, as we have already suggested, such ability can be enhanced by ongoing engagements with critical scholarship on the part of contemporary Christian communities. We are not claiming that all Christians must become biblical scholars in order to read Scripture well. Rather, in order that communities can embody wise readings of Scripture, they need to nurture and develop people who are capable of exercising the critical virtues of professional biblical scholarship.

What we did not mention earlier, and need to point out here, is that it will cost communities something to take seriously this responsibility of nurturing and developing people skilled in the application of critical biblical scholarship. For, as Ben Sira notes in the deutero-canonical book Ecclesiasticus, "The wisdom of the scholar depends on the opportunity of leisure and someone who has little business may become wise" (38:24 RSV). One does not become skilled as a critical exegete without the time to be devoted fully to that task. That time comes from being relieved of other duties. Others will have to pick up

29. Allan Boesak, *Black and Reformed* (Maryknoll, N.Y.: Orbis, 1984), 155–56. We are indebted to Gerald West for directing us to this passage.

30. We noted earlier that different communities adopt functional "canons within the canon" in providing readings of the texts. And we further suggested that such functional differences were not problematic so long as they were not allowed to become normative. Here we would note that, whereas different communities construct functional canons in their interpretation, we also need to allow the canon of Scripture to construct us. This would be the analogous move at the canonical level to our claim about allowing particular texts to interrogate us.

this slack if Christian communities are serious about nurturing biblical scholars. There is always a possibility that people in the community will resent this burden, especially if they don't see how the scholar is helping the community. In addition, there is a tremendous temptation to arrogance on the part of the would-be scholar.[31] Hence, communities must recognize these possibilities and choose people wisely for the task of scholarship.

Would-be scholars from Christian communities, for their part, must remember the cost to the communities that set them apart for a specific task. Such a task is a work of service to those communities, and only scholars who develop and retain the humility that this perspective demands will be able to handle faithfully the divided allegiances that will necessarily develop when they become full-fledged members of the scholarly community as well as members of particular Christian communities. In times of conflict between these allegiances, such scholars must remember that their primary allegiance is to the God who is worshipped in and through particular Christian communities. This allegiance to God must ultimately determine scholars' practice.

Throughout this section we have been arguing for the importance of providing "readings of the texts." We have understood that both in terms of the need for us to read the texts that constitute the Christian canon and in terms of the importance of allowing the texts to provide readings of us. We still need to address how Scripture is related both to the various contexts in which we live and to other possible sources for ethical guidance.

Readings of the World

We have argued that Scripture is best read in and through Christian communities. Such communities, however, find themselves within the political arrangements of wider societies. They need to understand these larger contexts and the ways in which they impinge on Christian communities if Christians' readings of Scripture are to enable them to live faithfully. Hence faithful interpretation requires not only readings of the texts but also "readings of the world." In a manner analogous to our argument about readings of the texts, believers need to provide readings of the world and also to allow the world to provide readings of us and of the politics of our communities.

It is important to provide readings of the world for at least three interrelated reasons. First, using a more restricted sense of the notion *world* than found in ordinary usage, we need to call the world to account for its unbelief. This sense of the world, derived from particular biblical passages, refers to all that which is opposed to God. So the Letter of James, for example, suggests that one who seeks to be a friend of the world puts himself at enmity with God

31. Ben Sira also recognizes this and reflects on the importance of maintaining a proper relationship between scholars and craftspeople for the continuing health of a society. See particularly Ecclesiasticus 38:31–34.

(James 4:4). Likewise in John's Gospel Jesus is quoted as saying that "[the world] hates me because I testify against it that its works are evil" (John 7:7). In this sense, providing a reading of the world entails calling to account all those who continue to be in rebellion against God. But before we can call them to account we must first understand what they are about.

Second, Christians need to provide readings of the world because the world remains a part of God's good creation to which God sent Jesus Christ and in which Christians are to serve (see John 17:15–19). The scope of God's work, particularly as focused in Jesus of Nazareth, remains the world. This world is not simply a spiritual abstraction. Rather, it is an arena of social, economic, and political interactions, conflicts, and cooperative endeavors. In particular, then, we need to discern and describe well the material conditions in which we find ourselves. No situation in which Christians (either now or in the past) find themselves is self-interpreting. The process of faithfully embodying an interpretation of Scripture presupposes that Christian communities have already analyzed and diagnosed the contexts in which they find themselves. Such analysis must be informed and directed by Scripture, but it is not simply an interpretation of Scripture.

In part our argument has to do with the now familiar claims about the importance of the "social location" of the interpreter. It makes a difference whether one is interpreting Scripture in the barrios of Los Angeles or the Houses of Parliament in Westminster, and we need to be aware of that difference. Nevertheless, diagnosing the material conditions in which we find ourselves goes beyond claims about social location. We need to analyze the ways in which the wider societies in which we live construct our identities and our relations with one another.

So, for example, in the contexts of modern Western societies, people's readings of the world ought to be informed by analyses of such features of contemporary life as individualism, consumerism, bureaucracy, reliance on managerial expertise, and the politics of our discursive practices.[32] These readings entail complex moral, political, economic, social-psychological, and historical issues. We need to consider, learn from, and also criticize sources and resources other than Scripture which address both the tasks of ethics and particular moral issues. For example, if we are addressing the problems of hunger in the world, we will need to utilize the resources of economic analyses as well as international politics. Or if we are addressing issues of medicine, we will need to draw on the resources of contemporary scientific investigations. We may also need to turn to the perspectives of other religious traditions in discerning approaches to moral

32. Many people have turned to such figures as Marx, Nietzsche, and Freud for their readings of the world (understanding *world* here in the context of modern Western societies), but to that list we might also add such (diverse and competing) theorists as Max Weber, Robert Bellah, Peter Berger, Michel Foucault, Jürgen Habermas, Julia Kristeva, and Alasdair MacIntyre. Moreover, we ought also to remember that some of the most powerful readings of the world come from artists as diverse as Angela Carter, Don DeLillo, Spike Lee, and Walker Percy.

questions or to an issue like the environment. If Christians' readings of Scripture for Christian ethics are to be wise, then we need to discern as wisely as possible the actual material conditions in which we find ourselves and the ways in which those conditions impinge not only on us but on others around the world.

We are contending that Scripture is the primary source and norm for Christian ethics. Thus our readings of the world should not be simply correlated with our readings of the texts as if each carries equal status in Christian ethical discernment. This is the danger of seeking to establish *methods* for relating Scripture to other sources and resources of moral guidance. The priority of readings of the texts does not in any way preclude drawing on other sources and resources. Indeed we are convinced that wise reading of the texts for Christian ethics actually *requires* that we provide readings of the world. But that conviction can too easily be misunderstood, and so we offer two caveats.

First, we need to recognize that Christians often disagree with one another about how best to read the world. We can and do need to learn from conversation and argument with fellow Christians. Further, Christians can and do need to learn from people in other disciplines and with other interests. When we do so, however, we need to remember that their readings of the world, whether in relation to economic analyses, moral judgments, or political calculations, are *not* descriptively neutral. We should not see them as neutral experts. Rather they are themselves providing readings from which we can learn and that we ought also to evaluate critically.

The second caveat is a reminder of something that we have already suggested, only this time with a different emphasis. Earlier we indicated that readings of the world ought to be informed by Scripture, but they are not themselves interpretations of Scripture. Now we need to emphasize the former part of that claim. Even when we are providing readings of the world, those readings ought to be informed and guided by our readings of Scripture. The ways we describe ourselves and the situations we face (let alone the world) are matters of controversy. Because of this, we need to remember that Scripture provides the primary context for our descriptions and the way we learn to make those descriptions.

One might object that Scripture is silent on numerous ethical issues that we face. While this is true, the force of the objection is overstated. Even where Scripture is silent in terms of any direct address to a moral issue, we can and ought to work analogically from the descriptions of Scripture to our descriptions and evaluations of particular concrete issues.[33]

Although these reasons indicate why we need to provide readings of the world, we need also to learn to allow the world to provide readings of us. That might seem odd, given our convictions about the centrality of providing readings

33. Medical ethics would seem to be one area where Scripture is silent on many of the issues we are now facing. But, as Richard Mouw has suggested, that does not imply that Scripture should not play an important role in how we "read" and describe the issues that are being raised. See "Biblical Revelation and Medical Decisions," in *Revisions,* ed. Stanley Hauerwas and Alasdair MacIntyre (Notre Dame: University of Notre Dame Press, 1983), 182–202.

of the texts. The world does not retain an independent authority over-against Scripture in discerning how we ought to live. Our primary task is learning to live faithfully before the Triune God by embodying the Scriptures. Even so, however, the world's readings of us present challenges as well as insights that can assist us in learning to live as scriptural people. This is so for several reasons.

First, in our judgment of the world we also judge ourselves. We discover the ways in which our own lives, as communities and individuals, continue to reflect that world of unbelief rather than the gospel of Jesus Christ. As James Wm. McClendon, Jr., has suggested, "the line between church and world passes right through each Christian's heart."[34] We need to allow the world to provide readings of us because we can too easily conflate the church and the Kingdom, presuming that the world is not — or at least is not any longer — a part of our lives. So, for example, when we condemn racism or sexism as incompatible with the gospel of Jesus Christ, we need to allow the world to "read" us by showing how the practices and institutions of Christian communities continue to be racist and sexist.

A second reason we need to allow the world to provide readings of us is that the material conditions in which we live not only shape our societies but shape our Christian communities in ways that are incompatible with Christian convictions. Christian communities too often and too easily reflect the material conditions of our societies and our culture instead of manifesting alternative ways of ordering common life. Christian communities in modern Western societies are beset by such problems as individualism, bureaucratic rationality, and consumerism. Hence, the analyses of social theorists are important not only for diagnosing the conditions in which we live but also for critically evaluating the practices and institutions of Christian communities and Christian lives.

Third, we also need to see what other disciplines and other readings of the world, including other religions, have to teach us. Other sources and resources of moral guidance contain wisdom from which we can enhance our own understandings of what it means to live faithfully before God. As Augustine puts it:

> In the same way all the teachings of the pagans contain not only simulated and superstitious imaginings and grave burdens of unnecessary labor, which each one of us leaving the society of pagans under the leadership of Christ ought to abominate and avoid, but also liberal disciplines more suited to the uses of truth, and some most useful precepts concerning morals. Even some truths concerning the worship of one God are discovered among them.[35]

We need to be open to the discovery of wisdom wherever it can be discerned.

Nevertheless, we need to pay attention to that wisdom's congruence with our readings of the scriptural texts. We sometimes mistake cultural presumptions

34. James Wm. McClendon, Jr., *Ethics: Systematic Theology, Volume I* (Nashville: Abingdon Press, 1986), 17.

35. Augustine, *On Christian Doctrine,* 75.

and societal fads for divine wisdom. Once again, there is no way to guarantee an adequate resolution of these issues in advance. As we have repeatedly insisted, there is no substitute for practical wisdom. That is, learning how to hold together readings of the texts and readings of the world is a lifelong project to be carried out in and through communities formed and transformed by the Holy Spirit.

Archbishop Oscar Romero's life and death provide an excellent example of someone who, through his participation in Christian communities, learned to embody Christian practical wisdom. He learned how to hold together powerful readings of both Scripture and the world. Romero was appointed archbishop of San Salvador in 1977 because he was considered to be politically safe. Yet over the next three years Romero developed powerful readings both of the biblical texts and of the world that were anything but politically safe.[36] Romero did not develop these readings in isolation; they emerged from worshipping, conversing, and living among fellow Christians, particularly poor Salvadorans who gathered together for worship and study in "base Christian communities." These readings led him to speak out prophetically against the spiral of violence that was ravaging El Salvador.[37] An assassin finally silenced Romero's voice on 24 March 1980 as he celebrated Holy Communion. Even so, the wisdom of Romero's readings, as embodied in his life and death, has enabled many people — both in El Salvador and beyond — to understand more clearly the interconnections between readings of the texts and readings of the world.

Conclusion

In this chapter we have argued that the interpretation of Scripture is a difficult task not because of the technical demands of biblical scholarship but because of the importance of character for wise readings. We pointed to the importance of Christian communities that are given their shape and form by the Triune God as the central contexts for learning to be wise readers of Scripture. We further suggested that in and through those Christian communities we need to engage both readings of the texts and readings of the world. Throughout, we have insisted on the importance of practical wisdom for both interpreting Scripture and discerning how we ought to live and what we ought to do.

Even though many people might acknowledge the importance of practical wisdom and Christian communities for understanding the place of Scripture in Christian ethics, there is still likely to be considerable uneasiness about staking too much on such notions. After all, we have not yet addressed the discontinuities between Scripture and our own contemporary settings. Isn't what we have argued for in this chapter undermined, or at least relativized, by the problems

36. See, for examples of Romero's readings, *The Violence of Love: The Pastoral Wisdom of Archbishop Oscar Romero,* ed. James R. Brockman (New York: Harper and Row, 1988).

37. Jon Sobrino has emphasized Romero's prophetic role in his *Archbishop Romero: Memories and Reflections,* trans. Robert R. Barr (Maryknoll, N.Y.: Orbis, 1990), especially 101–66.

of bridging the gap between the first centuries of the Common Era (when the Christian canon was formed) and the late twentieth?

Moreover, do we really want to place so much emphasis on Christian communities, given the ways in which people can become alienated from or marginalized by those communities? And how can we cope with the conflicts and fractured character not only within communities but among diverse and competing Christian communities? Have we failed to acknowledge the importance of individual believers in the midst of an emphasis on community?

We do not think that such questions are unanswerable or raise insuperable problems for our position. They do, however, call for further explication.[38]

Suggestions for Further Reading

Hauerwas, Stanley. *Unleashing the Scripture: Freeing the Bible from Captivity to America.* Nashville: Abingdon Press, 1993.

Hays, Richard B. *The Moral Vision of the New Testament: A Contemporary Introduction to New Testament Ethics.* New York: HarperSanFrancisco, 1996.

Meeks, Wayne A. *The Origins of Christian Morality: The First Two Centuries.* New Haven: Yale University Press, 1993.

Yoder, John Howard. "The Hermeneutics of Peoplehood: A Protestant Perspective." In *The Priestly Kingdom.* Notre Dame: University of Notre Dame Press, 1984.

38. See Stephen E. Fowl and L. Gregory Jones, *Reading in Communion: Scripture and Ethics in Christian Life* (Grand Rapids, Mich.: Wm. B. Eerdmans, 1991), where we pursue these issues.

Chapter 6

Practicing the Rule of Christ

John Howard Yoder

Editor's Introduction

We suggested in Chapter 2 that two of the practices constitutive of the church are discernment and discipling. (We used the term *discipling* for alliteration; Yoder refers to this practice as "binding and loosing.") In this chapter, Yoder argues that these two practices are inseparable and that above all else the practice of binding and loosing is definitive of the church. We might say that it is the *sine qua non* for maintaining the bonds of community. Discernment is the means by which the church finds guidance for its development and adaptation to new circumstances.

The practice of binding and loosing is based on Jesus' instructions (*rules*) in Matthew 18 to follow a series of steps in seeking reconciliation with a brother or sister who has sinned: first, go in private to talk; second, if that fails, take a few others along; finally, as a last resort bring the matter before the congregation. Yoder emphasizes that the purpose of the practice (the *internal good* at which it aims) is to bring about reconciliation (not, for instance, to vent frustration).

The justification for the practice comes from the Christian *story*. "The readiness not only to forgive but to make forgiveness the instrument and standard of all church experience is of a piece with the broader theme of suffering servanthood, the theme that stretches from Hosea and Isaiah 42, 49, 52–53 through Christ himself to the cross bearing of his disciples." The process is sensitive to the *life stories* of the participants. It requires that the one accused have the opportunity to explain extenuating circumstances, and is "concerned to see the fellow believer grow freely in the integrity with which he or she lives out the meaning of a freely made commitment to Christ."

Yoder emphasizes that the *virtue* of meekness is necessary if the practice is to avoid legalism and have a chance of attaining its true end. We can mention as a second virtue what MacIntyre refers to as the virtue of having an adequate sense of the tradition to which one belongs (*After Virtue,* 223). Yoder expresses this as follows: "There must be, if a decision is to be faithful, a way of informing it with full access to the biblical and theological heritage of Christian insight."

Yoder mentions briefly that "gifts" contribute to the Spirit-led decision process. An important area that needs development in a virtue ethic for Christians is the relation between virtues and gifts of the Spirit or grace.

Yoder makes a number of valuable remarks about the relation between the practice of binding and loosing and other practices we have mentioned as constitutive of the church. First, he argues on biblical grounds that binding and loosing is the defining feature of the church — Jesus uses the word *church* only in connection with this practice. Thus, as McClendon pointed out in Chapter 4, it is at the very center of the more encompassing practice of community formation.

Second, binding and loosing always involves discernment, and discernment always involves some degree of reconciliation, since matters of correct practice, doctrine, and morality cannot be settled in abstraction from the personal stakes of the participants in decision making. Discernment and a history of attempts to apply the instructions of Matthew 18 in particular cases together contribute to the ongoing development of the church's standards.

Third, the *interpretation of Scripture* cannot be understood apart from the practices of binding and loosing and discernment, since the Bible is for teaching, reproof, correction, and instruction in right behavior. So to attempt to understand the Bible apart from the specific questions of the people reading it is to do violence to the very purpose for which the Scriptures have been given (see chapter 5 above).

Fourth, personal reconciliation is a prerequisite for *worship*.

Fifth, the quality of personal relations within the church is a very powerful *witness* to the outsider.

Thus, we see that this pair of practices, discipling and discernment, is intrinsically related to two others we have characterized as essential to the identity of the church: witness and worship. It would be possible to show, for instance, by means of an account of Quaker life, that discernment and discipling are also essential for guiding the *works* of the church.

NANCEY MURPHY

1. Binding and Loosing: A Study Guide

Better a frank word of reproof than the love that will not speak; Faithful are the wounds of a friend. (Proverbs 27:5–6, Moffatt)

A study outline is intentionally a skeleton, unevenly filled out. It is not written for smooth and easy reading or for completeness and balance. The careful reader, evaluating it as an essay, will find the presentation fragmentary. The theologically alert reader will resent the absence of efforts to relate to the range of current schools of thought. Questions of historical or textual criticism are avoided. Texts are taken straightforwardly in a way that may seem naive. "How-to-do-it" concerns are mixed with the meaning of atonement with no respect for pigeonholing. No energy has been invested in explaining how this simplification differs from fundamentalism in method or motive.

The position suggested here may seem to gather together the dangers of several ecclesiastical scarecrows. It gives more authority to the church than does Rome, trusts more to the Holy Spirit than does Pentecostalism, has more respect for the individual than does humanism, makes moral standards more binding than does puritanism, is more open to the given situation than is the "new morality." If practiced it would change the life of churches more fundamentally than has yet been suggested by the perennially popular discussions of changing church structures.

Thus the path to the rediscovery of Christian faithfulness may lead right through some positions modern Christian "moderates" have been trying to avoid. The concern expressed here does not fit at any one point on the map of traditional denominational positions — which may just show that something is wrong with the map. The positions taken will seem strange to Christians of many schools of thought — and yet they echo a conviction historically present in many Christian traditions.

In leaving to one side other aspects of the problem of church renewal, and in opening up this one particular topic in this simple, generally accessible, apparently dogmatic way, I imply no claim that oversimplification is generally a way to solve problems. The naive form is a discussion-starting method and not a theological stance.

2. The Key Text — Matthew 18:15–20[1]

[15] If your brother or sister sins,
go[2] and reprimand that person
between the two of you, alone;

If that person listens, you have won your brother or sister.

[16] If not, take with you one or two more,
so that every matter may be established
by the mouth of two or three witnesses.[3]

[17] If the person will not listen to them,
tell it to the church.
If the person will not listen to the church either,
let such a person be to you as a pagan or a taxgatherer.

[18] I tell you[4] truly,
whatever you bind on earth shall be bound in heaven
and whatever you loose on earth shall be loosed in heaven. . . .

1. Author's own translation used throughout the essay. — Eds.
2. In the first four verses the "you" is always singular.
3. Deut. 19:15.
4. For the rest of the text, "you" is the plural.

Discussion questions on Matthew 18:15–20

- Note your first impressions of the passage under consideration before continuing with further study.
- What is the purpose of dealing with a brother or sister in this way?
- Is this way of dealing with a fellow Christian the responsibility of every Christian? Or only of the one sinned against? Or only of church officers?
- What do you take "binding" and "loosing" in verse 18 to mean?
- Can you think of other New Testament texts on this subject, or is it an isolated idea?
- Has the practice that Jesus describes here been a part of your experience as a Christian?

3. The Twofold Meaning of "Binding" and "Loosing"

In the sweeping summary authorization that he gives the church, Jesus uses the verbs *bind* and *loose* in a way that takes for granted that their meaning is clear to his listeners. Centuries later, when neither secular nor religious usage has retained the pair of terms, we must resurrect their meaning. Perhaps the very fact that the terms no longer have a customary sense in current language may permit us to use them now as a "technical" label for the practice Jesus commanded.

A. *Two aspects of meaning.* There are clearly two dimensions to the meaning of these verbs.

(1) Forgiveness: to "bind" is to withhold fellowship, to "loose" is to forgive. This is supported by the parallel texts in Luke 17:3 (based in turn on Lev. 19:17; note the other elements in Luke 17:14 that are also parallel to Matt. 18:14 and 18:21–22) and in John 20:25. It is supported as well by the other portions of Matthew 18 (10–14, the hundredth sheep; 21–22, seventy times seven; 23–35, the unmerciful servant).

(2) Moral discernment: To "bind" is to enjoin, to forbid or make obligatory; to "loose" is to leave free, to permit. We recognize the root *ligare* "to bind" in *obligate, ligament, league.* Thus the New English Bible translates "forbid" and "allow."

This was the current, precise technical meaning that the Aramaic equivalents of the terms *bind* and *loose* probably had in the language of the rabbis of Jesus' time. Moral teaching and decision making in Judaism took the form of rulings by the rabbis on problem cases brought to them, either "binding" or "loosing" depending on how they saw the Law applying to each case.[5]

Out of these decisions there accumulated a fund of precedents and principles called the *halakah,* the moral tradition, which continued from one generation to the next to be useful in relating the Law to current problems. By taking over

5. See below, sec. 15A.

these terms from rabbinic usage, Jesus assigns to his disciples an authority to bind and loose previously claimed only by the teachers in Israel.

This dimension of meaning is the one emphasized in the parallel phrasing of Matthew 16:19 and is further confirmed when we look at Matthew 18:15–20 more closely. Verses 15–17, describing the direct dealings with the brother, are spoken in the singular; but the following verses shift to the plural. This suggests that the authorization of 18–20 may have a broader import for the church than that of the immediate disciplinary context.

B. *The relation of forgiveness and discernment.* At first sight these two activities would seem not to be closely related; yet, on closer analysis their intimate interrelation becomes clear:

(1) Forgiving presupposes prior discernment. Jesus' words startle the modern reader with the simplicity of his beginning: "If your brother or sister sins . . . " In our age of tolerance and confusion we are not used to thinking of "sin" as so easily identifiable. Jesus assumes that the moral standards by which sin is to be identified are knowable and known. He further assumes that the offender and those who reprove him share a common moral yardstick.

(2) Forgiving furthers discernment. If the standards appealed to by those who would reprove someone are inappropriate, the best way to discover this is through the procedure of person-to-person conversation with reconciling intent. Thus the group's standards can be challenged, tested and confirmed, or changed as is found necessary, in the course of their being applied. The result of the process, whether it ends with the standards being changed or reconfirmed, is to record a new decision as part of the common background of the community, thus accumulating further moral insights by which to be guided in the future.

(3) Discernment necessitates forgiveness. There is in every serious problem a dimension of personal offense or estrangement. This is the case even when the issue at stake is quite "impersonal" or "technical" or "objective." Therefore, in every right decision there must be an element of reconciliation. The idea that questions of right and wrong could best be studied somehow "objectively" or "disinterestedly" is in itself an unrealistic misunderstanding of the personal character of every decision-making process.

(4) Forgiving concern sets the limits of our responsibility for one another's decisions. If I am a Christian at all, what I do is my brother's and my sister's business. We owe one another counsel and, sometimes, correction and pardon. Yet it is neither possible nor desirable for my brother or sister to be concerned with or responsible for all that I do. What then is the point where the search for a common mind ends and individual variation and personal responsibility begins?

The most current answer is that big sins are the church's business and small ones are not. Yet every effort to draw that line leads to legalism, and to concern with the deed rather than the doer, with guilt rather than restoration.

The correlation of the two concerns of forgiveness and discernment provides another answer, though not an abstract one, to this question. Differences of conviction and behavior are unacceptable *when they offend.* The "line" is not drawn theoretically but in terms of personality and interpersonal concern. If the difference destroys fellowship, it is for that reason a topic for reconciling concern. Any variance not dealt with, on the grounds that it is unimportant, becomes increasingly important with the passage of time. Unattended, it magnifies the next conflict as well.

But if, on the other hand, Christians have been accustomed to dealing with one another in love and have been finding that they are able to be reconciled whenever they deal with a matter in love, then they find as well that their "tolerance threshold" rises. A spirit of mutual trust grows, in which fewer differences offend.

Thus both the necessity of dealing with some differences and the possibility of leaving other matters to individual liberty are rooted in the very process of the reconciling approach.

"Forgiveness" and "discernment" do not point to two alternative meanings of the same words, whereby one would always need to choose which meaning applies. Forgiveness and discernment are not two poles of a tension but two sides of a coin. Each presupposes and includes the other. In the following pages we shall deal predominantly with the "forgiveness" face of the coin but never as if this excluded the other aspect of moral discernment.

Discussion questions on the meaning of binding and loosing

- Before reading further, note your first reactions on reading that Jesus authorizes his disciples: (1) to forgive sins; and (2) to make binding moral decisions.
- What place has forgiveness had until now in your concept of what the church is for in your experience of church?
- Can you be deeply reconciled with your brother or sister while disagreeing on moral decisions?
- Can you tolerate disagreement with someone you have forgiven or who has forgiven you?
- Can you agree on moral issues with someone you have not forgiven? Are you more critical of someone you have not forgiven?

4. The Source of the Authority to Bind and Loose

A. *The authority given the church is parallel to the authority of Christ himself* (John 20:19–23). Throughout Jesus' ministry, especially as recorded in the Fourth Gospel, Jesus scandalized the authorities by his claims to have been sent by the Father in a unique way (5:18ff., 6:30ff., 7:28ff., 8:36ff., 10:25ff.). Now he tells his disciples, "Just as the Father sent me, so I send you."

If it was possible to be yet more offensive to official reverence, it was when Jesus took it upon himself to forgive sins (Mark 2:7, Luke 7:48ff.); yet this too is what the disciples are charged to do. He lays upon them, and thereby upon us, the same power he claimed for himself.

B. *The scandal of the divine mandate.* We do not fully understand the grandeur of this commission if we are not first shocked by it as were Jesus' contemporaries. Not only were his contemporaries shocked (in Mark 1:7, they called it blasphemy); Protestants today are shocked, too. Reacting against the abuses of Roman Catholic penitential practice (see below, section 10E), Protestants have for centuries been arguing that "only God can forgive" and that the believer receives reassurance of forgiveness not from another person but in the secret of his or her own heart.

In the later development of Judaism as well, a distinction developed between interpersonal adjudication or reconciliation or forgiveness, which the community deals with, and Atonement, accorded by God alone, which is the theme of the annual Holy Day.

The heat and vigor of this old Protestant-Catholic debate point us to the difficulty we have in conceiving, and in believing, that God really can authorize ordinary humans to commit him, that is, to forbid and to forgive on his behalf with the assurance that the action stands "in heaven." How can it be, and what can it mean, that such powers are placed in the hands of ordinary people the likes of Peter? The jealous concern of religious leaders, and of all religion, for the transcendence of God, for his untouchability and his distance from us, might have been able to adjust, or to make an exception, for arrogant claims like this made on behalf of some most exceptional person, a high priest or a grand rabbi, a prophet or king. But the real scandal of the way God chose to work among humans — what we call the Incarnation — is that it was an ordinary working man from Nazareth who commissioned a crew of ordinary people — former fishermen and taxgatherers — *to forgive sins.*

C. *The church is empowered by the Holy Spirit.* The text in John 20 links the imparting of the Holy Spirit directly with the commission to forgive. According to John 14 and 16, the functions of the promised Spirit will be to "convince," to "lead into all truth," and to remind believers of teachings of Jesus that they had not grasped before.

In Acts 1 and 2 the function of the Spirit is to empower the disciples to be witnesses; but in the rest of the story of Acts, notably in the decisions of chapters 13 and 15, but also in the modest details of Paul's travel arrangements, the Spirit is active especially in making decisions. If the proportionate space given to various themes is indicative, the basic work of the Holy Spirit according to Acts is to guide in discernment. Prophecy, testimony, inward conviction, and empowerment for obedience are subordinate aspects of that work.

The promise of the presence of Christ "where two or three are gathered in my name" is often understood in modern Protestantism as meaning either that there are grounds for belief in the efficacy of prayer or that the gathered congregation may sense a spiritual presence in their midst. Yet in the original context of Matthew 18:19–20 its application is to the consensus (the verb is *sumphōnein,* from which we get "symphony") reached by the divinely authorized process of decision.[6] The "two or three others" are the witnesses required in the Mosaic law for a judicial proceeding to be formally valid (Deut. 17:6; 19:15; applied in Num. 35:30; 2 Cor. 13:1; 1 Tim. 5:19; Heb. 10:28).

D. *This mandate makes the church the church.* The Greek word *ekklēsia* ("church") is found only twice in the Gospels coming from Jesus' lips; the two times are the two "bind and loose" passages. The word *ekklēsia* itself (like the earlier Hebrew term and the Aramaic equivalent that Jesus probably used) does not refer to a specifically religious meeting or to a particular organization; rather it means the "assembly," the gathering of a people into a meeting for deliberation or for a public announcement. It is no accident that in Matthew 16 the assignment by Jesus of the power to bind and loose follows directly upon Peter's first confession of Christ as Messiah. The confession is the basis of the authority; the authorization given is the seal upon the confession. The church is where, because there Jesus is confessed as Christ, men and women are empowered to speak to one another in God's name.

Discussion questions on the church's authorization

- Are there many different activities, or only a few, that Jesus specifically ordered the church to carry out in his name?
- Read John 16 and the story in Acts to check on the statements made in section C, above, concerning the work of the Holy Spirit.
- What teaching do you remember in the past about who can forgive sin?

5. The Way of Dealing with the Brother or Sister Is Determined by the Reconciling Intent

A. *The reconciling approach is personal.* The entire section 18:15–17 is in the singular: it is a command to the individual. The point of the passage is not that there must be just three steps (rather than four or five) but that (1) the first encounter is "between the two of you alone"; and that (2) still another small group effort at mediation is made, if the first attempt has failed, before (3) the matter becomes public.

The personal approach first of all guarantees that the matter remains confidential. This is the scriptural prohibition of gossip and defamation. Anyone knows that there is something wrong with talebearing. But sometimes one may think it wrong only because it reveals secrets, or only when the reports one passes on are not true, or when the intention in passing them on is to hurt someone. Each of these explanations of what is wrong with gossip leaves a loophole. Each would permit some kinds of talking about the neighbor's faults to continue.

---

6. Rabbi Hananjah ben Teradion (d. 135) said, "when two sit and there are between them words of Torah, the Shechinah rests between them . . ." (*Aboth* Sayings of the Fathers III/3; other looser parallels in III/4, III/7, IV/10; brought to my attention by Michael Signer).

But if Jesus' command is that the thing to do with an unfavorable report is to go to the person herself or himself, then all one's temptations to pass the word along are blocked and confidentiality is demanded by the concern for the offender.

Second, it is hereby assured that the process is closely bound to the local situation. Either party can bring into the discussion aspects of the picture that would not be taken into account in general statements of rules. Thus there is a safeguard against the danger of legalism, which promulgates ethical generalities apart from the context where they must apply and then applies them strictly and uniformly to every case.

When dealing personally with the offender, in view of that person's problems, it is not possible to identify as virtues or vices whole categories of behavior without taking part with that person in the struggle and the tension of applying them to his or her situation. It is that person who must determine how to behave when he or she really faces the difficult choice. It may be that the one accused will be able to demonstrate that the action criticized as "sin" was right after all. Or perhaps the one admonishing may be able to help the accused find a better solution he or she had not seen.

This is a built-in way to assure that churches will not continue to proclaim rules that are no longer capable of application. Standards must constantly be tested by whether it is possible to show the brother or sister how he or she has sinned. If no one can show that person how he or she should have done differently, then the rules are inadequate and that person has been accused unfairly. The very process of conversation with that person is then the way to change the rules. If, on the other hand, the standards continue to be correct, it is in the conversation with the offending individual that the church will be obliged and enabled to give the most fruitful attention to finding other ways of meeting his or her needs and the temptations that led that person to fall.

Yet at the same time that legalism must be avoided, there is an equal danger of letting the situation provide its own rules. What modern writers call "situation ethics" or "relevance" or "contextualism" may mean simply allowing every individual full liberty to make his or her own decisions. This approach ends by sacrificing all moral bindingness and all community, adopting in advance a general "rule-against-rules." Binding and loosing achieves the same flexibility to fit each context, without being too sweepingly permissive.

The approach is made in a "spirit of meekness" (Gal. 6:1), that is, in recognition of the mutual need of all members for one another and for forgiveness. "Bearing one another's burdens" in Galatians 6:2 is centered not on economic needs, as it is often read, but on the need for this kind of mutual moral support.

B. *Everyone in the church shares responsibility for the reconciling approach.*

(1) The command of Matthew 18 assigns the initiative to anyone aware of the offense. The words "against thee," present in most older translations, are missing in the most reliable ancient manuscripts; no such limitation is present in Luke 17:3, Galatians 6:1–2, James 5:19–20.

Those who interpret the instructions to apply only to the person sinned against would shift the attention from the offender's need for reconciliation to the resentment of the person hurt in order to give vent to his or her feelings. If this shift is taken seriously, it could mean that for certain sins where there is no one specific person offended, or the offended person is absent, there would be nothing for anyone to do. Such a limiting interpretation would also lead the more "mature" or "tolerant" or "accepting" person to absorb the offense and suffer without response, claiming to be adult enough or magnanimous enough not to need to "blow off steam." However, according to Galatians 6, it is the spiritually mature person who is especially responsible to act in reconciliation.

(2) The instructions of Matthew 5:23ff. assign the same responsibility to the person who has offended, if that person becomes aware of the offense. His or her obligation to be reconciled is prior to any other righteous works, however worthy. If your fellow Christian has something against you, don't bring your sacrifice to the altar. It is thus the responsibility of every person — of the offender, of the offended, of every informed third party in the Christian fellowship when aware of any kind of offense — to take initiative toward the restoration of fellowship.

(3) There is no indication that this responsibility belongs in any particular way to "the ministry." "Forgiving" is never indicated in the New Testament as one of the "gifts" distributed within the congregation, nor as a specific responsibility of the pastor, elder, bishop, or deacon.

Now there are good commonsense reasons for assuming that anyone who is responsible for leadership in the life of the church will also be concerned for the proper exercise of this reconciling discipline. Thus church leaders might well be included among the "two or three" of Matthew 18:16, or the "wise among you" of 1 Corinthians 6:5, who seek to mediate in the second effort, or among the "more spiritual" of Galatians 6:1. Nevertheless these are only relative, commonsense considerations. They may be properly applied only after the first attempt at reconciliation, for to inform church leaders before that first attempt is counter to the letter and the intent of the demand for initial confidentiality: "between you and him or her alone."

For the pastor, the teacher, the elder, the preacher, or the deacon to be normally or exclusively the disciplinarian, to the extent that others no longer share in bearing the same burden, undermines both the reconciling process and this person's other leadership ministries. It is one of the main reasons for both the loss of authentic discipline in the churches and the discrediting of some kinds of ministerial leadership.

C. *This process belongs in the church.* The church's responsibility may not be turned over to the state (as in the age of the Reformation, according to the convinced theological opinions of Huldrych Zwingli and his followers) or to any other agency representing the total society.

Something like this is happening in our society. Although legalism in churches is going out of style, we are accustomed to the FBI and the draft board exercising moral oversight; we expect schools and social workers to develop the character of the persons they work with.[7]

Nor can the reconciling process in the church be properly replaced by secular psychotherapy. This study makes no attempt to investigate the complex interrelationships between the church and the mental health institution, between moral guilt and psychotic anxiety, and so on. There clearly can and should be no fixed wall between mental health and the church, yet neither may one be absorbed into the other. No definition of the interrelation of these areas can be accepted that takes the matter of guilt and grace completely away from the congregation, or that excludes conscious confession and forgiveness for known willful offenses, or that dissolves all moral measurement into self-adjustment. Not psychiatry and psychology but the caricature of these professions as secular agencies of forgiveness is the abuse we need to avoid.

D. *Reconciliation and restoration is the only worthy motive.* Any textbook discussion of "church discipline" aligns several other reasons for its application by the church: the purity of the church as a valuable goal in its own right; the need to protect the reputation of the church before the outside world; the obligation to testify to the righteous demands of God; the desire to dramatize the demands of church membership, especially to new or young members, assumed more likely to be tempted; and the wish to safeguard against relativization and the loss of common Christian moral standards.

Real as they are as by-products, and logical as they may well be in motivating the church, it is striking that these concerns are not part of the New Testament picture. These reasonings all put the church in a posture of maintaining its own righteousness, whereas the New Testament speaks of shared forgiveness.

Nevertheless there is, beyond Jesus' simple "you will have won your sister or brother," one deeper way of phrasing the motivation. 1 Corinthians 5:6ff. speaks of the discipline process in the image of "leaven": the church is the lump of dough, all of which will be caused to ferment by the presence of a few yeast cells within it. Paul thus says that there is a kind of moral solidarity linking all the members of the body so that if individuals persist in disobedience within the fellowship, their guilt is no longer the moral responsibility of those individuals alone but becomes a kind of collective blame shared by the whole body. I should deal with my fellow believer's sin because that person and I are members one of another; unless I am the agent of that person's sharing in restoration, he or she is the agent of my sharing guilt.

Discussion questions on the reconciling approach

- Would it be possible to maintain self-righteousness or judgmental attitudes if the principle of going directly to the offender were respected?

7. Concerning the way the nation takes over the moral authority of the church, see John Edwin Smylie, "The Christian Church and the National Ethos," in *Biblical Realism Confronts the Nation,* ed. Paul Peachey (Nyack, N.Y.: Fellowship Publications, 1963), 33–44.

- Would the concern for discipline be more effectively taken care of if it were assigned to one particular officer in the church?
- Are there certain kinds of questions to which the instructions of Matthew 18 should not apply? Certain sins that should not be so easily forgiven? Or certain others that do not call for this much attention?

6. The Centrality of This Forgiving Function in the New Testament

A. Reference to "binding and loosing" occurs at the only places in the Gospels where the word *church* is reported as used by Jesus. The church is, therefore, most centrally defined as the place where "binding and loosing" takes place. Where this does not happen, "church" is not fully present.

B. This is the only connection in which it is said of the church that it is authorized to "commit God." "What you bind on earth stands bound in heaven." The image is that of the ambassador plenipotentiary or of the "power of attorney"; the signature of the accredited representative binds the one who gave the commission.

C. It is in the context of this activity of the church that the promise is given (Matt. 18:19–20; John 14:26; 16:12ff., 20–23) that Christ (or the Spirit) is present where his followers meet in his name. It can be argued that in the New Testament the gift of the Spirit is more often spoken of in connection with discerning and forgiving than (as in Acts 1:8) in relation to witnessing.

D. This practical application of forgiveness (18:15–18) is the center of the teaching of the entire chapter 18 on forgiveness.

E. Both the only condition in the Lord's Prayer (Matt. 6:12) and the only commentary of Jesus on the prayer (Matt. 6:15) limit God's forgiveness to those who forgive others (also said in Matt. 18:35; Mark 11:25; Eph. 4:32; Col. 3:13; Sirach 28:2).

F. The reconciliation with one's brother or sister is prerequisite to valid worship (Matt. 5:23–24).

G. The promise of the presence of the Holy Spirit is related especially closely to binding and loosing as we saw above (sec. 4C, Matt. 18:19, 20).

H. It is a function of the "spiritual" people in the church that in a spirit of meekness they restore offenders; this is called "bearing one another's burdens" (Gal. 6:1–2). It is also described as "covering a multitude of sins" (James 5:19–20).

Discussion questions on the New Testament

- Do you see in the passages cited any localizing of this function as a "ministry" of specific officers of the church?
- Do you see in the narrative elements of the New Testament that this function was exercised?

- Do you see in the letters of the New Testament that the writer "admonishes" his readers in this way?
- As you pray the Lord's Prayer, does the phrase "as we forgive" draw your mind to whether you are in fact forgiving others as you ask to be forgiven?

7. The Centrality of Binding and Loosing in the Life of Free-Church Protestantism

A. The small group of followers of Huldrych Zwingli who after 1525 came to be known as Anabaptists are usually thought of as having begun their search for the form of the faithful church around the question of the state church or around infant baptism. It is, however, just as correct to say that the point at which the group of brethren became conscious of identity was a concern for dealing with offenders according to the pattern of Matthew 18. The term *rule of Christ,* with which they referred to the instructions of Matthew 18, was already a fixed phrase in their vocabulary in 1524, before they had reached any final conclusions about the form of the church, the practice of adult baptism, or the church's independence from the state.

The first Anabaptists did not say that infants should not be baptized because they cannot have an experience of faith and the new birth, nor did they reject infant baptism only because there was no biblical text commanding it.[8] Their belief was rather that one who requests baptism submits to the mutual obligation of giving and receiving counsel in the congregation; this is what a child cannot do.

In the first clear statement rejecting infant baptism, in September 1524, before going on to discuss whether water has a saving effect or whether unbaptized children are lost, Conrad Grebel wrote "even an adult is not to be baptized without Christ's rule of binding and loosing." Thus the issue is not the age of the one baptized but the commitment that person makes, entering into the covenant community with a clear understanding of its claims upon him or her.

Balthasar Hubmaier, the theologian of Anabaptism and the only first-generation leader to have the opportunity to draw up printed patterns of church order, likewise put the commitment character of baptism at the center of his view of reformation. It is clear in his catechism:

> Q. What is the baptismal pledge?
>
> A. It is a commitment which one makes to God publicly and orally before the church, in which he renounces Satan, and his thoughts and works. He pledges as well that he will henceforth set all his faith, hope and trust alone in God, and direct his life according to the divine Word, in the power of Jesus Christ our Lord and in case he should not do that, he promises hereby to the church that he desires

8. These are the reasons that most contemporary Baptists, Pentecostals, or Disciples of Christ would give.

virtuously to receive fraternal admonition from her members and from her, as is said above....

Q. What power do those in the church have over one another?

A. The authority of fraternal admonition.

Q. What is fraternal admonition?

A. The one who sees his brother sinning goes to him in love and admonishes him fraternally and quietly that he should abandon such sin. If he does so he has won his soul. If he does not, then he takes two or three witnesses with him and admonishes him before them once again. If he follows him, it is concluded, if not, he says it to the church. The same calls him forward and admonishes him for the third time. If he now abandons his sin, he has saved his soul.

Q. Whence does the church have this authority?

A. From the command of Christ, who said to his disciples, "all that you bind on earth shall be bound also in heaven and all that you loose on earth shall also be loosed in heaven."

Q. But what right has one brother to use this authority on another?

A. From the baptismal pledge in which one subjects oneself to the Church and all her members according to the word of Christ.[9]

Far from being the extreme expression of individualism, the baptism of believers is thus the foundation of the most sweeping communal responsibility of all members for the life of all members.

B. The Wesleyan revival may stand as a sample for the numerous renewal movements since the sixteenth century. John Wesley and his colleagues had some particular doctrinal emphases and some unique personal gifts. Their ministry came at a time of great need. Yet the fundamental local experience that the "methodist" believer had week by week, and the real reason for the movement's practical success, was the regular encounter with the "class." This was a circle of persons meeting regularly, committed to one another and bearing one another's burdens in every way, with special attention to reproof and restoration.[10]

This has been true of movements of revival and renewal in every age; they restore a new freedom in forgiving relationships within the local fellowship and a renewed ethical earnestness born not out of rigorous law but out of mutual concern.

---

9. For the entirety of Hubmaier's "A Christian Catechism," see H. Wayne Pipkin and J. Yoder, eds., *Balthasar Hubmaier: Theologian of Anabaptism* (Scottdale, Pa.: Herald Press, 1989), 339–71; the portions cited here are from pp. 350–53 of this volume. Another translation is available in *The Reformation Catechisms,* ed. Denis Janz (New York: Edwin Mellen Press, 1982), 135ff. See also Ervin Schlabach, "The Rule of Christ among the Early Swiss Anabaptists," Th.D. diss., Chicago Theological Seminary, 1977.

10. See "The Nature, Design, and General Rules of the United Societies..." (1743) in *The Works of John Wesley,* vol. 9 of *The Methodist Societies: History, Nature, and Design,* ed. Rupert Davies (Nashville: Abingdon, 1989), 69–73; and "Rules of the Band Societies," 77–78.

C. Contemporary examples may be found in the revivalism of Keswick and of East Africa, and in most renewal movements. By the nature of the case such movements, without fixed denominational authority, are open to various organizational, doctrinal, and personal peculiarities. Some of these are novel, and some perhaps are questionable. Yet what keeps these movements alive and lively is the renewed experience of the gift of openness, the capacity given by grace to be transparent with the brother about one's own sins and the brother's and thereby to make concrete the assurance of forgiveness.

Thus every revival and every renewal movement has begun by reestablishing among estranged brethren, by repentance, a possibility of communication that had been broken off by the pride and the power-hunger of those within the churches. This kind of renewal may happen at any time or place and within any kind of Christian group; but for the free churches it is constitutive, it defines their specific character. The free church is not simply an assembly of individuals with a common spiritual experience of personal forgiveness received directly from God; nor is it merely a kind of working committee, a tool to get certain kinds of work carried out. The church is also, as a social reality right in the midst of the world, that people through whose relationships God makes forgiveness visible.

Discussion questions on the histories of renewal

- What has been the record of breakthrough experiences of forgiveness and dialogical discernment in the history of your own community? In the biographies and novels you have read?
- What has been the place of failure to dialogue reconcilingly in the failures to "be church" that you have seen?

8. The Congregational Method of Decision Making

The mandate to forgive and to decide makes no formal prescriptions about how small or large groups (the "two or three with you" or "the church") are to discuss and decide. Shall the decisions for the group be made by authority personages, entitled by age or ordination to speak for all? Or by a numerical majority? This question applies not only to "discipline" but to other kinds of "discerning" decision making as well. This study does not seek to go deeply into this formal matter.

A. From the narrower realm of the forgiving process, we must carry over into the broader discussion of churchly decision making several elements that are not usually emphasized in discussions of church organization: (1) the abiding awareness that all decision involves elements of conflict and resentment that need to be dealt with in an atmosphere of abiding forgiveness; and (2) the situation-bound movement of an issue from the two through the few to the congregation.

B. From the few descriptions of congregational meetings we have in the New Testament, especially 1 Corinthians 12–14, it seems clear that every member has a right, perhaps a duty, to share in the process. This is not to say that the Corinthian type of church life, charismatically effervescent to the border of disorder, is normative in any formal way.

C. It is clear that specific "gifts" contribute to the Spirit-led decision process; it is an orderly and not a formless movement. Some "prophesy," others "preside" and "oversee" and "administer."[11]

D. The decision process, although it is often "illuminated" by some immediate inspiration, cannot go forward validly in a knowledge vacuum. There must be, if a decision is to be faithful, a way of informing it with full access to the biblical and theological heritage of Christian insight. If it is to be relevant, it must be equally informed about all the factual dimensions of the current problem. There is no basis for any dichotomy between "religious" and "secular" information, as if either could make decision making superfluous or as if Spirit guidance could get along without either. Holy Spirit guidance is not an alternative to correct information.

Discussion questions on decision making

- Does it ever happen that "religious knowledge" is held to settle a question so that no decision is needed?
- Does the same thing ever happen with "secular" knowledge? Do the "authorities" or the "law" settle a question without decision making?
- Do current ways of assigning tasks to individuals in our churches reflect the teaching of Romans 12, Ephesians 4, 1 Corinthians 12?

9. Misunderstandings of the Concept of "Discipline"

As central as is the commission to bind and to loose, both in the New Testament and in any sober view of the mission of the church, it has nevertheless been widely misunderstood, distorted, and neglected. How can this have come about? So universal a loss of so fundamental a function must be understood and evaluated. Otherwise we may well fall into the same traps and be unable to recover it, or, having grasped it, rapidly lose it again. We shall, therefore, have to devote a sizable part of our study to the encounter with other points of view.

We look first at misunderstandings connected to the word *discipline,* the label by which this work of community maintenance is most often designated.

A. *The attention may move from the reconciliation of the offender to his or her punishment.* Under this misunderstanding, instead of restoration, one seeks to inflict on the guilty party some suffering to compensate for the suffering caused; at least the suffering of public humiliation. This may be thought of as a right,

11. For a discussion of the "gifts" in the New Testament context, see my *The Fullness of Christ* (Elgin, Ill.: Brethren Press, 1989).

or a need, of the offended people or group for some kind of vengeance; or it may be thought that the "moral order" somehow demands it, or that the guilty one himself or herself needs chastisement.

B. *The attention may move from the person to the offense.* Big offenses call for big punishment, small ones for lesser measures. These standards are the same regardless of the person involved. Concern for "fairness," that is, uniformity in application, replaces the unpredictability of dealing with one offense at a time.

C. *Concern may move from the offender to the "standards."* Strict observance of the rules is thought of as necessary to reassure the group of its righteousness, or to teach other members the seriousness of the offense, or to justify to the surrounding world the church's seriousness. The brother is then less important to the church than its identity and reputation and standards or even than the power of its leaders that is threatened by the offender's not conforming.

D. *Responsibility moves from the brother or sister to the church disciplinarian.* The bishop or the deacon (in Protestantism) or the priest (in Catholicism) is charged *ex officio* with the duty of reprimand: (1) this depersonalizes the process, for the official disciplinarian will be farther from the offense and will be concerned to demonstrate fairness by treating all alike; (2) this furthermore undermines the other ministries that that minister should be exercising in the church; and (3) such delegation of power bypasses the express instruction of Matthew 18:15 to the effect that the first approach made to the guilty one by anyone should be "between the two of you, alone," that is, such an approach should exclude any discussion with a third party.

E. *In line with these misunderstandings, there may well develop the idea of a distinction between several categories of sin.* Public and scandalous offenses (sexual sins, theft, and murder) or ritual taboos (alcohol and dancing in pioneer Protestantism) can be dealt with in a depersonalized, puritan discipline. But talebearing, pride, and avarice cannot. The sins of the weak and sensual are magnified; those of the proud and strong are not named. Now if the New Testament authorizes any distinction at all between the several levels of different kinds of sin — which is challengeable — it would be the other way around.

We may sum up this constant temptation to deform the binding and loosing experience with the word *puritan.* It is this abuse that has given terms like *discipline, admonish,* and *reprove* a distasteful ring in our ears. The puritan is concerned to impose the right standards on a whole society; Jesus and the free church are concerned to see the fellow believer grow freely in the integrity with which he or she lives out the meaning of a freely made commitment to Christ.

Discussion questions on the misunderstanding of discipline

- Can you illustrate from experience any of the reformations listed above?

- Talk back; are there any understandings listed above as "misunderstandings" that you think are correct? Why?

- Can you see some other reasons for the repeated loss, with the passage of time, of the practice of fraternal discipline?
- Is the above outline right in rejecting the idea of "punishment"? Does society need to punish the offender? Does the offender need to feel punishment? Does the moral order call for it?

10. Misunderstandings of the Meaning of Love

The expression of evangelical forgiveness and discernment can just as easily be lost in the reaction against puritanism, which in the name of love leaves the individual alone with his or her struggles, guilt, uncertainty, and mistaken certainties. Once the puritanical approach has been discredited by its friends and undermined by the pressure of the larger society (which in its demands for conformity at other points is, however, also a backhanded kind of puritanism), the undiscerning and adolescent reaction that comes most easily is that of letting every individual be his or her own master.

A. This failure to intervene may be explained (sincerely or in cowardice) in terms of "love" or "acceptance" or "respect for individual difference" or "leaving him or her free to work it out for himself or herself." There is an element of truth in this feeling; it is understandable to the extent to which puritanism is assumed to be the only alternative. But the procedure commanded by Jesus is also an expression of "love" and "acceptance" and still "lets him or her work it out himself or herself."

During the first generation of reaction against a puritanical heritage, people may have sufficient moral rigor built into their reflexes that they may seem to be able to get along with a great degree of individual autonomy and still not loose their moorings. Yet once the backlog of puritanical certainties is no longer there to lean upon and to react against, it again becomes visible that individual freedom is a most deceptive and loose kind of conformity to the world.

B. There is the excuse of modesty. Who am I to say that he or she has sinned because I, too, am a sinner, because I don't know his or her situation ("sin" is, after all, a relative matter), or because everyone must find his or her own way?

We can agree that no one knows the offender's situation quite as he or she does. This is why the one who reproves the offender must "go to him or her alone" instead of judging the person a priori for what he or she is thought to have done. This approach thus safeguards all the valid concerns of what is currently advertised as "situation ethics."

It is true as well that we are all sinners; but Jesus does not let the duty to forgive depend on one's own sinlessness; he precisely says that it is those who are forgiven who must forgive.

C. The excuse of "maturity": if I am emotionally strong I can forgive and forget without bothering the brother, the sister, or the church. This attitude, which can be the sincere expression of a forgiving spirit and of wholesome emotional resilience, is based on the mistaken assumption (see above, sec. 5B[1]) that the concern of the process is for the one offended rather than for the offender.

D. The idea of blanket forgiveness by virtue of theological understanding or by liturgy:

1. Forms that prescribe the phrases for the routine confession of sin and the assurance of forgiveness are part of the regular liturgies of the Anglican and Lutheran communions.
2. Anyone who knows, as any Christian should know, that God is a forgiving God can apply this knowledge to herself or himself as a purely mental operation and thus have the assurance of one's own reconciliation.
3. Anyone accustomed to the diluted "lay" forms of popular contemporary psychology knows that "self-acceptance" is for the contemporary person a possibility, a virtue, or even a duty. Thus, knowing it should be done and therefore must be possible, one may seek consciously to "forgive oneself."

E. The anti-Roman Catholic argument that forgiveness is not within the authority of the church. As at other points, some Protestants have been driven by their anti-Catholicism to become unbiblical. The medieval Catholic penitential practice involved some definite abuses:

1. Limiting the forgiving function to a sacramentally authorized priest.
2. Tying it to a prescribed set of acts of penance.
3. Trying to make it consistent, legal, impersonal, impartial, so as to apply in the same way to all without favoritism (the same deformation as in puritan Protestantism).
4. Leaving room for the idea that the sin is "made right" not wholly by forgiveness but also partly by reparation or penance.
5. Linking absolution to the church hierarchy's control of the means of grace.

There is in all these abuses no reason to reject the offering of words of pardon from one believer to another.

F. Individualism seen in its various forms: as a modern humanist philosophy making each person a law unto himself; or as an antipuritan reaction denying that it is the business of the church to reach common decisions about contemporary faithfulness; or as a spiritualist glorification of guidance or illumination received immediately by the individual.

G. Arguing that the church should preach about sin or sinfulness but not deal with specific sins or specific sinners.

H. All of the above distortions relate to the application of reconciling concern to moral offense; the other possibility is to call into question the principle of morality itself as a common concern. Many contemporary currents of thought, within and without the church, challenge whether a common Christian moral position is attainable or desirable or binding.

This argument needs to be faced honestly. But for present purposes we must only recognize that it is a quite different question from the ones we have been dealing with thus far. The New Testament and Christians until modern times agreed that such moral consensus is desirable. With those who challenge this, the argument must be carried out on a different basis and a different level from the present outline.

11. Diversions and Evasions

A. The mechanical detour. Since, as we have seen, the two dimensions of discernment and forgiveness, or decision making and reconciliation, are intimately mingled, every estrangement between people also has about it a difference in discernment: a conflict about fact or about proper procedures or wrong policies. Differences in opinion or policy are both causes and effects of personal disharmony.

It is, therefore, no surprise that the "detour" of attention to mechanics is frequently resorted to. Divided about principles or people and unwilling to face the strain and threat of reconciliation, we concentrate instead on procedures. The prospect of loving frankness, with admonition and forgiveness flowing freely both ways, is threatening by its unfamiliarity. Ours is an age of great psychological and sociological self-awareness, which heightens the consciousness of the threat. Ours is also an age of great organizational concern, which increases our ability to find ways to avoid such an open meeting of souls.

(1) There is evasion by compromise, bypassing an issue without resolving it, hoping it will resolve itself.

(2) There is evasion by superior power, overcoming the other not by reconciliation but by maneuvering, by parliamentary or administrative methods.

(3) There is evasion by appeal to outside authority. That authority may be an expert in sociological theory or management methods, or in theological correctness or empirical research, who is called in to provide us an answer without opening up the personal dimensions.

Calling in the outsider depersonalizes the issue. Should the outsider take "our side," this is powerful confirmation of our rightness that we can ask everyone to submit to, whatever may have been the personal feelings. Should he or she take "the other side," we can bow to authority with less "loss of face" than would have been involved in listening and submitting to the sister or brother.

B. The therapy detour. A detour is also possible by taking the matter to a counselor whose solution is felt to be preferable because it is given by a "doctor figure" rather than a sister or brother:

(1) One is not otherwise personally or socially related to the healer figure; both "doctor" and "patient" deal with one another as roles rather than as people.

(2) The "doctor's" very involvement in the problem labels the trouble as "illness" rather than "blame," so that one feels less responsible.

(3) The "doctor" is sure to accept me, for that is his or her role.

(4) The "doctor" solves my problem by virtue of technical competence and not through personal commitment to me.

(5) The "doctor" serves me for payment; once payment is made there is no more hold on me, and I need feel no debt of commitment to the person or of gratitude.

(6) I can trust the "doctor" to keep my problem confidential.

This characterization of the therapeutic counselor is not meant to be an evaluation; our only point here is that this resource is different in kind and in function from that of the community.

C. Evaluations related to an incomplete view of human nature. In one way or another all of the misunderstandings that stand in the way of a confident and loving binding and loosing are variations on a basic misconception of human nature. If we think of ourselves as normally not in need of admonition and restoration and guidance from the brotherhood, then we think of the procedure described in Matthew 18 as exceptional, for use only in extreme cases.

(1) We would hope not to have to apply it often, and then only after other means of evasion or of indirect pressure had failed.

(2) We would hope, as serious, well-intentioned Christians, not to need such treatment ourselves.

(3) We would withdraw from exercising this ministry to others if in need of it ourselves.

(4) We would "hesitate to make an issue" of another's peculiarities, as long as they were within the limits of the tolerable.

(5) We consider the need for this admonition to be itself a sign of blameworthy weakness. We tend to look down on the person who needs it and respect instead the irreproachable person. Thus we are on the way toward the puritan deformation again.

(6) We see no direct connection between this matter and the gospel, since by *gospel* we mean a kind of general graciousness of God toward sinfulness in general rather than concrete forgiveness for oneself or one's sister or brother. We seek instead to fix a great gulf between divine and human forgiveness.

(7) We concentrate our attention on an initial Christian experience of conversion and regeneration, or on a specific second experience of sanctification brought about by God alone. These emphases in many cases can become a denomination's special emphasis and can be identified and spoken about more easily. They may even help us to think that, following this divine work, daily forgiveness should be less necessary.

D. Hindrances in unbelief: Thus far, our analysis of how churches lose the reality of forgiving fellowship has assumed the best of intentions, as if misinformation were keeping Christians from doing what would otherwise be easily attained. It certainly is possible that misunderstandings and erroneous teachings can stand in the way of knowing and thereby in the way of doing right. Yet ignorance or misinformation only complicate the problem; they do not create it. The real reason we do not go to our brother or sister lies in disobedience; that of the individual or of the community.

The individual neither loves sufficiently nor believes sufficiently in the renewing power of the Holy Spirit to go to the other when it is one's duty, when both the outer command and the inner awareness are clear despite all misunderstandings.

12. The Price of the Neglect of This Function of the Church

A. We are not faithful. This failure to be the real church in which the Spirit works shows up in a sense of formality and unreality in the life of the congregation. More and more we have the feeling that we are going through the motions of what was meaningful in another age and that the real depths of concern and of motivation are not touched in what we speak about when we are together.

In the absence of clear devotion to this central working of the Spirit by which the church is defined, we tend to take refuge in other good works and other manifestations of the presence of the Spirit, which, although good, constructive, and proper in their place, are nevertheless not equally indispensable.

In the more "respectable" segments of Christendom these secondary works are focused in the areas of Christian nurture and social action. In the more "enthusiastic" portions of the church the concentration is on the outwardly ecstatic aspects of the Spirit's working. The concentration on the "respectable" or on the "enthusiastic" works of the Spirit (as well as the almost universally accepted assumption that the two are mutually exclusive) is but a sign of the loss of the living center in which a functioning congregation would hold in genuine unity the entire range of the Spirit's gifts.

B. We are not forgiven, and we are not guided. The widespread success of secular and sub-Christian sources of forgiveness and guidance in society (psychiatry, Peale-ism, astrology, Ann Landers and Abigail Van Buren) are testimony to the lostness of living without the forgiving and discerning resources of fellowship. Here we see the desperate and irrational lengths to which people will go to find a substitute.

C. But the real tragedy is not that individuals within the larger society are without guidance and without forgiveness; it is that as church we have come to respect as a sign of maturity the willingness to live with directionlessness and with unreconciled divisions and conflicts. We reject as immature or impatient those who would argue that something definitely must or must not be done.

We make a virtue of the "acceptance" of intolerable situations rather than of the obedience in openness and forgiveness that could transform situations. Especially we have come to "live with" a situation in which, as a defense against "defenders of the faith" whose methods in the past were less than redemptive, we are satisfied with trying to do a decent job day by day without taking responsibility for the direction in which churches and their institutions are evolving. A sense of not knowing where to turn next is pervasive among denominational leaders.

D. The church that does not forgive is not a missionary church. A great mass of contradictory testimony springs out of the widespread recognition of the ineffectiveness of the Christian churches before their missionary task. For some, the corrective should be a renewed dedication to the forms of message and ministry found effective in other ages, in the confidence that it is adequate if preached with conviction.

For others, the message must be "translated" into another more relevant idiom in order to "communicate." For others, it is the "structure" of church activity that must change to fit the new urban world. For still others mission itself must be redefined to refer to all the wholesome contributions the church makes to society, independently of winning the allegiance of additional individuals.

These discussions are worthwhile in their own right, yet the danger is great that they become a substitute for the church's being the forgiving and discerning fellowship of which we are speaking. No juggling of vocabulary or of agencies or of times and places and forms of meeting can fill the vacuum where fellowship is missing. Yet where believers do interact in reconciling love, the tool is at hand for changing both societies and personalities.

13. Wider Implications

This outline has intentionally been kept simple and practice-oriented, since it is on the level of simple obedience to a clear duty that we usually go astray. Yet if this task were tested by and related to broader kinds of theological meditation, or other ways of understanding and helping humanity, the import of what we have been discussing would be all the stronger.

A. The human is a social being, not by error or by compromise but by nature and by divine intent.

After centuries of trying best to understand the person as a spirit in a hostile body or an individual in a hostile world, both theology and psychology are seeing that what one is is not separable from the network of one's social relationships. Thus healing, whether from sin or from sickness, is inseparable from the healing of human relationships.

B. The work of God in the whole biblical story, from Abraham to Pentecost and from Adam to the New Jerusalem, is the creation of covenant community, in which the loving relationships are the outworking of people's obedience to the reconciliation worked for them by God. Salvation is not just fishing single souls out of the mass for a privileged destiny; salvation is loving human relationships under God.

C. The witness of the church is not only the verbal message of public preaching; in a day of cheapened words this may become the least important language, especially for the outsider. The witness of the church always includes and may sometimes center upon the quality of personal relationships that even the outsider may observe.

D. We may be humiliated, but we should not be surprised to discover that Christian duty is also secular good sense. Current techniques in institutional and industrial management replacing hierarchical authority by group decision processes, commending frankness as more efficient than deviousness, are now recognized as good (that is, efficient) practice.

E. The readiness not only to forgive but to make forgiveness the instrument and the standard of all church experience is of a piece with the broader theme of suffering servanthood, the theme that stretches from Hosea and Isaiah 42, 49, 52–53 through Christ himself to the cross bearing of his disciples.

Forgiveness is not a generally accessible human possibility; it is the miraculous fruit of God's own bearing the cost of human rebellion. Forgiveness among us also costs a cross. One can go to one's brother or sister only as God came to us: not counting our trespasses against us. Forgiveness does not brush the offense off with a "think nothing of it"; it absorbs the offense in suffering love.

F. The process of binding and loosing in the local community of faith provides the practical and theological foundation for the centrality of the local congregation. It is not correct to say, as some extreme Baptist churches and Churches of Christ do, that only the local gathering of Christians can be called "the church." The Bible uses the term *church* for all of the Christians in a large city or even in a province. The concept of local congregational autonomy has, therefore, been misunderstood when it was held to deny mutual responsibilities between congregations or between Christians of different congregations.

We understand more clearly and correctly the priority of the congregation when we study what it is that it is to do. It is only in the local face-to-face meeting, with brothers and sisters in Christ who know one another well, that this process can take place of which Jesus says that what it has decided stands decided in heaven. Whether the outcome be the separating of fellowship or its restoration, the process is not one that can be carried on in a limited time and by means of judicial formalities; it demands conversation of a serious, patient, sustained, loving character. Only when people live together in the same city, meet together often, and know each other well can this "bearing of one another's burdens" be carried out in a fully loving way.

The church is defined by this process; not by a legal organization or by a purely spiritual doctrinal criterion. The church is where two or three or more are gathered in the name of Jesus around this kind of need. The synod, or the overseer from outside the congregation, may very well be of real assistance and may very well share something of the character of the "church"; but there is no way whereby such people or mechanisms could replace the process of loving and binding fraternal conversation.

G. If we understand deeply enough the way in which the promise of the Holy Spirit is linked to the church's gathering to bind and loose (Matt. 18:19–20), this may provide us as well with a more wholesome understanding of the use and authority of Scripture. One of the most enduring subjects of unfruitful controversy over the centuries has been whether the words of Scripture, when looked at purely as words, isolated from the context in which certain people read them at a certain time and place, have both the clear meaning and the absolute authority of revelation.

To speak of the Bible apart from people reading it and apart from the specific questions that those people reading need to answer is to do violence to the very purpose for which we have been given the Holy Scriptures. There is no such thing as an isolated word of the Bible carrying meaning in itself. It has meaning only when it is read by someone and then only when that reader and the society in which he or she lives can understand the issue to which it speaks.

Thus the most complete framework in which to affirm the authority of Scripture is the context of its being read and applied by a believing people that uses its guidance to respond to concrete issues in their witness and obedience. Our attention should center not on what theoretical ideas a theologian (isolated from the church) can dissect out of the text of Scripture in order to relate them to one another in a system of thought. As the apostle Paul says, it is for teaching, reproof, correction, and instruction in right behavior.

Let us, therefore, not be concerned, as amateur philosophers, to seek for truth "in itself," as if it were more true by its being more distant from real life. The Bible is the book of the congregation, the source of understanding and insight as, with the assistance of the same Spirit under whose guidance the apostolic church produced these texts, the congregation seeks to be the interpreter of the divine purpose in the church's own time and place.

14. Cavils and Caveats

The above basic outline has been found useful in the same form for a quarter century, with only minimal corrections needed. There has been no reason to change its account of the place of the message of Matthew 18 in the mainstream Protestant Reformation[12] or in the Anabaptist movement.

There would, however, be reason to move farther along in three directions than the original outline intended to do. None of these can be pursued in depth here, but each should be noted.

If taken seriously, simply in the practical life of Christian communities, would it work? The original outline intentionally left this question in the form of a simple exposition of the biblical message; but that should not mean that significant objections as to realistic feasibility would not need to be taken account of.

A. In the nineties there is a much more widespread awareness than obtained in the sixties concerning the way in which human relations are predisposed by considerations of power and status. The initial imperative, "Go to your brother or sister, between the two of you" may now be thought by some to be unrealistic. It seems to presuppose that the brothers and sisters are equals, so that anyone who is aware of an offense is empowered to admonish and anyone who needs admonition is committed, by virtue of the baptismal covenant, to be addressable. But if the offense itself involved an abuse of power, how can one

12. John H. Yoder, "Martin Luther's Forgotten Vision," *The Other Side* (April 1977): 66–70.

expect the victim to have the courage to address the perpetrator? Does such a requirement not merely reinforce the offender's control of a skewed relationship? In settings where the recovery of concern for reconciliation overlaps with awareness of power abuse, there are thus many who simply would set aside Jesus' guidance as not relevant. The issue is worthy of analysis.

(1) The level of dialogue where this point tends to be made is often superficial. One often sees the point argued in short letters to church papers, in which there is no serious wrestling with the possibility that behind the literal meaning of the words of Jesus (which the children of naive biblicists or fundamentalists enjoy setting aside) there might be a deep understanding of the nature of reconciling social process. "We need not take it literally" is just as naive a way of reading texts as is "we must take it literally."

(2) It is not the case that to respect Jesus' words would obligate the victim to make herself vulnerable to being overpowered again by the offender. As was already spelled out in the original version of the above text, it is a mistake to think that the first purpose of admonition is to meet the victim's need to purge her pain or resentment. In either of two ways, the straightforward meaning of Jesus' guidance compensates directly for that weakness.

The very first imperative empowers the victim with the mandate to confront; but the second imperative heightens the corrective. "If your brother or sister will not listen, take with you two or three." Here the power imbalance is radically reversed. Or one could also understand that the intervention of a third party, if informed about an offense whose victim does not feel capable to talk back, would constitute the first step of reconciling address.

(3) Those who so easily set aside the direct approach to the offender usually do not make clear what other alternatives are thereby opened up. Is the better recourse to call on the state? the press? a discreet ecclesiastical agency? Any other path decreases the likeliness of convincing and healing. Some alternative recourses might retain Jesus' stated concern for ultimate reconciliation and for the implicit room for truth-finding as to the original offense, which Jesus' guidance provides; but some do not. Some seek to correct for one unilateral use of power by another use, equally unilateral, of even greater power. Thereby what is sacrificed is not merely (as we were told at first) a superficial part of Jesus' procedural guidance but also Jesus' ultimate reconciling intention.

B. The procedure Jesus called for is radically decentralized, as was the life of the synagogue in the age of Jesus. "Tell it to the church" means that every local community is responsible. Will that not make for diversity that will confuse people and in fact even discredit the process?

(1) One pitfall under the heading of "decentralization, diversity" arises when we take stock of the fact that the criteria whereby people will state their belief that "your brother or sister has sinned" are often matters on which sincere believers differ. Killing in war is a sin for a Mennonite congregation and not for a Lutheran one. Knowing of the presence of other churches with different

standards may well undercut the readiness of the person being admonished to grant the nature of the offense.

A part of the answer to this worry is the fact that the admonition is based on the covenant of the congregation that the individual voluntarily joined. If he or she voluntarily joined a Mennonite congregation and not a Lutheran one, he or she is asking for pacifism to be part of the discipline.

Yet the membership covenant cannot involve a full prior catalog of all possible offenses to avoid. There may and should well be cases where the individual admonished does not grant the wrongness of the deed. This is not much of a problem in the first generation of the life of a very cohesive community. It becomes more delicate if the community in question maintains cooperative and fraternal relations with other Christian bodies who think otherwise. The problem may also get worse in the measure in which leadership separates the meaning of discipleship from the meaning of membership; that is, if the notion is accepted that some components of Christian obedience are optional, matters of idealism rather than obligation. This is a set of questions that Jesus was not addressing. It may well be that there will be some issues in the divided church on the modern scene where the Rule of Christ will not suffice to resolve all questions.

(2) A weightier handicap of local autonomy is the possibility that the regular application of this procedure might quash valid prophetic vocation. At first view the procedure seems to be biased in favor of enforcing recent customs, which often have much wisdom behind them but cannot be infallible. The process is also biased in favor of the squeaky wheel; it will give more of a hearing to those persons who are more ready to complain and to intervene. The history of discipline procedures that have gone wrong in the past should be sufficient to warn us that this danger is real.

The corrective for this danger is, however, not to abandon the vision (in favor of what alternative?) but to implement it with still greater understanding and sensitivity. To provide for ways to respect the rare but real possibility of the utterly isolated dissenting individual being right, the community must have ways to record the nuances of the more difficult decisions. Sometimes it should be recorded that a member submitted without being convinced, in the interest of the peace and the ongoing momentum of the community. Then the community thanks the member for that submissiveness and recognizes that he or she might in fact be right. Thereby the door is held open for reviewing the question later, especially if new evidence should arise. Sometimes the strong dissent of an individual who refuses to be convinced and also refuses simple withdrawal may be dealt with by a postponement.

This does not mean, however, that the communal decision structure would be crippled by every case of dissent or that some other mode of locating responsibilities (an absentee bishop? a synod?) would be more fair, more sure, or more loving.

C. One more reason, both practical and moral, for not bypassing the sinner in the process of admonition is that there needs to be a concern for clarifying the truth of the accusation. There are truths that are not "the whole truth" or "nothing but the truth." There are cases of dramatic memory, especially if the memory is retrieved after the passage of time or in a process of therapy, where the offense is seen in the light of other times or places or persons. Some accusations are only partly true by no fault of the accuser; even more so if the accounts are received indirectly.

Some sincerely intended accusations deal not only with what happened but also with what was intended; sometimes that is surmised rather than known firsthand. The guilty person should be allowed to say "that was not what I meant" as well as "that is not what happened." Some accusations are in fact inflated or slanderous or malevolent.

In this setting the secular courts recognize a truth-finding obligation that includes the accused's opportunity to "confront the accuser." If in a society aware of the psychodynamic biases the notion of "confronting" is less apt, out of concern for the victim's vulnerability, the concern for truth finding should be no less. The accused has a claim, and the stated reconciling intention of the process of admonition has a stake, in giving the accused an opportunity to test the fullness and the fairness of the accusation. If for special reasons the accuser and the accused cannot at first converse "between the two of you, alone" then the other parties who become involved in the second or the third phase have an obligation to make up for the gap in the process, rather than leapfrogging over the truth-finding phase.

15. Textual Fine Points

A. The phrases "to bind," *la'asor,* "to loose," *lehatir.*

The classic scholarly summary of the usage of this pair of terms in rabbinic Judaism is provided in the (German) commentary of Strack and Billerbeck (Munich, 1923, pp. 738ff. dealing with Matt. 16:18–19).

In the *Theological Dictionary of the New Testament*[13] Professor Büchsel, author of a very brief article on "binding and loosing," agrees that the *halakah* meaning of moral decision making was the standard usage yet denies that Jesus could have meant this. The denial is dictated, however, not by dictionary considerations but by Büchsel's own theology. The article by J. Jeremias on "keys" is more helpful.[14] He points out that the scribes claimed this same authority (Matt. 25:13).

B. The tense of Matthew 18:18.

The future perfect tense twice used in this verse would be rendered literally: "What you bind on earth shall have been bound in heaven; what you loose on earth shall have been loosed in heaven."

13. Ed. R. Kittel (Grand Rapids, Mich.: Wm. B. Eerdmans, 1964), 2:20.
14. *Theological Dictionary of the New Testament,* 3:749ff.

A few interpreters have sought to restrict considerably the scope of Jesus' mandate by using the future perfect restrictively, so as to mean "You should bind on earth only what has already been bound in heaven." Their practical pastoral and theological motivation is clear: a fear lest human office bearers speak unduly in God's name.

What "has already been bound in heaven" would be hard to know from the original context, but for the twentieth-century evangelicals who argue this point (with motivations like those cited in sections 9–11 above, especially 10E) it probably means "what is in the Bible."

This reading has been applied only in the modern version of the New Testament, translated by Charles B. Williams and printed by Moody Press (Chicago, 1952). It was argued most fully by J. R. Mantey in 1939 and refuted convincingly by Henry J. Cadbury in the same issue of the *Journal of Biblical Literature*.[15]

Suggestions for Further Reading

Jeschke, Marlin. *Discipling in the Church: Recovering a Ministry of the Gospel.* 3d ed. Scottdale, Pa.: Herald Press, 1988.

Oden, Thomas C. *Corrective Love: The Power of Communion Discipline.* St. Louis: Concordia Publishing House, 1995.

White, John, and Ken Blue. *Healing the Wounded: The Costly Love of Church Discipline.* Downers Grove, Ill.: InterVarsity Press, 1985.

Yoder, John Howard. *Body Politics: Five Practices of the Christian Community before the Watching World.* Nashville: Discipleship Resources, 1992.

15. J. R. Mantey, "The Mistranslation of the Perfect Tense . . . ," *Journal of Biblical Literature* 58 (1939): 243ff.; Henry J. Cadbury, "The Meaning of John 20:23, Matthew 16:19, and Matthew 18:18" (ibid., 251ff.).

Chapter 7

Reconceiving Practice in Theological Inquiry and Education

Craig Dykstra

Editor's Introduction

At first glance, it might seem a bit odd to include in an ethics textbook an essay about theological education. After all, what ethical issue is at stake? But since ethical reflection is far broader than the scope of moral quandaries, attention to practices that constitute the Christian tradition is entirely fitting. As "people of the book," we must think deeply and clearly about theological education, because it is one such tradition-constitutive practice. In this light, the following article by Craig Dykstra is instructive because it clarifies MacIntyre's analysis of practices and uses this analysis as the basis for constructive suggestions of ways that theological education might be bettered.

Theological education, argues Dykstra, is burdened with an ill-fitting load. Theology is commonly depicted as a form of technology; the lone theologian is a technician who through technical expertise (preaching the sermon, teaching the class, writing the article) causally effects change in the generic recipients of these activities. Excellence in theology in this view involves, at least in part, mastery of the techniques that are uncovered by the social sciences and by which the theologian finesses some desired outcome from his or her audience. But, objects Dykstra, human relations are not necessarily mechanical, nor is knowledge necessarily technical. How well one does theology, and how clearly one sees theological truths, is a function of one's personal character and involvement in the subject matter. Therefore, this way of construing theology remains "harmfully individualistic, technological, ahistorical, and abstract."

Dykstra prescribes an appropriation of MacIntyre's notion of practice in order to give us fresh tracks to run upon. The salient features of this alternative contrast strikingly with the received account. First, the theologian-as-practitioner does not aim primarily at *unilateral* dissemination of information. Rather, when theological education is understood in terms of a MacIntyrean practice, what comes into view is a complex interplay of human activity that depends upon intentional participation of *parishioners* as well as pastors, *students* as well as professors, and the engagement of all with voices from their common history. This way of putting things illustrates the narrative weave of the Christian community in which individual life stories intersect in such practices as worship, witness, and theological education.

Second, only by a participation of the sort that involves one's whole self can the moral and cognitive faculties of each community member be adequately sensitized to recognize what is *good* about theology. The goods of a practice cannot be seen from the outside (that is, from the side of triflers and other nonplayers). The goods of a practice can be seen only from the inside, from the side of the practitioner. Therefore, far from being an abstract enterprise, theology is a very practical exercise whose good is nothing less than a way of life. As this good has been championed by each generation of Christians and handed down from one generation to the next, conversation with our theological forebears is essential to our understanding of what human life is all about. Another way of making this same point is to say that the Christian tradition is a narratively extended quest for a singular *telos.*

Third, not only does this model overcome the individualistic, abstract, and ahistorical tendencies of the standard view, because theological education aims at cultivating a practiced way of living, but Dykstra's model abandons the technological criterion (namely, "effecting change") for the practical skill of living faithfully to our tradition. As traditions are constituted, at least in part, by their practices, living faithful to the tradition is identical to participating in the practices. If Dykstra is correct in identifying theological education as one such distinctive practice of the Christian tradition, then he is consistent to conclude that theology, thus construed, cannot be given up without sacrificing our very identity: "Communities do not just engage in practices; in a sense, they *are* practices."

Dykstra's application is not without practical difficulties. For example, the fact that we live in a pluralistic context implies that the integrity of Christian practices may be threatened by the sheer number of diverse *non*theological (which is to say, *secular*) practices (for example, vocation and politics) which are also part of our contemporary lives. Nevertheless, Dykstra remains faithful to the MacIntyrean view by reminding us that since practices contribute to our identity as Christians, participation in the theological form of life is not simply appropriate, it is nonnegotiable.

BRAD J. KALLENBERG

A Fundamental Problem in Theological Education

Theology and theological education are burdened by a picture of practice that is harmfully individualistic, technological, ahistorical, and abstract. This conventional current picture, implicit in our imaginations and explicit in our actual ways of doing things, is implicated in many of the problems that communities of faith, theology as a body and activity of thought, and theological education in all its contexts are now struggling to overcome.

With regard to the theological education of clergy, the main focus has been on problems in "practical theology" as a department of teaching or area of study. Some (particularly professors in other departments) say that practical theology is too much oriented to teaching people how to carry out certain procedures in church life (such as managing conflict in a group, organizing budgets, teaching a class, giving a sermon, or counseling a couple having marital difficulties). Others (particularly recent graduates who don't know how to do these things) plead for more of such teaching, not less. Some regard practical theology as far too untheological and overly dependent upon such nontheological disciplines as psychology and sociology and studies in organizational behavior and communications theory. Others say that practical theology is not disciplined enough by the social sciences, is always picking up what has become popularized and out of date, and thus is trailing years behind and is superficial at that.

The confusion regarding these and many other problems is so great that, according to Edward Farley,

> "practical theology" may prove not to be a salvageable term. The term is still in use as a term some seminary faculty members use to locate their teaching in the curriculum of clergy education. As such it functions more as a rubric for self-interpretation and location on the curricular map than a name for a discrete phenomenon. So varied are the approaches and proffered definitions of practical theology in recent literature that it is not even clear what is under discussion.[1]

The problems redound not only on practical theology, however. The inadequacy of our current picture of practice also creates problems for other areas of theological study and theological education. When practice means the application of theory to contemporary procedure, then biblical studies, history, systematic theology, philosophy, and ethics all become theoretical disciplines in which practice has no intrinsic place. This is a problem not only because of the usual pedagogical complaints heard about such disciplines by those who want from them something immediately usable but also for reasons intrinsic to the meaning of the disciplines themselves. For when practice is rightly understood, the "academic" disciplines are themselves seen to be practices; it also becomes clear how their subject matter includes practices. Thus, when "practice" is entirely relegated to something called "practical theology," certain features intrinsic to the "academic" theological fields are hidden; they themselves become distorted, fragmented, and overly dependent upon and conformed to university

1. See "Interpreting Situations: An Inquiry into the Nature of Practical Theology," in *Formation and Reflection: The Promise of Practical Theology,* ed. Lewis S. Mudge and James N. Poling (Philadelphia: Fortress Press, 1987), 1. For a sampling of some of the proposals Farley refers to, including Farley's own, see the various chapters in *Formation and Reflection;* Don S. Browning, ed., *Practical Theology: The Emerging Field in Theology, Church, and World* (San Francisco: Harper and Row, 1983); and the many articles and books referred to in the bibliographies included in these two works.

disciplines and their secular, Enlightenment assumptions; and their own point, or *telos,* as dimensions of theological study is then obscured.

A major problem for congregations, as Farley has pointed out, is that congregations are left without theological study altogether when theological study is identified with "clergy education."[2] This is a tragic loss. But the answer is not simply to reduplicate clergy education in churches. This is sometimes attempted, but the outcome is almost always the transmission of some of the tips and techniques clergy may have picked up from their own studies of "practice" plus some of the "contents" garnered from their studies in the "academic" fields. And both are watered down and left bereft of the understandings, assumptions, and skills that make theological inquiry sustainable in local church settings. As a result, communities of faith are left with the effluvium of theological study.

The current picture of practice is not, of course, alone responsible for these problems. But our conception of practice does plague communities of faith, theology, and theological education in seminaries and divinity schools and needs to be revised.

An alternative to the conventional current picture is available to us, one that has potential to reorient our ways of thinking theologically about practice. Then certain dimensions of our understandings and practice of theological education, not only in seminaries and divinity schools but also in congregations, may be improved.

The Conventional Picture of Practice

What is the current picture? When we imagine practice, we see someone doing something. And when we think of practice in relation to theology and theological education, we see, I would suspect, someone doing something like preaching to a congregation, teaching a class, moderating a meeting, or visiting someone in the hospital. Usually, the person in our mind's eye is a clergyperson. This is the picture of practice that much of the church and almost all of theological education takes for granted.

The fact that we focus on clergy so readily is evidence of the pervasiveness of what Edward Farley calls "the clerical paradigm," which he says governs theological education in general and practical theology in particular.[3] This is surely a problem, for the many good reasons Farley discusses. But it is not a problem intrinsic to our understanding of practice. Were we to substitute a layperson in our minds (or in the actual situation), the basic problem with our view of practice would not be solved.[4] The emphasis on clergy is only a symptom and manifestation of deeper issues.

2. See Edward Farley, *Theologia: The Fragmentation and Unity of Theological Education* (Philadelphia: Fortress Press, 1983), chaps. 2 and 7; and esp. *The Fragility of Knowledge: Theological Education in the Church and the University* (Philadelphia: Fortress Press, 1988), chap. 5.

3. See Farley, *Theologia,* esp. 84–88, 127–35.

4. One attempted solution to problems of practice in the church is the "lay ministry" movement.

Closer to the heart of the problem is the fact that we almost automatically see some*one* doing something. It is true, of course, that the one doing something (let us call him or her the practitioner) is often doing it in the presence of others.[5] Indeed, the practitioner is doing it *to* the others, often *for the sake of* the others who are there. But notice the assumptions here. The person doing something to and for others is the one engaged in the practice. The preacher, the teacher, the counselor is the one who is doing the thing we are interested in. The others are objects or recipients of the practice. If we pay any attention at all to what the others are doing, it is in terms of the effects generated in them by the practice of the practitioner. The others are not themselves engaged in the practice. Our assumptive vision of practice is that it is something *individuals* do. This points to what I mean when I say that our current picture of practice is individualistic.

Why does our assumption that practice involves individuals doing something make the picture individualistic? After all, there is no getting away from the fact that practice does involve individuals doing things. But the problem is not what is included in the picture but what is left out. Our point of focus is the individual actor. Left out is the larger social and historical context in which individual actions take place.[6] In the alternative understanding of practice that I will be developing, practice is not the activity of a single person. One person's action becomes practice only insofar as it is participation in the larger practice of a community and a tradition.

When we think of practice, we also picture the practitioner as someone who knows what he or she is doing, and we expect that person to carry out his or her practice effectively. "Good practice" does not mean just the exercise of routine, mechanical technique. It means knowledgeable, thoughtful action. This is why we invest so heavily in the professional education of practitioners. We want them to know what to do and how to do it; we want them to recognize the point of what they are doing and to be aware of the reasons for doing something one way rather than another. They should be able to give explanations of their action. We want them, in short, to be guided in their practice by theory.

This is all good, of course — it is not desirable that people be stupid and ineffectual in their practice. But this picture is problematic in its suggestion of what most aids and forms intelligent practice.

In the case of the professional education of ministers, the social sciences have played a fairly considerable role — particularly in that part of theological education we call practical theology. These sciences seem to be quite useful in providing the kind of theory (the reasons and explanations and predictions)

Movements in this direction are important, but they often lead only to the quasi-clericalization of laypeople. This does not solve the problems inherent in our picture of practice; it only abets them.

5. When we think of practice, in fact, we rarely think of someone doing something alone, like praying or meditating on Scripture or studying a work of theology.

6. See Alasdair MacIntyre, *After Virtue: A Study in Moral Theory* (Notre Dame: University of Notre Dame Press, 1981), chap. 15, on the necessity of a social and narrative-historical account of any action that is to be rendered intelligible.

that helpfully guide action. The value of other theoretical disciplines — biblical studies, history, systematic theology — in guiding action is more difficult to discern. Usually, in fact, we cannot find ways to think of them in that role at all. These areas of study are therefore relegated to providing the "content" for practice, that is, what is preached and taught.[7] Or we take the tack that these "academic" disciplines shape the practitioners' character; teach them to be better, clearer thinkers; or help them become more discerning in their perceptions and interpretations of the people and situations in which they work — all examples of influencing practice in some indirect way.[8] Even so, making connections between the so-called academic and practical fields seems difficult, not only to students but to teachers and scholars as well.[9]

The problem, again, is with the assumptions behind the conventional picture. The picture is a technological one. We assume the theory-practice relation to be a form of the science-technology relation. "Practice" means for us "making something happen." Practitioners are not supposed just to be doing something. They are supposed to be doing something to something or someone *in order to gain some desired outcome or result.* The reasons we consider for doing any particular thing are the *effects* it generates. The criterion by which practice is evaluated is whether it produces the effects we expect. That is, the criterion is effectiveness.

When theory and practice are related in this way, the kind of theory that is particularly relevant to practice is theory that helps us understand and trace causal relationships. Under the power of this picture, what we need to know from theory is how things work. When we know that, we can see how best to intervene in their workings and influence the course of events. Theory that can help us do that is highly valued. Theory that cannot do that (or can do so only marginally) is not valuable to practice.

This way of understanding practice not only focuses our attention on issues of cause and effect; it prescinds moral questions. Moral issues are not so much excluded as kept hidden or extraneous. This is because moral questions are

---

7. It is harder to see how they provide content for what is counseled or organized, but attempts along these lines are also made.

8. In a few cases, more sophisticated connections are made, so that ways such studies can indeed provide theoretical guidance to practice become more evident. I have in mind here, as an example, Marianne Sawicki, *The Gospel in History* (New York: Paulist Press, 1988). Sawicki both rethinks what practice is (though she does not use this language to talk about what she is doing) and uses revisionist historiographical methods to get at it in the Bible and in the Christian tradition. See also two of her essays: "Historical Methods and Religious Education," *Religious Education* 82, no. 3 (summer 1987): 375–89 and "Recognizing the Risen Lord," *Theology Today* 44, no. 4 (January 1988): 441–49. The kind of thing Sawicki does requires, however, that we see the "academic" disciplines as involving practice — both as method and subject matter. And this, in turn, presses toward an understanding of practice different from that contained within the prevailing picture. It leads, I believe, to the kind of alternative I suggest below.

9. In view of this difficulty, some have simply defined the problem away by substituting the single word *praxis* for the phrase *theory and practice.* But "thought-filled practice," which is what many seem to mean by praxis, is what good practice involves anyway, and the regular appearance of the oddity "theory and praxis" proves that nothing is really solved by a name change.

made extrinsic to cause-and-effect relations, and thus to both theory and practice understood this way. When practice is procedure, its value depends upon its utility. Morality, then, has to do with the value of the results or effects of practice rather than with anything intrinsic to practice itself. Morality and practice thus become separate issues.

Again, the problem concerns focus and exclusion. We do not want people to be *in*effective. Nor should we deny the often causal relations among events, which, if we understand them, are important to know about and do something with. The problem is our too-easy assumption that *all* relations are causal; that practice is fundamentally intervention into a causal network and thus always the purposeful creation of change (especially in other people or in groups and institutions); that the creation of such change is both within our power and the point or purpose of any and every practice; and that the criterion of all practice must be an extrinsic one like effectiveness. And with these assumptions we are forced to conclude that if we do not know how or do not have the power to intervene in certain causal relations in order to make change, there is nothing to do. Lacking such understanding and ability, we are left with no practice, or else what practice there is, is mere habit or technique with no point. This is what I mean by a technological understanding of practice.

If we conceive of practice technologically, it is likely that our conception will also be ahistorical and abstract. When *practice* refers to what someone does to and for someone or something else in order to create change, and if we come to know how to do that by understanding the causal relations involved, our tendency is to focus primarily on *present* circumstances and the possibilities inherent in them. We do, of course, often try to trace what has led up to the present circumstances in order to discern better the causal relations involved, but our interest in the past is exhausted by what it can tell us about this. Furthermore, our historical interest is in the history of the current situation, not in the history of practice. Practice is *applied* to a situation — perhaps historically (or better, genetically) understood — but the practice itself is not regarded as part of the situation to be understood historically. Indeed, practice, technologically understood, can have no real history. Practices may be repeated (that is, one may do the same kind of thing in sufficiently similar situations), but each practice is essentially a singular event, beginning and ending upon its intervention into each situation. Practice has no internal history of its own.

In theological schools, the assumed ahistoricism of practice is evident in how little work is done in the various subfields of practical theology on the history of Christian education, homiletics, pastoral care, and church administration.[10] We

10. Another indication is the inattention to practice that prevails in most history departments in theological schools. Such departments normally do not give systematic attention to the practices of, say, Christian education, homiletics, or pastoral care. Nor do they seem to attempt systematic connection between the history they teach and the practices their students are supposedly going to be engaged in after graduation. There are several possible reasons. One may be that historians simply do not care about practice. Another may be that they assume that it is taken care of by

see little reason to analyze carefully the continuities and discontinuities of practice in various historical periods, traditions, and cultures. The research of this kind that does exist is marginal to the curriculum largely because its relevance to contemporary practice is so difficult to discern. When it is perceived to be relevant, it is usually as data out of which certain methods and techniques or, more generally, principles and guidelines may be recovered from earlier periods for use today.

The assumption that the value of history is the current usability of technical resources found there is an indication of what I mean by the abstractness of the current picture of practice. What we are seeking are theoretical principles and guidelines, together with tested methods, approaches, and techniques, which we regard as historically and culturally neutral.[11] We get these principles and methods mainly from contemporary theory-building and experimentation. If we turn to historical documents for help at all, we do so assuming that our task is to abstract the principles and methods from any historical narrative or tradition of which they may be a part. The tradition or context is, intentionally or unintentionally, distilled out. When we have these principles and methods, we may then employ them in our contemporary action. We understand, of course, that situations vary considerably and that our principles, guidelines, methods, and techniques must be applied differently in different situations, but we rely on theory together with direct observation rather than history or tradition to help us do this.

An Alternative Understanding of Practice

The above picture, I suggest, currently governs our understanding of practice in theology, in theological education, and to a large extent in the life of the church — particularly in the First World. This is not the only picture at all operative on the contemporary scene; nor do all of its dimensions as articulated here prevail equally in every situation. Correctives to the tendencies I have lifted up do exist in many actual situations as well as in the minds of many thinkers. Various aspects of the conventional picture and many of its implications and effects have numerous critics. Nevertheless, this remains the dominant picture and the one around which most ministers and members of congregations orient church

---

the people in the practical department. More likely, however, the current picture of practice, which both historians and practical theologians assume, keeps each at some distance from the concerns of the other, giving neither group much to think historically about. An alternative understanding of practice may provide a basis for considerable discourse. But it may also imply that the standard rubrics (Christian education, homiletics, pastoral care, etc.) are not really practices.

11. See related comments on this point in Farley, *The Fragility of Knowledge,* 10–11: "Empirical method has stunning success in understanding very specific causal relations. When isolated from all correctives, [however,] it loses the concrete reality in its complexity and, with this, the conditions of criticizing itself. Isolated, it tends to become a paradigm of reality itself, but of reality without the social and political contexts of knowledge, reality dispersed into abstract formulas or causal sequences, reality absented from the deposits of the past's wisdom. . . . Praxis isolated becomes situational abstraction."

life. It is the one that most faculty in theological seminaries take for granted. It defines for many in the "academic" fields what the "practical" department is concerned with, and few in practical departments really question that definition, even when they chafe under its effects. This picture so naturally comes to mind for so many that conscious resistance to and articulated criticism of it is required before one can function on the basis of any other.

Criticism of this picture may take place on two levels. One may criticize its implications and effects, or one may criticize the assumptions implicit in it. Both kinds of criticism are available across a broad literature.[12] But criticism, even if it is thoroughgoing, can take us only so far. What we really need is an alternative. Fortunately, an alternative is being put forward by some who have been most involved in the kind of criticism just mentioned. The picture of practice being suggested is quite different from the conventional picture in each of the aspects we have discussed. Its clearest formulation is provided by Alasdair MacIntyre, who defines a practice as

> any coherent and complex form of socially established cooperative human activity through which goods internal to that form of activity are realized in the course of trying to achieve those standards of excellence which are appropriate to, and partially definitive of, that form of activity, with the result that human powers to achieve excellence, and human conceptions of the ends and goods involved, are systematically extended.[13]

In the picture of practice carried by this definition, we do not first see an individual doing something. Rather, practice is inherently *cooperative,* so the lens broadens to include numbers of people. And these people are not doing things *to* one another so much as they are doing things *with* one another. Though each may be engaged in different specific actions, they are not doing different things. Individual actions interrelate in such a way that they constitute engagement in a common practice.

---

12. Important sources of this criticism are Robert N. Bellah, Richard Madsen, William M. Sullivan, Ann Swidler, and Steven M. Tipton, *Habits of the Heart: Individualism and Commitment in American Life* (Berkeley and Los Angeles: University of California Press, 1985); Hans-Georg Gadamer, *Truth and Method* (New York: Crossroad, 1975), and *Reason in the Age of Science* (Cambridge: MIT Press, 1981); Stanley Hauerwas, *Vision and Virtue* (Notre Dame: Fides Publishers, 1974), and *The Peaceable Kingdom: A Primer in Christian Ethics* (Notre Dame: University of Notre Dame Press, 1983); Christopher Lasch, "The Communitarian Critique of Liberalism," *Soundings* 69 (1986): 60–76; Alasdair MacIntyre, *Against the Self-Images of the Age* (Notre Dame: University of Notre Dame Press, 1978), and *Whose Justice? Which Rationality?* (Notre Dame: University of Notre Dame Press, 1988); Michael Sandel, *Liberalism and the Limits of Justice* (Cambridge: Cambridge University Press, 1982); Thomas L. Shaffer, *Faith and the Professions* (Provo, Utah: Brigham Young University Press, 1987); and Jeffrey Stout, *The Flight from Authority* (Notre Dame: University of Notre Dame Press, 1981), and *Ethics after Babel* (Boston: Beacon Press, 1988). The most important single text, however, is Alasdair MacIntyre's *After Virtue.*

13. MacIntyre, *After Virtue,* 175. MacIntyre's understanding of practice comes in the middle of chap. 14, "The Nature of the Virtues," and is developed in important ways in the next chapter, "The Virtues, the Unity of a Human Life, and the Concept of a Tradition." I am not able to discuss all the important connections between these ideas in this brief essay, but they provide an important context for understanding what this picture of practice involves and implies. For a briefer but extremely helpful presentation of MacIntyre's understanding of practice, see Stout, *Ethics after Babel,* chap. 12.

Jeffrey Stout's favorite example of a practice is baseball.[14] Baseball simply cannot be played alone. It is fundamentally cooperative. If you can't get a team together, you can't play the game. The players are gathered together, however, not in order to do different things *to* each other but to do one thing together — play baseball. Each player does, of course, do many things individually. We might see, for instance, Nolan Ryan pitching and Jose Canseco batting, while others are fielding, stealing bases, or watching from the dugout. Each of them, at a particular time, is doing something distinctive and individual. But at the level of practice, they are all doing the same thing — playing baseball.

Even this formulation may be too limiting, however; for the practice we have just been describing is "playing baseball" rather than "baseball itself." In the practice of baseball itself, Tommy Lasorda managing, Vin Scully and Joe Garagiola doing the play-by-play, and even my sons and I watching games on television and Roger Angell writing about it in *The New Yorker* are all included as well. A practice involves people doing things with one another, and normally at least some part of the time people will be doing what they do in physical proximity to one another. But not everyone engaged in a practice need be physically with others in order to participate.

Practice does not reduce to group activity. On the one hand, you do not have to be in a group to be participating in a practice. Prayer is a practice of the church. People praying by themselves are involved in this practice. Even though they are not at the moment involved in a group activity, they are involved in a "coherent and complex form of socially established cooperative human activity." It is cooperative because we pray, even when praying alone, as participants in the praying of the church. The principle is illustrated by an example MacIntyre uses — portrait painting.[15] Painting is something an individual does, so it is hard to see how this is a cooperative human activity. But the cooperation comes not primarily through persons interacting physically so much as it does through persons in activities that gain their meaning from the *form* that emerges through a complex tradition of interactions among many people sustained over a long period of time. Portrait painting and private prayer are in this way socially established forms of human activity, just as baseball is.

Conversely, the mere fact of a group of people doing something together does not mean we necessarily have a practice. Practice is participation in a cooperatively formed pattern of activity that emerges out of a complex tradition of interactions among many people sustained over a long period of time. This is what MacIntyre means when he says that a practice is "socially established." What is socially established is a "form" of human activity. Some cooperative human activities build up, over time, patterns of reciprocal expectations among participants, ways of doing things together by which the cooperative activity is given not only direction but also meaning and significance. The form itself

14. See Stout, *Ethics after Babel,* esp. 276 and 303.
15. MacIntyre, *After Virtue,* 177.

comes to embody the reasons for the practice and the values intrinsic to it. This is why, in order to participate in a practice intelligently, one must become aware of the *history* of the practice.

A practice cannot be abstracted from its past, because the past is embedded in the practice itself. To abstract the practice from its tradition is to reduce the practice to a group activity. An implication of this feature of practices is that a practice cannot be made up, created on the spot by an individual or even a group. Because practices come into existence through a process of interaction among many people over a sustained period of time, individuals can only participate in them; they cannot create them. This does not mean, of course, that new practices never emerge or that established practices do not change. As people participate in practices, they are involved in their ongoing history and may in the process significantly reshape them. Practices may be deepened, enriched, extended, and to various extents be reformed and transformed. Individuals, usually persons profoundly competent in a practice, may have considerable historical effect on its shape and direction.

The "form" of a practice is related to its value. In order for a socially established activity to be a practice, its form must be "coherent" and "complex" enough to generate "goods internal to that form" that may be realized through participation in the practice. Taking long showers, says Stout, is not a practice.[16] As an activity, it lacks the coherence and complexity necessary for generating value internal to the activity itself. It can certainly generate "external goods" (smelling better, feeling more relaxed), but the activity itself cannot simply through our participation in it make us better people or involve us in a kind of life that is itself good. A practice may do this.

MacIntyre uses his example of the practice of portrait painting to make this point. There are two different kinds of goods internal to painting, he says. The first kind is "the excellence of the products, both the excellence in performance by the painters and that of each portrait itself." The second kind is "what the artist discovers within the pursuit of excellence in portrait painting," namely, "the good of a certain kind of life."[17] That is, things of value arise through engagement in the practice itself. Some of these things are products emerging from the practice; others are the effects of the practice on the practicing persons and their communities — including the effects on their minds, imaginations, and spirits.[18]

The goods internal to a practice can be realized, according to MacIntyre, only by participating in it, and participating well.[19] Baseball often seems an utter waste of time to those who do not participate in the practice. Only by getting inside the world of baseball, through playing the game and attending to its nu-

16. Stout, *Ethics after Babel,* 303.

17. MacIntyre, *After Virtue,* 177.

18. Or consider what Stout says about the goods internal to the practice of baseball; they are "what Mattingly achieves, Red Smith appreciated, and Steinbrenner violates." *Ethics after Babel,* 303.

19. MacIntyre, *After Virtue,* 176.

ances, do its intrinsic values become evident. And, according to MacIntyre, we come to identify and recognize these goods more clearly and powerfully as we more fully satisfy the standards of excellence "appropriate to and, partially definitive of, that form of activity." Baseball may be played well or badly. It is baseball "at its best" that most clearly reveals the values embedded in it.

Furthermore, the criteria revealed, and by which a practice is ultimately to be judged, are not entirely external criteria. Some of the criteria — indeed, often the most significant criteria — are intrinsic to the practice, criteria that constitute the practice as the practice it is. Moral standards and values are built into practices. Practices themselves bear moral weight.

We must go beyond MacIntyre, however, to make another claim about practices. Practices bear more than moral weight; they also bear epistemological weight. In the context of participation in certain practices we come to see more than just the value, the "good" of certain human activities: we may come to awareness of certain *realities* that outside of these practices are beyond our ken. Engagement in certain practices may give rise to new knowledge.

Some of this knowledge may be almost entirely somatic. A fine batter comes to "know" what a ball will do, and his body will "know" what to do to hit it. It is possible that without such somatic knowledge, other forms of cognition for which this is a prerequisite become impossible. Edward Farley reminds us also how "social relationships mediate realities [through] their capacity to effect new powers of perceptiveness" and suggests that "what is true for physical perception carries over, it seems, into the more subtle realms of insight or perceptiveness into various regions of reality; the nuances of poetry, the complex interrelations of a bureaucracy, the shadings of human vocabulary."[20]

But Farley points this out while making a deeper theological point. He argues that under certain conditions changes in perceptivity may take place that bring more than simply new perspectives on things. Sometimes new *realities* appear on the horizon to be apprehended, thus generating new knowledge. More specifically, within what Farley calls "the situation of faith" there come into being "states of affairs which at one time had no existence and which now have emerged in the course of history and individual existence."[21] In the situation of faith, these new realities include a new way of life, a new form of existence which in turn presupposes a transcendent source and ground.

It is important to ask whether participation in certain practices provides physical, social, and even intellectual conditions necessary to the knowledge intrinsic to the life of faith.[22] Marianne Sawicki has argued that the New Testament it-

20. Edward Farley, *Ecclesial Man* (Philadelphia: Fortress Press, 1975), 213.

21. Ibid., 214, 215. See also pp. 215–31 for Farley's argument concerning apprehended "realities-at-hand" and the realities they "appresent" that are not accessible to direct apprehension.

22. In raising this point, we are not suggesting that any practice in and of itself provides *sufficient* conditions. As Farley makes clear, these conditions are many and deeply interrelated. They are comprised in what he calls the "faith-world," the key structures of which are its language, the co-intentionalities of its intersubjectivity, and its experience of the redemptive modification of existence.

self makes clear that certain practices are in fact conditions to the possibility of "recognizing the risen Lord." She contends that both Luke-Acts and Matthew posit the insufficiency of their own words and stipulate that "action on behalf of the needy is not an implication of resurrection faith, but a precondition for it. Talk about resurrection is literally meaningless in the absence of such action."[23] The claim is that engagement in the practice of service is a *condition* for the knowledge of a reality absolutely central to faith — the reality of resurrection presence.

The Place of Practices in the Christian Life

We have put forward an understanding of practice that is quite different from the standard current picture. Alasdair MacIntyre's discussion of the nature of "practices" as fundamental features of the moral life has provided us a way to move forward. But in order to discern the significance of practice for Christian life, we needed to move beyond MacIntyre's historical-moral claim to make epistemological-theological suggestions. Once we have reached this level of discussion, it begins to become clear how intrinsic practices are to the life of faith.

In the prevailing picture, practice cannot be intrinsic to or constitutive of a way of life. Practice understood technologically, individualistically, and ahistorically is practice reduced to the merely functional. But things are different in the alternative picture. Our identities as persons are constituted by practices and the knowledge and relationships they mediate. Some of these are so central to who we are that we cannot give them up without being transformed. Correlatively, communal life is constituted by practices. Communities do not just engage in practices; in a sense, they *are* practices.[24]

Lacking the category of "practices," however, Farley is forced to leap from these deep-structural levels to institutions and situations or events without benefit of any mediating form of concrete social structure. His accurate awareness of the dangers to the faith-world of institutionalization makes him sometimes pessimistic about the sustainability of the life-world of Christian faith, as well as frustratingly abstract to his readers. The idea of "practices," we would suggest, provides a level of analysis more concrete than "life-worlds," less rigid than institutions, and more sustained and sustainable than situations and events.

23. Sawicki, "Recognizing the Risen Lord," 449.

24. "Practices" names what I believe Lewis S. Mudge tries to lift up as the key to understanding the social fact that "recognizably Christian communities of faith continue to exist" but must be understood as "network[s] of signifying action and interaction, both scattered and gathered" rather than as an institution or cluster of institutions. (See "Thinking in the Community of Faith: Toward an Ecclesial Hermeneutic," in *Formation and Reflection,* ed. Mudge and Poling, 107, 116–17.) Practices are indeed "networks of signifying action and interaction," and they are not to be identified with institutions. As Stout points out: "Social practices are often embodied in institutions.... Without some sort of sustaining institutions, [a] practice would change dramatically for the worse, if not collapse altogether." But institutions also "typically pose significant moral threats to the social practices they make possible," primarily because "institutions necessarily trade heavily in external goods," and such goods "can compete with and even engulf goods internal to [a] practice" *(Ethics after Babel,* 274).

Our suggestions obviously raise a host of questions on all fronts. What status do practices so defined really have? Under what conditions do certain practices in fact have power to create new perceptivities and even make accessible to us such realities as are central to the life of faith? What have been the practices by which Christian life in the world has been sustained across the centuries? What have people done, and what has their doing meant? How have their practices taken on different shape and meaning in various historical and cultural contexts? What have people come to see and know and be through participation in these practices? How has that happened? What agencies are involved — both immanent and transcendent — and how? Where are these practices still alive in some form in the contemporary world? What does participation in them involve? What are their consequences and effects? What are the grounds of their possibility?

These questions admit of no easy answers, but there are good reasons to raise them here. First, the prevailing conception of practice fails even to generate such questions. That is a sign of its poverty. Second, to answer such questions we must cross the lines that now divide biblical studies, European church history, Reformed systematic theology, and religious education — to cite a few specific curriculum areas in contemporary theological study — from one another. And clearly, a list of pastoral activities will do us no good.

The identification, study, and pursuit of practices that are central to and constitutive of Christian faith and life are, in my view, among the signal tasks of Christian theological study. This is especially true today, when this task has been singularly neglected. Answers to questions about practices are relatively simple when we are talking about baseball or even portrait painting. But matters become quite complicated when we attend to practices that have histories often going as far back as biblical times and further, practices that have been embodied in various ways in societies and situations around the globe. Moreover, in the context of theological study, we attend to practices of a form of life that claims to bear intimacy with God as well as world-transforming power.

That there would ever be unanimity on what the constitutive practices of Christian life are or at what levels of discourse they ought to be identified is unlikely. But it is best not to strive for common agreement in any case, because some ways of construing practices may serve some specific purposes and occasions better than others. My own list includes such practices as interpreting Scripture, worship and prayer, confession and reconciliation, service, witness, social criticism, and the mutual bearing of suffering.[25] Margaret Miles's recent book *Practicing Christianity: Critical Perspectives for an Embodied Spirituality* includes a section on "practices of Christian life." What she means by "practice" is

25. I articulated this list in a previously published essay. See "No Longer Strangers," *Princeton Seminary Bulletin* 6, no. 3 (November 1985): 188–200. A revised version of this listing plus some discussion of the rationale for it appears in a paper adopted for study by the General Assembly of The Presbyterian Church (U.S.A.), which I helped to write. See "Growing in the Life of Christian Faith," *Minutes of the 201st General Assembly* (1989), Part 11 (Louisville: Office of the Stated Clerk, 1990), 38.087–38.231.

consistent with the meaning we have been discussing here, and our lists overlap. She mentions a number of practices in her introduction and devotes a chapter each to ascetic practices, worship and sacraments, service, and prayer.[26] In these chapters, she poses some of the important questions that I have suggested need to be pursued.

An essay by Michael Welker provides an excellent example of the analysis that the historical and theological intricacy of practice in Christian life demands.[27] He asks what law is and how it relates to gospel. But rather than providing an intellectual history of the concepts, he engages in an acute multidisciplinary investigation of the basic human practice of securing expectations. The question Welker pursues is this: How do people commit themselves and others to obligations to one another in such a way that public security and a social future can be corporately secured? All human communities must find some way to do this. Welker shows how a distinctive practice of securing expectations lies at the heart of Christian life, and he traces how this practice emerges from cultic and legal practices reflected in Deuteronomy, everyday social issues refracted through the narratives recounted in Exodus, as well as the theological struggles engaged by Paul in the face of Christ's death.

I wish here to recommend neither a specific list of practices nor a particular way of identifying and studying them. The point is to call for their recognition and to suggest their centrality in Christian life and, hence, in theological study and theological education. Suppose that practices central to Christian life are conditions under which various kinds and forms of knowledge emerge — knowledge of God, of ourselves, and of the world; knowledge that is not only personal but also public. Suppose that through such practices, the virtues and character and wisdom of the communities and individuals who participate in them are formed. Suppose that through participation in practices of Christian life, the community of faith comes continually to awareness of and participation in the creative and redemptive activity of God in the world. If these suppositions are sustainable, practices deserve a pivotal place in Christian formation, theological study, and theological education.

Learning Practices

Edward Farley has suggested that we recover an understanding of theology as *habitus*, "a state and disposition of the soul which has the character of knowl-

---

26. Margaret Miles, *Practicing Christianity: Critical Perspectives for an Embodied Spirituality* (New York: Crossroad, 1988), 87–144. Miles's "introduction to Part Two" contains some very helpful comments concerning the importance of both studying and participating in practices. Although her understanding of practice is usually quite compatible with the one we have been putting forward, it is not well developed, and at times she exhibits a tendency to equate practices with "exercises." This collapses a distinction that needs to be made.

27. See Michael Welker, "Security of Expectations: Reformulating the Theology of Law and Gospel," *Journal of Religion* 66, no. 3 (July 1986): 237–60.

edge."[28] I suggest that what such habitus involves is profound, life-orienting, identity-shaping participation in the constitutive practices of Christian life. If theology is habitus, then it follows that we learn theology (are formed in this habitus) by participation in these practices.

Such participation, certainly participation at any significant level of depth and understanding, must be learned. We need more than just to be included in the practices. We need to come to understand them from the inside and to study and interpret carefully the realities we encounter through engagement in them.

In order to learn them and learn in the context of them, we need others who are competent in these practices to help us, to be our models, mentors, teachers, and partners in practice. We need people who will include us in these practices as they themselves are engaged in them and who will show us how to do what the practices require. We also need them to explain to us what these practices mean, what the reasons, understandings, insights, and values embedded in them are. And we need them to lure us and press us beyond our current understandings of and competence in these practices, to the point where we together may extend and deepen the practices themselves.

People best learn practices such as these when conditions like the following pertain:

1. When we are active in them, actually *doing* what these practices involve, engaging in them personally in particular physical and material settings and in face-to-face interaction with other people;

2. When we participate in them *jointly* with others, especially with others who are skilled in them and are able to teach them to us;

3. When the people involved in them with us are, or are becoming, personally significant to us — and we to them;

4. When we are involved in increasingly broader, more varied, and more complex dimensions of them, and when the activities we engage in during these practices become increasingly more wide-ranging in their context and impact;

5. When we come more and more to connect articulations of the significance and meaning of these practices and the ways the various practices are related to one another with our own activities in them and with the reasons we ourselves have for engaging in them; and

6. When we come to take increasing personal responsibility for initiating, pursuing, and sustaining these practices, and for including and guiding others in them.

---

28. See Farley, *Theologia,* 31, 35–36, 151–73. The nature of this knowledge is "*practical,* not theoretical, habit having the primary character of wisdom" (35). Later, in *The Fragility of Knowledge,* Farley defines theology as "the reflectively procured insight and understanding which encounter with a specific religious faith evokes" (64). I prefer his earlier understanding of theology as wisdom, which includes, in my view, not only insight and understanding but also the kind of judgment, skill, commitment, and character that full participation in practices both requires and nurtures.

Participation in some of the practices of Christian life can and should occur naturally in the context of everyday life in a community constituted by them. But communities, especially in such culturally and socially fragmented situations as our own, cannot depend entirely upon natural occurrences for initiating people into these practices and guiding them in them. The situation requires planned and systematic education in these practices. But such education must never be detached from participation in the practices; it cannot be satisfactory simply to describe and analyze them from afar.[29] Nonetheless, education must order this participation in such a way that all the practices are engaged in meaningfully and with understanding at increasingly broader and more complex levels. And that presupposes systematic and comprehensive education in the history and wider reaches of the practices as well as in the interpretation and criticism of the reasons and values embedded in the practices. This is true in the theological education of children and youth as well as in the education of adults.

The range of such education is still more extensive, however. None of us lives only in communities constituted by such practices as we have articulated, and such practices never exist in a vacuum. We both live and learn in multiple social contexts and institutions, each of which is constituted by a much broader plurality of practices than those on which we have focused. Our wider intellectual, political, social, and occupational lives involve us all in a great variety of practices. And because such contexts naturally infiltrate faith communities, this broad spectrum of practices is internal to congregations, to theological seminaries, and even to convents. We all live our lives in an intersection of many practices.

29. Note Farley's discussion of the issue of education in *The Fragility of Knowledge,* 97–100, where he criticizes a current overgeneralizing of the meaning of the word *education* to the point where it encompasses every form of participation in ecclesial life. Farley calls for a more specific understanding of education, which he calls "ordered learning." The focus of ordered learning is not participation, which it presupposes, but interpretation: systematic, linguistically mediated, critical inquiry.

Though Farley is right about the need for ordered learning, he seems to restrict it primarily to the analysis and interpretation of the cognitive products of practices. Significant connections between actual engagements in the practices and inquiry carried out in a context formed through them is vastly underemphasized by Farley. Some criticize Farley's approach as being thereby too cognitive in orientation. I do not have that quarrel with him; I believe that theological education ought to be very cognitive. The reason, however, is not that our subject matter is the cognitive products of practices but that cognition is vitally important to and involved in the practices themselves.

Further, we must be careful not to fall into understandings of cognition (and interpretation) that are too limited in scope, as I believe Farley has done. Howard Gardner, in *Frames of Mind: The Theory of Multiple Intelligences* (New York: Basic Books, 1985), articulates seven different kinds of intelligence: linguistic, musical, logical-mathematical, spatial, bodily-kinesthetic, and two personal forms (one, the capacity to have access to the shape and range of one's own feeling life, and the other, "the ability to notice and make distinctions among other individuals and, in particular, among their moods, temperaments, motivations, and intentions" [239]). Each of these intelligences is somewhat distinct, according to Gardner, and each involves modes of insight, interpretation, and expression characteristic of it. Farley seems to identify both cognition and interpretation with linguistic and logical-mathematical intelligence, leaving the others completely unattended to. I would argue that *all* these forms of intelligence are involved in theology-habitus and that all of them must be systematically engaged in theological education at every level.

Theological education must concern itself with the mutual influences that various practices have on each other, as well as whatever complementarity or conflict there may be between the goods internal to ecclesial practices and others. Because we are all citizens, for example, we must inquire into the nature, effects, and implications of our simultaneous engagement in practices constitutive of Christian life and those central to public politics. We need to inquire into the continuities and discontinuities between medical practice in our society and practices of care for the ill and the dying that now are and have in the past been characteristic of the church. Various intellectual disciplines (such as physics, literary studies, and psychology) are also practices in the sense we mean. Inquiries into the relations between disciplines (including those that are theological and those that are secular) engage us in similar issues and are thus central to theological study and theological education.[30]

An Agenda for Theological Education

The understanding of practice we have been developing has manifold implications for theological inquiry and theological education. The constriction of the range of appropriate participants in theological education will need to be broken. The organization of theological study might well need to change significantly. And in response to both of these alterations, the kind of institutions responsible for theological education might well need to be significantly expanded and the educational processes structured by them considerably enriched.

Farley has ably critiqued the clerical paradigm in theological studies and the reduction of theological education to schools for clergy.[31] Theological study and theological education are appropriate to and necessary for all Christians. Once we recognize that a more significant and fruitful conception of practice refers to the ongoing and central practices that constitute the community's very life and that all its members are called to be participants in that practice, we are led to a broad vision of theological inquiry and education. The idea that theological inquiry and education are only for scholarly researchers and clergy begins to evaporate. But clergy, like others, do require theological education, and the patterns of study that now obtain in those schools powerfully influence most other institutions of theological education presently existing or likely to emerge. So I conclude by developing some of the implications of our work on practice for these schools.

Clergy, like all Christians, need to be formed and schooled in the practices of the life of Christian faith. This should not be just beginning when candidates enter a theological seminary or divinity school. Prerequisite to seminary education are not just certain studies in the liberal arts and sciences, but education in

30. Parallel observations, though couched in terms of "elemental modes of interpretation," are made by Farley, *The Fragility of Knowledge,* esp. 140–41.

31. See notes 1 and 2.

ecclesial practices. The theological education of clergy is dependent upon and should be continuous with the theological education these same people receive as laypeople.

To presuppose much of an education along these lines may be, under present circumstances, to traffic in an ideal. Seminary or divinity school education is not the first context for people's participation in the practices of the life of Christian faith; otherwise, they would not be enrolled. But it may well be their first exposure to some of them. And it is likely to be their first opportunity to explore ways in which all of the practices are carried out in contexts beyond those they have personally experienced. Because these practices, understood as practices that take place worldwide and over a long history, are so central to Christian life and community, a key task in clergy education is to insure that all students are exposed to and participate in all of these practices in some context and at some level and become aware of the breadth and depth to which these practices may extend.

The continuity of the theological education of clergy with their previous theological education is premised on the fact that clergy are involved in the same fundamental practices as are all other Christians. But clergy have some responsibilities and roles that not all of us have. They are not only responsible for their own participation in the practices of Christian life but uniquely responsible for the participation of whole communities in them. This requires that they organize these practices corporately in a particular situation and insure that the people of that community, young and old, are initiated into them, guided in them, and led in them. It requires that they work to insure that all the practices are learned by everyone in breadth and in depth, in their increasing complexity, and with ever more profound understanding. It requires that they work to insure that the practices happen and that the dangerous proclivities of the institutionalization necessary to sustaining a community in these practices do not subvert them.

Because clergy must be teachers of these practices in their own communities, it is essential that they know and understand the histories of these practices and the reasons, insights, values, and forms of judgment borne both by the traditions of which they are a part and by competent and wise contemporary engagement in them. But not only this. These insights, values, and forms of judgment are borne in Christian practices only because new perceptivities and the apprehension of distinctive, life-transforming realities gave rise to them. If the ever-fresh promise in the context of these practices is that new perceptivities are shaped and life-transforming realities are made available for apprehension in each new day, then this must be the heart of what is taught. Christian teachers are not ultimately teachers of practices; they are teachers of the gospel. The education that clergy are responsible for is education in truth and reality in and through those practices by which truth and reality may be made manifest.

This is what clergy are called to articulate and explain (or, better, expose and reveal) to others. Teachers, as they guide others in their participation in the practices of Christian life, must be able to make the inner workings and qualities of each practice available to those they teach in such a way that those workings and qualities open up to the reality and truth on which they are founded. Clergy ought to be teachers who can do this, and the theological education that clergy receive ought to help them.

The present system of curricular fields and departments of seminaries and divinity schools leaves much of this unattended. Under the dominance of the current picture of practice, practical theology attends either to other issues or to a stripped down form of practice as mere know-how. The other fields disregard practice almost entirely. But we do not have to reform the structure of departments and fields in order to ameliorate this situation considerably. Every field of seminary education currently existing has contributions to make to the understanding and interpretation of every one of these practices — if they become aware that these practices actually permeate their own subject matters and are, to various extents, actually or potentially implicated in the practice of their own disciplines.

In the Bible, for example, we can see all of these practices being carried out — and in a great variety of situations and circumstances. Moreover, the coming of the Bible into its present form is itself the engagement of a people in many of these practices, as the various forms of criticism clearly show. The case is similar with respect to the historical study of any era, dimension, text, or community of the Christian tradition. But historical studies are not the only relevant ones. The practices carry a broad and complex range of theological, ethical, and philosophical assumptions, convictions, insights, and reasonings, all of which are in need of exposure, display, and continuing scrutiny. Here the systematic disciplines come heavily into play. They are essential for helping communities and persons know what they are doing and why as they engage in these practices. They are also essential for the continuing criticism and reform of these practices, the goods internal to them, and the knowledge that they make possible.

This is not to assert that the curriculum of seminary education can or should be exhausted by attention to these practices or that the historical, theological, and philosophical investigation of these practices should define and circumscribe every field. It is more than enough to say that all of these fields and disciplines are relevant and necessary to the kind of systematic investigation and understanding of these practices that clergy require. And all of these fields could be enhanced by recognizing and making explicit this relevance and necessity.

At this point, one might ask, If education in the history and inner workings and meanings of these practices were actually taking place in the Bible, history, and theology departments of a school, and especially if this were done in relation to actual engagement in these practices, would there be anything left for a practical theology department to do? My own response to this question is ambivalent. Ideally, I am inclined to think probably not.

Realistically speaking, however, and short of an entire reformulation of the departmental structure of theological education, attending to the history, inner rationality, and truth of the practices may be enough to ask of the "academic" fields. For the time being at least, disciplined reflection on and engagement in the practices as such may have to fall to those who teach in the departments and curriculum area we now gather under such rubrics as social ethics, church and society, and practical theology.[32] This would provide a context in which the practices and their engagement in the various concrete, contemporary situations and environments in which they are carried out would be the focusing subject matter.[33] It would be the responsibility of such fields to articulate these practices, describe them, analyze them, interpret them, evaluate them, and aid in their reformation. It would also be their focal responsibility to help students participate actively in them in actual situations of the kind they do and will face in their roles as clergy.

This is a somewhat more traditional understanding of the function of practical theology departments than I myself am happy with, but even this would call for significant change in the way we currently conceive practical theology and social ethics. Furthermore, I believe that more radical revision of the current curriculum structure is unlikely, and I am sure that we will not get from where we are to where we might someday be in a single leap. Where these functions and issues do not yet permeate the curriculum as a whole, they must not be left unattended. At present, there may be no other choice than to give them to some particular curriculum area.

Even were it possible to expect these practices — and the understandings and skills intrinsic to them — to be taught within the context of other fields, there still might be some need for something in addition. MacIntyre says that "politics in the Aristotelian sense" is a practice.[34] And what politics in this sense turns out to be is the practice of "the making and sustaining of forms of human community — and therefore of institutions"; it is the practice of "sustaining the institutional forms which are the social bearers of the practice[s]" constitutive of a community's form of life.[35] This is a difficult business, precisely because of the threat that institutionalization can pose to every practice. Thus, the practice of politics requires specific understandings, skills, and virtues intrinsic to itself. And this practice, carried out in the context of the life of a particular Christian community, may well be the particular practice that defines what it means to be clergy.

MacIntyre has said that "a living tradition . . . is an historically extended, socially embodied argument" and that the argument is "precisely in part about the goods which constitute that tradition."[36] I would add that it is also about the

32. In my view, it would be helpful if ethics and church-and-society fields were regularly gathered together with the so-called practical fields under a common departmental umbrella, at least until a more radical reorganization could be configured.

33. In his essay in *Formation and Reflection* (ed. Mudge and Poling), Farley has important things to say about the theological task of interpreting situations. What I am suggesting is that the interpretation of situations be focused and ordered by their relations to practices.

34. MacIntyre, *After Virtue,* 175.

35. Ibid., 181, 182.

36. Ibid., 207.

shape of the practices in the context of which those goods emerge and the truth and reality on which they are grounded and to which they point. If all this is what a living tradition is, then the shape of theological study and the contours of theological education ought to engage deeply the elements that are vital to it. Eminent among these for the Christian tradition are the practices central to its life.

Suggestions for Further Reading

Hauerwas, Stanley. "Clerical Character." In *Christian Existence Today,* 133–48. Durham, N.C.: Labyrinth Press, 1988.

Kelsey, David H. *To Understand God Truly: What's Theological about a Theological School.* Louisville: Westminster/John Knox Press, 1992.

———. *Between Athens and Berlin: The Theological Education Debate.* Grand Rapids, Mich.: Wm. B. Eerdmans, 1993.

Willimon, William H. "Clergy Ethics: Getting Our Story Straight." In *Against the Grain: New Approaches to Professional Ethics,* ed. Michael Goldberg, 161–84. Valley Forge, Pa.: Trinity Press International, 1993.

Wood, Charles M. *Vision and Discernment: An Orientation in Theological Study.* Atlanta: Scholars Press, 1985.

———. *An Invitation to Theological Study.* Valley Forge, Pa.: Trinity Press International, 1994.

PART III

Perspectives on Contemporary Issues

Chapter 8

From Family Values to Family Virtues

Rodney Clapp

Editor's Introduction

Rodney Clapp's chapter on family and sexual ethics draws explicitly on MacIntyre's work in several ways. He uses MacIntyre's recognition of the plurality of traditions to call into question the very phrase "traditional family." In particular, he points out that the mid-twentieth-century bourgeois nuclear family is strikingly different from any traditional family that writers of the Bible would have known. One of the differences is the extent to which public and private have been distinguished in modern times and the family designated as the sphere of the private. In our day, the purpose of the family has been reduced to provision of intimacy and affection—not a function it can well serve without any more significant *telos* to hold it together.

Clapp suggests that a MacIntyrean tack on the "family values" debate would urge us to pay attention to the Christian family tradition exactly as a tradition—a historically extended, socially embodied argument. And the social embodiment of the Christian tradition is the church. In fact, he suggests, the church is the Christian's primary family.

There is irony in the fact that political conservatives couch the debate in terms of family "values." As MacIntyre would point out, to substitute the word *value* for more substantive moral language such as *virtue* is to accede to the *liberal* political agenda—the project of "founding a form of social order in which individuals could emancipate themselves from the contingency and particularity of tradition" (*Whose Justice?* 335). Furthermore, since values have no source beyond personal choice, the assertion of one set of family values over another can be nothing more than the assertion of preference.

In the second half of his chapter, Clapp attends to the charged issue of sex. Sexual attraction is not a mere biological urge but something shaped by narrative traditions. Clapp develops James McClendon's thesis that modern Christians' understanding of sex, love, and marriage has been shaped not by the Christian story but by the myth of romantic love. Only by recognizing as normative the Christian story, with its world-transforming goal, can we find adventure enough to make marital virtue more appealing than romantic yearning.

NANCEY MURPHY

The Family Values Debate

Since at least the summer of 1991, when Vice President Dan Quayle attacked a television character for her loose living, Americans have been heatedly involved in a debate over "family values." It has been a debate about profoundly important matters, usually conducted shallowly and histrionically. Sadly, though Christians have been among the main players in the debate, they have brought little real theological orientation or perspective to it. I brazenly propose, in what follows, to do exactly that — to ask what, if any, business Christians, exactly as Christians, have in fighting for family values. Brazen, but not entirely foolish, I will theologically appropriate the esteemed work of philosopher Alasdair MacIntyre. Christian convictions (for example, that Jesus' cross calls his followers to a cruciformly nonviolent way of life) will precede and adjust MacIntyre's terms and arguments. But MacIntyre's terms and arguments will help to crystallize and, I hope, point beyond limitations in the family values debate. So equipped, and focusing on a specific aspect of the family values debate, I will be enabled to suggest that the view of human sexuality presupposed in the family values debate — the sexual person as consumer — is profoundly in tension with a more decidedly Christian understanding of sexuality and family life.

The Historicity of "Family"

From at least as early as 1966, with the publication of his *Short History of Ethics*, Alasdair MacIntyre has emphasized the historical situatedness of ethics — and indeed, of all philosophy and ways of life.[1] Human beings, as historical creatures, simply cannot escape to timeless and placeless vantage points from which to view "reality" or "the way things are actually." MacIntyre has instead argued, compellingly and in detail, that particular persons and communities see and respond to the world as they do because they are situated in a tradition that significantly determines the shape of the world for them. He has accordingly rejected post-Enlightenment attempts to belittle and escape tradition, attempts to appeal instead to a universal, timeless, and placeless Reason. Without capitulating to any radical relativism (a persuasive tradition must, after all, account for physical objects, events, and other phenomena that really are "out there"), he has worked to revive respect for tradition, and to interpret tradition as something dynamic and flexible enough to negotiate the undeniable changes of history. Hence MacIntyre's famous definition of a *tradition* as a "historically extended, socially embodied argument."[2] It is "historically extended" in that the argument goes

1. Alasdair MacIntyre, *A Short History of Ethics* (New York: Collier Books, 1966).

2. MacIntyre, *After Virtue,* 2d ed. (Notre Dame: University of Notre Dame Press, 1984), 222. MacIntyre offers another, and complementary, definition in *Whose Justice? Which Rationality?* (Notre Dame: University of Notre Dame Press, 1988), 12: "A tradition is an argument extended over time in which certain fundamental agreements are defined and redefined in terms of two kinds of conflict: those with critics and enemies external to the tradition who reject all or at least key parts of those fundamental agreements, and those internal, interpretative debates through which the meaning and

on over time and "socially embodied" in that it is carried on by a community dedicated to pursuing the good as understood by that tradition.

In stark contrast, the family values debate has been carried on with blithe indifference to historical particularities. It is arguable, in fact, that much of the popularity of the term is due to its vacuousness. "Family values" are something that almost everyone can rally around, because they can in the end be defined almost as anyone would like. In the speech that ignited the debate, Vice President Quayle apparently referred to the bourgeois, heterosexual nuclear family. He worried over the "breakdown of family structure" due to "a welfare ethos that impedes individual efforts to move ahead in society." He protested against women bearing children outside marriage and quipped that "a welfare check is not a husband."[3] Quayle's references to welfare and illegitimate births were understood as thinly veiled code words for black, and especially ghetto, families.

But beyond this reference and apparent indication that true families are not on welfare, the vice president did not specify what he meant by "family values." MacIntyre would drive us to push the definition, and in so doing to pay attention to social and historical contexts. For instance, does it exemplify family values to build hardness into boys by compelling them to disturb a hornets' nest, be repeatedly stung, and suffer punishment if they cry? The Sioux believed so.[4] Does it exemplify family values to suppress a child's willfulness through fierce beatings, exhibition of corpses, and tales of castration and abandonment? The Puritans were so convinced.[5]

The debate subsequent to Quayle's speech has continued with indifference to the family values of any actual traditions, with the implicit pretense that family values are absolutely objective and obvious to anyone, anywhere, at any time. Christian proponents of family values have been especially apt to refer to the "traditional family," but without any deep MacIntyrean sense that a "traditional family" must belong to one or another specifiable tradition. Thus many of these Christians have easily elided "the traditional family" into "the natural family."

When we examine what clues we can about the "traditional family" called for by such Christian proponents of family values as James Dobson, Pat Robertson, and James Robison, it seems that they long for the bourgeois traditional family: the nuclear family, with home as an emotional haven from the heartless realities of commerce and politics, providing all religious and moral "values"

---

rationale of the fundamental agreements come to be expressed and by whose progress a tradition is constituted."

A generally compelling application of MacIntyre's understanding of tradition to theological methodology is Trevor Hart's *Faith Thinking: The Dynamics of Christian Theology* (Downers Grove, Ill.: InterVarsity Press, 1995). Hart makes the important critical point that not all Christian engagement with its own or other traditions need or should be belligerent, so that a tradition might be better thought of as a "dialogue" than an "argument" (228).

3. Cited in Lance Morrow, "But Seriously, Folks . . . ," *Time,* 1 June 1992, 29.

4. See Frances Kartunnen, *Between Worlds: Interpreters, Guides, and Survivors* (New Brunswick, N.J.: Rutgers University Press, 1994), 139.

5. Steven Mintz and Susan Kellogg, *Domestic Revolutions: A Social History of American Family Life* (New York: Free Press, 1988), 1–23, particularly 15.

for its members — values that are by definition "private" and "personal."[6] In so doing, they exalt a "traditional family" that is hardly two centuries old, a kind of family decisively shaped by the advent of capitalism and industrialization. It was these historical developments that separated nuclear families from their extended families, severely divided the world into public and private spheres, and pushed Christianity (and any other religion) out of the public sphere into the cozier but much less significant private sphere.

This says enough to suggest that Christians, with only a bit of theological reflection, ought to have some suspicions about this particular "traditional family." After all, how can we fit the confession that Israel's and Jesus' God is the Lord of the entire universe with the bourgeois relegation of God to the status of (private) household idol? It simply will not do to assume, as many eager Christian proponents of family values have, that this "traditional family" is identical with "the biblical family." It will not do, at least, if we actually pay attention to the shape and substance of biblical households. The ancient Hebrews, for instance, did not even conceive of what we call the nuclear unit apart from the extended family of kin and even servants. The average North American household of today consists of two to five people. The average Hebrew household, on the other hand, numbered 50 to 100 inhabitants. Jacob's family, we are told in the Book of Genesis (46:26) consisted of 66 people. What we call the nuclear family the Israelites saw seamlessly woven into the multigenerational extended family. Every family centered on a patriarch. Each son, with his wife, children, and (in some cases) servants, lived in a separate shelter. So a Hebrew family or household would in effect have been a small village of several adjacent buildings. What's more, these households would sometimes induct and include as members of the family aliens or sojourners who had permanently taken shelter with them.[7] The same sorts of points could be made regarding the other defining traits of the bourgeois traditional family. Hebrew culture made no sharp separation between public and private life and certainly regarded Yahweh as something much more than a household god.

Likewise, the Roman society of the New Testament period made no sharp separation between public and private life. Household relationships that bourgeois moderns consider private carried important social and political baggage in the Roman world. No doubt the home was a place of comfort and rest for family members, especially the paterfamilias, or male head. But streams of commerce and politics flowed daily through the home. There the paterfamilias paid court to clients. Clients were those he sponsored in public life, such as poets and philosophers dependent on patrons for a livelihood. So the paterfamilias's social and political obligations did not end when he crossed the threshold into

---

6. For documentation and further discussion, see my *Families at the Crossroads: Beyond Traditional and Modern Options* (Downers Grove, Ill.: InterVarsity Press, 1993), 30–34.

7. See, e.g., Judges 17:12. For information and understanding of the Israelite household, see especially Hans Walter Wolff, *Anthropology of the Old Testament* (Philadelphia: Fortress, 1974), and Norman K. Gottwald, *The Tribes of Yahweh* (Maryknoll, N.Y.: Orbis Books, 1979).

his home. If anything, they began there. These facts rehearsed, we do well to remember that the early church was based in the households of Rome. The Christians of the New Testament worshipped together in their homes, welcomed and supported missionaries in homes, assisted the poor in homes, and challenged the undue claim of Caesar in homes. On all counts, they regarded the home as something more significant, more challenging, and more exciting than a privatized, sentimentalized haven.[8]

Now none of this suggests that we could (or should want to) simply graft the Hebrew or New Testament family tradition onto our current, late modern setting. Among other things, both of these families were harshly patriarchical, even by the terms of those "traditionalists" who would today argue for a modified and milder patriarchicalism.[9] But again, MacIntyre has reminded us that traditions are not static and changeless. Standing in the Christian tradition, we are called to formation by the profound theological convictions originally embodied — however partially or imperfectly at points — in the convictions and practices of Israel and the New Testament church. Consequently a MacIntyrean tack on "family values" would urge us to problematize the family values debate by first determining *whose* or which tradition's family values are being promoted.[10] It would then pay more attention to the Christian family tradition exactly as a tradition — "a historically extended, socially embodied argument." Consequently we would have to devote more focus to the social embodiment of the Christian argument, namely the church, and much less to the isolated nuclear family (or the "American family," whatever that is).

Though I do not have luxury here to make the case in detail, I would hold that Christians should in fact understand the church as their first, or primary, family — the social allegiance most determinative of their identity and aspirations in life. N. T. Wright nicely encapsulates the theological basis of this case when he notes that, for the earliest Christians, "from baptism onwards, one's basic family consisted of one's fellow-Christians. The fact of widespread per-

8. See Paul Veyne, ed., *A History of Private Life,* vol. 1, *From Pagan Rome to Byzantium,* trans. Arthur Goldhammer (Cambridge, Mass.: Belknap, 1989), 2–205; David L. Balch, *Let Wives Be Submissive: The Domestic Code in 1 Peter* (Chico, Calif.: Scholars, 1981); and O. Larry Yarbrough, *Not Like the Gentiles: Marriage Rules in the Letters of Paul* (Atlanta: Scholars, 1985).

9. These traditionalists support what sociologists call "patriarchy of the last instance," a view of men and women that is largely egalitarian but that insists that in the event of an irresolvable disagreement between husband and wife, the husband's decision is final. Albeit certainly objectionable, this is a form of patriarchy considerably diluted and moderated from earlier, robust patriarchy, which forthrightly understood and treated women as the property of men. See Judith Stacey, *Brave New Families* (New York: Basic Books, 1990), 133–46.

10. Historian John Gillis rightly notes, "Ironically, we are . . . in the habit of updating the traditional community and family periodically so that the location of the golden age is constantly changing. For the Victorians, the traditional family, imagined to be rooted and extended, was located sometime before industrialization and urbanization, but for those who came of age during the First World War, tradition was associated with the Victorians themselves; today we think of the 1950s and early 1960s as the location of the family and community life we imagine we have lost." See Gillis, *A World of Their Own Making: Myth, Ritual, and the Quest for Family Values* (New York: Basic Books, 1996), 4–5.

secution, regarded by both pagans and Christians as the normal state of affairs within a century of the beginnings of Christianity, is powerful evidence of the sort of thing Christianity was, and was perceived to be. It was a new family, a third 'race,' neither Jew nor Gentile but 'in Christ.'"[11]

The Family Values Platform as Hanging Gallows

It seems to me that a Christian focus on the church as First Family — or the primary community and *polis* of those baptized in the name of Father, Son, and Holy Spirit — is congruent with MacIntyre's insistence that we are shaped and formed by particular communities, specific living and active traditions. In the now famous closing passage of *After Virtue,* MacIntyre called for the "construction of local forms of community within which civility and the intellectual and moral life can be sustained through the new dark ages that are already upon us.... We are waiting not for a Godot, but for another — doubtless very different — St. Benedict."[12] What I am here suggesting is that Christians already have (or are possessed by) such a community: the community called church.

So from a Christian theological standpoint, we must first of all and most determinatively ask what "family values" mean for the church. The vacuous, exceedingly fuzzy, sentimental family values of the 1990s debate do not help here because they do not locate a community whose tradition and embodiment of family they purport to represent. As I have noted with reference to Dan Quayle, when "family values" have been specified at all, they have been specified mainly in negative and oppositional terms — for example, by denouncing homosexuals or employing racist code words — and so their major effect has been to batter the already precarious civility of the American public square. Significantly, for Christians, not only do such family values fail in helping us to behave civilly (to love our neighbors and even our enemies), but they take any self-critical eyes off ourselves. Focusing debate about family values on supposed ghetto behavior and the immorality glorified in the popular media neatly lets affluent American Christians off the hook.

In truth, we live in and too often in accordance with a culture a good deal more corrupt than graphic entertainment or ghetto crime alone can indicate. It is a culture almost entirely defined by what MacIntyre calls the "bureaucratic manager," seeing people as means rather than ends, and obsessed with maximal profits as the real "bottom line."[13] So it is a culture in which family (and friendships) are viewed from the managerial vantage point of "productivity" and

11. N. T. Wright, *The New Testament and the People of God* (Minneapolis: Fortress, 1992), 449–50. For an extended biblical and theological argument of this theme, see my *Families at the Crossroads,* 67–88.

12. *After Virtue,* 263.

13. See *After Virtue,* 23–35. For an extended discussion applying this MacIntyrean insight to the subject of Christian friendship, see my *A Peculiar People: The Church as Culture in a Post-Christian Society* (Downers Grove, Ill.: InterVarsity Press, 1996), 204–11.

therefore are "invested" in until they no longer serve productivity, then are "terminated." It is a culture in which elite economists can seriously propose solving the adoption shortage by quoting baby prices like soybean futures, and where a day-care franchise can unironically call itself Precious Commodities. In the prophetic words of a post–World War II retailing analyst, we have made "consumption our way of life" and converted "the buying and use of goods into rituals" from which we seek "spiritual satisfaction."[14] In short, if we are actually going to be capable of such Christian family practices as fidelity and commitment, we need to be a good deal more radical and self-critical than sentimentalized family values will make us.

The family values sloganeering, so far, then, has foreclosed debate at just the point where it should begin for Christians. We need to ask hard questions about exactly what kind of people — what kind of families — we want to be, and whether those goals are promoted or retarded not just by our popular entertainment but by our economics as well. Family values as they are usually sketched concede the game at the start to an advanced capitalist way of life. Yet it is capitalism and industrialization that isolated and insulated the nuclear family. "Family values" as we have known them in the 1990s assume this isolation but hope to make it palatable by rendering it magnificent. The family is now not only atomized, broken off from any comprehensive institution that might give it content and purpose, but is made the very foundation of all order and morality. So Dan Quayle contended that "the single most critical threat" to society is "the dissolution of the family."[15] And the vice president's speech to the 1992 Republican National Convention was titled "The Family Comes First."[16]

How strange it is to take a family that is now a pale shadow of its former self — a postindustrial family no longer serving primary educational, economically productive, or welfare functions, one reduced to the private promotion of affection — how strange to take this family and place on it the weight of the entire society. The household that once served major social and economic purpose is now a "haven" from the "real world." It is a retreat for the wage earners and a nest for children who await true personhood in the form of maturity and independence. All it can provide is affection and intimacy, which tend to be cheapened and sentimentalized because they are not seen to have a tie to the truly significant wider world. This is affection and intimacy powerless to affect

14. Victor Lebow, cited in Alan During, "How Much Is Enough?" *The Utne Reader*, July/August 1991, 73.

15. Quoted in Steve Daley, "Quayle's rehash of 'family values' falls way short on specifics," *Chicago Tribune*, 11 September 1994, DuPage edition, sec. 4, p. 4.

16. *Vital Speeches of the Day*, 15 September 1992, 711–12. Quayle closed the speech with a promise that the Republican ticket would "build an America more secure in the values of faith, family and freedom," apparently with no sense of how these three "values" might conflict. I say more about such tensions below. Here I note that it is disastrously shortsighted not to recognize that rising divorce rates and child abandonment have something to do with the liberal, democratic, and individualistic apotheosis of freedom. This freedom is negative, only a freedom *from* community, tradition, and other strictures. As such it actively corrodes the virtues of fidelity and commitment, and it breeds no sense of constructive freedom, freedom *for* the service of some community's or tradition's purpose.

reality, affection and intimacy that quickly erode into the triviality of "warm fuzzies."

Family values, then, work against a more Christian conception of the family as a quite public and political good, family based in and defined by the *polis* of the church. And they most directly threaten to kill the family by conceding and even promoting its privatization. So doing, family values elevate the family to a platform without realizing that the platform is a hanging gallows. Family needs purpose beyond itself and its mere sentimentality to survive and prosper. As sociologist Robert Nisbet writes,

> To suppose that the present family, or any other group, can perpetually vitalize itself through some indwelling affectional tie, in the absence of concrete, perceived functions, is like supposing that the comradely ties of mutual aid which have grown up incidentally in a military unit will outlast a condition in which war is plainly and irrevocably banished....
>
> The family is a major problem in our culture simply because we are attempting to make it perform psychological and symbolic functions with a structure that has become fragile and an institutional importance that is almost totally unrelated to the economic and political realities of our society.[17]

The Trouble with Values

We are brought at last to what may be the preeminent irony of the family values debate. Though they were later touted by the likes of Bill Clinton, family values were originally presented and promoted by ostensible conservatives. But in fact the terms of the debate have been set on thoroughly liberal grounds. I refer here to the classical liberalism undergirded or championed by such Enlightenment luminaries as Immanuel Kant, John Locke, and Adam Smith. This is the liberalism that defines (and now, at least in some ways, stunts) most contemporary political argument. As MacIntyre observes, "It is of the first importance to remember that the project of founding a form of social order in which individuals could emancipate themselves from the contingency and particularity of tradition...was and is not only, *and not principally,* a project of philosophers. It was and is the project of modern liberal, individualistic society."[18]

It was classical liberalism, after all, that enshrined the privatization of family (and faith). It also enshrined the concomitant distinction of *fact* and *value. Fact* was understood, and still is widely understood, to be that which is public, universal, and self-evident to "reason." *Value,* on the other hand, was and is thought to be private, particular, and chosen by the individual.

Thus the surest sign that Quayle and company are involved in internecine liberal warfare is their very language. They battle for family *values.* MacIntyre,

17. Robert Nisbet, *The Quest for Community: A Study in the Ethics of Order and Freedom* (New York: Oxford University Press, 1953), 61.

18. *Whose Justice?* 335 (emphasis added).

of course, would call us to a quite different language — the language of family *virtues*. Classical virtues, as opposed to modern and liberal values, are not preferences that the autonomous individual creates or validates but are instead excellences or skills that precede the individual and remain objectively praiseworthy even if a particular (vicious) individual would never choose them. To accept the privatization of family, to strive for family values rather than the contentful family virtues of a particular tradition, to designate said "values" with little more than sentimental commonplaces — all this is to champion family with an unmistakable liberal pedigree. And despite liberalism's purported neutrality, the consequences of such a view for our political and common life are considerable. As Michael Sandel comments in another context, "As long as it is assumed that man is by nature a being who chooses his ends [the liberal view inherent to "values" language] rather than a being, as the ancients conceived him, who discovers his ends, then his fundamental preference must necessarily be for conditions of choice. . . ."[19]

In short, we are unavoidably mired in liberal emotivism, the view that any morality or faith or philosophy is simply the private preference of the one who professes it. And as MacIntyre notes, emotivism entails that "the choice of any one particular evaluative stance or commitment can be no more rational than any other."[20] Thus "family *values*" ironically casts matters in terms that cannot consider any type of family (or nonfamily, or anti-family) any better than another. So-called conservatives who stand on this ground are consequently poised, not even on sinking sand, but on thin air. Such proponents of "family values" are accused of being coercive, of imposing their favored picture of family on everyone else. And indeed the emotivist terms of their argument and attempted persuasion can finally allow for nothing but coercion and imposition. Emotivism, in MacIntyre's words, "entails the obliteration of any genuine distinction between manipulative and non-manipulative social relations."[21] My values — even my family values — are simply and finally only that: what I prefer or value above all other options. You, on the other hand, have your own values or preferences, determined by yourself. With no effective appeal to anything other than individually self-determined preferences, I can only "win" you to my values by trickery (manipulation) or sheer force.

So it is that the terms, conceptualities, and aims of the family values debate serve to disarm the family of what little defense it has left in a liberal, capitalistic, consumer society. After all, no one can really "choose" a mother, a father, or a particular child. Yet in liberal eyes family (like faith) can be only, at best, akin to a hobby. Blood is supposed to be thicker than water, but in the terms of liberal and family values devotion to one's family means nothing more substantial than a personal preference for blood over water.

19. *Liberalism and the Limits of Justice* (Cambridge: Cambridge University Press, 1982), 22.

20. *After Virtue*, 26. See his entire criticism of emotivism, pp. 11–35.

21. Ibid., 23.

Consumer Sexuality

In short, those Christians who argue for family values cannot help being drawn into forms of expression — and ways of life — that are radically at odds with their own professed aspirations. Perhaps this point will make more concrete sense, and gain more credibility, if we dwell at some length on a single aspect of the family values debate. I have in mind the contentious subject of sex.

Many Christian proponents of family values believe that sexuality is best constrained and channeled, and that the best place for genital sexual expression is within the bonds of marriage. Sexual fidelity is, in fact, one of the primary family "values" they are fighting for. Yet the very same champions, buying into the inherently liberal, emotivist, consumeristic conceptuality that undergirds values language, publish books and magazine articles insisting that sex is really more pleasurable if you save it until after you are married. Evangelical Christian marriage seminars, for example, offer T-shirts with the legend, "I'm having a wonderful affair — with my wife." Such attitudes make the most prominent apologia for Christian marital fidelity the argument that monogamy is an aphrodisiac superior to free love. In other words: choose the "value" of fidelity for the sake of better sex.

MacIntyre's contextualized, historicized account of ethics helps us to ask what view of human sexuality is at work here. Rather than simply and grossly assuming that human sexuality is a given, an instinct identical in all times and places, we can ask what account of sexuality and marriage lies behind the propensity of (even) some Christians to make fidelity an aphrodisiac, and thus a commodity more appealing to the sovereign consumer. Accordingly, I argue that what lies behind it is the tradition of romantic love, a tradition that is part of the bourgeois package of family values but one that Christians more mindful of their own tradition would do well to challenge.[22]

The Myth of Romantic Love

It may not be hyperbolic to say that romantic love is one of the master stories or traditions of liberal, advanced capitalistic society. Think of it this way: As historian Eamon Duffy shows in a richly detailed account, fifteenth-century English folk could hardly make it through a waking hour of the day without encountering living manifestations of the Christian tradition. Church bells rang. Processions recalling Christ's sacrifice paraded by homes. Duffy writes,

> With the liturgy, birth, copulation, and death, journeying and homecoming, guilt and forgiveness, the blessing of homely things and the call to pass beyond them were all located, tested, and sanctioned. In the liturgy and the sacramental celebra-

22. Brigitte and Peter Berger, writing in defense of the bourgeois family, list six primary characteristics of that form of family, including romantic love as the major motive for marriage. See *The War over the Family* (Garden City, N.Y.: Doubleday, 1983), 101–2.

tions that were its central moments, medieval people found the key to the meaning and purpose of their lives.[23]

Now compare how easy it is to pass through an hour of the Western, late-twentieth-century day without any reminders of the Christian tradition, but how difficult it would be to avoid fragments of the tradition of romantic love. Popular, jazz, and country radio stations are saturated with it, heralding it in song around the clock. Escaping it would mean never turning on the television, watching a movie, or overhearing office gossip. It's apparent on billboards and in magazines and newspapers and, as I've observed, barely less prominent in Christian literature and media.

Inherent to the ethos of romantic love is the notion that it is "natural" and universally inevitable. People fall in love as surely as the earth orbits the sun and heavy objects roll down hills. No doubt much of the uncritical acceptance of romantic love among Christians is due to the perception that it is natural, rather than a contestable tradition. It has been second nature to most moderns to think of emotions (like romantic love) as somehow deeper, truer, less contrived than thoughts or behavior. But emotions have histories and social origins too. They are, after all, more than mere sensations — else how do we distinguish between abject fear and cheerful excitement? In either case, heartbeat speeds up, stomach tightens, lungs draw air more rapidly. What sorts of things will frighten or happily excite someone? Who should feel fear (or excitement), and when? How is fear (or excitement) expressed — is it hidden, demurely shown, displayed in weeping or laughter? Emotions are interpretations of objects and circumstances, and as such they are always culturally formed and informed. "Feelings," anthropologist Michelle Rosaldo has well said, "are not substances to be discovered in our blood but social practices organized by stories we both enact and tell." Feelings, like selves in general, are shaped by culture and may be understood as the "creation of particular sorts of polities" or embodied traditions.[24] The emotional life, it turns out, is no less political and traditional than the thought life.

Accordingly, women and men everywhere may be sexually attracted, have intercourse, and often produce offspring. But romantic love is far more complicated than that. How is sexual attraction experienced? Is it considered to be mere animal magnetism (as in paganism); is it simultaneously alluring and a disgusting temptation (as in antiphysical accounts); or is it, among other possibilities, part and parcel of "falling in love"? Is attraction to be resisted, indulged, or somehow channeled? Where may it lead, what potential does it present — is it apt to suggest a one-night stand or marriage, possible and eventual satisfaction or unending though sometimes delicious frustration? This is the level at which cultural and political traditions must come into play.

23. Eamon Duffy, *The Stripping of the Altars* (New Haven: Yale University Press, 1992), 11.

24. Michelle Z. Rosaldo, "Toward an Anthropology of Self and Feeling," in *Culture Theory,* ed. Richard A. Shweder and Robert A. Levine (Cambridge: Cambridge University Press, 1984), 143.

The Roots of Romantic Love

Once we recognize as much, we may not be in a position simply to shake off the spell of romantic love. It is far too potent magic for that. But at least we are in a position to assess its narrative in Christian terms and begin concocting an antidote. Then we are poised to remember that it is only since the Middle Ages that romantic love has been prized as an ideal, the *sine qua non* for marriage and the fully vital human life. Marriage in history has more typically been arranged between families than chosen merely by a man and a woman "in love." In fact, in most of Western history the sweeping intensity, confusion, and absorption of what we have come to know as romantic love was considered a misfortune. Friendship was the higher love.

The roots of romantic love lie in heresy. Denis de Rougemont traces it back to the Cathari, who emerged in twelfth-century Germany.[25] True to their name (which means "pure ones"), the Cathari were obsessed with evil and believed its origins were found in physical matter. Accordingly, they prohibited sexual intercourse even within marriage. Certain of the Cathari's themes were picked up by twelfth-century court bands. From there they made their way into written verse romances, and finally into modern romantic literature. Perhaps the tidiest way to lay out the narrative tradition of romantic love is to recount the story of Tristan and Iseult, memorialized in so many medieval poems and songs.

Tristan and Iseult, Carolyn and Scott

In the tale Tristan, an orphan, becomes the adopted son of King Mark (in some accounts he is the nephew of the king). Early on he proves to be a fine warrior. With this attribute in mind, the king sends Tristan to fetch the king's bride-to-be, Iseult, from Ireland to Mark's realm of Cornwall. Returning from Ireland, Tristan and Iseult drink the love potion intended for her and King Mark. They fall in love and succumb to temptation. Yet both attempt to remain loyal to the king, so Iseult is delivered to Mark. Tristan and Iseult's duplicitous sexual adventures continue in the castle, until the couple flees to the forest of Morrois, to live for three years in the hardship of poverty. Then the couple repents, and Iseult returns to Mark. But Tristan and Iseult soon plot reunion. Before they are reunited and manage to manifest their love in its fullness, both die.

Once the core narrative is exposed, even in such sketchy detail, several enduring dynamics of supposedly natural romantic love rise into view. True love is something that falls on people, like a spell. The couple on which it falls is special, admirable at least from outside the social circles where their love wreaks havoc, and yet the couple is tragically ill-fated. To the limited extent that romantic love can be realized, it is realized fitfully and fleetingly, clandestinely, in poverty, and in opposition to society. Quintessential love is understood as

25. Rougemont's classic account is found in his *Love in the Western World,* rev. and augmented ed., trans. Hazel E. Barnes (Princeton: Princeton University Press, 1983); first published in French, 1939.

unsatisified yearning, as desire exquisitely deprived. It cannot end in consummation or steady, unfolding fulfillment but only in death. According to the myth of romantic love, true love is too good for this sordid world.

In an illuminating chapter of his *Ethics*, James McClendon demonstrates how these themes of the narrative of romantic love remain prominent in massively popular tales like Erich Segal's *Love Story* and in sturdier, more sophisticated work like the novels of John Updike.[26] For my purposes and more abbreviated space, I turn to a true life story.

The spring and summer 1988 odyssey of Carolyn MacLean and Scott Swanson serves my purposes because Carolyn and Scott were students at Wheaton College, that midwestern bastion of Protestant evangelicalism, and as such an institution devoted to the intentional cultivation of the Christian story and its attendant traits of character. So it is all the more striking that Carolyn and Scott, seniors about to graduate from the college, fell in love and then disappeared one April day. Both came from wealthy families, and Carolyn's BMW was found abandoned in a Chicago alley. A harried, highly publicized four-month search ensued. Then, late in July, Carolyn and Scott turned up in San Diego. It seems their intended marriage was opposed by their families. In addition, Scott's education was partly financed by his participation in ROTC, and in a few months military service would separate him from Carolyn.

What could this couple, this Christian couple, do? They knew the romantic script well. As a *Chicago Tribune* headline later reported, "Missing Wheaton couple did it all for love."[27] Scott and Carolyn eloped and ran off because, Carolyn said, "We loved each other so much that we wanted to give up everything for each other." They left behind the encumbrances of wealth, lived in a cut-rate apartment, and waited tables in restaurants to experience "unadorned love." Their safe return was a relief to police, friends, and family but also the occasion for anger at all the unnecessary worry and expense Tristan and Iseult — I mean, Scott and Carolyn — had put them through. In response, Scott averred that their extraordinary relationship simply wasn't understood: "We feel like we're on a different level than a lot of people... Carolyn's my life, and me to her, her to me. I would die for her and she would die for me."

The couple admitted that they modeled the entire episode on *A Severe Mercy*, Sheldon Vanauken's intensely romantic account of his love affair and marriage, in which he and his wife rejected any interference with their love, including material goods or children. Vanauken creates an admittedly moving account of his and lover Jean's rapture, replete with starlit nights on a sailboat, and then her wrenching, untimely death. But Scott and Carolyn apparently missed the ultimate point of the book. After Jean's death, and counseled by C. S. Lewis, Vanauken comes to see that his and Jean's attachment was too exclusive, too

---

26. See James Wm. McClendon, Jr., *Ethics: Systematic Theology, Volume I* (Nashville: Abingdon Press, 1986), 133–55.

27. "Missing Wheaton couple did it all for love," by George Papajohn and James Warren, *Chicago Tribune*, 28 July 1988.

all-encompassing, and finally just plainly and destructively selfish. The book's title comes from Lewis's penetrating insight that Sheldon's forced, agonizing separation from Jean might be perceived as "a severe mercy" rescuing the pair from the poisonous effects of extreme romantic love.

The Fallout of a Tradition

But perhaps I should not be too hard on Carolyn's and Scott's reading of the book. In the end, Vanauken (and Lewis too) remained a committed if chastened romantic. Though with the help of such brilliant guides as Lewis (and his friend Charles Williams), Christians might well appropriate aspects of romantic love, I suspect our environment is now so completely corrupted by this myth that whatever remains redeemable of it lies only on the other side of more radical, thoroughgoing critique than Lewis ever suggested.

For what the narrative of romantic love tells us is that we are powerless to "make" and sustain real love. Remember, according to this tradition true love can never last. We simply fall into it and are swept into the arms of that special person destined just for us. (The feeble Christianization of this romantic plotline is the supposition that God has somewhere out there that one person exactly right for each of us to find and marry. Hence the widespread and heightened anxiety that "I might be making a mistake," for well you might if there is only a single person genuinely fit for you in a world of several billion. This is searching for a unique needle in a haystack full of needles.) Even at its most sentimentalized, when the tale of romantic love ends with the couple living "happily ever after," the marrow of the fairytale is never about actually living happily ever after; romantic love cannot even provide us with a description of "ever after." It is all about a goal, a goal that can never be achieved but is by definition best dreamed about and pined after.

I think of a friend who tells about warding off her husband's lovemaking advances so that she might rather read, in bed beside him, her latest romance novel. That's romantic love in its essence. It is first and finally gnostic, anti-physical, drawn more to fantasies than any actual, particular body near to hand. A pernicious irony of the narrative of romantic love is that, for all its supposed adoration of the love object, romantic love is not really about loving a particular person — it is about being in love with love.

Romantic love is based on inconstancy, on feelings unanchored in reality. That is why so many popular romantic love songs protest of illicit affairs, "How can this be wrong when it feels so right?" Of course, many of those who have succumbed wholeheartedly to this myth realize, at least when they're not in the throes of love's latest spell, that they said exactly the same thing to the earlier lover they're now betraying. So it is that romantic love leaves us prey to both sensuality and cynicism. And in that regard it's worth noting how well the narrative of romantic love supports the ethos of advanced capitalism, which demands that the ideal consumer be perpetually frustrated and never really contented. It's not for nothing that the story still flourishes in a day far removed from the courtly world of Tristan and Iseult.

The now faintly quaint custom of dating, after all, is a preeminently capitalistic practice, a sign of just how far the market has transgressed beyond any proper boundaries. In theory a young man or woman dates in order to grow in the knowledge and ability to make a more informed marital choice. Yet we have little or no sociological evidence that dating, after almost a century of its practice, reliably results in happier, longer-lasting marriages. What is clear is that dating's inexorable consumerist logic has been extended to encompass premarital cohabitation. If romanticized sexual compatibility is so important to the success of a marriage, and if it is more found or "fallen into" than made, it only makes sense to experiment before taking any vows. No sensible consumer would buy a car without test-driving it, or a stereo without first listening to it. So how dare choose a mate without first living with him or her? I say all this by way of suggesting that challenging the myth of romantic love is a matter not merely of confronting Grace Livingston Hill or Danielle Steel; it's a matter of going toe-to-toe with Wall Street and Madison Avenue. And there's something that may be more interesting than falling in and out of love *ad nauseum.*

McClendon properly reorients Christians for just such a fight when he writes, "While the romantic myth moves from love to death, the Christian master story moves (through death) to newfound life — in the body."[28] In the shadow of Christ's death and the light of his resurrection, the Christian master story recasts the story of love so that it does not *end* at the wedding and the commencement of "ever after" but instead *begins* there. As Michael Ignatieff puts it, the Christian marriage ceremony, with its vows to love in sickness or health, until death, replaces the romantic tale of falling in love with the "arduous drama of staying in love."[29] Romantics make love in private, at best oblivious to the welfare of the surrounding community. Christians make love in public, realizing that Christian love is much more than mere sexual passion and trusting that they can build an enduring, open, and generous love only through participation in the surrounding community called church.

I suspect that we might best de-idolize romantic love by giving more attention to friendship in the context of *koinōnia,* or churchly community. I have in mind Aristotle's highest form of friendship — the friendship of those devoted to a common cause. Christians are those people caught up in an adventure involving nothing less than the destiny of the world. As such, we hardly need the comparatively puny and petty adventure of romantic love. Christians do not get married because monogamy is an aphrodisiac; they get married because this is the key way they participate as sexual beings in an adventure far surpassing the potentials of any aphrodisiac, the adventure of witnessing to and building up God's kingdom on earth.

28. *Ethics,* 150.
29. As quoted in Martin E. Marty, "Who says all you need is love?" *Context,* 1 July 1988, 5–6.

The important question for Christians, then, after five, ten, fifty years of marriage, is not, "Am I still in love with my spouse?" The better question is, "Are we stronger, deeper, continuing Christian friends?" That is to say, are we supporting and challenging each other in the faith, in service to one another, to our children, to our church, to our neighbors? In the words of Diogenes Allen, when Christian marriage is friendship rather than romance, "We do not fight dragons or villains, as in 'love stories,' but fight with ourselves, as more and more of ourself and our partner is revealed with time and through the ups and downs of life. We face an inward struggle with what we are [and, I would add, a political struggle with what the world wants us to be]. What is won is oneself and the other. Married people *become* people who love each other."[30] In short, the sex lives of Christians can improve. But they can improve only once we learn how to make love after we have fallen out of love.

The Noncommodified Christian Family

We have now theologically viewed the family values debate with a MacIntyrean lens and devoted considerable attention to what is literally the "sexiest" aspect of that debate. My conclusion is that if there is any hope for living such Christian family virtues as fidelity and commitment, it will be only in a community that can stand in some considerable tension with the liberal, advanced capitalistic way of life. Believing this would mean taking seriously a number of Christian convictions that can only appear odd in the veiled liberal terms of the family values debate. We do not, for instance, hear much in that debate about certain statements of Jesus, such as, "I have come to set a man against his father, and a daughter against her mother . . . and one's foes will be members of one's own household" (Matt. 10:34–36) or St. Paul's, "So then, he who marries . . . does well; and he who refrains from marriage will do better" (1 Cor. 7:38 NIV). We do not hear much about the biblical, and ancient Christian, conviction that the church is the Christian's first and primary family, that through baptism we are grafted into a community of adopted siblings who are our truest sisters and brothers because they do the will of the God of Israel and Jesus the Nazarene (Mark 3:31–35; Gal. 4:1–7).

Christians, in the end, can do much better than fight for family values. We can strive better to discern and live out distinctively Christian family virtues, and through this way of life demonstrate that there is an alternative to the liberal capitalistic way of life. Only such an imaginative and costly embodiment can provoke and encourage other (that is, non-Christian) families. Only such a flesh-and-blood embodiment can free people to dream and hope for a better way of living together. If Christians live out Christian family, if we even to a degree make the church our first family, then at least others will know that fam-

30. Diogenes Allen, *Love: Christian Romance, Marriage, Friendship* (Cambridge, Mass.: Cowley Press, 1987), 79.

ily can be other than — and more than — a feckless haven, a commodity, or a personal hobby.

Suggestions for Further Reading

Barton, Stephen C., ed. *The Family in Theological Perspective.* Edinburgh: T. & T. Clark, 1996.

Charry, Ellen T. "Raising Christian Children in a Pagan Culture." *Christian Century* 111 (16 February 1994): 166–68.

Clapp, Rodney. *Families at the Crossroads: Beyond Traditional and Modern Options.* Downers Grove, Ill.: InterVarsity Press, 1993.

Dawn, Marva J. *Sexual Character: Beyond Technique to Intimacy.* Grand Rapids, Mich.: Wm. B. Eerdmans, 1993.

Eerdman, Chris William. *Beyond Chaos: Living the Christian Family in a World like Ours.* Grand Rapids, Mich.: Wm. B. Eerdmans, 1997.

Hauerwas, Stanley. "The Family: Theological and Ethical Reflections" and "The Moral Value of the Family." In *A Community of Character,* 167–74 and 155–66. Notre Dame: University of Notre Dame Press, 1981.

Meilaender, Gilbert. "A Christian View of the Family." In *Rebuilding the Nest: A New Commitment to the American Family,* ed. David B. Blankenhorn, Steven Bayme, and Jean Bethke Elshtain, 133–48. Milwaukee: Family Service American, 1990.

Chapter 9

Character and Conversation in the Homosexuality Debate

Editor's Introduction

We, the editors, have warned ourselves — and been forewarned by our peers — that the inclusion of a single chapter on homosexuality and the church is risky business indeed. On the one hand, it would have been safer to say nothing at all, for one who occupies an unknown position is an invisible target. On the other hand, it would have been safer to say much more than we have done: a reader is rarely alienated by an anthology of fifty essays, since he or she can surely find refuge in at least one. Alas, we opted for the hazardous road. The following chapter comprises a scant two essays, a selection thin enough for virtually anyone to find at least one major point of disagreement! But our purpose in including these two essays is entirely pedagogical. We are not attempting to spell out *the* Christian position regarding homosexuality in the church but rather to *illustrate* the types of issues (moral virtue, faithfulness to the story of Jesus, right reading of biblical texts, congruence with the Christian tradition, and so on) necessary for the manner of one's moral reflection to be genuinely Christian.

Whether or not MacIntyre's conceptual scheme will ultimately prove useful for untangling the rhetorical skein surrounding homosexuality in the church, his conception of a tradition as a socially embodied *argument* prepares us to be neither surprised by, nor entirely dismayed at, the volatility and polarizing tendencies of this issue. We have tried to capture the dialectical flavor of this debate by selecting authors who would certainly be seen as having "mortgaged the farm" by *both* of the far ends of the spectrum, and yet who differ enough from each other to make their conversation productive. Each author seems nervous to have taken a stand at all, and not simply nervous that he has taken the particular stance he has. Because of this uneasiness, each author tries to temper the stance of his essay with a title that points in the opposite direction. Richard Hays's title, "Awaiting the Redemption of Our Bodies," is prospective, hopeful, and eschatological, while the essay itself is purposefully historical, drawing on the staid resources of Scripture and tradition for elucidating the grammatical boundaries of the churchly debate. In contrast, Luke Timothy Johnson's title, "Debate and Discernment, Scripture and the Spirit" is retrospective, cautious, and biblical, while his essay is explicitly innovative, asking under what conditions might the church be willing to consider homosexuals as a social class akin to Gentiles, an admission that would seemingly obligate the church to judge some version of "homosexual Christianity" as an authentic work of God's Spirit, just as Gentile Christianity was so judged after Acts 15. Whether the tentativeness of these authors is real or imagined, it is significant for the vitality of the argument, and hence to the vitality of the tradition, that they explicate their respective views distinctively enough so that their positions not be confused; an argument promises to be most constructive when the sides are separated by real difference.

In addition to exemplifying the *dialectical* nature of the conversation, these authors speak *with* each other (rather than *past* each other, as MacIntyre has shown to be the case with the traditionless voices of post-Enlightenment ethicists) because they share a commitment to the sorts of things that show them to be, in MacIntyrean terms, members of the same tradition. First, both are committed to the biblical text as functioning authoritatively for the shaping of Christian identity (although they differ in the details of what phrases such as "according to Scripture" mean). Because Johnson's essay assumes knowledge of the biblical exegesis that Hays's article makes explicit, Hays's essay is presented first. But the reader should not be misled into thinking that Johnson thereby has the last word. Remember, both authors are included for the way they exemplify the use of such concepts as virtue, narrative, practice, *telos,* and tradition.

Second, *character* is of central concern to the conversation in two senses. On the one hand, both authors ponder what contribution to the Christian narrative, as lived out in the community of faith, is made by the presence of self-proclaimed homosexuals: does their presence suggest the possibility of ongoing revelation (Johnson), or is it a reminder of the tragic, though redeemable, human predicament (Hays)? On the other hand, both authors inquire into the present character of the *church,* asking whether the greater body of Christ has what it takes to respond with Christlike grace and justice.

Third, both approaches are teleological in the sense that God's creative intention (*telos*) for human life, while yet to be fully realized, provides present direction for moral life and reasoning. Hays reminds readers of the eschatological character of Christian existence, which awaits the redemption of human sexuality with hopeful expectancy and sees the testimony of those who have been "healed of their homosexuality" (however they understand their former condition) as forerunners of the bodily transformation which all believers eagerly anticipate. Johnson reminds his readers that the adjective *eschatological* also applies to the present, forward-moving character of the church; the church, like a MacIntyrean tradition, makes genuine progress toward its *telos.* However, this progress can be made only by overcoming obstacles, such as that posed by the issue of homosexuality.

By no stretch of the imagination do I think that this summary treatment even begins to frame the discussion of such a complex and explosive issue. Yet both authors' narrative employment of Scripture, together with their respective focus on the question(s) of character and their teleological hope for the church, illustrate that the conversation between them is rendered both possible and fruitful because of the recovery of the very resources to which MacIntyre has so successfully drawn our attention.

Hays's essay originally appeared in the July 1991 issue of *Sojourners* magazine (vol. 20, no. 6). *Sojourners* has asked us to make clear that the essay was one of several printed as a debate on the issue. We republish here their accompanying commentary from pages 10–11 of the same issue.

> In our July 1985 issue, *Sojourners* published an article on sexual ethics. It contained a short section on homosexuality, which became the overwhelming focus of the response to the piece. The essay's broader discussion on Christian ethics and human sexuality was unfortunately lost in the controversy that followed, and, even more regrettable, a number of our readers felt angered by what they regarded as a very brief—and to some insensitive—treatment of gay and lesbian sexuality. Others liked the article, and we were literally deluged with letters to the editor, many filled with great emotion.
>
> Neither the magazine staff nor Sojourners Community had discussed the topic of homosexuality before that article was run, and its publication generated much discussion, strong feelings, and divided opinions here at home. We said in subsequent issues of *Sojourners* that we would continue the dialogue among ourselves, while publishing articles that reflected the consensus we did have on issues such as the just and equitable treatment of gay and lesbian people in regard to civil and human rights and the urgency of addressing the AIDS crisis — a special concern to members of the gay community—with compassion, sensitivity, and political commitment.
>
> We now find ourselves in a dialogue and debate that has swept up the churches in one of the most painful, anguishing, and perplexing questions the Christian community has encountered in a long time. How should the churches respond to homosexuality and, most important, to gay and lesbian Christians in their midst? *Sojourners'* own constituency is not of one opinion on this issue. Christians deeply and passionately committed to justice and reconciliation find themselves at different places on the complicated questions raised by gay and lesbian sexuality.
>
> That most churches are dealing with the question and listening to people involved is a very good and positive thing. But the dialogue has often been quite impoverished, with too much hasty rhetoric, ideology, fear, and insensitivity replacing honest and sincere wrestling with the hard questions and difficult dilemmas the controversy poses.
>
> In many conservative churches and seminaries, gay and lesbian voices simply cannot be heard, producing a cultural orthodoxy that requires an enforced silence. In more liberal church sectors and seminaries, gay and lesbian sexuality is affirmed and no challenging questions or concerns are tolerated by the prevailing political orthodoxy. Neither climate breeds good, helpful, and ultimately healing dialogue. Neither homophobic fears nor politically correct ideologies will allow the open space for real conversation to occur.
>
> We need a better dialogue — more open, listening, searching, and, most of all, more humble than most of us have been. We offer this forum on the subject of gay and lesbian sexuality and the church's response as a small contribution toward a better dialogue. *Sojourners* isn't taking a position in this forum, in part because

as a staff we all haven't reached clarity or agreement; but also because we're not sure it would best serve our constituency and the churches at this moment. Some issues are so profoundly pastoral that the first requirement is to make sure that we have listened carefully. Our editorial perspective at this moment is that people on different sides of the question need to do a much better job of talking together.

We asked people to write who have different perspectives and life experiences. We asked only those who, despite their differences, share a common commitment to justice and human rights for all people, regardless of their sexual orientation, and to an inclusive church open to all who know their need for the grace of God. We asked our authors to focus on the theological, biblical, and pastoral issues at stake in the churches' debate, being careful to keep the personal nature of the issues at the center of the conversation — that we not forget the human beings at the heart of the controversy.

We are aware that the individual opinions expressed here may be difficult for some to read and will probably create strong reactions — on all sides. But we feel that they are fair in their representation of a spectrum of voices in the debate sweeping the churches. If we are to find any common ground, especially in the churches, we shall have to grant an integrity to the convictions and concerns of others with whom we may not agree. The practice of attacking, caricaturing, and name-calling — on all sides — must come to an end.

The discussion of gay and lesbian sexuality raises questions of sexual ethics for heterosexuals as well, which is where this conversation in *Sojourners* began some time ago. What are the gospel imperatives and Christian characteristics that should shape and guide our sexual relationships? To that subject we must certainly turn.

Because of *Sojourners'* own tradition, our approach to the questions of gay and lesbian sexuality, and sexual ethics more generally, must have biblical and theological integrity, must be pastorally concerned with the people most affected, must make justice a central priority, and must respond especially to those who have suffered and been abused. Our commitment is to seek to be more faithful to those principles in the days ahead.

We offer this issue of *Sojourners* with prayers for those people and places in the churches now seeking to find their way through the thicket of contention and controversy surrounding any discussion of these matters — and for all of us who seek the mind and heart of God in relation to our sexuality.

This long commentary has been included because it helps set the context for the articles that follow.

BRAD J. KALLENBERG

Awaiting the Redemption of Our Bodies

Richard B. Hays

Speaking the Truth in Love

Gary came to New Haven in the summer of 1989 to say a proper farewell. My best friend from undergraduate years at Yale was dying of AIDS.

During the week he stayed with my family, we went to films together, we drank wine and laughed, we had long, sober talks about politics and literature and the gospel and sex and such. Above all, we listened to music. Some of it was nostalgic music: the record of our college singing group, which Gary had directed with passionate precision; music of the sixties, recalling the years when we marched together against the Vietnam War — Beatles, Byrds, Bob Dylan, Joni Mitchell.

We prayed together often that week, and we talked theology. It became clear that Gary had come not only to say goodbye but also to think hard, before God, about the relation between his homosexuality and his Christian faith. He was angry at the self-affirming gay Christian groups, because he regarded his own situation as more complex and tragic than their stance could acknowledge. He also worried that the gay subculture encouraged homosexual believers to "draw their identity from their sexuality" and thus to shift the ground of their identity subtly and idolatrously away from God.

For more than twenty years, Gary had grappled with his homosexuality, experiencing it as a compulsion and an affliction. Now, as he faced death, he wanted to talk it all through again from the beginning, because he knew my love for him and trusted me to speak without dissembling. For Gary, there was no time to dance around the hard questions. As Dylan had urged, "Let us not talk falsely now; the hour is getting late."

In particular, Gary wanted to discuss the biblical passages that deal with homosexual acts. Among Gary's many gifts was his skill as a reader of texts. After leaving Yale and helping to found a community-based Christian theater group in Toronto, he had eventually completed a master's degree in French literature.

He had read hopefully through the standard bibliography of the burgeoning movement advocating the acceptance of homosexuality in the church: John J.

McNeill, *The Church and the Homosexual;*[1] James B. Nelson, *Embodiment;*[2] Letha Scanzoni and Virginia Ramey Mollenkott, *Is the Homosexual My Neighbor?;*[3] John Boswell, *Christianity, Social Tolerance, and Homosexuality.*[4] In the end, he came away disappointed, believing that these authors, despite their good intentions, had imposed a wishful interpretation on the biblical passages. However much he wanted to believe that the Bible did not condemn homosexuality, he would not violate his own stubborn intellectual integrity by pretending to find their arguments persuasive.

The more we talked, the more we found our perspectives interlocking. Both of us had serious misgivings about the mounting pressure for the church to recognize homosexuality as a legitimate Christian lifestyle. As a New Testament scholar, I was concerned about certain questionable exegetical and theological strategies of the gay apologists. Gary, as a homosexual Christian, believed that their writings did justice neither to the biblical texts nor to the depressing reality of the gay subculture that he had moved in and out of for twenty years.

We concluded that our witnesses were complementary and that we had a word to speak to the churches. The public discussion of this matter has been dominated by insistently ideological voices: on one side, gay rights activists demanding the church's unqualified acceptance of homosexuality; on the other, unqualified homophobic condemnation of homosexual Christians. Gary and I agreed that we should try to encourage a more nuanced discourse within the community of faith. He was going to write an article about his own experience, and I agreed to write a response to it.

Tragically, Gary soon became too sick to carry out his intention. His last letter to me was an effort to get some of his thoughts on paper while he was still able to write. By May of 1990 he was dead.

This article, then, is an act of keeping covenant with a beloved brother in Christ who will not speak again on this side of the resurrection. I commit it to print sorrowfully aware that it will outrage some. At the same time, I commit it to print praying that it will encourage others as Gary was encouraged, and that it will foster compassionate and carefully reasoned theological reflection within the community of faith.

What Does the Bible Say?

The Bible hardly ever discusses homosexual behavior. There are perhaps half a dozen brief references to it in all of Scripture. In terms of emphasis, it is a

1. 4th ed. (Boston: Beacon Press, 1993).
2. *Embodiment: An Approach to Sexuality and Christian Theology* (Minneapolis: Augsburg Fortress, 1979).
3. *Is the Homosexual My Neighbor? A Positive Christian Response,* rev. ed. (San Francisco: Harper, 1994).
4. *Christianity, Social Tolerance, and Homosexuality: Gay People in Western Europe from the Beginning of the Christian Era to the Fourteenth Century* (Chicago: University of Chicago Press, 1981).

minor concern, in contrast, for example, to economic injustice. What the Bible does say should be heeded carefully, but any ethic that intends to be biblical will seek to get the accents in the right place.

Genesis 19:1–29. The notorious story of Sodom and Gomorrah—often cited in connection with homosexuality—is actually irrelevant to the topic. The "men of Sodom" come pounding on Lot's door, apparently with the intention of gang-raping Lot's two visitors — who, as we readers know, are actually angels. The gang-rape scenario exemplifies the wickedness of the city, but there is nothing in the passage pertinent to a judgment about the morality of consensual homosexual intercourse. In fact, the clearest statement about the sin of Sodom is to be found in an oracle of the prophet Ezekiel: "This was the guilt of your sister Sodom: She and her daughters had pride, excess of food, and prosperous ease, but did not aid the poor and needy" (Ezekiel 16:49).

Leviticus 18:22, 20:13. The Holiness Code in Leviticus explicitly prohibits male homosexual intercourse: "You shall not lie with a male as with a woman; it is an abomination" (Leviticus 18:22). In Leviticus 20:10–16, the same act is listed as one of a series of sexual offenses — along with adultery, incest, and bestiality — that are punishable by death. It is worth noting that the *act* of "lying with a male as with a woman" is categorically proscribed; motives for the act are not treated as a morally significant factor.

Quoting a law from Leviticus, of course, does not settle the question for Christian ethics. The Old Testament contains many prohibitions and commandments that have, ever since the first century, generally been disregarded or deemed obsolete by the church, most notably rules concerning circumcision and dietary practices. Some ethicists have argued that the prohibition of homosexuality is similarly superseded for Christians: It is merely part of the Old Testament's ritual "purity rules" and therefore morally irrelevant today.

The Old Testament, however, makes no systematic distinction between ritual law and moral law. The same section of the Holiness Code also contains, for instance, the prohibition of incest (Leviticus 18:6–18). Is that a purity law or a moral law? In each case, the church is faced with the task of discerning whether Israel's traditional norms remain in force for the new community of Jesus' followers.

1 Corinthians 6:9; 1 Timothy 1:10. The early church did, in fact, consistently adopt the Old Testament's teaching on matters of sexual morality and on homosexual acts in particular. In 1 Corinthians 6:9 and 1 Timothy 1:10, we find homosexuals included in lists of persons who do things unacceptable to God.

In 1 Corinthians 6, Paul, exasperated with the Corinthians—some of whom apparently believe themselves to have entered a spiritually exalted state in which the moral rules of their old existence no longer apply to them (see 1 Corinthians 4:8, 5:12, 8:1–9) — confronts them with a blunt rhetorical question: "Do you not know that wrongdoers will not inherit the kingdom of God?" He then gives an illustrative list of the sorts of persons he means: "fornicators, idolaters, adulterers, *malakoi, arsenokoitai,* thieves, the greedy, drunkards, revilers, robbers."

I have left the terms pertinent to the present issue untranslated, because their translation has been disputed recently by Boswell and others. The word *malakoi* is not a technical term meaning "homosexuals" (no such term existed either in Greek or in Hebrew), but it appears often in Hellenistic Greek as pejorative slang to describe the "passive" partners — often young boys — in homosexual activity.

The other word, *arsenokoitai,* is not found in any extant Greek text earlier than 1 Corinthians. Some scholars have suggested that its meaning is uncertain, but Robin Scroggs has shown that the word is a translation of the Hebrew *mishkav zakur* ("lying with a male"), derived directly from Leviticus 18:22 and 20:13 and used in rabbinic texts to refer to homosexual intercourse.[5] The Septuagint (Greek Old Testament) of Leviticus 20:13 reads, "Whoever lies with a man as with a woman [*meta arsenos koitēn gynaikos*], they have both done an abomination." This is almost certainly the idiom from which the noun *arsenokoitai* was coined. Thus, Paul's use of the term presupposes and reaffirms the Holiness Code's condemnation of homosexual acts.

In 1 Corinthians 6:11, Paul asserts that the sinful behaviors catalogued in the vice list were formerly practiced by some of the Corinthians. Now, however, since they have been transferred into the sphere of Christ's lordship, they ought to have left these practices behind. The remainder of the chapter counsels the Corinthians to glorify God in their bodies, because they belong now to God and no longer to themselves.

The 1 Timothy passage includes *arsenokoitai* in a list of "the lawless and disobedient," whose behavior is specified in a vice list that includes everything from lying to murdering one's parents, under the rubric of actions "contrary to sound teaching that conforms to the glorious gospel." Here again, the Old Testament prohibition is presupposed.

Romans 1:18–32. The most crucial text for Christian ethics concerning homosexuality remains Romans 1, because this is the only passage in the New Testament that places the condemnation of homosexual behavior in an explicitly theological context.

> Therefore God gave them up in the lusts of their hearts to impurity, to the degrading of their bodies among themselves, because they exchanged the truth about God for a lie and worshiped and served the creature rather than the Creator.... Their women exchanged natural intercourse for unnatural, and in the same way also the men, giving up natural intercourse with women, were consumed with passion for one another. Men committed shameless acts with men and received in their own persons the due penalty for their own error. (Romans 1:24–27)

(This is, incidentally, the only passage in the Bible that refers to lesbian sexual relations.)

The aim of Romans 1 is not to teach a code of sexual ethics; nor is the passage a warning of God's judgment against those who are guilty of particular

5. *The New Testament and Homosexuality* (Philadelphia: Fortress Press, 1983).

sins. Rather, Paul is offering a *diagnosis* of the disordered human condition: He adduces the fact of widespread homosexual behavior as evidence that human beings are indeed in rebellion against their creator.

The fundamental human sin is the refusal to honor God and give God thanks (1:21); consequently, God's wrath takes the form of letting human idolatry run its own self-destructive course. Homosexuality, then, is not a *provocation* of "the wrath of God" (Romans 1:18); rather, it is a *consequence* of God's decision to "give up" rebellious creatures to follow their own futile thinking and desires.

The unrighteous behavior catalogued in Romans 1:26–31 is a list of *symptoms:* The underlying sickness of humanity as a whole, Jews and Greeks alike, is that they have turned away from God and fallen under the power of sin (see Romans 3:9).

Paul singles out homosexual intercourse for special attention because he regards it as providing a particularly graphic image of the way in which human fallenness distorts God's created order. God the creator made man and woman for each other, to cleave together, to be fruitful and multiply. When human beings engage in homosexual activity, they enact an outward and visible sign of an inward and spiritual reality: the rejection of the Creator's design. They *embody* the spiritual condition of those who have "exchanged the truth about God for a lie."

Homosexual acts are not, however, specially reprehensible sins; they are no worse than any of the other manifestations of human unrighteousness listed in the passage (verses 29–31), no worse in principle than covetousness or gossip or disrespect for parents.

Repeated again and again in recent debate is the claim that Paul condemns only homosexual acts committed promiscuously by heterosexual persons — because they *"exchanged* natural intercourse for unnatural." Paul's negative judgment, so the argument goes, does *not* apply to persons who are "naturally" of homosexual orientation. The "exchange," however, is not a matter of individual life-decisions; rather, it is Paul's characterization of the fallen condition of the pagan world. In any case, neither Paul nor anyone else in antiquity had a concept of "sexual orientation." To introduce this concept into the passage (by suggesting that Paul disapproves only those who act contrary to their individual sexual orientations) is to lapse into an anachronism.

The expression *para physin* ("contrary to nature"), used here by Paul, is the standard terminology in dozens of ancient texts for referring to homoerotic acts.[6] The fact is that Paul treats *all* homosexual activity as *prima facie* evidence of humanity's tragic confusion and alienation from God the Creator.

One more thing must be said: Romans 1:18–32 performs a homiletical sting operation. The passage builds a crescendo of condemnation, declaring God's wrath upon human unrighteousness, whipping the reader into a frenzy of indig-

6. For details, see my article "Relations Natural and Unnatural: A Response to John Boswell's Exegesis of Romans 1" in the *Journal of Religious Ethics,* spring 1986.

nation against others. But then, in Romans 2:1, the sting strikes: "Therefore you have no excuse, whoever you are, when you judge others; for in passing judgment on another you condemn yourself, because you, the judge, are doing the very same things."

We all stand without excuse under God's judgment. Self-righteous judgment of homosexuality is just as sinful as the homosexual behavior itself. That does not mean that Paul is disingenuous in his rejection of homosexual acts and all the other sinful activities mentioned in Romans 1. But no one should presume to be above God's judgment; all of us stand in radical need of God's mercy. That warning must temper the tone of our debate about homosexuality.

The Wider Biblical Framework

Though only a few biblical texts speak of homoerotic activity, all of them express unqualified disapproval. In this respect, the issue of homosexuality differs significantly from matters such as slavery or the subordination of women, concerning which the Bible contains internal tensions and counterposed witnesses. No theological consideration of homosexuality can rest content, however, with a short list of passages that treat the matter explicitly. We must consider how Scripture frames the discussion more broadly.

1. *God's creative intention for human sexuality.* From Genesis 1 onward, Scripture affirms repeatedly that God has made man and woman for one another and that our sexual desires rightly find fulfillment within heterosexual marriage (see, for instance, Mark 10:2–9; 1 Thess. 4:3–8; 1 Cor. 7:1–9; Eph. 5:21–33; Heb. 13:4).

2. *The fallen human condition.* The biblical analysis of the human predicament, most sharply expressed in Pauline theology, offers an account of human bondage to sin. As great-grandchildren of the Enlightenment, we like to think of ourselves as free moral agents, choosing rationally among possible actions, but Scripture unmasks that cheerful illusion and teaches us that we are deeply infected by the tendency to self-deception. We are "slaves of sin" (Rom. 6:17), which distorts our perceptions, overpowers our will, and renders us incapable of obedience (Rom. 7). *Redemption* (a word that means "being emancipated from slavery") is God's act of liberation, setting us free from the power of sin and placing us within the sphere of God's transforming power for righteousness (Rom. 6:20–22, 8:1–11; see Rom. 12:1–2).

Thus we must reject the apparently commonsensical assumption that only freely chosen acts are morally culpable. Quite the reverse: The very nature of sin is that it is *not* freely chosen. We are in bondage to sin but still accountable to God's righteous judgment of our actions. In light of this theological anthropology, it cannot be maintained that homosexuality is morally neutral because it is involuntary.

3. *The eschatological character of Christian existence.* The Christian community lives in a time of tension between "already" and "not yet." Already we have the

joy of the Holy Spirit; already we experience the transforming grace of God. But at the same time, we do not yet experience the fullness of redemption: We walk by faith, not by sight.

The creation groans in pain and bondage, "and not only the creation, but we ourselves, who have the first fruits of the Spirit, groan inwardly while we wait for adoption, the redemption of our bodies" (Romans 8:23). This means, among other things, that Christians must continue to struggle to live faithfully in the present time. The "redemption of our bodies" remains a future hope. The transforming power of the Spirit is present in our midst; the testimonies of those who claim to have been healed and transformed into a heterosexual orientation should be taken seriously. If we do not continue to live with that hope, we may be hoping for too little from God.

On the other hand, the "not yet" looms large; the testimonies of those like Gary who pray and struggle in Christian community and seek healing unsuccessfully for years must be taken with no less seriousness. Perhaps for many the best outcome that is attainable in this time between the times will be a life of disciplined abstinence.

That seems to be the spiritual condition Gary reached near the end of his life. He wrote in his last letter:

> Since All Saints Day I have felt myself being transformed. I no longer consider myself homosexual. Many would say, big deal, you're 42 . . . and are dying of AIDS. Big sacrifice. No, I didn't do this of my will, of an effort to improve myself, to make myself acceptable to God. No, he did this for me. I feel a great weight has been lifted off me. I have not turned "straight." I guess I'm like St. Paul's phrase, a eunuch for Christ.[7]

4. Demythologizing the idolatry of sex. The Bible undercuts our cultural obsession with sexual fulfillment. Despite the smooth illusions perpetrated by American mass culture, sexual gratification is not a sacred right, and celibacy is not a fate worse than death. Scripture, along with many subsequent generations of faithful Christians, bears witness that lives of freedom, joy, and service are possible without sexual relations. Indeed, however odd it may seem to contemporary sensibilities, some New Testament passages (Matt. 19:10–12; 1 Cor. 7) clearly commend the celibate life as a way of faithfulness.

Biblical Authority and Other Voices

We must consider how the Bible's teaching is to be weighted in relation to other sources of moral wisdom. I offer only some brief reflections as places to start the discussion.

1. *The Christian tradition.* Far more emphatically than Scripture itself, the moral teaching tradition of the Christian church has for more than nineteen hundred years declared homosexual behavior to be contrary to the will of God.

7. Actually, Gary's phrase rather elegantly conflates 1 Cor. 4:10 with Matt. 19:12.

Only within the past twenty years has any serious question been raised about the church's universal prohibition of such conduct. If anything, a passage like Romans 1 might serve to moderate the tradition's harsh judgments.

2. *Reason and scientific evidence.* Here the picture is cloudy. Some studies have claimed that as much as 10 percent of the population is inclined to same-sex erotic preference, and some theorists hold that homosexual orientation is innate (or formed by a very early age) and unchangeable. This is the opinion espoused by most advocates of full acceptance of homosexuality in the church: If homosexual orientation is a genetically determined trait, then any disapproval of it is a form of discrimination analogous to racism.

Others, however, regard homosexual orientation as a form of developmental maladjustment or "symbolic confusion." Some therapists claim significant clinical success rates in helping homosexual persons develop a heterosexual orientation; others challenge such claims. A major cross-cultural study published in 1990 by David F. Greenberg, professor of sociology at New York University (*The Construction of Homosexuality*[8]), contends that homosexual identity is socially constructed rather than inborn.

Even if it could be shown that same-sex preference is somehow genetically programmed, that would not necessarily make homosexual behavior morally appropriate. Surely Christian ethics does not want to hold that all inborn traits are good and desirable.

The argument from statistical incidence of homosexual behavior is even less useful in ethical deliberation. Even if 10 percent of the people in the United States should declare themselves to be of homosexual orientation, that would not settle the *normative* issue; it is impossible to argue simply from an "is" to an "ought."

3. *The experience of the community of faith.* This is the place where the advocates of homosexuality in the church have their most serious case. Robin Scroggs argues that the New Testament's condemnation of homosexuality applies only to a certain "model" of exploitative pederasty that was common in Hellenistic culture; hence, it is not applicable to the modern world's experience of mutual, loving homosexual relationships. I think that Scroggs's position fails to reckon adequately with Romans 1, where the relations are not described as pederastic and where Paul's disapproval has nothing to do with exploitation.

But the fact remains that there are numerous homosexual Christians — like my friend Gary and some of my ablest students at Yale — whose lives show signs of the presence of God, whose work in ministry is genuine and effective. They are evidence that God gives the Spirit to broken people and ministers grace even through us sinners, without thereby endorsing our sin.

In view of the considerable uncertainty surrounding the scientific and experiential evidence, in view of our culture's present swirling confusion about gender roles, in view of our propensity for self-deception, I think it prudent and neces-

8. Chicago: University of Chicago Press, 1990.

sary to let the univocal testimony of Scripture and the Christian tradition order the life of the church on this painfully controversial matter. We must affirm that the New Testament tells us the truth about ourselves as sinners and as God's sexual creatures: Marriage between man and woman is the normative form for human sexual fulfillment, and homosexuality is one among many tragic signs that we are a broken people, alienated from God's loving purpose.

Living under the Cross

Having said that the church cannot condone homosexual behavior, we still find ourselves confronted by complex problems that demand rigorous and compassionate solutions. On the issue of civil rights, there is no reason at all for the church to single out homosexual persons for malicious discriminatory treatment: Insofar as Christians have done so in the past, we must repent and seek instead to live out the gospel of reconciliation.

Those who uphold the biblical teaching against homosexuality must remember Paul's warning in Romans 2:1–3: We are all "without excuse"; we all stand or fall under God's judgment and mercy. If homosexual persons are not welcome in the church, I will have to walk out the door along with them, leaving in the sanctuary only those entitled to cast the first stone.

We live, then, as a community that embraces sinners as Jesus did, without waiving God's righteousness. We live confessing that God's grace claims us out of confusion and alienation and sets about making us whole. We live knowing that wholeness remains a hope rather than an attainment in this life. The homosexual Christians in our midst may teach us something about our true condition as people living between the cross and the final redemption of our bodies.

Gary wrote urgently of the imperatives of discipleship: "Are homosexuals to be excluded from the community of faith? Certainly not. But anyone who joins such a community should know that it is a place of transformation, of discipline, of learning, and not merely a place to be comforted or indulged."

In the midst of a culture that worships self-gratification, and a church that preaches a false Jesus who panders to our desires, those who seek the narrow way of obedience have a powerful word to speak. Just as Paul saw in pagan homosexuality a symbol of human fallenness, so I saw conversely in Gary, as I have seen in other homosexual friends and colleagues, a symbol of God's power made perfect in weakness (2 Cor. 12:9).

Gary knew through experience the bitter power of sin in a twisted world, and he trusted in God's love anyway. Thus he embodied the "sufferings of this present time" of which Paul speaks in Romans 8: living in the joyful freedom of the "first fruits of the Spirit," even while groaning along with a creation in bondage to decay.

Debate and Discernment, Scripture and the Spirit

Luke Timothy Johnson

Clearing Space for Debate

Homosexuality as an issue internal to the life of the church poses a fundamental challenge not only to moral discernment and pastoral care (the two aspects touched on in the recent *Catechism of the Catholic Church*) but to the self-understanding of the church as at once inclusive ("catholic") and separate ("holy"). The question is not only how we feel or think or act concerning homosexuality but also how those feelings, thoughts, and actions relate to the canonical texts that we take as normative for our lives together. Homosexuality in the church presents a hermeneutical problem.

The present essay has the modest goal of clearing some space for debate and discernment by setting out appropriate boundary markers for what promises to be a long and difficult discussion. I proceed by staking out three basic premises concerning ecclesial hermeneutics, and then a number of theses pertinent to the issue of homosexuality.

I take it as a given, first, that any process of discernment within the church uses as its fundamental framework the Irenaean triad of ecclesial self-definition: the canon of Scripture, the rule of faith, and the teaching authority of bishops. To step outside this framework is to shift the debate to other grounds entirely. Conservatism in commitment to canon, creed, and council is paradoxically the necessary condition for genuine freedom in scriptural interpretation.

Second, I take it as basic that hermeneutics involves the complex task of negotiating normative texts and continuing human experiences. Within the faith community, this means an openness to the ways in which God's revelation continues in human experience as well as a deep commitment to the conviction that such revelation, while often, at first, perceived as dissonant with the symbols of Scripture, will, by God's grace directing human fidelity, be seen as consonant with those symbols and God's own fidelity. Essentially, however, the call of faith is to the living God whose revelation continues, rather than to *our previous understanding* of the texts. Faith in the living God seeks understanding; theological understanding does not define faith or the living God.

My third premise is that Scripture does not characteristically speak with a single voice. Rather, as an anthology of compositions it contains an irreducible and precious pluralism of "voices," shaped by literary genre, theme, and perspective. The *authority* of these texts, furthermore, is most properly distinguished in terms of their function. Their highest authority is found in their capacity to reliably "author" Christian identity. Almost as important is the way in which these texts "authorize" a certain freedom in interpretation, by presenting a model of how Torah was reinterpreted in the light of new experiences. A third sort of authority is important but not as fundamental. The Scripture contains a wide range of "authorities" in the sense of *auctoritates,* or "opinions," not on all the subjects we could desire, but on many of great significance. Responsible hermeneutics claims the "freedom of the children of God" authorized by the New Testament. It seeks to negotiate the various voices or authorities within the texts in an effort to conform to that "mind of Christ" (1 Cor. 2:16) that is the authentic form of Christian identity which those texts are, through the power of the Holy Spirit, capable of "authoring."

I would like to think that these three premises, though perhaps nontraditional in formulation, are in essence profoundly Catholic, fairly and accurately representing the implications not only of the New Testament's own origin and canonization but also of much loyal and creative interpretation within the tradition.

Before moving to the specific case of homosexuality, it may be helpful to amplify slightly two aspects of these premises which without explication may appear careless if not cavalier. The first concerns the experience of God in human lives. Nothing could be more offensive than to challenge tradition on the basis of casual or unexamined experience, as though God's revelation were obvious or easy, or reducible to popularity polls. The call to the discernment of human experience is not a call to carelessness but its opposite; it is a call to the rigorous asceticism of attentiveness. I repeat: an appeal to some populist claim such as "everyone does it," or "surveys indicate" is theologically meaningless. What counts is whether *God* is up to something in human lives. Discernment of experience in this sense is for the detection of good news in surprising places, not for the disguising of old sins in novel faces.

Yet it is important to assert that God *does,* on the record, act in surprising and unanticipated ways and upset human perceptions of God's scriptural precedents. The most fundamental instance for the very existence of Christianity is the unexpected, crucified, and raised Messiah, Jesus. A considerable amount of what we call the New Testament derives from the attempt to resolve the cognitive dissonance between the experience of Jesus as the source of God's Holy Spirit, and the text of Torah that disqualifies him from that role, since "cursed be every one that hangs upon a tree" (Deut. 23:21; see Gal. 3:13).

Another example is the spread of the gospel to the Gentiles. It is easy for us at this distance, and with little understanding of the importance of the body language of table fellowship, to take for granted such a breaking of precedent that allowed Gentiles to share fully in the life of the Messianic community without being circumcised or practicing observance of Torah. Good for us, also, therefore, to read Acts 10–15 to see just how agonizing and difficult a task it was for that first generation of Christians to allow their perception of God's activity to change their perceptions, and use that new experience as the basis for reinterpreting Scripture.

The second aspect of the premises I want to amplify slightly is the requirement for responsible hermeneutics to take every voice of Scripture seriously. I spoke of the *auctoritates* as diverse and sometimes contradictory. But every ecclesial decision to live by one rather than another of these voices, to privilege one over another, to suppress one in order to live by another, must be willing to state the grounds of that decision and demonstrate how the experience of God and the more fundamental principles of "the mind of Christ" and "freedom of the children of God" (principles also rooted in the authority of the text) legitimate the distance between ecclesial decision and a clear statement of Scripture. Do we allow divorce (even if we don't openly call it that) when Jesus forbade it? We must be willing to support our decision by an appeal not simply to changing circumstances but to a deeper wisdom given by the Spirit into the meaning of human covenant, and therefore a better understanding of the sayings of Jesus. This is never easy. It is sometimes — as in the case of taking oaths and vows — not even possible. But it is the task of responsible ecclesial hermeneutics.

The Hermeneutics of Homosexuality

How does this approach provide a context for the hermeneutics of homosexuality? First, it cautions us against trying to suppress biblical texts that condemn homosexual behavior (Lev. 18:22; Wisd. 14:26; Rom. 1:26–27; 1 Cor. 6:9) or to make them say something other than what they say. I think it fair to conclude that early Christianity knew about homosexuality as it was practiced in Greco-Roman culture, shared Judaism's association of it with the "abominations" of idolatry, and regarded it as incompatible with life in the kingdom of God. These *auctoritates* emphatically define homosexuality as a vice, and they cannot simply be dismissed.

Second, however, Scripture itself "authorizes" us to exercise the freedom of the children of God in our interpretation of such passages. We are freed, for example, to evaluate the relative paucity of such condemnations. Compared to the extensive and detailed condemnation of economic oppression at virtually every level of tradition, the off-handed rejection of homosexuality appears instinctive and relatively unreflective. We are freed as well to assess the contexts of the condemnations: the rejection of homosexuality, as of other sexual sins, is connected to the incompatibility of *porneia* with life in the Kingdom. We can further observe that the flat rejection of *porneia* (any form of sexual immorality) is more frequent and general than any of its specific manifestations. We are freed, finally, to consider the grounds on which the texts seem to include homosexuality within *porneia,* namely that it is "against nature," an abomination offensive to God's created order.

Such considerations, in turn, provide an opening for a conversation between our human experience (including our religious experience) and the texts of our tradition. Does our experience now support or challenge the assumption that homosexuality is, simply and without exception, an "offense against nature"? Leviticus and Paul considered homosexuality a vice because they assumed it was a deliberate choice that "suppressed the truth about God." Is that a fair assessment of homosexuality as we have come to understand it? It is, of course, grossly distorting even to talk about homosexuality as though one clearly definable thing were meant. But many of us who have gay and lesbian friends and relatives have arrived with them at the opposite conclusion: for many persons the acceptance of their homosexuality *is* an acceptance of creation as it applies to them. It is emphatically *not* a vice that is chosen. If this conclusion is correct, what is the hermeneutical implication?

Another order of questions concerns the connection of homosexuality to *porneia.* The church, it is clear, cannot accept *porneia.* But what is the essence of "sexual immorality"? Is the moral quality of sexual behavior defined biologically in terms of the use of certain body parts, or is it defined in terms of personal commitment and attitudes? Is not *porneia* essentially sexual activity that ruptures covenant, just as *castitas* is sexual virtue within or outside marriage because it is sexuality in service to covenant?

If sexual virtue and vice are defined covenantally rather than biologically, then it is possible to place homosexual and heterosexual activity in the same context. Certainly, the church must reject the *porneia* that glorifies sex for its own sake, indulges in promiscuity, destroys the bonds of commitment, and seduces the innocent. Insofar as a "gay lifestyle" has these connotations, the church must emphatically and always say "no" to it. But the church must say "no" with equal emphasis to the heterosexual "*Playboy/Cosmo* lifestyle" version. In both cases, also, the church can acknowledge that human sexual activity, while of real and great significance, is not wholly determinative of human existence or worth, and can perhaps begin to ask whether the church's concentration on sexual behavior corresponds proportionally to the modest emphasis placed by Scripture.

The harder question, of course, is whether the church can recognize the possibility of homosexual committed and covenantal love, in the way that it recognizes such sexual and personal love in the sacrament of marriage. This is a harder question because it pertains not simply to moral attitudes or pastoral care but to the social symbolization of the community. The issue here is analogous to the one facing earliest Christianity after Gentiles started being converted. Granted that they had been given the Holy Spirit, could they be accepted into the people of God just as they were, or must they first "become Jewish" by being circumcised and obeying all the ritual demands of Torah? Remember, please, the stakes: the Gentiles were "by nature" unclean and were "by practice" polluted by idolatry. We are obsessed by the sexual dimensions of the body. The first-century

Mediterranean world was obsessed by the social implications of food and table fellowship. The decision to let the Gentiles in "as is" and to establish a more inclusive form of table fellowship, we should note, came into direct conflict with the accepted interpretation of Torah and what God wanted of humans.

The decision, furthermore, was not easy to reach. Paul's Letter to the Galatians suggests some of the conflict it generated. Even the irenic Luke devotes six full chapters of Acts (10–15) to the account of how the community caught up with God's intentions, stumbling every step of the way through confusion, doubt, challenge, disagreements, divisions, and debate. Much suffering had to be endured before the implications of Peter's question, "If then God gave them the same gift that he gave us when we believed in the Lord Jesus Christ, who was I that could hinder God?" (Acts 11:17), could be fully answered: "We believe that we [Jews] will be saved through the grace of the Lord Jesus, just as they [Gentiles] will" (Acts 15:11).

The grounds of the church's decision then was the work that God was doing among the Gentiles, bringing them to salvation through faith. On the basis of this experience of God's work, the church made bold to reinterpret Torah, finding there unexpected legitimation for its fidelity to God's surprising ways (Acts 15:15–18). How was that work of God made known to the church? Through the narratives of faith related by Paul and Barnabas and Peter, their personal testimony of how "signs and wonders" had been worked among the Gentiles (Acts 15:4, 6–11, 12–13).

Such witness is what the church now needs from homosexual Christians. Are homosexuality and holiness of life compatible? Is homosexual covenantal love according to "the mind of Christ," an authentic realization of that Christian identity authored by the Holy Spirit, and therefore "authored" as well by the Scripture despite the "authorities" speaking against it? The church can discern this only on the basis of faithful witness. The burden of proof required to overturn scriptural precedents is heavy, but it is a burden that has been borne before. The church cannot, should not, define itself in response to political pressure or popularity polls. But it is called to discern the work of God in human lives and adapt its self-understanding in response to the work of God. Inclusivity must follow from evidence of holiness; are there narratives of homosexual holiness to which we must begin to listen?

Suggestions for Further Reading

Boswell, John. *Christianity, Social Tolerance, and Homosexuality: Gay People in Western Europe from the Beginning of the Christian Era to the Fourteenth Century.* Chicago: University of Chicago Press, 1980.

Comstock, Gary D. *Unrepentant, Self-Affirming, Practicing: Lesbian/Bisexual/Gay People within Organized Religion.* New York: Continuum, 1996.

Greenberg, David F. *The Construction of Homosexuality.* Chicago: University of Chicago Press, 1990.

Hays, Richard B. "Homosexuality." In *The Moral Vision of the New Testament,* 379–406. New York: HarperSanFrancisco, 1996.

Kotva, Joseph J., Jr. "Scripture, Ethics, and the Local Church: Homosexuality as a Case Study." *Conrad Grebel Review* 7 (winter 1989): 41–61.

Schmidt, Thomas E. *Straight and Narrow? Compassion and Clarity in the Homosexuality Debate.* Downers Grove, Ill.: InterVarsity Press, 1995.

Sikes, Jeffrey S., ed. *Homosexuality in the Church: Both Sides of the Debate.* Louisville: Westminster John Knox Press, 1994.

Chapter 10

Abortion Theologically Understood

Stanley Hauerwas

Editor's Introduction

Stanley Hauerwas holds the conviction that Christians do *Christian* ethics. This shows itself in several ways in the following essay, and, at each point, resonates strongly with MacIntyrean themes. First, the essay is an "occasional" document. Originally delivered as a lecture for the meeting of the United Methodist Church's Evangelical Fellowship during its North Carolina Annual Conference in June 1990, Hauerwas's message is explicitly directed to a Christian readership. One does not commonly find a journal article (which, by nature of the genre, is crafted for a generic audience) beginning with a sermon—especially one written by someone other than the author of the article! But Hauerwas's inclusion of Rev. Terry Hamilton-Poore's homily shows the way Hauerwas has joined a much longer conversation. This conversation began as soon as there were biblical texts for preaching, such as Matthew 25, and has continued ever since. The discussion has revolved around the meaning and implication that such texts hold for Christian lives, that is, for the corporate life of those whose identity is determinatively shaped by their joint allegiance to these very texts. As you will recall, MacIntyre has dubbed this long-standing conversation about the role of authoritative texts and prophetic voices a "tradition."

Second, Hauerwas can be seen doing Christian ethics when he insists that the question facing Christians at every turn is "What kind of people ought we be?" And his emphasis is on the "we." What kind of people ought *we* be?—we who take seriously the task to "care for the least of these" in the same manner Jesus cared. The primary issue for Christians is not rendering a decision (for example, concerning when life begins, or regarding whose rights have priority) but responding in a manner consonant with Christian identity. In MacIntyre's terms, Christians cannot answer "What ought *we* do?" until they first identify who constitutes the "we." This identification is made by recognizing of which stories Christians are a part. Not only are Christians embedded in the life stories of other community members—including this pregnant teenage girl, that irresponsible teenage boy, and those unborn children—and therefore required to respond fittingly, Christians are also characters in the ongoing story of the gospel. Their actions, therefore, must be faithful to the gospel narrative.

Third, Christians do Christian ethics by refusing to debate issues except on Christian terms. The standard contemporary way of framing the abortion debate is unacceptable to Christians because it pits the unborn child against the pregnant mother and says, "Now, choose!" In stark contrast, Christians maintain that they are for *both*. If Christians are to retain their distinctive identity, they must recast the language of the debate so as to be able to champion both victims. This move mirrors the way MacIntyre wrested the meaning of moral concepts such as *goodness* and *justice* out of the coarse hands of post-Enlightenment thinkers by demonstrating the rightful use of these terms *within the tradition* of Aristotelianism. The similarity between Hauerwas's admonition and MacIntyre's example is clear: for Christians, moral reflection must occur by means of concepts internal to the Christian tradition.

Finally, Hauerwas's approach to abortion is shown to be a distinctively Christian one by his plea that Christians tackle the problem corporately, as "Church." Not only do Christians have a distinctive identity according to which their response must be fashioned in a Christlike manner, the *mode* of this response must be corporate rather than individual. As MacIntyre has shown, the notion that the individual is the fundamental unit of social reality (that is, one logically prior to the existence of community) was one of the central mistakes of the Enlightenment project. (Ironically, this mistake could not be propagated except by means of political liberalism, a communal tradition in its own right!) The Christian community is most threatened by the dangers of individualism when it unwisely appropriates for its own moral reflection liberalism's "rights" terminology, because rights are always held *against* others, a fact which renders impossible a genuine common good. However, authentic Christian existence is not a privatized one. Hauerwas is shockingly clear on this: "In the Church we tell you what you can and cannot do with your genitals. They are not your own. They are not private. That means you cannot commit adultery. If you do, you are no longer a member of 'us.'" Hauerwas reminds Christians that, as the church, they are dependent upon each other. On the one hand, this means that within the Christian community, all is public. On the other hand, this means that the Christian response to abortion requires a joint effort. Only by acting corporately can individual members of the church be sustained in practices, such as hospitality, by means of virtues, such as courage.

BRAD J. KALLENBERG

Text and Sermon

I am going to start with a sermon. Every once in a while you get a wonderful gift. Recently a former student, who is now a Presbyterian minister, mailed to me a copy of a sermon on abortion. I could not do better than offer this sermon and an ethical commentary on it. The author of the following sermon is the Reverend Terry Hamilton-Poore, formerly the chaplain of Queens College, Charlotte, North Carolina, and now of Kansas City, Missouri.

The text for the sermon is Matthew 25:31–46, from the Revised Standard Version.

> When the Son of man comes in his glory, and all the angels with him, then he will sit on his glorious throne. Before him will be gathered all the nations, and he will separate them one from another as a shepherd separates the sheep from the goats, and he will place the sheep at his right hand, but the goats at the left. Then the King will say to those at his right hand, "Come, O blessed of my Father, inherit the kingdom prepared for you from the foundation of the world; for I was hungry and you gave me food, I was thirsty and you gave me drink, I was a stranger and you welcomed me, I was naked and you clothed me, I was sick and you visited me, I was in prison and you came to me." Then the righteous will answer him, "Lord, when did we see thee hungry and feed thee, or thirsty and give thee drink? And when did we see thee a stranger and welcome thee, or naked and clothe thee? And when did we see thee sick or in prison and visit thee?" And the King will answer them, "Truly, I say to you, as you did it to one of the least of these my brethren, you did it to me." Then he will say to those at his left hand. "Depart from me, you cursed, into the eternal fire prepared for the devil and his angels; for I was hungry and you gave me no food, I was thirsty and you gave me no drink, I was a stranger and you did not welcome me, naked and you did not clothe me, sick and in prison and you did not visit me." Then they also will answer, "Lord, when did we see thee hungry or thirsty or a stranger and naked or sick or in prison, and did not minister to thee?" Then he will answer them, "Truly, I say to you, as you did it not to one of the least of these, you did it not to me." And they will go away into eternal punishment, but the righteous into eternal life.

"As a Christian and a woman, I find abortion a very difficult subject to address. Even so, I believe that it is essential that the Church face the issue of abortion in a distinctly Christian manner. Because of that, I am hereby addressing not society in general but those of us who call ourselves Christians. I also want to be clear that I am not addressing abortion as a legal issue. I believe the issue, for the Church, must be framed not around the banners of 'pro-choice' or 'pro-life' but around God's call to care for the least among us whom Jesus calls his sisters and brothers.

"So, in this sermon, I will make three points. The first point is that the gospel favors women and children. The second point is that the customary framing of the abortion issue by both pro-choice and pro-life groups is unbiblical because it assumes that the woman is ultimately responsible for both herself and for any child she might carry. The third point is that a Christian response must reframe the issue to focus on responsibility rather than rights."

Gospel, Women, and Children

"Point number one: the gospel favors women and children. The gospel is feminist. In Matthew, Mark, Luke, and John, Jesus treats women as thinking people who are worthy of respect. This was not, of course, the usual attitude of that time. In addition, it is to the women among Jesus' followers, not to the men, that he entrusts the initial proclamation of his resurrection. It is not only Jesus himself who sees the gospel making all people equal, for St. Paul wrote, 'There is neither Jew nor Greek, there is neither slave nor free, there is neither male nor female; for you are all one in Christ Jesus' (Gal. 3:28 RSV).

"And yet, women have been oppressed through recorded history and continue to be oppressed today. So when Jesus says, 'as you did it to one of the least of these my brethren, you did it to me' (Matt. 25:40 RSV), I have to believe that Jesus includes women among 'the least of these.' Anything that helps women, therefore, helps Jesus. When Jesus says, 'as you did it to one of the least of these,' he is also talking about children, because children are literally 'the least of these.' Children lack the three things the world values most — power, wealth, and influence. If we concern ourselves with people who are powerless, then children should obviously be at the top of our list. One irony of the abortion debate, as it now stands in our church and society, is that it frames these two groups, women and children, as enemies of one another."

The Woman Alone

"This brings me to my second point. The usual framing of the abortion issue, by both pro-choice and pro-life groups, is unbiblical because it assumes that the woman is ultimately responsible both for herself and for any child she might carry. Why is it that women have abortions? Women I know, and those I know about, have had abortions for two basic reasons: the fear that they could not handle the financial and physical demands of the child, and the fear that having the child would destroy relationships that are important to them.

"An example of the first fear, the inability to handle the child financially or physically, is the divorced mother of two children, the younger of whom has Down syndrome. This woman recently discovered that she was pregnant. She believed abortion was wrong. However, the father of the child would not commit himself to help raise this child, and she was afraid she could not handle raising another child on her own.

"An example of the second fear, the fear of destroying relationships, is the woman who became pregnant and was told by her husband that he would leave her if she did not have an abortion. She did not want to lose her husband, so she had the abortion. Later, her husband left her anyway.

"In both of these cases, and in others I have known, the woman has had an abortion not because she was exercising her free choice but because she felt she had no choice. In each case the responsibility for caring for the child, had she had the child, would have rested squarely and solely on the woman."

Reframing with Responsibility

"Which brings me to my third point: the Christian response to abortion must reframe the issue to focus on responsibility rather than rights. The pro-choice/pro-life debate presently pits the right of the mother to choose against the right of the fetus to live. The Christian response, on the other hand, centers on the responsibility of the whole Christian community to care for 'the least of these.'

"According to the Presbyterian Church's *Book* of *Order* of 1983–1985, when a person is baptized, the congregation answers this question: 'Do you, the members of this congregation, in the name of the whole Church of Christ, undertake the responsibility for the continued Christian nurture of this person, promising to be an example of the new life in Christ and to pray for him or her in this new life?' We make this promise because we know that no adult belongs to himself or herself, and that no child belongs to his or her parents, but that every person is a child of God. Because of that, every young one is our child, the church's child to care for. This is not an option. It is a responsibility.

"Let me tell you two stories about what it is like when the Church takes this responsibility seriously. The first is a story that Will Willimon, the Dean of Duke University Chapel, tells about a black church. In this church, when a teenager has a baby that she cannot care for, the church baptizes the baby and gives him or her to an older couple in the church that has the time and wisdom to raise the child. That way, says the pastor, the couple can raise the teenage mother along with the baby. 'That,' the pastor says, 'is how we do it.'

"The second story involves something that happened to a woman named Deborah. A member of her church, a divorced woman, became pregnant, and the father dropped out of the picture. The woman decided to keep the child. But as the pregnancy progressed and began to show, she became upset because she felt she could not go to church anymore. After all, here she was, a Sunday School teacher, unmarried and pregnant. So she called Deborah. Deborah told her to come to church and sit in the pew with Deborah's family, and, no matter how the church reacted, the family would support her. Well, the church rallied around when the woman's doctor told her at her six-month checkup that she owed him the remaining balance of fifteen hundred dollars by the next month; otherwise, he would not deliver the baby. The church held a baby shower and raised the money. When the time came for her to deliver, another woman in the church was her labor coach. When the woman's mother refused to come and help after the baby was born, the church brought food and helped clean her house while she recovered from the birth. Now the woman's little girl is the child of the parish.

"This is what the Church looks like when it takes seriously its call to care for 'the least of these.' These two churches differ in certain ways: one is Methodist, the other Roman Catholic; one has a carefully planned strategy for supporting women and babies, the other simply reacted spontaneously to a particular woman and her baby. But in each case the church acted with creativity and compassion to live out the gospel.

"In our Scripture lesson today, Jesus gives a preview of the Last Judgment:

> Then the King will say to those at his right hand, "Come, O blessed of my Father, inherit the kingdom prepared for you from the foundation of the world; for I

> was hungry and you gave me food, I was thirsty and you gave me drink, I was a stranger and you welcomed me, I was naked and you clothed me, I was sick and you visited me, I was in prison and you came to me." Then the righteous will answer him, "Lord, when did we see thee hungry and feed thee, or thirsty and give thee drink? And when did we see thee a stranger and welcome thee, or naked and clothe thee? And when did we see thee sick or in prison and visit thee?" And the King will answer them, "Truly, I say to you, as you did it to one of the least of these my brethren, you did it to me." (Matthew 25:34–40 RSV)

"We cannot simply throw the issue of abortion in the faces of women and say, 'You decide and you bear the consequences of your decision.' As the Church, our response to the abortion issue must be to shoulder the responsibility to care for women and children. We cannot do otherwise and still be the Church. If we close our doors in the faces of women and children, then we close our doors in the face of Christ."

An Ethical Commentary

I begin with this sermon because I suspect that most ministers have not preached about abortion. Most ministers have not preached about abortion because they have not had the slightest idea how to do it in a way that would not make everyone in their congregations mad. Most ministers considering a sermon on abortion have mistakenly thought that they would have to take up the terms that are given by the wider society.

Above you have a young minister cutting through the kind of pro-choice and pro-life rhetoric that is given in the wider society. She preached a sermon on abortion that derives directly from the gospel. Her sermon is a reminder about what the Church is to be about when addressing this issue in a Christian way. That is the primary thing that I want to underline: the Church's refusal to use society's terms for the abortion debate, and the churches' willingness to take on the abortion problem as Church. This sermon suggests that abortion is a question not about the law but about what kind of people we are to be as the Church and as Christians.

Abortion forces the Church to recognize the fallacy of a key presumption of many Christians in this society—namely, that what Christians believe about the moral life is what any right-thinking person, whether he or she is Christian or not, also believes. Again, that presumption is false. We Christians have thought that when we address the issue of abortion and when we say "we," we are talking about anybody who is a good, decent American. But that is not who "we" Christians are. If any issue is going to help us discover that, it is going to be the issue of abortion.

Beyond Rights

Christians in America are tempted to think of issues like abortion primarily in legal terms such as "rights." This is because the legal mode, as Tocqueville pointed out long ago, provides the constituting morality in liberal societies. In other words, when you live in a liberal society like ours, the fundamental problem is how you can achieve cooperative agreements between individuals who share nothing other than their fear of death. In liberal society the law has the function of securing such agreements. That is the reason that lawyers are to America what priests were to the medieval world. The law is our way of negotiating safe agreements between autonomous individuals who have nothing in common other than their fear of death and their mutual desire for protection.

Therefore, rights language is fundamental in our political and moral context. In America, we oftentimes pride ourselves, as Americans, on being pragmatic people who are not ideological. But that is absolutely false. No country has ever been more theory-dependent on a public philosophy than America.

Indeed I want to argue that America is the only country that has the misfortune of being founded on a philosophical mistake — namely, the notion of inalienable rights. We Christians do not believe that we have inalienable rights. That is the false presumption of Enlightenment individualism, and it opposes everything that Christians believe about what it means to be a creature. Notice that the issue is *inalienable* rights. Rights make a certain sense when they are correlative to duties and goods, but they are not inalienable. For example, when the barons protested against the king in the Magna Carta, they did so in the name of their duties to their underlings. Duties, not rights, were primary. The rights were simply ways of remembering what the duties were.

Christians, to be more specific, do not believe that we have a right to do with our bodies whatever we want. We do not believe that we have a right to our bodies because when we are baptized we become members of one another; then we can tell one another what it is that we should, and should not, do with our bodies. I had a colleague at the University of Notre Dame who taught Judaica. He was Jewish and always said that any religion that does not tell you what to do with your genitals and pots and pans cannot be interesting. That is exactly true. In the Church we tell you what you can and cannot do with your genitals. They are not your own. They are not private. That means that you cannot commit adultery. If you do, you are no longer a member of "us." Of course pots and pans are equally important.

I was recently giving a talk at a very conservative university, Houston Baptist University. Since its business school has an ethics program, I called my talk "Why Business Ethics Is a Bad Idea." When I had finished, one of the business-school people asked, "Well, goodness, what then can we Christians do about business ethics?" I said, "A place to start would be the local church. It might be established that before anyone joins a Baptist church in Houston, he or she would have to declare in public what his or her annual income is." The only people whose incomes are known in the United Methodist Church today are ordained ministers. Why should we make the ministers' salaries public and not the laity's? Most people would rather tell you what they do in the bedroom than how much they make. With these things in mind, you can see how the

Church is being destroyed by the privatization of individual lives, legitimated by the American ethos. If you want to know who or what is destroying the babies of this country through abortion, look at privatization, which is learned in the economic arena.

Under the veil of American privatization, we are encouraging people to believe in the same way that Andrew Carnegie believed. He thought that he had a right to his steel mills. In the same sense, people think that they have a right to their bodies. The body is then a piece of property in a capitalist sense. Unfortunately, that is antithetical to the way we Christians think that we have to share as members of the same body of Christ.

So you cannot separate these issues. If you think that you can be very concerned about abortion and not concerned about the privatization of American life generally, you are making a mistake. So the problem is: how should we, as Christians, think about abortion without the rights rhetoric that we have been given — right to my body, right to life, pro-choice, pro-life, and so on? In this respect, we Christians must try to make the abortion issue our issue.

Learning the Language

We must remember that the first question is not, Is abortion right or wrong? or, Is this abortion right or wrong? Rather, the first question is, Why do Christians call abortion *abortion?* And with the first question goes a second, Why do Christians think that *abortion* is a morally problematic term? To call abortion by that name is already a moral achievement. The reason that people are pro-*choice* rather than pro-*abortion* is that nobody really wants to be pro-abortion. The use of *choice* rather than *abortion* is an attempt at a linguistic transformation to avoid the reality of abortion, because most people do not want to use that description. So, instead of *abortion,* another term is used, something like *termination of pregnancy.* Now, the Church can live more easily in a world with "terminated pregnancies," because in that world the Church no longer claims power, even linguistic power, over that medically described part of life; instead, doctors do.

One of the interesting cultural currents is the medicalization of abortion. It is one of the ways that the medical profession is continuing to secure power against the Church. Ordained ministers can sense this when they are in hospital situations. In a hospital today, the minister feels less power than the doctor, right?

My way of explaining medicine's power over the Church is to refer to the training of ministers and doctors. When someone goes to seminary today, she or he can say, "I'm not into Christology this year. I'm just into relating. After all, relating is what the ministry is really about, isn't it? Ministry is about helping people relate to one another, isn't it? So I want to take some more Clinical Pastoral Education (CPE) courses." And the seminary replies, "Go ahead and do it. Right, get your head straight, and so on." A kid can go to medical school and say, "I'm not into anatomy this year. I'm into relating. So I'd like to take a few more courses in psychology, because I need to know how to relate better to people." The medical school replies, "Who in the hell do you think you are, kid? We're not interested in your interests. You're going to take anatomy. If you don't like it, that's tough."

Now, what that shows you is that people believe incompetent physicians can hurt them. Therefore, people expect medical schools to hold their students responsible for the kind of training that's necessary for them to be competent physicians. On the other hand, few people believe an incompetent minister can damage their salvation. This helps you see that what people want today is not salvation but health. And that helps you see why the medical profession has, as a matter of fact, so much power over the churches and their ministry. The medical establishment is the counter-salvation-promising group in our society today.

So when you innocently say "termination of pregnancy," while it sounds like a neutral term, you are placing your thinking under the sway of the medical profession. In contrast to the medical profession, Christians maintain that the description "abortion" is more accurate and determinative than the description "termination of pregnancy." That is, morally, a most serious matter.

Morally speaking, the first issue is never what we are to do but what we should see. Here is the way it works: You can act only in the world that you can see, and you must be taught to see by learning to say. Therefore, using the language of abortion is one way of training ourselves as Christians to see and to practice its opposite—hospitality, and particularly hospitality to children and the vulnerable. Therefore, *abortion* is a word that reminds us how Christians are to speak about, to envision, and to live life—and that is to be a baptizing people that is ready to welcome new life into our communities.

In that sense *abortion* is as much a moral description as *suicide*. Exactly why does a community maintain a description like *suicide?* Because it reminds the community of its practice of enhancing life, even under duress. The language of suicide also reminds you that even when you are in pain, even when you are sick, you have an obligation to remain with the People of God, vulnerable and yet present.

When we joined the United Methodist Church, we promised to uphold it with "our prayers, our presence, our gifts, and our service." We often think that "our presence" is the easy one. In fact, it is the hardest one. I can illustrate this by speaking about the church I belonged to in South Bend, Indiana. It was a small group of people that originally was an Evangelical United Brethren congregation. Every Sunday we had Eucharist, prayers from the congregation, and a noon meal for the neighborhood. When the usual congregation would pray, we would pray for the hungry in Ethiopia and for an end to the war in the Near East, and so on. Well, this bag lady started coming to church and she would pray things like, "Lord, I have a cold, and I would really like you to cure it." Or, "I've just had a horrible week and I'm depressed. Lord, would you please raise my spirits?" You never hear prayers like that in most of our churches. Why? Because the last thing that Christians want to do is show one another that they are vulnerable. People go to church because they are strong; they want to reinforce the presumption of strength.

One of the crucial issues here is how we learn to be a people dependent on one another. We must learn to confess that, as a hospitable people, we need one another because we are dependent on one another. The last thing that the Church wants is a bunch of autonomous, free individuals. We want people who know how to express authentic need, because that creates community.

So the language of abortion is a reminder about the kind of community that we need to be. Abortion language reminds the Church to be ready to receive new life as Church.

The Church as True Family

We, as church, are ready to be challenged by one another. This has to do with the fact that in the Church, every adult, whether single or married, is called to be parent. All Christian adults have parental responsibility because of baptism. Biology does not make parents in the Church; baptism does. Baptism makes all adult Christians parents and gives them the obligation to help introduce these children to the gospel. Listen to the baptismal vows; in them the whole Church promises to be parent. In this regard the Church reinvents the family.

The assumption here is that the first enemy of the family is the Church. When I taught a marriage course at Notre Dame, I used to read to my students a letter. It went something like this, "Our son had done well. He had gone to good schools, had gone through the military, had gotten out, had looked like he had a very promising career ahead. Unfortunately, he has joined some Eastern religious sect. Now he does not want to have anything to do with us because we are people of 'the world.' He is never going to marry because now his true family is this funny group of people he associates with. We are heartsick. We do not know what to do about this." Then I would ask the class, "Who wrote this letter?" The students would guess, "Probably some family whose kid became a Moonie or a Hare Krishna." In fact, this is an account by a fourth-century Roman senatorial family about their son's conversion to Christianity.

From the beginning we Christians have made singleness as valid a way of life as marriage. This is how. What it means to be the Church is to be a group of people called out of the world, and back into the world, to embody the hope of the kingdom of God. Children are not necessary for the growth of the Kingdom, because the Church can call the stranger into its midst. That makes both singleness and marriage possible vocations. If everybody has to marry, then marriage is a terrible burden. But the Church does not believe that everybody has to marry. Even so, those who do not marry are also parents within the Church, because the Church is now the true family. The Church is a family into which children are brought and received. It is only within that context that it makes sense for the Church to say, "We are always ready to receive children." The People of God know no enemy when it comes to children.

From the Pro-Life Side: When Life Begins

Against the background of the Church as family, you can see that the Christian language of abortion challenges the modern tendency to reduce morality to moral dilemmas and discrete units of behavior. If that tendency is followed, you get the questions, "What is really wrong with abortion?" and "Isn't abortion a separate problem that can be settled on its own grounds?" And then you get the termination-of-pregnancy language that wants to see abortion as solely a medical problem. At the same time, you get abortion framed in a legalistic way.

When many people start talking about abortion, what is the first thing they talk about? When life begins. And why do they get into the question of when life begins? Because they think that the abortion issue is determined primarily by the claims that life is sacred and that life is never to be taken. They assume that these claims let you know how you ought to think about abortion.

Well, I want to know where Christians get the notion that life is sacred. That notion seems to have no reference at all to God. Any good secularist can think life is sacred. Of course what the secularist means by the word *sacred* is interesting, but the idea that Christians are about the maintenance of some principle separate from our understanding of God is just crazy. As a matter of fact, Christians do not believe that life is sacred. I often remind my right-to-life friends that Christians took their children with them to martyrdom rather than have them raised pagan. Christians believe there is much worth dying for. We do not believe that human life is an absolute good in and of itself. Of course our desire to protect human life is part of our seeing each human being as God's creature. But that does not mean that we believe that life is an overriding good.

To say that life is an overriding good is to underwrite the modern sentimentality that there is absolutely nothing in this world for which it is worth dying. Christians know that Christianity is simply extended training in dying early. That is what we have always been about. Listen to the gospel! I know that today we use the Church primarily as a means of safety, but life in the Church should actually involve extended training in learning to die early.

When you frame the abortion issue in sacredness-of-life language, you get into intractable debates about when life begins. Notice that here we have an issue for legalists. For the legalists, the fundamental question becomes, How do you avoid doing the wrong thing?

In contrast, the Christian approach is not one of deciding when life has begun, but hoping that it has. We hope that human life has begun! We are not the kind of people who ask, Does human life start at the blastocyst stage, or at implantation? Instead, we are the kind of people who hope life has started, because we are ready to believe that this new life will enrich our community. We believe this not because we have sentimental views about children. Honestly, I cannot imagine anything worse than people saying that they have children because their hope for the future is in their children. You would never have children if you had them for that reason. We are able to have children because our hope is in God, who makes it possible to do the absurd thing of having children. In a world of such terrible injustice, in a world of such terrible misery, in a world that may well be about the killing of our children, having children is an extraordinary act of faith and hope. But as Christians our hope is from the God who urges us to welcome children. When children are welcomed, it is an extraordinary testimony of faith.

From the Pro-Choice Side: When Personhood Begins

On the pro-choice side you also get the abortion issue framed in a noncommunitarian way. On the pro-choice side you get the question about when the fetus becomes a "person," because only persons supposedly have citizenship rights. That is the issue of *Roe v. Wade.*

It is odd for Christians to take this approach since we believe that we are first of all citizens of a kingdom far different from something called the United States of America. If we end up identifying personhood with the ability to reason — which, I think, finally renders all of our lives deeply problematic — then we cannot tell why we ought to care for the profoundly retarded. One of the most chilling aspects of the current abortion debate in the wider society is the general acceptance, even among pro-life people, of the legitimacy of aborting severely defective children. Where do people get that idea? Where do people get the idea that severely defective children are somehow less than God's creatures? People get that idea by privileging rationality. We privilege our ability to reason. I find that unbelievable.

We must remember that as Christians we do not believe in the inherent sacredness of life or in personhood. Instead we believe that there is much for which to die. Christians do not believe that life is a right or that we have inherent dignity. Instead we believe that life is the gift of a gracious God. That is our primary Christian language regarding abortion: Life is the gift of a gracious God. As part of our understanding life as gift, we believe that we ought to live in a profound awe of the other's existence, knowing that in the other we find God. So abortion is a description maintained by Christians to remind us of the kind of community we must be to sustain the practice of hospitality to new life. That is related to everything else that we do and that I believe.

Slipping down the Slope

We have all heard the argument that if you let abortion start occurring for the late-developed fetus, sooner or later you cannot prohibit infanticide. This is the slippery-slope argument. H. Tristram Engelhardt, a prominent, well-respected philosopher in this country, argues in his *Foundations of Bioethics* that, as far as he can see, there is absolutely no reason that we should not kill children up to a year and a half old, since they are not yet persons.[1] *Foundations* is a text

1. 2d ed. (1986; Oxford: Oxford University Press, 1995).

widely used in our universities today by people having to deal with all kinds of bioethical problems.

I have no doubt that bioethical problems exist. After all, today you can run into all kinds of anomalies. For example, in hospitals, on one side of the hall, doctors and nurses are working very hard to save a prematurely born, 500-gram child — while, on the other side of the hall, they are aborting a similar child. There are many such anomalies, and you can build up a collection of these horror stories. But people can get used to horror. Also, opposition to the horrible should not be the final, decisive ground on which Christians stand while tackling these issues. Instead, the issue is how we as a Christian community can live in affirmation of the kind of hospitality that will be a witness to the society we live in. That will open up a discourse that otherwise would be impossible.

One of the reasons that the Church's position on abortion has not been authentic is that the Church has not lived and witnessed as a community in a way that challenges the fundamental secular presuppositions of both the pro-life side and the pro-choice side. We are going to have to become that kind of community if our witness is to have the integrity that will make a difference.

The Male Issue

When addressing abortion, we must engage the crucial question of the relationship between men and women, and thus sexual ethics. The church has tried — and this is typical of the liberal social order in which we live — to isolate the issue of abortion from the issue of sexual ethics. We cannot do that.

As the above sermon suggests, the legalization of abortion can be seen as the further abandonment of women by men. One of the cruelest things to happen in the last few years is the convincing of women that "yes" is as good as "no." That gives great power to men, especially in societies, like ours, where men continue to have domination. Women's greatest power is the power of the "no." This simply has to be understood. The Church has to make it clear its understanding that sexual relations are relations of power.

Unfortunately, one of the worst things that Christians have done is to underwrite romantic presuppositions about marriage. Even Christians now think that we ought to marry people simply because we are "in love." Wrong, wrong, wrong! What could being in love possibly mean? The romantic view underwrites the presumption that, because people are in love, it is therefore legitimate for them to have sexual intercourse, whether they are married or not. Contrary to this is the Church's view of marriage. Marriage, according to the Church, is the public declaration that two people have pledged to live together faithfully for a lifetime.

One of the good things about the Church's understanding of marriage is that it helps us to get a handle on making men take responsibility for their progeny. It is a great challenge for any society to get its men to take up this responsibility. As far as today's Church is concerned, we must start condemning male promiscuity. A church will not have a valid voice on abortion until it attacks male promiscuity with the ferocity it deserves. And we have got to get over being afraid of appearing prudish. Male promiscuity is nothing but the exercise of reckless power. It is injustice. And by God we have to go after it. There is no compromise on this: men must pay their dues.

Christians must challenge the romanticization of sex in our society. After all, the romanticization of sex ends up with high school kids having sexual intercourse because they think they love one another. To the contrary, we must often say that this is rape. Let us be clear about it. No unattractive, fourteen-year-old woman — who is not part of the social clique of a high school, who is suddenly dated by some male, who falls all over herself with the need for approval, and who ends up in bed with him — can be said to have had anything other than rape happen to her. Let the Church speak honestly about these matters and quit pussyfooting around. Until we speak clearly on male promiscuity, we will simply continue to make the problems of teenage pregnancy and abortion female problems. Males have to be put in their place. There is no way we as a church can have an authentic voice without this clear witness.

The "Wanted Child" Syndrome

One other issue is worth highlighting. It concerns how abortion in our society has dramatically affected the practice of having children. In discussions about abortion, one often hears that "no unwanted child ought to be born." But I can think of no greater burden than having to be a wanted child.

When I taught the marriage course at the Notre Dame, the parents of my students wanted me to teach their kids what the parents did not want them to do. The kids, on the other hand, approached the course from the perspective of whether they should feel guilty for what they had already done. Not wanting to privilege either approach, I started the course with the question, "What reason would you give for you or for someone else wanting to have a child?" I would get answers like, "Well, children are fun." In that case I would ask them to think about their brothers or sisters. Another answer was, "Children are a hedge against loneliness." Then I recommended getting a dog. Also I would note that if they really wanted to feel lonely, they should think about someone that they had raised turning out to be a stranger. Another common student reply to my question was, "Kids are a manifestation of our love." "Well," I responded, "what happens when your love changes and you are still stuck with them?" In effect, these students' answers show that people today do not know why they are having children.

It happened three or four times that someone in the class, usually a young woman, would raise her hand and say, "I don't want to talk about this anymore." I took this to mean that she knew she was going to have children, didn't have the slightest idea why, and did not want it examined. You can talk in your classes about whether God exists all semester and no one cares, because it does not seem to make any difference. But having children makes a difference, and the students are frightened that they do not know about these matters.

Then my students would come up with that one big answer that sounds good. They would say, "We want to have children in order to make the world a better place." They are thinking, of course, that they ought to have a perfect child. And then you get into the notion that you can have a child only if you have everything set — that is, if you are in a good "relationship," if you have your finances in good shape, the house, and so on. As a result, we absolutely destroy our children, so to speak, because we do not know how to appreciate them or their differences.

Now who knows what we could possibly want when we "want a child"? The idea of want in that context is about as silly as the idea that we can marry the right person. That just does not happen. Wanting a child is particularly troubling because it finally results in a deep distrust of children with physical and mental handicaps. The crucial issue for us, as Christians, is what kind of people we need to be to be capable of welcoming children into this world, some of whom may be born with disabilities and even die.

Too often we assume that compassion means preventing suffering. Too often we think that we ought to prevent suffering even if it means eliminating the sufferer. In the abortion debate, the Church's fundamental challenge is to challenge this ethics of compassion. There is no more fundamental issue. People who defend abortion defend it in the name of compassion. "We do not want any unwanted children born into the world," they say. But Christians are people who believe that any compassion that is not formed by the truthful worship of the true God cannot help being accursed. Christians must challenge the misbegotten compassion of this world. That is not going to be easy.

Common Questions, Uncommon Answers

Question 1: What about abortion in American society at large? That is, in your opinion, what would be the best abortion law for our society?

Hauerwas: The Church is not nearly at the point where it can concern itself with what kind of abortion law we should have in the United States or even in the state of North Carolina. Instead, we should start thinking about what it means for Christians to be the kind of community that can make a witness to the wider society about these matters.

Once I was giving a lecture on medical ethics at the University of Chicago Medical School. During the week before the lecture, the school's students and faculty had been discussing abortion. They had decided that if a woman asked them to perform an abortion, they would do it because a doctor ought to do whatever a patient asks. So I said, "Let's not talk about abortion. Let's talk about suicide. Imagine that you are a doctor in the Emergency Room (E.R.) at Cook County Hospital, here on the edge of Lake Michigan. It's winter; the patient they have pulled out of the lake is cold; and he is brought to the E.R. He has a note attached to his clothing. It says, 'I've been studying the literature of suicide for the past thirty years. I now agree completely with Seneca on these matters.

After careful consideration, I've decided to end my life. If I am rescued prior to my complete death, please do not resuscitate.'"

I said, "What would you do?"

"We'd try to save him, of course," they answered.

So I followed, "On what grounds? If you are going to do whatever the consumer asks you to do, you have no reason at all to save him."

So they countered, "But it's our job as doctors to save life."

And I said, "Even if that is the case, why do you have the right to impose your role, your specific duties, on this man?"

After quite a bit of argument, they decided that the way to solve this problem would be to save this man the first time he came into the E.R. The second time they would let him die.

My sense of the matter is that secular society, which assumes that you have a right to your body, has absolutely no basis for suicide prevention centers. In other words, the wider secular society has no public moral discourse about these matters.

In this kind of a setting, Christians witness to wider society, first of all, not by lobbying for a law against abortion but by welcoming the children that the wider society does not want. Part of that witness might be to say to our pro-choice friends, "You are absolutely right. I don't think that any poor woman ought to be forced to have a child that she cannot afford. So let's work hard for an adequate child allowance in this country." That may not be entirely satisfactory, but that is one approach.

Question 2: Should the Church be creating more abortion-prevention ministries, such as homes for children?

Hauerwas: I think that would be fine.

Let me add that I have a lot of respect for the people in Operation Rescue. However, intervention in an abortion-clinic context is so humanly painful that I'm not sure what kind of witness Christians make there. But if we go to a rescue, one of the things that I think that we ought to be ready to say to a woman considering an abortion is, "Will you come home and live with me until you have your child? And if you want me to raise the child, I will." I think that that kind of witness would make a very powerful statement. The children's homes are good, but we as Christians should also be the kind of people who can open our homes to a mother and her child. A lot of single people are ready to do that.

Question 3: How should the Church assist a woman who was raped and is pregnant? Where is justice, in a Niebuhrian sense, for her?

Hauerwas: First, I am not a Niebuhrian. One of the problems with [Reinhold] Niebuhr's account of sin is that it gets you into a lesser-of-two-evils argument. Because I am a pacifist, I do not want to entertain lesser-of-two-evils arguments. As you know, Christians are not about compromise. We are about being faithful.

Second, I do know some women who have been raped and who have had their children and become remarkable mothers. I am profoundly humbled by their witness.

Now, stop and think. Why is it that the United Methodist Church has not had much of a witness about abortion, suicide, or other such matters? We must face it: moral discourse in most of our churches is but a pale reflection of what you find in *Time* magazine. For example, when the United Methodist bishops drafted their pastoral letter on peace, they said that most Methodist people have been pacifists or just-war people. Well that was, quite frankly, not true. I sat in on a continuing-education session at Duke right after the peace pastoral came out. I asked how many of the ministers present had heard of just-war theory prior to the pastoral. Two-thirds of the approximately one hundred ministers indicated that they had never heard of just war. The United Methodist Church has not had disciplined discourse about any of these matters.

Does our church have disciplined discourse, even about marriage? No. We let our children grow up believing that what Christians believe about marriage is the same thing that the wider society believes about marriage — that is, if you are in love with someone, you probably ought to get married. It is a crazy idea. Being in love has nothing whatsoever to do with their vocation as Christians.

When was the last time you heard of a United Methodist minister who refused to marry a couple because they were new to the congregation? People should be married within our congregations if and only if they have lived in those congregations for at least a year. After all, those getting married are making serious promises.

Furthermore, when was the last time you preached or heard a sermon on abortion? When was the last time you preached or heard a sermon on war? When was the last time you preached or heard a sermon on the kind of care we ought to give to the ill? When was the last time you preached or heard a sermon about death and dying? When was the last time you preached or heard a sermon on the political responsibilities of Christians? The problem is that we feel at a loss about how to make these matters part of the whole Church. So, in effect, our preaching betrays the Church. I do not mean to put all the blame on preaching, but ministers do have a bully pulpit that almost no one else in this society has — except for those on television. It is not much, but it is something. At least preachers can enliven a discourse that is not alive anywhere else, and people are hungering to be led by people of courage.

One of the deepest problems concerning these issues is that ministers fear their own congregations. But we see from the Reverend Hamilton-Poore's sermon that this kind of sermon can be preached. And people will respond to it. And it will enhance a discourse that will make possible practices that otherwise would not be there.

This brings me to comment on how we conduct our annual conferences. I think that the lack of discussion of serious theological and moral matters at annual conferences is an outrage. It is an outrage! That is the one place where the United Methodist ministry comes together every year, and yet very little serious theological and moral challenge takes place. Annual conference today is like any other gathering of people in a business organization. Of course we have Bible study and all of that, but it is pietistic. It is pietism. It is all individualism. It is about how I can find my soul's relationship with God. But God is not just interested in our little souls. God has bigger fish to fry. If all we are interested in is our little souls, we shortchange the extraordinary adventure that the gospel calls us to be part of.

You might wonder what this means in terms of supporting a constitutional amendment on abortion. More important than that is what Christians owe our fellow participants — I do not want to use the word *citizens* because I do not believe we are citizens — in this strange society in which we find ourselves.

Suggestions for Further Reading

Callahan, Sidney, and Daniel Callahan, eds. *Abortion: Understanding the Differences.* New York: Plenum Press, 1984.

Hauerwas, Stanley. "Why Abortion Is a Religious Issue" and "Abortion: Why the Arguments Fail." In *A Community of Character,* 196–211, 212–29. Notre Dame: University of Notre Dame Press, 1981.

Rudy, Kathy. *Beyond Pro-life and Pro-choice: Moral Diversity in the Abortion Debate.* Boston: Beacon Press, 1996.

———. "Thinking Through the Ethics of Abortion." *Theology Today* 51 (July 1994): 235–48.

Stallsworth, Paul T., ed. *The Church and Abortion: In Search of New Ground for Response.* Nashville: Abingdon Press, 1993.

Chapter 11

Pacifism as a Vocation

Grady Scott Davis

Editor's Introduction

Grady Scott Davis begins his essay by summarizing arguments against any pacifist position based on rights, duties, justice, or utility. Then he examines John Howard Yoder's argument for Christian pacifism as a witness to the character and purposes of God. The alternatives are set out starkly: either something like Yoder's account of Jesus is true and its entailed pacifist ethic is obligatory, or pacifist arguments are incoherent and pacifism itself is morally abhorrent.

Davis makes use of an analysis by Jan Narveson to argue for the unintelligibility of pacifism in light of an ethic based on principles, rules, rights, and duties. According to Narveson, if pacifism is to be made plausible as a duty it must be shown to follow from our best analysis of justice. The pacifist seems to have to deny that a person has the right to defense against unprovoked attack, for if any sort of defense is justifiable, then why draw a line between violent and nonviolent defense?

Furthermore, to claim to have a duty not to defend innocent friends and family members against rape, murder, enslavement is to claim to have a duty to let myself or others be raped, murdered, enslaved. This, Narveson says, "borders on the perverse"; as long as we retain our basic moral vocabulary, the pacifist's position is incoherent. It advances as a duty a principle of action that asks us to give up the very rights that make duties intelligible.

On the other side, Yoder's short answer to the question of why Christians must be pacifists is that it is a part of their witness. Christians are called to be members of a revolutionary community whose existence and way of life testifies to the character of the God who sacrificed himself on the cross out of love. True disciples, therefore, need to undergo a character change, a transformation that enables them to "resemble God in the character of this love." Their willingness to give up attempting to make history come out right is a testimony to their belief that Jesus Christ is Lord of creation and that human life can be understood only in terms of that Lord's intentions. Thus, the story of Jesus is essential justification for pacifism.

For our purposes Davis's is an exceptionally interesting essay. Not only does it present two sides of a significant issue in Christian ethics, but it well illustrates how differently the arguments will be formulated in MacIntyrean terms versus terms of standard modern philosophical approaches. Perhaps Davis is right that the pacifist argument can be made only in MacIntyrean terms.

We have to confess that the reader may feel set up at this point. Readers who have come this far with us should be disposed to be convinced by MacIntyrean arguments, and it is the MacIntyrean terms that are used for the pacifist argument. It is therefore important to point out that a MacIntyrean conception of the terms of ethical debate does not necessitate a pacifist conclusion. MacIntyre himself rejects pacifism not only as unrealistic but as immoral. We believe that the difference comes down to theology. As Davis says: "Yoder must couch his pacifism in the larger picture of disciples following a God who not only comes to them in human form but also sacrifices himself on the cross out of love. . . . The gospel narrative and Yoder's way of reading that narrative are indispensable to the moral integrity of discipleship." MacIntyre, we believe, would take issue with Yoder's retelling of the gospel story.

NANCEY MURPHY

Why We Should Want to Be Pacifists

Most of us, most of the time, want to be pacifists, for most of us, most of the time, cannot consider war without focusing, with the eye of imagination, on the puzzled face of the first enemy we kill at close quarters. This, I think, more than the image of our own death, begets horror. Even the courageous, at the last moment, shut their eyes on their own death, and cowards never look at all. But the face of the victim demands, whether in memory or anticipation, its due consideration.

Soldiers needn't be particularly reflective to butt up against such thoughts. Fighting alongside their comrades cannot help leading them into contemplation. The situation is only compounded by the knowledge, and perhaps the firsthand experience, of the ways that battle contrives to turn them from the decent sort they think themselves to be into killers, capable not only of defending themselves and their cause but also of vengeful slaughter, plain if not altogether simple.[1] "But, say they, the wise man will wage just wars." This, Augustine notes caustically, is little consolation, "as if he would not all the rather lament the necessity of just wars, if he remembers that he is a man; for if they were not just he would not wage them, and would therefore be delivered from all wars."[2] Modern methods of war make it possible to distance ourselves from the immediacy of death, not altogether unlike the way a supermarket distances us

1. Cf. John Keegan, *The Face of Battle: A Study of Agincourt, Waterloo, and the Somme* (London: Penguin Books, 1976), 45–52.

2. Augustine of Hippo, *City of God,* trans. Marcus Dods (Edinburgh: T. & T. Clark, 1872), 19, 5.

from the slaughterhouse, but this detachment is self-deception. We distinguish, in bad faith, the death from the killing in order to contemplate the conditions for and prosecution of war without the moral discomfort. But, as Augustine goes on to remark, should a person contemplate the miseries of war "without mental pain, this is a more miserable plight still, for he thinks himself happy because he has lost human feeling." The more decent the soldier, the more horrified at the prospect of killing. The soldier's predicament is not unlike Oedipus's as he confronts the consequences of his fate. E. R. Dodds is correct in insisting that Oedipus cannot, morally, be held culpable but that this doesn't matter: "the great king, 'the first of men,' the man whose intuitive genius had saved Thebes, is suddenly revealed to himself as a thing so unclean that 'neither the earth can receive it, nor the holy rain nor the sunshine endure its presence' (line 1426)."[3] In what ways does killing approach for us the repugnance we associate with Oedipus's unwitting patricide and incest?

Some acts, even when innocently done, undermine the ability of the society, and sometimes the agent himself, to accept that person as a full member of the community. To kill your father and then to commit incest are not simply infractions but acts that cannot be incorporated into the fabric of society; and when Oedipus, the most thoughtful, just, and courageous of men, recognizes that these are his acts he rips himself, a loathsome pollution, from human society. The incest specially swims before the imagination: images of what was previously a delight now transformed into inescapable reproach. Similarly, as children, boys in particular, we revel in games of war, conquest, and heroic prowess, but as we grow and attain a clearer sense of the fragility of the body, the permanence of death, and how much there is to lose for someone caught up in violent conflict, the less comfortable we become with the naivete of childish games. To imagine yourself a killer without feeling the enormity of the act is a sure sign of corruption. With his usual eye for contemporary analogy, Dodds notes that a driver who has, even innocently, killed another should feel the full weight of his act, regardless of any formal finding of guilt.[4] There is a stain of homicide indifferent to responsibility or intent. If only because so few of us have ever been party to killing, homicide comes close to incest in its power to provoke not merely disapproval but revulsion, and this seems to be true even for soldiers engaged in a plausibly just war. Michael Walzer reports that "in the course of a study of combat behavior in World War II, S. L. A. Marshall discovered that the majority of men on the front lines never fired their guns."[5] Justification, opportunity, and need must be pushed to the extreme to overcome our deeply ingrained reluctance to mete out death.

We should, therefore, hold suspect anyone who is not drawn by the voice

3. E. R. Dodds, *The Ancient Concept of Progress and Other Essays on Greek Literature and Belief* (Oxford: Oxford University Press, 1973), 73.

4. Ibid., 72.

5. Michael Walzer, *Just and Unjust Wars: A Moral Argument with Historical Illustrations* (New York: Basic Books, 1977), 138.

of pacifism. When conflict escalates to deadly force, I risk my person, which inspires a reasonable fear. But when I knowingly enter into such a conflict, I risk injuring and even killing another, which is a horrifying prospect. How can I take a life if I do not have the power to return it? I cannot reasonably answer for, or expect on my own initiative to transform, my entire society, but one step within my power is refusing to be a part of such conflicts. I say, in effect, that I am not and will not become the sort of creature who willingly risks the lives of others. But merely to say this, as Sophocles makes painfully clear, cannot shield us from the contingencies of human existence. As long as we share a communal life, we risk implicating ourselves in those very acts that most horrify us.

For Oedipus, it is clear what needs to be done. Regardless of his intentions, relations existed between Jocasta, Laius, and himself that precluded certain further involvements. Specifically, Oedipus could under no circumstances undertake deadly force against his father or have sexual relations with his mother. In one sense, of course, he could because he did, but emphasizing the physical possibility of sleeping with a woman who also happens to be your mother betrays a modern narrowness of vision. For Oedipus, the consequences of action are more complex. The world is such that a patricide, even an unwitting one, puts him at odds with the fabric of life. He is no longer fit for human interaction; and if the community is to protect itself, then the offender must be cast out. Failure to remove the pollution risks destruction for the whole of Thebes. Not unlike present-day pollutants, Oedipus's transgressions exercise a corrosive force, invisible except to experts, that gnaws secretly at our very makeup, threatening unimagined future generations. The toxins must be removed. The distinction between the supernatural and the material, or between the divine and the secular, has no purchase here; that is just the way the world is.[6]

Made desperate, Oedipus removes himself from the society of others. The pacifist, horrified by the prospect of taking life, rejects war because it is the organized practice of killing. But war is not the only activity that makes up my life or the life of the community. If asked how my pacifism relates to the rest of my practical activity, what should I respond? The concept of pollution no longer plays the role it did in traditional thought. Recent moral theories elaborate the relation of the internal to the external act in different ways, but by and large they agree in emphasizing the importance of will and intention in ways that would interpret Oedipus's self-destructive despair as morally inappropriate. This seems, in fact, to be Oedipus's view in Sophocles' later *Oedipus at Colonus.* "How was I

6. The limits of such distinctions as "natural/supernatural" and such analogues as "moral/physical" are familiar to anyone who has spent much time reading non-European or premodern European materials. Mary Douglas's classic *Purity and Danger* (London: Routledge and Kegan Paul, 1966) sheds much light on the complex ways in which peoples understand their worlds and the interrelations between practical reasoning, self-perception, and cosmic order. Jeffrey Stout has employed Douglas's work to illuminate ethical debate in "Moral Abominations," reprinted in Jeffrey Stout's *Ethics after Babel: The Languages of Morals and Their Discontents* (Boston: Beacon Press, 1988) as chap. 7.

evil in myself?" he asks the chorus. "I had been wronged, I retaliated.... Then, knowing nothing, I went on."[7] If revulsion at killing is, for some moderns, analogous to Oedipus's revulsion at patricide and incest, and if pacifism rests merely on this revulsion, then perhaps such pacifism is as misplaced as Oedipus's despair.

Jan Narveson on the Incoherence of Pacifism

Such, at least, is Jan Narveson's argument. Take pacifism to be the position that recourse to war is wrong. What, Narveson asks, makes such action wrong? Some may be squeamish at the thought of killing and others may simply be unwilling to employ deadly force, but neither stance constitutes a moral position, properly speaking. These responses, so far, register nothing more than individual preference. Narveson rightly rejects appeals to violence in the abstract as in themselves irrelevant.[8] Nor will it do to argue that war rarely achieves a good end. Particular failures are not by themselves arguments that a course of action is wrong. Unless it rests on a principle that establishes a duty independent of personal preference, it is not clear what would make war wrong as opposed to being messy or imprudent. It would surely be reasonable to adopt the rule that war is to be avoided as generally not in the best interests of the many. I suppose, in fact, that almost everybody already maintains something like this. For even Napoleon, as Clausewitz remarked, "is always peace-loving.... he would prefer to take over our country unopposed."[9] But neither Napoleon nor Augustine, whose wise man wishes to be delivered from war, can properly be called a pacifist. Napoleon will certainly, faced with resistance, give up his irenic stance in order to subdue his prey, and the bishop of Hippo will insist on the regrettable necessity of war in order to protect the innocent against Napoleon's aggression. It is a Pickwickian pacifism indeed that can incorporate these exceptions.

To give moral weight to the idea, Narveson asks: what moral reasons might lead to someone's becoming a pacifist? And he suggests that one response open to the pacifist is "that pacifism as such is a duty, that is, that meeting violence with force is, as such, wrong."[10] Only if violent response is wrong does pacifism move beyond the realm of habit or preference and constitute a recognizable moral duty. It is important for Narveson's argument that this duty cannot be one that applies only to a particular subset of the populace or be taken on voluntarily. Thus, for me to argue that I am a pacifist but that it is perfectly acceptable for others to defend their family and friends brands my rejection of force as pref-

7. Sophocles, *Oedipus at Colonus,* trans. Robert Fitzgerald (Chicago: University of Chicago Press, 1941), 11, 270ff.

8. Jan Narveson, "Pacifism: A Philosophical Analysis," in *War and Morality,* ed. Richard A. Wasserstrom (Belmont, Calif.: Wadsworth Publishing, 1970).

9. Carl Von Clausewitz, *On War,* ed. and trans. Michael Howard and Peter Paret (Princeton: Princeton University Press, 1976), 370.

10. Narveson, "Pacifism," 66.

erential as opposed to moral. If a course of action is wrong, then it is wrong even for those who don't realize it. Similarly, should I as the erstwhile pacifist reject recourse to violence until there is a direct threat to my immediate family, I am not, morally speaking, a pacifist. Restricting use of force to certain reasonably well-defined situations is not the same as rejecting it altogether. If pacifism is to be made plausible as a duty it must be shown to follow from our best analysis of justice. But among our most secure intuitions about justice is the view that defending self, family, and friends is not only reasonable but obligatory. After all, as long as my family and I have not otherwise violated the requirements of justice, why shouldn't I use whatever force is reasonable against an attacker? Whom do I have better reasons for defending? What kind of person would I be just to stand by? Thus the pacifist must argue, against these intuitions, "that no one ought ever to be defended against attack. The right of self-defense can be denied coherently only if the right of defense, in general, is denied."[11]

Here Narveson's argument depends upon introducing the language of "rights." Rights seem to be of two sorts: those that accrue to individuals or groups by virtue of some acknowledged contractual relationship and those devolving upon someone by virtue of the sort of creature she is. Leaving aside, for the moment, how we recognize and from whence we derive these natural rights, we may agree that if something is a right then we are justified in maintaining and protecting it. One of our natural rights, Narveson suggests, is that to security of our persons against gratuitous attack.[12] It follows from this that should someone be attacked without cause she would be within her rights to exert herself against her attacker. But this seems to fly in the face of the pacifist's contention that defense is not a right.

Could, perhaps, the pacifist retreat to the weaker position that defense *with force* is wrong but that means short of force are acceptable? This won't do, for if the voice of reason and sympathy should fail, then recourse to force may be a last resort. Consider, for example, a woman confronting a would-be rapist. What more unwarranted attack could we imagine? Now suppose that she attempts to reason with her attacker, arguing that his action is vicious and a gross violation of her rights. What if reason fails? When he grabs her, is she duty-bound not to resist? Two points. First, the pacifist cannot argue that it is a bad idea for her to resist, since it may provoke her assailant to greater violence. Perhaps it would, but this is not relevant. The pacifist must insist that resort to force is wrong, whatever the consequences. Second, it is equally beside the point that my victim *may forgo* any resistance. Perhaps she believes that rape is a symptom of a systemic social disease and that the behavior of the rapist is determined by social and biochemical forces over which he has no control. She might, in other words, be a Skinnerian behaviorist, capable of analyzing her assailant purely in

11. Ibid., 71.
12. Ibid., 72.

terms of immediate stimulus and response. In doing this she would attribute to the rapist no reflection or responsibility beyond that of a rutting dog. But to be consistent she should attribute nothing more to herself. Thus, the pacifist appeal to duty, right, or the moral law is otiose. This is just her animal response. For her pacifist claim to be compelling, in the sense required by Narveson, she must view both herself and her attacker as bound by duties and hedged round with rights, and as yet she has not been given any plausible reason to forgo protecting her right to her person.

Suppose the pacifist retreats once again, to the still weaker position that *deadly* force is prohibited but other forms of struggle are theoretically allowable. This position has two failings. First, it is not evident what should count as deadly force. If hitting him with her fists is acceptable, what about using the stick that happens to be on the path? It is a minimal weapon, but surely people have been killed with sticks. If the fortuitous stick is an acceptable instrument, what about the billy club she carries against just such eventualities? If the club, why not the knife, and so on? In short, if she is justified in using any form of force at all, it would seem that there is no nonarbitrary way of drawing the line short of whatever "might be necessary."[13] Perhaps she may not justly intend to kill the rapist, but this is a different matter.[14] The force she is driven to use may turn out to be deadly despite her best intentions.

But the pacifist has a more difficult problem than drawing the line between increments of force. If force of any sort may be employed in defense of rights, then why should the victim be prohibited from using *deadly* force if that is necessary to preserve a right? Perhaps some rights are not sufficiently important to justify such force; still, this admission leaves open the possibility that other rights, such as security against murder, rape, and being enslaved, are that important. All three attack my integrity as a person, and all three provoke a response similar to Oedipus's when first confronted with his patricide and incest. Being murdered, on reflection, seems to be the least revolting because as a victim I am no longer aware. The slave and the rape victim must live with the knowledge of that attack through which they were rendered objects, instruments for the will of another. This points up the importance of placing acts within the larger context of human interaction. Descriptively there may be no visible distinction between being raped and eagerly engaging in acts of sexual expression. But to pretend that there is no difference between the two is delusion, and to say that I have a duty to let myself be raped borders on the perverse. Thus, Narveson concludes that as long as we retain our basic moral vocabulary the pacifist's position is incoherent. It advances as a duty a principle of action which asks that we give up the very rights that make duties intelligible.

---

13. Ibid., 73.

14. On this subject, see Grady Scott Davis, *Warcraft and the Fragility of Virtue: An Essay in Aristotelian Ethics* (Moscow: University of Idaho Press, 1992), chap. 3.

The Limitations of Narveson's Arguments

But how much has Narveson accomplished? Has he shown, as he maintains, that "the pacifist's central position is untenable"?[15] I don't think so. His critique of pacifism works only if his antagonist grants the primacy of an ethics based on principles, rules, rights, and duties. Pacifists have the option of rejecting, as does MacIntyre in *After Virtue,* the vocabulary of natural rights as a philosophical fiction and belief in such rights as "one with belief in witches and in unicorns."[16] Or they can adopt the position that justice is, on the one hand, a prerequisite of any sustainable communal enterprise and, on the other, capable of progressive elaboration in ways that make the recognition of just practices nontransitive.[17] Pacifists can then go on to say that although earlier societies did not achieve the rejection of deadly force, theirs has. Their awareness of the injustice of killing, they now argue, is analogous to my understanding of slavery vis-à-vis the eighteenth-century slaver. However elaborate they become, the slave-trader's arguments will not prevail against my clarity of conscience. That I, had I lived in the eighteenth century, might not have been able to convince the slaver of the injustice of his livelihood is not an argument in favor of slavery; it merely points up the limits of the eighteenth-century moral vocabulary.

On the surface this strategy seems promising, for it emphasizes the capacity of practical agents to acknowledge that norms of action are supplied by the community and sustained by tradition while still being open to self-critical scrutiny. It rejects unargued metaphysical warrants for practical action and insists on a minimal level of pluralistic tolerance based on a pragmatic fallibilism. The nondogmatic pacifist can maintain that a rejection of deadly force is truly consonant with justice while admitting that the conceptual situation may be such that other reasonable and upright agents cannot be brought to see this fact.

But closer scrutiny reveals more serious problems even when we reject the vocabulary of rights. Justice, I have argued, renders each his due. Specifying the demands of justice in particular cases requires knowledge of fact and a mature grasp of the relevant social practices, values, and virtues.[18] I granted that the agent in times of crisis, or the investigator caught between two social worlds, might find herself unsure about how to respond to incommensurable virtues and values, although I insisted, agreeing with Aquinas, that she was finally answerable to her conscience, and that that might mean acting against the prevailing norms of the community in which she found herself. The one thing that ensured a measure of continuity between communities, however, was the consensus that persons of practical wisdom consider the practices, virtues, and values of their community conducive to an acceptable quality of life. It is this last requirement

15. Narveson, "Pacifism," 77.

16. *After Virtue: A Study in Moral Theory* (Notre Dame: University of Notre Dame Press, 1981), 67.

17. See Davis, *Warcraft,* chap. 1.

18. Ibid.

that, when pressed, leads the pacifist into difficulties. Return to the rapist and his intended victim. Imagine that she is my pacifist. Then part of what she believes is that the good life for humans is such that it incorporates a disposition to refrain from undertaking deadly force against anyone, even if that means forsaking goods to which she might otherwise be entitled. Note here that the entitlement is a positive and not a natural one. It requires no warrant beyond the presupposition that my pacifist holds a particular position within a community and that part and parcel of that is the positive right to withhold sexual favors. In the example given, the good of choosing her sexual partners is being set aside in favor of the greater good of refusing to undertake deadly force. While this is understandable, it is scarcely a demand of right reason; rape is so heinous an attack that a forceful defense is more than reasonable; it is what we would advocate were the situation to permit it. But perhaps her community has come to see the injury of forced sex as minor, not much different from being cheated out of five dollars in three-card monte. This would require a major transformation of human values, but it is not inconceivable. It would imply a dramatic shift away from our community's concepts of love, marriage, personal integrity, and the unimpeded pursuit of our own ends; but for the moment let's grant the point. We would then find ourselves in the position of the anthropologist. This is a remarkable and intriguing society, no doubt, but hardly one whose practices we have good reason to embrace.

Suppose, though, that the injury was not rape but murder. Confronted with an impending murder my pacifist might, I suppose, maintain that her assailant is being driven by forces that have obscured the ability to see what justice demands. She might then be willing to die rather than undertake the injustice of killing, forsaking herself in favor of the deluded other. But now she comes upon an unfolding murder that involves not herself as victim but some third party. Staying her hand would seem to favor the life of the murderer over that of her innocent compatriot. Why is such restraint due the one and intervention not hers to offer the other? Is the one life more worthy?

Here, the following strategy may present itself. Her community, she might say, is one for which the use of force is inconceivable. She and her fellows could not even consider such acts. But what is the strength of this "could not"? It might come to pass that the community of rational beings achieved a presently unimaginable habit of justice, bringing it about that none of its number ever overstepped the bounds of justice. It might further be the case that, in the evolution of science, therapies had been developed which made it possible to cure all physical and psychological pathologies (they might even be the same) which led to inflicting harm on one's fellows. We might imagine that such a thirst for justice developed that even in cases of accident or unforeseen conflict the overwhelming inclination of community members was to redress any injury, forestalling resentment and deprivation. With the passing of time it might come about that no one ever thought to assault anyone. But even here it is possible to *consider* resort to force in the abstract. It simply doesn't occur as a live option in deliberation. If the resort to force were strictly incapable of being conceived, then the community would have passed beyond justice. It would no longer be able to consider the concept of attack. When confronted by my so-called rapist, a member of this community would have to view the experience as either rather like being caught in a summer shower or like being somewhat too close to an erupting volcano. The one is a minor discomfort and the other likely to vaporize me, but only a crude anthropomorphism would see in either an attack. An attack, to fall under the scope of justice, requires an object of pursuit and the intent to injure that object. It is only by extension from the realm of human experience that we say that a virus "attacks" the DNA of healthy cells or that a swarm of bees "attacks" an intruder to the hive. A community that lacks the resources for such contemplation lacks the resources for formulating the concept of justice. It would also, of course, lack a great many other concepts, such as "rape." In a sense, members of this community would not be able to recognize my rapist as a person, for he would be undertaking acts that *people* just don't perform. It is not difficult to see that this community would lack most, if not all, the concepts we typically consider ethical; and we would soon begin to wonder, appearances notwithstanding, whether we were justified in calling it a human community. Narveson makes the point more polemically, writing that, were we to discover a society such as this, "we should have to conclude, I think, not that this was a community of saints, but rather that this community lacked the concept of justice — or perhaps that their nervous systems were oddly different from ours."[19]

John Howard Yoder's Pacifism of Vocation

Still, we haven't exhausted the options for a coherent pacifism. Under what circumstances, to follow up Narveson's hint, might a community of saints be justified in adopting pacifism, and how should this be understood? In a deliberately provocative extension of the meaning of the term, John Howard Yoder has catalogued various of the ways that "pacifism" has been argued. I say provocative because his *Nevertheless: The Varieties and Shortcomings of Religious Pacifism* extends the scope of pacifism to include arguments from justice (chap. 2), political strategy (chaps. 4 and 5), and what he calls "Utopian Purism" (chap. 8), none of which would traditionally count as forms of pacifism.[20] Nonetheless, Yoder's own position is the most subtle and far-reaching of any contemporary pacifism. As such, it offers the most interesting available response to Narveson's claim that "the pacifist's central position is untenable." First, however, a little history is in order.

Christian pacifism has rarely, if ever, viewed itself in terms that would satisfy Narveson's philosophical presuppositions. Early Christian rejection of military

19. Narveson, "Pacifism," 75–76.
20. Scottdale, Pa.: Herald Press, 1971.

service and the tradition of martyrdom, as opposed to armed resistance, do not seem to have stemmed from a rejection of war or violence as contrary to the principles of justice. In his response to the pagan Celsus, for instance, Origen insists that Christians are not, as his adversary claimed, antisocial and unpatriotic; they are merely following the law laid down for them by their Lord. Unlike the Jews,

> for whom it was lawful to take up arms in defence of their families and to serve in the wars, the lawgiver of the Christians... taught that it was never right for his disciples to go so far against a man, even if he should be very wicked; for he did not consider it compatible with his inspired legislation to allow the taking of human life in any form at all.[21]

This passage testifies to several important aspects of the early Christian rejection of deadly force. Central to Origen's understanding is the particularism of law. Jesus' prohibition of killing applies only to Christians. God left the Jews free to protect their community, and there is no suggestion that this is improper. True, all people would be better off if they embraced Christianity, but until that happens all may legitimately exist together. Furthermore, the prohibition, as Origen understands it, does not represent a rejection of political community. He seems to take for granted that political community is a necessity and that wars will occur. In this, Origen does not differ from his pagan contemporaries. What restrains the Christian from killing is discipleship, a special vocation that is not different in kind from the exemption granted pagan priests.[22] Christian prayers, in fact, serve as a first line of defense against the demons of discord.

By and large it is the sense of vocation that animates the Christian refusal to serve, even after military service becomes common. Later, in an era when bishops were known to lead men into battle, the monastic orders persevered in their pacifism, but it was a militant pacifism. Orderic Vitalis, recommending the foundation of a monastery, advises an earl to "look carefully at the things which are provided for you by trained monks.... Strenuous is the warfare which these castellans of Christ wage against the Devil.... The cowled champions will resist Behemoth in constant warfare for your soul."[23] All life is a struggle, and the invisible struggles are the most difficult. The monk eschews physical force because he is in training for a more profound battle, with more powerful tools, and cannot risk the diminution of his energy.

The rejection of killing takes on a more exclusivist complexion among the radical Reformers. The eponymous founder of the Mennonite tradition proclaimed an acceptance of any secular involvement a capitulation to the prince of darkness, whose servants "are born to torture and corruption, for their hearts,

---

21. Origen of Alexandria, *Contra Celsum,* ed. and trans. Henry Chadwick (Cambridge: Cambridge University Press, 1953), 132.

22. Ibid., 509.

23. R. W. Southern, *Western Society and the Church in the Middle Ages* (Harmondsworth, England: Penguin Books, 1970), 225.

mouths, and hands drip and reek with blood."[24] Despite their differences, all these positions on killing reflect not a theory of justice so much as an interpretation of Christian vocation. Christians are called out of the world because it can no longer house them. It is ruled by a lord of vengeance and destruction, and if we attempt to match him at his own game we cannot avoid losing our souls. The only refuge is with Jesus, and those who do not hear are, finally, beyond our help.

A vocation, obviously, is a calling, but a calling of a rather special sort. The person called is enjoined to take on a particular task and bound to the faithful pursuit of that task even if it should lead into difficulties or require forsaking other goods. A vocation thus differs from a principle or duty in two distinct ways. Narveson rightly notes that principles, and the duties they generate, hold generally, regardless of whether we believe ourselves bound by them. Thus, if there is a duty to respect parents, it is binding on me regardless of my beliefs about, or attitudes toward, my parents. It is this understanding of principles that leads Narveson to write of the person who holds "that only he himself ought not to meet force with force, although it is quite all right for others to do so," that "we may continue to call him a 'pacifist,' in a somewhat attenuated sense, but he is then no longer holding pacifism as a *moral* principle or, indeed, as a principle at all."[25] To talk about adopting something as a "principle for me" is to misunderstand the concept. Principles are norms of a practice, not of the participants.[26] Narveson is wrong, however, to move from the insight that pacifism cannot be a principle to the claim that the pacifist's rejection of violence "is essentially just a matter of taste."[27] This reflects an all too common blunder not unlike that made in epistemology when the only alternative to foundationalism (be it positivist or Cartesian) is thought to be an inexplicable relativism. Consider a paradigm example of calling, that of Moses called to redeem the Israelites. "But suppose they do not believe me or listen to me," Moses responds in an attempt to beg off. And when that doesn't work, he protests that "I have never been eloquent, neither in the past nor even now that you have spoken to your servant" (Exod. 4:1–11). Despite running counter to his own inclinations, Moses cannot avoid God's call. When finally he acquiesces, Moses acts as someone who has voluntarily, if reluctantly, undertaken a task that must be seen to its end. A vocation once acknowledged has perhaps a greater power over the individual than action from principle or virtue because it involves accepting a task as his own, in which his identity and merit are involved. Moses accepts

24. Arthur F. Holmes, *War and Christian Ethics* (Grand Rapids, Mich.: Baker Book House, 1975), 189.

25. Narveson, "Pacifism," 67.

26. I should note that the same would hold for virtues as excellences of a practice. Participants either achieve or fall short of virtues in much the same way that they abide by, or fail to act in accord with, the principles of a given activity. Nonetheless, there are many things about the ethics of principles, rights, and duties that do not sit well with the ethics of virtue. See Davis, *Warcraft,* chap. 4.

27. Narveson, "Pacifism," 67.

responsibility for leading the Israelites. The bodhisattva, to take a non-Western example, forsakes entry into Nirvana in order to help all other sentient beings free themselves from the rounds of karmic suffering. Evaluating an individual and her vocation involves a rather different procedure than that appropriate to an ethic of principles and duties. Even if there is no compelling duty, the bodhisattva chooses a worthy task, and by persevering in that task becomes an example of greatness that creates not an obligation but an option for human striving. Accepting the kingship, Oedipus takes on responsibilities most cannot bear, and when he is crushed it is genuinely tragic. Imagine that Moses had weaseled out. He might have lived a perfectly decent life herding sheep in Midian, but he would not have merited a special place in the sacred books of the Israelites.

A vocation, then, is felt by an individual to be personally binding, regardless of the position of others, and in this it differs from a principle or a virtue. By the same token a vocation requires the forsaking of genuine goods that remain available to others. A mafioso cannot, this side of farce, forsake the mob, although he can leave it and risk the consequences. To forsake a particular goal, status, or enterprise is to acknowledge its legitimate claims and allures while nonetheless choosing to distance yourself, perhaps forever, from them. Familiar examples are not hard to find. How much did Schweitzer the scholar, musicologist, musician give up to work in Africa? To think that these other pursuits did not matter is to miss the impact of Schweitzer's choices.

When it comes to pacifism, at least three goods are being forsaken. Least of these is my person, but it is a good nonetheless. My ability to pursue reasonable ends without undue fear of attack is a presupposition of social life. Protecting myself from the occasional attack is a regrettable eventuality but one in accord with reason should the attack be unwarranted. Who, after all, would it be more reasonable to protect? One answer, and a second good the pacifist wishes me to forsake, would be my family and friends. Unlike certain theorists of the natural law, I don't believe that individuals have functions by nature that impel them toward any particular form of sexual activity or that lead naturally to forming certain kinds of socially recognized bonds. This having been said, there are, nonetheless, goods of fellowship, child rearing, sexual satisfaction, and friendship that marriage and parenthood are well designed to serve. Not only this, but one of the best candidates for genuine moral progress in recent centuries is the changing status of relations in marriage. It is true that Aristotle maintained that "between man and wife friendship seems to exist by nature.... Human beings live together not only for the sake of reproduction but also for the various purposes of life.... they help each other by throwing their peculiar gifts into the common stock."[28] Still, for the most part, this view of

28. Aristotle, *Nicomachean Ethics,* trans. W. D. Ross, rev. ed., ed. J. L. Ackrill and J. O. Urmson (Oxford: Oxford University Press, 1980), 1162a.

married virtue seems more a peripatetic ideal than a practical reality.[29] But relations between men and women, at least in much of the modern West, have reached a level at which it is at least possible to imagine friendships of genuine virtue arising between husband and wife. Marriage and parenthood are goods; the friendship that can emerge between family members is a good in which individuals acknowledge the intrinsic worthiness of others. Having entered into these relations and invested self and energy in fostering their attendant goods, I am henceforth disposed to maintain and protect them. That is part and parcel of achieving a lasting good. When my family is subjected to attack, the reasonable thing would be to protect it. Failure smacks of cowardice or indifference, and these are attributes of character that render me unworthy of the relationships themselves.

Pacifists, then, want me to forsake both the goods attendant on my person and the family that I love. They ask me to do this in the name of an abstraction, "human life," which I encounter only as embodied by individuals whom I love, am indifferent to, or view as actively undertaking to injure those I love. Not only this, but the pacifist is asking me to draw no distinction between these classes. This seems to run contrary to right reason.

A striking aspect of John Yoder's pacifism is his willingness to embrace this conclusion. Sensitive as he is to the demands of consistency, Yoder does not attempt to argue that his Mennonite pacifism meets the demands of justice and right reason in anything like the commonsense meanings of the terms. Instead, he argues that Jesus initiated a revolution, Yoder's "original revolution," in which the participants acknowledge God's call by giving themselves over to his providential will. Part of this response is forsaking the traditional human ways of coping with an unjust political order. Rather than attempting to impose order and justice on the social world, Jesus called his followers to leave that world and enter another:

> He gave them a new way to deal with offenders — by forgiving them. He gave them a new way to deal with violence — by suffering. He gave them a new way

29. The history of marriage provides a particularly instructive introduction to the concept of progress in ethics. Christopher Brooke (in *The Medieval Idea of Marriage* [Oxford: Oxford University Press, 1989]) presents an overview of the changing concept in the Middle Ages. Much fascinating information and analysis on marriage is to be found in the volumes of *A History of Private Life.* The discussions by Paul Veyne and Peter Brown in *From Pagan Rome to Byzantium,* trans. Arthur Goldhammer, vol. 1 of *A History of the Private Life,* ed. Paul Veyne (Cambridge: Harvard University Press, 1987), are extremely interesting. Marriage from antiquity to the recent past was more often than not a matter of establishing alliances, concluding financial transactions, and ensuring the continued exercise of power through wealth passed down to progeny. The interaction of powerful characters that engenders affection and self-knowledge between Jane Austen's Emma and Knightley would have been uncommon to the point of unbelievability for much of history. More indicative of the status of marriage is Duby's account of the ways in which women were promised, taken back, and reallotted among the barony of medieval England. (See Georges Duby, *William Marshal, the Flower of Chivalry,* trans. Richard Howard [New York: Pantheon Books, 1985], 118–37.) Many recent studies of women and the family in Islam provide an illuminating comparison. Of contemporary writers on marriage and the family, Stanley Hauerwas seems to me consistently the most rewarding.

> to deal with money — by sharing it. . . . He gave them a new way to deal with a corrupt society — by building a new order, not smashing the old.[30]

To say, however, that Jesus invites his followers to form a new community is scarcely the end of the matter. We need to investigate the nature of this community and the structure of the vocation to which its members are called. For the sake of clarity, we can divide this into three related questions. What, morally speaking, is the nature of this community? In what ways can that community affect the political life of the society it rejects? And what is the relation of the pacifist community to those communities or individuals who at least profess a desire for justice?

To answer these questions means introducing a new and unfamiliar vocabulary. Central to the very idea of Christian pacifism, as Yoder understands it, is an eschatological perspective. To be a Christian is to proclaim that Jesus is the Christ and that Christ is Lord of creation. To acknowledge that Christ is Lord is to admit that human life can be understood only in terms of the Lord's intentions for creation, and in Yoder's reading of the gospel message this means perceiving Jesus' activity for the world as pervaded by *agapē*. Christ's *agapē* is nonresistant, seeking neither justice nor results, but reveals itself instead "in the uncomplaining and forgiving death of the innocent at the hands of the guilty" (56). Individuals responding to the call of Jesus take upon themselves the burden of forgiving the guilty, even when what is attacked is what they most love. True, there is the promise of eternal life, but, as Yoder notes, "before the resurrection there was the cross, and the Christian must follow his Master in suffering for the sake of love" (57). Jesus displayed, in willingly accepting the cross, the nature and depth of his love, and from this love he issues his call to repentance. The would-be disciple must repent the sins of the past and prepare for the Kingdom (37–38). Accepting this message is primary, and it is a message that refuses to be judged by the standards of the world; the old standards no longer apply.

It should be clear that Jesus, as Yoder interprets him, advocates pacifism neither as a strategic means to an end nor as obedience to principle. Yoder takes great care "to combat one of the most widespread interpretations of the contemporary pacifist commitment," namely that it is "a logical, deductive, impersonal kind of legalism taking certain biblical texts or certain ethical principles with utmost rigor, without asking whether it be possible or not to live up to such demanding ideals" (34). The world is not made just in Christ's crucifixion; it goes on pretty much the same as always. Nonetheless, the Christian is called to persist in love, even when it is rejected. This is a pacifism, in other words, based not on principle but on the desire to live in a way that reflects the life of the master, regardless of any practical achievements in the world. In any case, only an ethics wedded overmuch to Kantian universalism would be tempted to deny that Yoder's is a compelling moral vision.

30. John Howard Yoder, *The Original Revolution: Essays on Christian Pacifism* (Scottdale, Pa.: Herald Press, 1977), 29. Parenthetical page references that follow are to this volume.

To undertake discipleship means to live in a way that reflects Christ's lordship and to rejoice in Christ as Lord (39). Honesty requires that entry into this way of life be voluntary. This requires reflection on and interpretation of Jesus' career, as opposed to mindless emulation; but central to that career is the belief that God's will does not go unfulfilled. True disciples, in fact, have undergone a transformation at Jesus' hand, a healing that enables them to fit, to be "at home" in God's kingdom (40). When they feel at home, they find rules and rewards irrelevant. Having been healed of the ills of the world, they strive to resemble God in the character of their love (47). Part of this task means rejecting preference and calculation and striving to love the other person, even should he be her enemy.

This is indeed, as Yoder insists, "an ethic of excess" (49), but it is one to which the Christian is now disposed as a matter of character. In confronting a situation, disciples of Jesus do not ask what principles of Christian morality apply or what duties they are called to perform but rather how to "reach beyond available models and options to do a new thing whose very newness will be a witness to divine presence" (49). Or, as Yoder pithily puts it: "We do not, ultimately, love our neighbor because Jesus told us to. We love our neighbor because God is like that" (51).

The vocabulary of this new community, then, rests heavily on such terms as *repentance, discipleship,* and *love.* But how do these concepts come together in social action? Answering this question requires the addition of a fourth vocabulary entry: *witness.* Members of the new community seek to perform acts that "witness to divine presence," and it behooves us to recall the Greek background in the term *martyr.* To be a martyr is to witness, in the most active fashion, to the consequences of belief. The martyr testifies to the transforming power of God; and given the historical resonances of martyrdom and persecution in the Christian tradition, the concept of witness establishes the central connection in Yoder's pacifism between putting forward the evidence of Jesus' healing activity and accepting the unjust suffering imposed upon the disciple by an unbelieving world.

To make sense of her actions, the witness must take an eschatological perspective on the world. This perspective must be a minority one, and the consequences of its being true must be sufficiently profound to bring its adherents into conflict with the majority. If the likelihood of the minority belief's being true is unimpressive or if the consequences are comparatively unimportant, then witnessing in a manner approaching martyrdom is remote. Here I am not making a sociological prediction about the likelihood of believers dying for their beliefs. Suppose that, proclaiming their position at the local airport, the Christians sufficiently aggravated travelers to the point that irate fliers started shooting them in order to proceed unmolested to the shuttle. This would be an aberrant form of martyrdom, for the commuters are indifferent to the beliefs involved; they just don't want to be bothered. What makes it possible for Christian pacifists to be martyrs is that the majority culture takes seriously the import of their belief, rejects it, and expresses a willingness to impose some form of sanction or injury on them as a consequence of continuing to maintain the belief.[31]

Yoder's Christian is a pacifist not by design but by default. Were the majority, and hence the political organization that represents the majority, to acknowledge the lordship of Jesus and to reject recourse to violence in favor of Christlike *agapē,* then there would be no special vocation for the disciples to adopt. There would equally be no special witness for them to make. For should everyone adopt the Christian perspective on history there would exist a consensus that all things serve God and that, appearances to the contrary, the Lamb did indeed triumph in the Cross.[32] Under those conditions the state would not be demonic and thus not be a power over and against which Christians needed to affirm the *agapē* of Jesus.

It takes no particular historical knowledge or sociological acumen, however, to recognize that such is not the case. If Jesus is who Yoder says he is and if his will is even remotely like what Yoder suggests it is, then the state remains a power to which the disciple of Jesus must remain opposed. This is not the place to assess the quality of Yoder's biblical exegesis or the details of his account of the falling away of the church from Jesus' original revolutionary vision.[33] Nonetheless, it is important to sketch the steps of "demonization," if only because they come to represent the paradigm of temptation for those who lose sight of the revolutionary nature of Jesus' message.

When, for reasons of history and social affiliation, the Roman Empire gave up its persecution of the Christians and when the Christian community came to incorporate within its ranks members of the political and intellectual elite, it became natural, as Yoder sees it, that "the next step in the union of church and world was the conscious abandon of eschatology."[34] It is a virtue of Yoder's analysis that he can present this move toward "disavowal and apostasy"[35] as undertaken by Christians of good faith, such as Augustine. Transformations in ecclesiology, social expectation, and even metaphysics[36] need not be seen as the machinations of demagogues and heresiarchs but may be accounted for in social and historical terms sufficient to explain how such changes, when noticed at all, could be viewed as the natural consequences "of time and organic

---

31. It is this, more than the absence of any prior pacifist tradition, that would have made Jewish pacifists anomalous martyrs in the context of the Holocaust. The intention to commit genocide, as opposed to "religiocide," renders pacifism pointless. Hitler's Final Solution was directed at race and consequently indifferent to principle, virtue, or vocation. For their pacifism to be meaningful, paradoxically, Jewish pacifists would have had to take extraordinary steps to flee the Holocaust.

32. Yoder, *Original Revolution,* 58–61.

33. The primary source for Yoder's interpretation of Jesus is his 1972 work. See *The Politics of Jesus,* 2d ed. (Grand Rapids, Mich.: Wm. B. Eerdmans, 1994). Several of Yoder's historical essays on the transformation of the tradition and its relation to the Radical Reformation are reprinted in *When War Is Unjust* (Minneapolis: Augsburg, 1984; rev. ed., Maryknoll, N.Y.: Orbis, 1996). See especially part 2, "History." The notes contain a useful bibliography.

34. Yoder, *Original Revolution,* 66.

35. Yoder, *When War Is Unjust,* 144.

36. Ibid., 136–44.

development."[37] Augustine, on this account, can be absolutely clear on the pervasiveness of sin and still see the Roman Empire as providentially ordained. If Augustine's thought constitutes a watershed, and later a fountainhead, for interpretations and movements contrary, as Yoder would have it, to the original gospel message, it is not because the saint fails to recognize sinfulness but because "he seriously overestimated the adequacy of the available institutional and sacramental means for overcoming it."[38] Fourth-century Christians were no less men and women of their time, and their interpretations of their Christian commitment were no less dependent on the new and inherited forces that made their interpretations possible. This doesn't mean, however, that those interpretations are sound or that later generations must remain uncritically bound to them. If Yoder is correct, the heirs of the fourth century remain trapped in the "Constantinian" understanding of political life precisely because of the deforming powers of that interpretation.

Once the original eschatological vision is given up, what replaces it for the Christian community, and what are the components of "Constantinianism"? First, no longer at odds with the state, the church loses the impetus to speak out against it. The church can even endorse the basic premises of political activity as part of God's providential order. As the relation between the church and the state changes so does that between the individual believer and the demands of the state. "After Constantine," Yoder writes, "not only is the ruler the bearer of history; the nonsovereign ethical agent has changed as well."[39] The simple believer is called merely to do his or her duty and abide in the established practices of the church. In these changed circumstances the Christian finds it less immediately necessary, and then less plausible, to "witness." A new question, "What if everyone did that?" begins to intervene in deliberations, which "would have been preposterous in the early church and remains ludicrous wherever committed Christians accept realistically their minority status."[40] Since the church has identified itself with the political order, the sort of witnessing envisioned no longer operates. It becomes, instead, "sectarianism." Christianity has ceased to be a vocation.

If pacifism as a vocation is no longer operative, Christians will need an alternative way of interpreting their role in political society. But however well-intentioned such alternatives might be, forces of sin work from the very beginning to undermine their efforts. As soon as the Christian community gives up its minority status, the state loses a powerful voice of criticism, which had previously acted as a check against easy self-justification by the political authorities. Given the pervasiveness of sin in the structures of human society, the state reinterprets the Christian message as endorsing its political agenda. The church, in its turn, risks being coopted into the establishment. Rather than testing the

37. Ibid., 144.
38. Yoder, *Original Revolution,* 66.
39. Yoder, *When War Is Unjust,* 139.
40. Ibid.

state, there is pressure toward first condoning and then advocating force in God's name. The consequences are first the rise of the crusader mentality and ultimately "a purely pagan view of God as a tribal deity,"[41] represented on the field of battle by the armies of Christian Rome, for whom the church, as a matter of civic duty, provides a chaplain (113–15). The mission of the Christian community becomes in this moment the mission of the state, be it Constantine's Rome or Reagan's America.[42] The church, in other words, has given up its minority status and in so doing directs itself to establishing an ecumenical and natural theology that makes evident the work of the state as God's work, carrying out a providentially appointed task. Once this transformation has taken place, Yoder suggests, the conviction of our own mission, as bearers of the burden of righteousness in history, becomes so pervasive that "the imperative itself 'Thou shalt make history come out right,' is so deeply founded in our culture that we cannot even perceive that it might be in need of verification" (133). At this moment, both state and church become demonic because both are now bent on replacing God's will in history with their own.

Yoder maintains that a pervasive will to power continuously reasserts itself, in the state and in the individual (135). Did Paul not speak of "the principalities and powers" as "those structures of the present world order in whose autonomy mankind has become enslaved" (140)? In saying that we have been freed from bondage to these powers, the apostle implies that the followers of Christ are "freed from the temptation to sanctify the power structures" (141). But since those powers continue, for the time being, to rule this world, the Christian must give up the quest for efficacy in history—that, after all, is God's business—and accept once again the minority function of witnessing, even to the point of martyrdom, to the original revolution in which humanity is called to acknowledge the absolute lordship of Christ (175).

Yoder's biblical exegesis and his reading of Christian history may be contested, but they are not implausible or without justification in the central texts of the tradition. Exactly how to go about shaping a life on the basis of this vocation is, of course, susceptible to various interpretations, but the particulars of the witnessing community are not the concern of this essay. Yoder himself clearly thinks that those possibilities are given the community by the contingencies of history, which are themselves shaped by the time and place in which people hear Christ's call. But he insists that the contingencies may be distinguished from the communal response to the essentials of Christ's message.

First and foremost, the community forsakes the person of the other. Despite the love that the disciple has for her fellow citizen she will not come to his aid with the offer of protective force. This is to forsake justice, and Yoder properly terms it the "scandal of the Cross." My family and friends do not, contrary to

41. Yoder, *Original Revolution,* 71. Parenthetical page references that follow are to this volume.

42. Yoder's remarks on America as a surrogate church (Yoder, *When War Is Unjust,* 119) are even more apposite to the 1980s perhaps than they were to the late 1960s and 1970s.

common sense, have a privileged status that should, morally speaking, incline me to protect them against injustice. Nor will I press the just attack against the aggressor, regardless of the scope of his depravity. Despite my love for family and friends and despite my reverence for justice, I do not merely avoid, indeed I actively refuse, to accept political responsibility for preventing evil. In short, when it comes to engaging political force against injustice, I deny that "letting evil happen is as blameworthy as committing it" (81). To be faithful to my vocation I must admit no exceptions, for God's claim on me, as on all of creation, is absolute and overriding.

These are harsh demands, but they must be met by the aspirant to pacifism as a vocation. And such pacifism is, unlike that criticized by Narveson, an intelligible stance to take in pursuit of human good. First, on the persuasive side of the issue, Yoder's pacifism of vocation is founded on divine revelation. God himself has, in the eyes of the believer, displayed his will for humanity and called people to acknowledge and faithfully to attempt to do his will. Not only this, but the gospel in which this revelation is embedded tells the story of a loving God, a God, in fact, whose love is so unfathomably great that having taken on human nature he sacrificed himself for humanity. Here, Yoder can explicate his point effectively through analyzing the Gospel narrative, for in the crucifixion the disciples of Jesus themselves lose heart, and even Peter cannot sustain faithfulness. It appears as though at the moment of expected triumph all hope perishes, much as it must have seemed to Abraham, called to sacrifice his son. The question becomes, as Yoder puts it, "'Can I obey God when He seems to be willing to jeopardize his own purposes?' The answer, 'God will provide,' is thus a reassurance not of our own survival or comfort, but of the rationality of obedience which seems to jeopardize God's own purposes" (96). God is loving beyond what human beings could reasonably hope and, even when submitting to God's will seems contrary to love and right reason, he nonetheless provides. What better grounds could be asked for my persistence in faithfully doing his will? As pacifist I do not paradoxically claim that I have discovered a principle which demands that I act contrary to a well-established principle but that I have discovered a power for good which can achieve ends I could never have imagined and which is willing to welcome me among the flock if only I will serve in strict obedience to divine will. Once I am convinced of the will of a benevolent deity, it is hard to imagine what further requirements I might have for acting in accord with that will.[43]

---

43. Implicit in these remarks is a rejection of most variations of the Euthyphro dilemma. If you have been apprised of the will of God and if this God is not nasty, capricious, or demonic in its behavior, then it is no more reasonable to question its authority than it is for a child to question the authority of a parent who has proved to be faithful and caring. On this point see Peter Geach, *God and the Soul* (New York: Schocken Books, 1969). Robert M. Adams, *The Virtue of Faith and Other Essays in Philosophical Theology* (Oxford: Oxford University Press, 1987), has incorporated the nature of God into his attempt to elaborate a divine-command theory of moral action. For some problems with Adams's account of the status of moral terms vis-à-vis revelation, see my article "Ethical Properties and Divine Commands," *Journal of Religious Ethics* 11, no. 2 (1983): 280–300.

Nevertheless, to the extent that discipleship rests on faith, it seems not just to supplement what can be discovered by any reasonably intelligent person but to go beyond what the consensus of the community maintains about the way the world is. Here the Christian risks falling into a trap in many ways analogous to the pacifist caught up in the language of rights. It is true that Yoder's disciple is the member of an embattled minority and that this group proclaims foolishness to the larger world, but he need not admit that "that wider society is itself the universe, or that its ways of testing validity beyond the provincial have succeeded, by dint of a harder and more thorough hauling away at one's own definitional bootstraps, in transcending particularity."[44] If believers allow themselves to be saddled with secular standards of believability, by which religious belief is presumed incredible unless it meets conditions to which the secular culture never holds its own analogous beliefs, then they will always be found wanting. But why do this?[45] Outside the limited arena of technological proficiency, the establishment vocabulary can make no claims to universality or *a priori* justification. Just the opposite. The inflated claims for "scientific method" have not shown themselves resilient to criticism. The various reductive "isms" have all been found to have feet of clay or to fail to address the real issues motivating religious life and thought. When placed within the context of its historical particularity and the tradition through which it develops, Christian belief is a rival to, not a subordinate of, economics or biology in its account of "wholeness, coherence, happiness [and] self-fulfillment" in human life. If it is currently a minority position, that need not be the result of any incoherence; it may as easily be that the failure to believe on the part of the majority reflects their own waywardness and desire to serve their own inclinations rather than God's will. That, at least, is how the Christian story interprets the situation. And while granting that there is room for honest dispute, the Christian tradition is under no obligation of reason to proclaim itself "a hypothesis needing to verify itself by someone else's standards."[46]

Yoder concludes that the "real issue is not whether Jesus can make sense in a world far from Galilee, but whether... we want to follow him."[47]

Conclusion

The aim of this chapter has not been to advocate following Jesus, though even in dissent I believe that doing so is a live option in William James's sense of the term.[48] As long as Christian belief remains a live option, the burden of

44. Yoder, *When War Is Unjust,* 49.

45. Cf. Nicholas Wolterstorff, *Reason within the Bounds of Religion* (Grand Rapids, Mich.: Wm. B. Eerdmans, 1976).

46. Yoder, *When War Is Unjust,* 58.

47. Ibid., 62.

48. See William James, "The Will to Believe," in *"The Will to Believe" and Other Essays in Popular Philosophy* (New York: Longman, Green, 1896).

proof in contests of rationality will lie with the nonbeliever, and it is one I do not wish to pick up. My goal has been to show that the only morally acceptable form of pacifism, properly so called, is pacifism as a vocation. Pacifism as a strategy rises and falls with the likelihood of success, like any other means to an end. Pacifism as a principle cannot be made coherent; Narveson is right about this. But if ethics is about living that life which is best for people, it remains a possibility that God will call and that people will listen to that call. If it is God's voice, they would be foolish to ignore it. Nonetheless, pacifists should not be allowed to forget the enormousness of what they forsake in heeding that summons. In renouncing any recourse to killing they willingly forsake their physical selves, their families, and their friends. They abandon as well their moral selves to the extent that they will not raise their hands against rape, slavery, torture, and oppression. Thus, pacifism represents, from any view other than the disciples', the forsaking of justice and all that implies. This Yoder rightly acknowledges as scandal. To ignore the ties of family and community goes beyond any particular act of wickedness, for these are the very relationships that constitute and sustain any human community. This worst of scandals is tolerable only so long as it can be viewed as a genuine response to a good even more worthy than the justice of human community. The only good that presents a plausible claim to such transcendence must be divine. Yoder must couch his pacifism in the larger picture of disciples following a god who not only comes among them in human form but also sacrifices himself on the cross out of love. The disciples of this god act as they do in acknowledgment of that sacrificial love which alone makes it conceivable that they should give up what they do. The Gospel narrative and Yoder's way of reading that narrative are indispensable to the moral integrity of discipleship, and they must, to sustain that integrity, be true in all essentials. Pacifism as a vocation stands or falls with belief in Jesus and the substantive historical truth of something very like Yoder's interpretation of that truth. In the absence of a story about human relations to the divine that provides a context for such renunciation, pacifism itself is a source of pollution altogether on a par with the crimes of Oedipus. This extreme way of putting the point can be true only if the Gospel narrative is false, and can be false only if it is true. For the nonbeliever, or for the Christian who does not endorse Yoder's reading, pacifism cannot become a genuine option without some sort of conversion. The theological presuppositions are that important. Consequently, it will always skew the discussion to attempt an analysis of pacifism cut off from analysis of Christian vocation in general.[49]

---

49. There seems to me no better contemporary argument for this view than that of Paul Ramsey and Stanley Hauerwas in *Speak Up for Just War or Pacifism, with an Epilogue by Stanley Hauerwas* (University Park: Pennsylvania State University Press, 1988). It's unfortunate that failure to come to grips with the theological sources of Yoder's pacifism vitiates Ramsey's discussion (96–113). There is need for a more comprehensive account of Yoder's pacifism and its relations to his theology, hermeneutics, and social ethics as a whole. Despite refusing to participate in the political structures of

Suggestions for Further Reading

Cahill, Lisa Sowle. *Love Your Enemies: Discipleship, Pacifism, and Just War Theory.* Minneapolis: Fortress Press, 1994.

Carmody, Denise Lardner, et al. "Review Symposium [on Love Your Enemies]." *Horizons* 22 (fall 1995): 266–90.

Davis, Grady Scott. *Warcraft and the Fragility of Virtue: An Essay in Aristotelian Ethics.* Moscow: University of Idaho Press, 1992.

Hauerwas, Stanley. *Against the Nations: War and Survival in a Liberal Society.* Notre Dame: University of Notre Dame Press, 1992.

———. "Whose Just War? Which Peace?" In *But Was It Just? Reflections on the Morality of the Persian Gulf War,* ed. David E. Decosse, 83–105. New York: Doubleday, 1992.

Yoder, John Howard. *The Politics of Jesus.* 2d ed. Grand Rapids, Mich.: Wm. B. Eerdmans, 1994.

---

the wider world, Christian love remains operative and directed toward that world. Furthermore, the good will directed toward the world continues to be formed by God's will. Thus, it is not enough to live as the Messianic community in moral isolation from others, although, as a matter of discipline, physical removal may be prudent. If Yoder's reading of the Gospel narrative is sound, then that community is obliged to witness to the world and to lead it to acknowledge God's sovereignty. Only in this larger context, for example, is it possible to understand how Yoder can speak against pacifism as strategy or principle in *The Original Revolution* while giving it a qualified endorsement in *Nevertheless.* The argumentative strategy of the latter volume is to present the pros and cons of various ways of limiting war with an eye to undermining simplistic distinctions between pacifism and its rivals. This is a strategy dictated by Christian love because it paves the way for at least a gradual approach to God through approximating the kind of community he desires for humanity. If the Gospel narrative were not true, then the varieties of pacifism beyond that of "the honest study of cases" would be no more than strategies for securing justice and would have to be judged in that light. (Cf. *Nevertheless,* chap. 2.) From the Gospel perspective, the just war tradition is, however, a strategy for containing human sinfulness, and this the pacifist of vocation desires as part of Jesus' love even when he does not believe that he is capable of achieving it himself. It is this position that informs Yoder's critique of current just war thinking in *When War Is Unjust* and thus ties the three volumes together. In general, there is a remarkable coherence to all of Yoder's work, and a full analysis of it would repay the effort manyfold. James Gustafson, in *Ethics from a Theocentric Perspective,* Vol. 1, *Theology and Ethics* (Chicago: University of Chicago Press, 1981), and Thomas Ogletree, in *The Use of the Bible in Christian Ethics* (Philadelphia: Fortress Press, 1983), have already begun to recognize the power of Yoder's position, although as a worrisome rival to their own. Stanley Hauerwas has gone further than anyone in absorbing and expanding on the implications of Yoder's thought, not only in his writings on war, gathered in his *Against the Nations: War and Survival in a Liberal Society* (Notre Dame: University of Notre Dame Press, 1992), but also in *The Peaceable Kingdom* (Notre Dame: University of Notre Dame Press, 1983).

Chapter 12

After Racism

Tammy Williams

Editor's Introduction

Tammy Williams is a good example of a writer who employs Alasdair MacIntyre's conceptual hardware without feeling constrained by any normative ethical theory imagined by some to be lurking beneath the surface of *After Virtue.* This freedom allows Williams to express her views imaginatively, if not in outright tension with MacIntyre at some points. For example, Williams argues that Christians are obligated to oppose racism for reasons that are particular to the Christian narrative, yet the character of this opposition is not a stance taken against the liberal political community, for racism must be opposed *from within liberalism.* Likewise Williams gets good mileage out of MacIntyre's notion of virtue, but distances herself from the intimate tie MacIntyre sees between virtues and practices. Thus, she admits that distinctively Christian virtues (like forgiveness) are habituated by active participation in the resistance of racism, but she is reticent to describe an anti-racist venture as a MacIntyrean practice. In fact, the primary use Williams makes of *practice* is in illustrating the fact that racism (and resistance to it) has a socially rooted character analogous to, but not identical with, practices. Williams concedes that her reluctance to think explicitly in terms of practices stems from her Christian conviction that racism is *evil* and her Christian hope that racism is *eliminable.* Williams asks, if racism is an "evil practice," for which tradition could it be thought of as constitutive? Further, if racism is eliminable, then how can the resistance to racism be conceived as a *perpetually* constitutive component for some other tradition?

Despite the limits of MacIntyre's notion of practices for Williams's account, she finds rich resources in his conception of virtue, historicism, and narrative. Williams notes that, from the Christian perspective, the trouble with racism is not determining *whether* and *why* racism is morally reprehensible—that is easy. Rather, the trouble is to account for the ways in which racists are vulnerable to profound self-deception. In addition to racism's "incognito" character, postmodern thinking has raised current awareness of the fact that racism does not admit to a general definition. Rather, there are multiple racisms. For these two reasons, *virtue* is a useful concept. The term not only names the sort of Teflon coating and stalwart integrity people need in an age permeated with prejudice;

virtue also serves as a synonym for the moral skills necessary for recognizing racism in all its multifarious, and nefarious, disguises.

Second, Williams finds MacIntyre's historicism crucial for her analysis. Williams holds that Christians must come to terms with the perennial presence of racism in their own churchly history. Disregard for these (countless) negative examples trades on the prior assumption of an ahistorical stance. But to take such a stance simultaneously distances from Christians the opportunity to identify as their own both the *positive* anti-racist examples and the prophetic voices in their history. Only by owning up to their *entire* history can Christians hope to have a mess worth sorting through in order to locate those positive examples that are normative for maintaining authentic Christian identity.

Having made this second point, Williams employs the narrative of Christian activist John Perkins to stimulate our imagination in a third way that resonates with MacIntyre's conceptual scheme. MacIntyre clearly argues that no one can ask, "What am I to do?" without first considering, "Of which stories am I a part?" Williams finds this valuable in two ways. On the one hand, the "good" of the Christian tradition is the formation of a particular kind of community, one that can inculcate those virtues necessary to the task of living out an authentically Christian resistance to racism. But on the other hand, Williams contends that the narrative web in which Perkins found himself embedded lay at the interface *between* two communities. Therefore, concludes Williams, MacIntyre's admonition to attend to one's communal narratives for learning truthful ways to live necessitates that the distinctively Christian response to racism be to construct an alternative *within* liberalism, rather than an alternative *to* liberalism.

BRAD J. KALLENBERG

Introduction

In this essay I seek to answer the following question: What kind of moral reasoning must the church employ in order to understand the nature of racism, to combat it, and, more important, to *end* it? I argue that the form of reasoning will be community-based in a broad sense and will emphasize the cultivation of the virtues as the centerpiece of moral life. My treatment of community focuses on the church as the reconciling community; in particular, I highlight the role of the black church in light of its unique history and locus with respect to racism.

My understanding and use of virtue ethics is dependent upon Alasdair MacIntyre's elaboration and critique of it, primarily in *After Virtue.* However, my use of virtue theory will be from *within* liberalism and admittedly will fall short of a full-blown implementation of the neo-Aristotelianism that MacIntyre advocates. Nonetheless, I argue that virtue-centered moral reasoning provides an alternative to "racial reasoning" and to the polemical discourse that at times characterizes partisan politics. MacIntyre's own constructive proposal for contemporary ethics is framed within an integrated schema of practices, tradition, community, *telos,* virtues, and narrative. I, however, make selective use of MacIntyre, build in part upon elements of his paradigm, and propose a virtue-centered response to racism that is both creative and indebted to MacIntyre's thought. To this end, I give special place to the concept of practices and the role of the virtues in moral development.

First, the issue of practices. I begin by examining MacIntyre's conception of a practice as the social backdrop for the display of the virtues, and the arguments of his respondents who challenge him with a critique of "evil practices." I then pursue an understanding of racism as a "social project" in which exclusion is a primary goal. By proffering racism as a participatory project, I seek to underscore the social rootedness of racism; by highlighting exclusion as a central feature, I hope to show that the biblical narrative provides the primary means by which Christians can judge racism as evil. I conclude the section by briefly exploring postmodern understandings of racism, which cohere with MacIntyre's general understanding of morality's dependence upon social life.

With respect to the second area of development, I hope to demonstrate how virtue theory can serve as an ethical resource in the church's ongoing reflection upon and resistance to racism. In light of this goal, I focus on moral agents rather than political "solutions" to racism. More concretely, I emphasize how communities can nurture moral agents who are *anti-racist* in their interpretation of the world and in their practices; such agents through their lifelong training are thereby "equipped" to devise concrete ways of opposing racism. To develop my stress on "agent morality," I present an account of the virtues, rooted in the community of the black church, which exemplifies how virtue theory can be appropriated by a particular community to sustain the moral training of its members. By portraying the life of John Perkins in narrative form, I show how the interplay of racism and practices of anti-racism provide the setting in which the virtues are displayed in a life. I conclude by highlighting ways that the virtues can help to sustain our moral imaginations so that we might be the kind of people who can envisage a society *after racism.*

The State of Racial Discourse

In observing the truncated character of public discourse on race, Cornel West in *Race Matters* notes that the rancor of contemporary debate leaves us both personally disillusioned and morally disempowered.[1] The resulting paralysis in discussions on race stems from a reductionist analysis that limits the conversation on race to "'problems' black people pose for whites" and, equally detrimental, from continued use of a narrow, liberal-conservative framework to debate race relations. Moving beyond the flawed partisan framework is mandatory if we are to converse critically about race, for "*[h]ow we set up the terms for discussing racial*

1. Cornel West, *Race Matters* (Boston: Beacon Press, 1993), 2.

issues shapes our perception and response to these issues" (italics mine).[2] A case in point was the Clarence Thomas/Anita Hill hearings in which the appeal to *racial reasoning* by black leaders inevitably led to questions about black authenticity, for example, "Is Thomas really black?" rather than "Is he a qualified candidate?"[3] What such inquiries failed to take into account was that the very rubric of racial reasoning should be not only questioned but *dismantled,* West contends, and replaced with a form of moral reasoning within a prophetic framework.

It strikes me that certain parallels can be drawn between West's albeit brief characterization of the state of contemporary racial discourse and its inadequate categories of analysis, and Alasdair MacIntyre's sweeping indictment of post-Enlightenment moral discourse. Moreover, racial discourse is symptomatic of the larger pathology of moral discourse.

The State of Moral Discourse

MacIntyre speaks of the language of morality as being in a state of grave disorder and notes how much of moral language is used to express disagreements that tend to be interminable.[4] Not only do the debates never end; more critically, there appears to be no rational way of obtaining moral consensus on issues. The problem is not that we are confused over particular moral issues like racism. Rather, the dilemma is more profound: we have lost the basis for formulating coherent moral arguments. This is because our moral vocabulary has lost the shared conceptual structure that originally imbued it with relevance and significance. With our moral terminology dislodged from its context, we are left with the residual fragments of the original schema that gave meaning to moral utterances. The relegation of race, in particular, to the realm of the problematic happens when moral issues become divorced from the larger social contexts and practices that give them intelligibility. While we continue to use moral phraseology in everyday discourse, we, unknowingly, have lost our comprehension of morality.

How we set up the terms for discussing moral issues *does* shape our perception and response to these issues. For MacIntyre, the only credible understanding

---

2. Ibid., 3.

3. Ibid., 23–25, 28. West uses the term *racial reasoning* to describe the process through which some black leaders rationalized and justified their support of Thomas's nomination. By appealing to the notion of *black authenticity,* supporters could point to Thomas's poverty-stricken childhood in the segregationist South, his determination, and consequent achievement as credentials of his blackness. This led to a *closing ranks for survival mentality* in which supporters felt the need to advocate for Thomas in the face of white opposition. In such a scenario the interests of black women tend to be subordinated in the name of protecting the interests of the larger community. West points out that Thomas could have been opposed simply on the basis of his qualifications; the fact that black leaders failed to speak publicly of his lack of credentials reflects how captive many blacks are to white racist stereotypes about black intellect. I use the term *racial reasoning* in a more general way to describe the "racialization" of discourse, that is, the ways in which race is referred to that preempt the appeal to other grounds of argument.

4. The following synopsis is based upon Alasdair MacIntyre, *After Virtue,* 2d ed. (Notre Dame: University of Notre Dame Press, 1984), 2–12. Also Peter McMylor, *Alasdair MacIntyre: Critic of Modernity* (London: Routledge, 1994), 23.

of morality is that of the Aristotelian teleological tradition, which emphasized the primacy of the virtues in the moral life.[5] This was the relinquished ethical framework that had earlier infused morality with meaning, and this is *the* tradition, he contends, that must be revived if we are to emerge from our current state of moral disarray.

But does Aristotelianism as a tradition, however reconstituted (for example, as Thomist Aristotelianism), have the moral resources to address the disturbing reality that *race* matters in this pluralistic society? Or does MacIntyre's attempt to recover Aristotelian ethics as a response to current moral debacles amount to nothing more than "nostalgic yearnings for holistic schema and contexts" and reflect an "elitist disengagement from present political and economic struggles"?—the latter being the more serious of the two charges leveled by West.[6] Although the particular terms and configuration of MacIntyre's moral vision continue to be fiercely debated by West and others in academic circles, I believe that appropriation of some significant aspects of MacIntyre's proposal allows us to transcend both the pitfalls of racial reasoning and the commonplace moralizing by liberals and conservatives on the issue of race.

Practices

In an effort to provide the necessary social background that renders the exercise of the virtues comprehensible, MacIntyre outlines the concept of a practice to underscore "that the exercise of the virtues is and always has been actually rooted in practices."[7] While social practices tend to be peripheral, if not negligible, to contemporary understanding of morality or political life, comprehensive human endeavors (such as mathematics or music) serve as the settings where the virtues can be displayed and excellence defined. To clarify the relationship between virtues and practices, MacIntyre offers a terse definition of a practice as

> any coherent and complex form of socially established cooperative human activity through which goods internal to that form of activity are realized in the course of trying to achieve those standards of excellence which are appropriate to, and partially definitive of, that form of activity, with the result that human powers to achieve excellence, and human conceptions of the ends and goods involved, are systematically extended.[8]

---

5. See MacIntyre's defense of *After Virtue*'s thesis in "Bernstein's Distorting Mirrors: A Rejoinder," *Soundings* 67 (spring 1984): 39, where he writes that "Aristotelianism provides the only standpoint from which in the end a true and adequate moral history of modernity can be written."

6. See Cornel West's critique of *After Virtue* titled "Alasdair MacIntyre, Liberalism, and Socialism: A Christian Perspective," in *Prophetic Fragments* (Grand Rapids, Mich.: Wm B. Eerdmans, 1988), 126–27. Unlike MacIntyre, West believes that any alternative to our current social disorder must be found *within* liberalism. We must therefore challenge liberalism's accepted assumptions, work within its framework, and build upon it.

7. MacIntyre, "Bernstein's Distorting Mirrors," 34.

8. MacIntyre, *After Virtue,* 187. The following discussion is based upon pp. 186–96.

Practices, examples of which include medicine, architecture, academic writing, football, and the formation of communities and families, provide the arenas in which the virtues are exhibited.

Two features intrinsic to a practice are standards of excellence and the achievement of goods "internal" to the practice. To say that someone has performed a surgical procedure "well" or played a "good" round of golf implies that there are certain standards determined not solely by the participant but by the practice. Likewise, to recognize that certain skills, attitudes, and goods can be identified and acquired only by participating in the particular practice, so that those outside the practice lack the expertise to judge it, is to speak of "internal goods." External goods, in contrast, are those goods such as money and status that are attained while participating in the practice but can also be acquired apart from it.

A graduate student, for example, who writes an article on MacIntyre, exclusively in the hope that a published paper will bring her recognition and further her incipient academic career, will not experience the *kinds* of challenges and joys associated with engaging with a seminal philosopher and learning new ways of reasoning, because she is pursuing external goods. Yet she can acquire internal goods by acknowledging the contributions of other practitioners to the craft of academic writing and her relationship to them; in so doing, she must recognize what she owes to whom, she must learn from her more experienced mentor and colleagues when confronted with her flawed reasoning, and yet continue to take the ongoing risks requisite to mastering the art. Without these virtues of justice, honesty, and courage the practice of scholarship and, indeed, any practice could not be sustained.

But practices are not to be confused with technical skills or with the institutions that support them, although MacIntyre describes the relationship between practices and institutions as intimate. Without institutions like hospitals, such practices as medicine could not be sustained, and without the exercise of the virtues, the practices themselves would be tainted by the power of the institution inasmuch as it is characteristic of institutions to be concerned with external goods; indeed they must be if they are to sustain themselves and the practices they undergird.

The implications for ethics are important. First, we should understand morality as being rooted in the ordinary aspects of our lives, such as practices, whereby "acting morally well, like playing chess well, is not a matter of individual preference or decision. Rather, the criteria for acting well are determined by the kind of practice in which we are engaged."[9] Moreover, the distinction between internal and external goods points to the fact that the virtues are to be exercised for their own sake and not for the sake of benefits or rewards that might accrue

9. John Horton and Susan Mendus, eds., "Alasdair MacIntyre: *After Virtue* and After," in *After MacIntyre: Critical Perspectives on the Work of Alasdair MacIntyre* (Notre Dame: University of Notre Dame Press, 1994), 10.

from that exercise. In fact, it is by means of exercising the virtues that we are enabled to achieve the internal goods of the practices and without them we are prevented from achieving those goods.

Evil Practices?

MacIntyre himself concedes that his discussion of practices is inadequate in providing a complete account of the role of the virtues in the moral life and therefore supplements his account by relating virtues to the narrative unity of a human life and to the content of a moral tradition. This three-tiered definition of a virtue stipulates that no disposition can be deemed a virtue unless it meets the criteria *at each of the three stages.*[10] Yet the very description of a practice has raised questions whether some practices that are inherently *evil,* for example, torture, can in fact satisfy MacIntyre's criteria.[11]

In a feminist critique of MacIntyre's depiction of practices, Elizabeth Frazer and Nicola Lacey raise the following issues regarding the political relevance of practices, namely:

> the terms on which social actors do or do not participate in a practice; second, their differential power to alter a practice; third, the existence and status of competing interpretations of the nature of the good internal to a practice....[12]

Because MacIntyre's depiction of practices lacks an analysis of power relationships in society, he does not account for how some participants in practices are not accorded the same status or degree of power as other practitioners, or how many practices, in contrast, exclude would-be participants (for example, a disabled child may be excluded from playing football unless the practice is altered; women have been denied access to institutions such as the university, whose conception of the good has been related to the exclusion of women).[13]

---

10. MacIntyre, *After Virtue,* 275.

11. Ibid., 199–200; see also Richard J. Bernstein, "Nietzsche or Aristotle? Reflections on Alasdair MacIntyre's *After Virtue,*" *Soundings* 67 (spring 1984): 13, 23. Bernstein questions whether practices like spying, smuggling, safecracking, and the art of the executioner would not qualify as practices given MacIntyre's definition. He then extends the argument to traditions, by asking whether there may be traditions that are evil. "Do we not have to recognize that there have been vital traditions that have been used to legitimate the moral inferiority of the poor, women, and minorities?"; see also MacIntyre's response to Bernstein in "Bernstein's Distorting Mirrors: A Rejoinder," *Soundings* 67 (spring 1984): 36. He argues that Bernstein's list is one not of evil practices but of activities defined by the use of multiple skills to reach a given type of end; of equal import is how they do not "involve systematic extension of our conceptions of the ends and goals which excellence may serve."

12. Elizabeth Frazer and Nicola Lacey, "MacIntyre, Feminism, and the Concept of Practice," in *After MacIntyre,* 276.

13. Ibid., 275, 277; see also MacIntyre's response to Frazer and Lacey in the same volume, 289–90. While acknowledging the exclusion of women that has occurred because of "externally based judgements deriving from unrecognized prejudice" of some participants (289) and the corrupting impact that institutions can have on practices, MacIntyre comments that Frazer and Lacey could also have remarked on the amount of harm done not only to women but also to practices when institutions are corrupted. Similarly, one can note that when certain participants, e.g., racial minorities,

We are then faced with the question which MacIntyre himself anticipates: "How can a disposition be a virtue and sustain practices, some of which issue in evil?" Despite MacIntyre's reluctance to concede the existence of evil practices, he does allow the *possibility* as such, and responds accordingly. We ought not to excuse such evils, he says, or consider that whatever flows from a virtue is right (for example, that courage can sustain injustice). Further, we cannot approve of all practices in all circumstances and must recognize that practices stand in need of moral criticism; in fact, it is not circular to appeal to the requirements of a virtue such as justice to criticize a practice. And finally, though justice may be initially defined as a virtue that is necessary to sustain practices, it does not rule out the need to condemn violations of justice that may arise.[14]

We are now left to consider how practices might relate to the issue of racism.

Spying, Smuggling, Safecracking, and Torture: Why Racism Is a *Different Kind* of Evil

Although the concerns that Frazer, Lacey, and others raise regarding power relations and exclusion within practices and traditions directly relate to the issue of racism,[15] to define racism *as a practice in the MacIntyrean sense* is problematic. Two difficulties arise from defining racism as a practice. First, if racism is defined as a practice according to MacIntyre's definition, the relationship between practices and virtues is troublesome inasmuch as the virtues are displayed in, and help to sustain, practices. Likewise, the relationship between practices and traditions must also be questioned. If practices constitute traditions and if racism is a practice, then we must ask "for which tradition is it constitutive?" The fact that racism has existed during periods of Christianity is not enough to identify it as a practice. Rather, it is a cancer that is diametrically opposed to the Christian narrative and, therefore, must be excised. To define racism as an *evil* practice in the sense of its being a "fallen" or "distorted" practice is equally problematic, for racism, according to this description, is construed as the shadow side or deficiency of a virtuous practice such as community building. This type of development, in my estimate, robs racism of its efficacy as a system of exclusion in its own right. Moreover, fallen practices by definition envision the possibility of redemption or restoration, whereas racism must be *eliminated.*

---

achieve *set* standards of excellence within a given practice, on occasion, the criteria for measuring excellence are questioned (the judging was "biased") or the practitioner's performance is demeaned (the essay wasn't *that* good).

14. MacIntyre, *After Virtue,* 200.

15. Bernstein, "Nietzsche or Aristotle?" 25. Bernstein notes MacIntyre's awareness that the virtue tradition has always been based on *exclusion* — that of barbarians, slaves, women, and others — by citing MacIntyre's acknowledgment of the blindness Aristotle shared with his culture as well as the ahistorical character of Aristotle's understanding of human nature. Yet Bernstein observes that MacIntyre himself explicitly rejects the idea that anyone in principle should be prevented from attaining the good life and embodying the virtues. See also David Theo Goldberg, *Racist Culture* (Cambridge, Mass.: Blackwell Publishers, 1993), 22, 38.

I will, however, employ the imagery of racism as a "social project"[16] that functions on many levels (interpersonal, institutional) with a wide range of participants (willing, unwitting), who have varying motivations. The advantage of this illustration is that it allows us to explore the aforementioned issues of social embeddedness and evil as they directly relate to racism.

To understand racism as a participatory project removes racism from the realm of the abstract, the order of the supernatural, the sphere of the individual, and the domain of the rational, to that of the *social.* Simply put, the ongoing existence of racism is perhaps most adequately, though not exclusively, accounted for not as a *demonic* stronghold by which its power lies in the invisible realm, nor as a feature that is innate in human beings, so that racism is viewed as *natural,* nor as rooted in rationality, so that personal prejudice is viewed as *irrational* behavior, but as a matter of shared human activities that are socially constituted and sustained. All three understandings of racism are inadequate as explanations or descriptions but also in generating meaningful ways of combating it. If racism is viewed as a demonic stronghold, it is all too easy for "spiritual warfare" to become the primary means of engaging with it, thereby minimizing other means of combating it. Second, a perspective on racism that views it as a matter of individual behavior, preferences, and choices downplays how institutional and social infrastructures aid and prolong racism. Likewise, the viewpoint that racism is "something we're born with" undermines the fact that a racist society is created by actions and political choices. It also denies that we as moral agents can repudiate racist thinking.[17] Finally, with respect to racism's irrationality, David Theo Goldberg argues that racial identifications and exclusions have been features of modernity, and at times such exclusions are rationally authorized and endorsed. To define racism as inherently irrational is to deny that appeals to race can be made to achieve well-defined ends and that power relations are often central to racism. To suggest that racism may be rational, however, does not commit us to claiming that racism is *moral.* A claim of irrationality undermines moral condemnation of racism, he believes, because the "mentally ill" cannot be held responsible for acts that stem from their sickness.[18]

If we extend the metaphor, racism can be conceptualized *as a social project in which one primary end is exclusion: in many instances, the exclusion of individuals and groups from a variety of social activities and institutions.* Implicit is the understanding that racially defined exclusions can assume a variety of forms. As an extreme manifestation, *elimination,* often in the form of "ethnic cleansing," requires that the other be expelled or killed; *assimilation* demands that identity be exchanged for acceptance; *domination* entails subjugation and exploitation by labeling the other as inferior and assigning her to her "proper place," as reflected

16. I use the word *project* in the everyday sense of a cooperative task or activity, not in the technical sense in which some authors use the word with respect to racial formation.

17. See bell hooks, *Killing Rage: Ending Racism* (New York: Henry Holt, 1995), 270.

18. See Goldberg, *Racist Culture,* 94, 117.

in education, employment, housing policies, and lack of social mobility; *abandonment* results by means of both distance and indifference, so that the other is prevented from intruding and making claims upon us.[19] Some exclusions may occur only to hold the racially different at a distance.[20] Various reasons such as discomfort with strangeness within ourselves, fear of the unknown, cultural preservation, or safeguarding economic distribution patterns may account for exclusions.[21]

It is on account of such exclusion (although other grounds can be cited) that Christians, alongside adherents of other traditions, can judge racism as evil because of the biblical narrative. Refuting claims that all judgments themselves are, in fact, acts of exclusion and that judgments are merely emotivist expressions of personal preference, Miroslav Volf roots his rejection of exclusion in the Christian tradition and bases it upon the biblical story:

> I do not reject exclusion because of a contingent preference for a certain kind of society. . . . I reject exclusion because the prophets, evangelists, and apostles tell me that this a wrong way to treat human beings, any human being, anywhere, and I am persuaded to have good reasons to believe them. . . . In my vocabulary, in any case, "exclusion" does not express a preference; it names an objective evil.[22]

Yet, unlike an undertaking such as torture, which is more readily evident and therefore socially identifiable as malicious, what is characteristic of racism is its form: its ability to cloak and camouflage itself, *so that it is seen as something other than racism.*[23] This is why David Theo Goldberg speaks of racism as "chameleonic and parasitic in character: It insinuates itself into and appropriates as its own mode more legitimate forms of social and scientific expression."[24]

The *incognito* quality of racism not only facilitates racism's formidability but also, in part, accounts for the self-deception of racists and clashing views about

19. Miroslav Volf, *Exclusion and Embrace: A Theological Exploration of Identity, Otherness, and Reconciliation* (Nashville: Abingdon Press, 1996), 74–75.

20. See Michael Eric Dyson, *Race Rules* (Reading, Mass.: Addison-Wesley, 1996), 55–56. In response to the question of why black public intellectuals seem to talk only about race, Dyson takes up the issue of racialized exclusion from an interesting angle and details how black thinkers have been discouraged from publicly debating issues *other* than race: "Black intellectuals are rarely asked about the collapse of communism, the crisis of capitalism . . . the Palestinian-Israeli conflict, the state of modern Islam, the transcendentalist vision of Emerson, Walt Whitman's beliefs about erotic friendship, the impact of Heisenberg's uncertainty principle on the debate about postmodernism, Foucault's notion of power, fin-de-siecle apocalyptic thinking, Russian formalism, Murray Perahia's Beethoven concertos, and a world of things besides. We're rarely even asked about the unusual things black folk do, like scuba diving, writing histories of German warplanes, studying ancient Chinese cultures, and so on."

21. Goldberg, *Racist Culture,* 95; Volf, *Exclusion,* 77–78.

22. Volf, *Exclusion,* 68.

23. A factor other than form that accounts for why racism is not universally recognizable as evil is the *observers* of racism. Only those with adequate narrative resources and virtues can recognize it as evil. Christians, and other communities, possess the necessary resources that enable them to *see* racism *differently* from others, for example, the Klan.

24. Goldberg, *Racist Culture,* 107.

race relations. Although golfers, math teachers, and concert pianists would explicitly acknowledge that they are engaged in sports, education, and music, the nature of racism is such that some engage in the activity without acknowledging it as racism and, it follows, without identifying themselves as "team players." Clearly, many choose to engage in the project of racism *qua* the project. Yet I would suggest that racism's mutative dimension may help to explain why it endures and how it can be historically extended under the cover of legitimate, social endeavors.

Finally, a word about the relationship between project participants and the *excluded others* — those who have been excluded in whatever way as a result of racism. There is a tendency on the part of those who either engage in racist activities or have never experienced racial discrimination to deny the reality of racism or to point to *other* social projects that would seem to discredit the charge of the excluded.[25]

This may be one reason that those who have an easy time catching a cab in New York City may be skeptical of Cornel West's anecdote and his interpretation of being bypassed by nine taxis and having the tenth one pick up a white female standing next to him, as a racist incident.[26] I know better. I have "faked out" more than one cab driver in Washington, D.C., appearing to be alone, only to have a male friend take my place once the cab stopped. It is "common" knowledge in D.C. that black men have difficulty hailing cabs, with the exception of William Raspberry, perhaps![27] It follows from this that one way of understanding divergent viewpoints between ethnic minorities and whites on "race relations" is to understand those responses not simply as emotivist speech acts or examples of racial reasoning, that is, expressions of "group loyalty," but in terms of concrete experiences of the excluded with racism or lack of such experiences on the part of all others.

West's taxi episode is instructive for another reason. It not only reflects a racist rejection at the macro-level but also reveals how race inserts itself at the micro-social level of everyday experience where it functions as *common sense* — a way of interpreting, explaining, and acting in the world.[28] Therefore, just as we use race to provide clues about "who" someone is, we often expect people to act out their racial identities. Examples of the Latino professional who is ha-

25. In the face of accusations of police brutality by members of a community who claim to be constantly harassed by the police, the pointing to the presence of minority police officers and community policing efforts by sectors of the community who enjoy cordial relations with the police is a common example of how the claims of the other are either minimized or discredited by those who have no experience with the said activity.

26. West, *Race Matters,* x.

27. William Raspberry is a Pulitzer Prize-winning journalist for the *Washington Post,* whose columns typically feature extended dialogue with "the cabbie."

28. My simplified discussion and several illustrations are taken from Michael Omi and Howard Winant, *Racial Formation in the United States: From the 1960s to the 1990s,* 2d ed. (New York: Routledge, 1994), 59–60. The authors insert racialized common sense (referred to as "common-sense racism" by other authors) into a broader and more sophisticated framework of racial formation. See also Goldberg, *Racist Culture,* 96.

rassed by police while walking in his own suburban neighborhood; the belief that Asians are naturally gifted in math; the look of disbelief given to the Korean kid who can out-rap Dr. Dre; the belief that black men are predisposed to violence — all reflect how our social structure is, in fact, "racialized." It shapes our experiences of race and impacts racial interpretations and meanings to the extent that aspects of our lives such as romantic preferences, tastes in music, films, sports, and ways of talking and walking become "racially coded." Because we live in a society where racial cognizance is so prevalent, "everybody learns some combination, some version, of the rules of racial classification, and of her own racial identity, often without obvious teaching or conscious inculcation."[29]

Racism — An Evil Beyond Definition? Postmodern Understandings of Racism

Throughout his career MacIntyre has maintained that moral concepts cannot be examined and understood apart from their history since "moral concepts are embodied in and are partially constitutive of forms of social life."[30] Just as the limitations of racial discourse cannot rightly be perceived apart from the larger arena of moral discourse, racism, like morality, cannot be comprehended apart from particular historical periods and societies.

While the category of race has come to be understood as "timeless," "unchanging," and "having the same features throughout its history"[31] — the very ways in which ethics was characterized that MacIntyre debunked in his early critique of modern moral philosophy — it is not an immutable, transhistorical category that is the same in all contexts.[32] In fact, different social groups in various historical periods have understood race in radically different ways. Consider the U.S. census and how its racial categories have varied each decade:

> Groups such as Japanese Americans have moved from categories such as "nonwhite," "Oriental," or simply "Other" to recent inclusion as a specific "ethnic" group under the broader category of "Asian and Pacific Islanders." The variation both reflects and in turn shapes racial understanding and dynamics. It establishes often contradictory parameters of racial identity into which both individuals and groups must fit.[33]

The concept of race, far from being static, is too complex and multilayered to be reduced to a single, simple definition.[34] Rather, race is better understood

29. Omi and Winant, *Racial Formation,* 60.

30. Alasdair MacIntyre, *A Short History of Ethics: A History of Moral Philosophy from the Homeric Age to the Twentieth Century* (London: Routledge and Kegan Paul, 1967), 1.

31. Ibid.

32. John Solomos and Les Back, *Racism and Society* (London: Macmillan, 1996), 27.

33. Omi and Winant, *Racial Formation,* 3.

34. Kenan Malik, *The Meaning of Race: Race, History, and Culture in Western Society* (London: Macmillan, 1996), 71. Although I disagree with Malik's "universalist" solution to racism, his analysis of race is informative. It should be noted that although race is intimately linked with class and gender, its uniqueness demands that it not be reduced to any one socioeconomic relationship.

as "a medium through which the changing relationship between humanity, society, and nature has been understood in various ways. *What is important to understand are the ways in which this changing relationship has been, and still is, expressed through the discourse of race*" (emphasis mine).[35] Michael Omi and Howard Winant, who understand race as an "unstable and 'decentered' complex of social meanings," define race as "*a concept which signifies and symbolizes social conflicts and interests by referring to different types of human bodies.*"[36] By defining race in this manner, and understanding it as "an element of social structure" (rather than a "problem" within it), Omi and Winant hope to counter notions of race as an *essence* (something fixed, objective) or as an *illusion* (an ideological construct).

Race as a Social Construct

One glaring omission that I admit to is the absence of any mention of race in terms of a biological or genetic foundation. Although the traits ("phenotypes"—visible, physical characteristics) chosen to define race (such as skin color) are biological, "selection of these particular human features for purposes of racial signification is always and necessarily a social and historical process."[37] To state this is to underscore that the categories employed to divide human groups along racial lines are imprecise and arbitrary. For example, throughout history different anthropologists have arrived at varying numbers of races by appealing to different criteria such as geography or skin color.[38] Rather than a classification based on phenotype, humankind could be divided on the basis of blood groups (type A race, type O race), which would be more biologically significant but would lack any meaningful social significance. Likewise, human characteristics such as nose shape or head shape could equally be appealed to as criteria for division. The fact that sharp racial boundaries are based upon certain selected characteristics such as skin color and not others is predicated upon the fact that people respond to racial groups in quite different and socially important ways. In light of this, it can be asserted that race is not a valid *biological* concept but a *social* construct—for the creation of the notion of race is the product of social need.[39]

If the concept of race is multifaceted, it follows then that racism can have no single, universal meaning, such as "prejudice and power."[40] A more critical view of racism must depose assumptions of a *monolithic racism* by speaking of

35. Ibid., 71.

36. Omi and Winant, *Racial Formation,* 55.

37. Ibid.

38. For a good introductory discussion of scientific support for understanding race as a social phenomenon rather than a genetic fact, see S. Dale McLemore, *Racial and Ethnic Relations in America,* 3d ed. (Boston: Allyn and Bacon, 1991), 107–11. See also Robert Lee Hotz, "Scientists Say Race Has No Biological Basis," *Los Angeles Times,* 20 February 1995, sec. A1, 1, 10.

39. Malik, *Meaning of Race,* 4–5.

40. Omi and Winant, *Racial Formation,* 73, 188 n. 65. One flaw of this definition of racism is that it views power as absolute (whites have it; blacks don't) versus relational (blacks may have more power relative to Native Americans). It has consequently been used to support the claim that only whites can be racist—an assertion that both authors rightly argue against.

historically specific *racisms.*[41] To delineate *multiple racisms* is to grasp what race signifies at different times and to acknowledge that various racisms have different effects and ramifications. There may be different racisms in the same place at different times, that is, the racism that sustained slavery in the United States differed from that of Jim Crow segregation, and both can be distinguished from contemporary racist practice. Therefore, to inquire about the causes of racism is not particularly meaningful, for there is no one set of determinants that invariably accounts for the occurrence of racism.[42] Moreover, there is a need to situate racisms within specific settings and social contexts before setting forth a larger account of their wider significance.[43]

One example of "contextualized" racism is that of *new racism,* also known as *cultural racism,* which some British sociologists believe has its origins in the emergence of the political right in British politics in the 1980s.[44] What characterizes new racism is that contemporary expressions of race are coded in a language that seeks to avoid accusations of racism. The nonracial rhetoric of "culture" or "nation" is the coded language that invokes a hidden racial narrative. The central feature of this reconfiguration is that the identities of racial groups are seen as "fixed" or "natural."[45] Put differently, new racism can be characterized by its ability to infuse old concepts with racialized meanings, so that the term *equality,* once understood as "equal opportunity for all," now signifies "preference for unqualified blacks."[46] Why bother to use the infamous "N-word" when the code words *rapper* or *urban* can conjure up the same image and serve the same purpose? The crucial property of these configurations is their ability to produce a racist effect while denying that this effect is the result of racism. As a result the advocates of this form of racism can claim that they are by no means racist but merely interested in guarding "their way of life" and that the issue of "color" is irrelevant to their arguments.[47]

From our brief overview of more contemporary modes of racism, it should be evident that the more monolithic racism of the 1950s or 1960s has given way to a more convoluted mapping of racisms or a "messy" racial hegemony.[48] Such complexity requires that we move beyond racial dichotomizing — the analyzing and conceptualizing of race solely in terms of black and white relationships — that we might recognize alliances among groups, differentiation within groups, and the evolving dynamics of white identity. Moreover, a bipolar framework is inadequate in addressing how policies like immigration have different impacts on various racial minorities; for example, affirmative action may have differ-

41. Goldberg, *Racist Culture,* 90–91.
42. Ibid., 90.
43. Solomos and Back, *Racism and Society,* 29.
44. Ibid., 18.
45. Ibid., 18–19.
46. Steven Small, *Racialized Barriers* (London: Routledge, 1994), 85.
47. Solomos and Back, *Racism and Society,* 27.
48. The discussion is taken from Omi and Winant, *Racial Formation,* 75, 153–55.

ent significance for Latinos than for Asian Americans. Likewise, an exclusive black-white focus cannot address such issues as racial scapegoating or anti-immigration backlash directed primarily against Latinos and Asians, who are viewed as partially "responsible" for economic and cultural decline. Not only must moral discourse move beyond the boundaries of racial reasoning, it must also transcend the bipolar model of race that has heavily influenced it.

Ethical Implications of Postmodern Understandings of Racism

If racism is neither monolithic nor universal, it is not surprising that no one set of principles can be relied upon to combat it. Instead, the new and improved forms of multiple racisms and their adaptations to new social and demographic circumstances require the nurturing of moral agents who are able to *recognize, interpret,* and *respond* to personal and institutional modes of racism by drawing upon the moral resources and skills that duty-based rules do not provide: namely, perception, judgment, moral insight, training, and practice. Of equal import is the prevalence of commonsense racism in our society, which suggests that although the removal of racist structures is necessary, the reeducation of moral agents who will subvert racial codes by learning new versions of the rules, thereby undermining accepted notions of racial classification, is imperative. A lifelong commitment to anti-racism can be sustained through the cultivation and exercise of the virtues within a community committed to an inclusive vision of the world. It is to the *community* component of MacIntyre's paradigm that I now turn.

"Been There, Done That": What the Church Has to Offer the World on Racism

If any one community in American society is in a unique position to understand how and why race matters so much, it is the church.[49] Moreover, the church's exceptional station results not so much from its moral leadership on racism as from its own long-documented history of aiding and abetting racism, while engaging in *bona fide* practices of the Christian faith. Through the practice of hermeneutics, the Hamitic Curse was used in the nineteenth century to validate black inferiority and slavery; through the practice of preaching, slaves were exhorted to obey their masters; in defense of the practice of worship, blacks

49. I adhere to the view that Christian ethics is community-dependent and therefore church-based. I base my discussion of the church on Stanley Hauerwas's well-known positions that Christian ethics is not a "minimalist ethic" written for everyone. It makes sense only because of the person and ministry of Jesus. The task of Christian ethics is to enable us properly to envision the world; it helps us to see. Our ability to act is based upon our being trained to see the world and ask, "What is going on?" See Stanley Hauerwas, *The Peaceable Kingdom: A Primer in Christian Ethics* (Notre Dame: University of Notre Dame Press, 1983), 97, 102; Stanley Hauerwas and William H. Willimon, *Resident Aliens: Life in the Christian Colony* (Nashville: Abingdon Press, 1989), 71.

were denied admission to or forcibly expelled from white services.[50] By means of denominational structures such as Sunday school boards, publishing boards, missions agencies,[51] seminaries, and Bible institutions, racialized oppression can all too easily become institutionalized through legitimate practices in our own contemporary settings.

The church's track record is important for us to remember: Christian leadership has been as captive to racism's seduction as the pew. Lest we forget, King's matchless "Letter from a Birmingham Jail" was addressed not directly to the nation at large or to the recalcitrant South but to eight fellow clergy who questioned King's motivations and the propriety of his actions.[52] The fact that Christians throughout the centuries have found ways to tolerate the peaceful coexistence of Christianity and racism should warn us that "we are no better than our forbears."

Yet can the children of the "third and fourth generation" be held accountable for the sins of the church fathers and mothers—when, in fact, *we* weren't there? *We* didn't do that. MacIntyre, I believe, can be helpful in this regard because he reminds us that to refer to ourselves as Christians is not only to acknowledge a personal "decision" but to identify ourselves with a historical tradition transmitted over generations and to recognize ourselves as its bearers.[53] To take seriously the fact that our identity is bound up with our embeddedness in a narrative longer than our own is to call into question modernity's assumption that we can choose or exclude those things for which we will be morally responsible. He therefore outlines liberalism's position:

> I can always, if I wish to, put in question what are taken to be the merely contingent social features of my existence. I may biologically be my father's son; but I cannot be held responsible for what he did unless I choose implicitly or explicitly to assume such responsibility. I may legally be a citizen of a certain country; but I cannot be held responsible for what my country does.... Such individualism is expressed by those modern Americans who deny any responsibility for the effects of

50. My argument is not that practices like preaching are inherently racist but that racial exclusions and domination were achieved under the cover of and were validated by various Christian practices. The Hamitic Curse, also known as the Hamitic hypothesis, is based upon Genesis 9:25, which says that Canaan shall be the servant of his brother Shem. Although Canaan is cursed, it is understood that it is for the sins of Ham, his father, that he is to be punished, hence the name of the hypothesis. This justification for slavery was based upon the assumption that all Africans were descendants of Canaan. The story of Abraham as a wealthy slave owner, New Testament passages such as Eph. 6:5–9, Col. 3:22, and Philemon were widely used as preaching texts by white preachers for black slaves. See James H. Evans, Jr., *We Have Been Believers: An African-American Systematic Theology* (Minneapolis: Fortress Press, 1992), 36–39. The impetus for Richard Allen's founding of a separate church for black Methodists in 1794 was the removal of his fellow worshippers during prayers from the gallery of St. George's Methodist Church in Philadelphia. See Milton C. Sernett, ed., *Afro-American Religious History: A Documentary Witness* (Durham, N.C.: Duke University Press, 1985), 142. For a similar experience nearly a century and a half later, see C. Eric Lincoln, *Coming through the Fire* (Durham, N.C.: Duke University Press, 1995), 35–36.

51. Spencer Perkins and Chris Rice, *More than Equals: Racial Healing for the Sake of the Gospel* (Downers Grove, Ill.: InterVarsity Press, 1993), 111–12.

52. Martin Luther King, Jr., *Why We Can't Wait* (New York: Harper and Row, 1963), 77–100.

53. The following is based upon MacIntyre, *After Virtue,* 220–23.

> slavery upon black Americans, saying "I never owned any slaves." It is more subtly the standpoint of those other modern Americans who accept a nicely calculated responsibility for such effects measured precisely by the benefits they themselves as individuals have indirectly received from slavery. In both cases "being an American" is not in itself taken to be part of the moral identity of the individual.[54]

In contrast to embracing liberalism, to embrace one's Methodism or Lutheranism or Pentecostalism is to situate oneself in the midst of "an historically extended, socially embodied argument, an argument precisely in part about the goods which constitute that tradition."[55] What is required in order to participate in the argument is the virtue of having an adequate understanding of the tradition to which one belongs in order to realize the possibilities of extending or modifying the tradition.[56] Such an informed understanding would insist that I supplement my account of Baptist slave-owning missionaries with that of abolitionist Quakers and manumitting "railroad engineers." It would point out that the church has a long tradition of *anti-racism* with its related practices of inclusive hermeneutics, forgiveness, conversion, reconciliation, group repentance,[57] multiracial church planting, not to mention our teleological practices of baptism and communion.[58] Having a historical understanding of our denominations' or nondenominations' journeys reminds us that the Christian tradition is not without resources or dissenting voices or "subversive" traditions within traditions that can confront racism within and outside the church. To acknowledge that this is so is to be without excuse.

Virtue Theory as Social Theory

By seeking to retrieve an Aristotelian-based theory of ethics, not only must MacIntyre converse in a new moral vocabulary but, more fundamentally, he must reconstruct the entire moral project, together with its history, for the notion of "virtue," though used in our moral speech, cannot be merely appended to our current ethical models.[59] Because much of our ethical energy as individuals

54. MacIntyre, *After Virtue,* 220.
55. Ibid., 222.
56. Ibid., 223.
57. Perkins and Rice, *More than Equals,* 113–14.
58. Though baptism and communion are perhaps more essential to our witness against racism than the activities of sit-ins, pray-ins, and marches that millions of Christians have participated in throughout history, I remain unconvinced, despite Hauerwas's contention that baptism and communion as they are practiced and understood in many of our churches carry "political" weight.
59. With respect to how virtue theory is reflected in the practices of the African American community, see Peter J. Paris, *The Spirituality of African Peoples: The Search for a Common Moral Discourse* (Minneapolis: Fortress Press, 1995), 129–54, who uses moral virtue as an ethic that underscores the pursuit of the common good for both the agent and the community. By identifying six virtues that are highly praised by Africans and African Americans, Paris seeks to construct a social ethic that is teleological and culturally specific and therefore shares some incidental commonalities with Aristotelian virtue theory. He goes on to show how each virtue is narratively displayed in the lives of Nelson Mandela and Martin Luther King, Jr., and in their public practices. In his earlier work, *The*

is expended in understanding rules or principles that will guide us in decision making, "What ought I to do?" becomes the primary moral question in modern morality. For Aristotle, who understood ethics as a means of unfolding the ways and means of living a life that could be called "good" — one that is lived in accordance with virtue — the principal issue was "What is the end or purpose of human life?" or "What is the good for human beings?" The concept of purpose or end, which is indispensable to Aristotle's theory, is conveyed by the term *telos.*[60] Inasmuch as the Aristotelian *telos* is socially rooted, our own good can never be "privatized" or merely be the outcome of our own use of reason: it is shaped by the society and the situations we inhabit.[61] It is this *teleological* understanding that humans have a particular nature and correspondingly an end (*telos*) toward which they aim that allows Aristotle to distinguish between "humans as they are" and "humans as they could be" (if they realized their *telos*).[62] To accept this distinction is to acknowledge that we can fail to achieve our purpose.

In Aristotle's view, the virtues were those qualities, acquired through habit and training, that assisted humans in achieving their *telos.*[63] By disposing the agent to act morally well or as reason directed in *specific* situations, the exercise of the virtues required the moral agent develop skills of perception and judgment in order "to do the right thing in the right place at the right time in the right way."[64] Therefore, being virtuous could never be a matter of simply following basic principles; one had to obtain experience and habits that could discern situational nuances through learning from the exemplary lives of others and from practice.

The Exercise of the Virtues and Moral Imagination

Examining the lives of those Christians who have engaged in practices and founded institutions to combat racism reveals the component that is often overlooked in the moral life: moral *imagination* — the ability to envision and form a

Social Teaching of the Black Churches (Philadelphia: Fortress Press, 1985), Paris identifies the locus of the racial and moral virtues of self-reliance, self-support, self-determination, and self-respect as "black resistance to racism by black people and their institutions" (15). For an interesting discussion of the seven "principles" of Kwanzaa (unity, self-determination, collective work and responsibility, cooperative economics, purpose, creativity, and faith), that have been likened to a virtue list, see Gerald Early, "Dreaming of a Black Christmas: Kwanzaa bestows the gifts of therapy," *Harper's,* January 1997, 55–61. Early indirectly raises the issue of criteria for deciding what constitutes a virtue by describing Kwanzaa's principles not as a philosophical system but as slogans that are "simplistic, banal, and vague" (56).

60. MacIntyre, *After Virtue,* 148.

61. Alasdair MacIntyre, "The Privatization of the Good: An Inaugural Lecture," in *The Liberalism-Communitarianism Debate,* ed. C. F. Delaney (Lanham, Md.: Rowman and Littlefield, 1994), 9–10.

62. MacIntyre, *After Virtue,* 52–53.

63. Ibid., 148–50.

64. Ibid., 150.

way of life consistent with our convictions.[65] Such skillful re-visioning leads to a moral creativity that is teleological inasmuch as it "*transforms what is into what ought to be* by displaying through the virtues the implication of our obligation to witness to God's rule."[66]

John Howard Yoder helps us to see how an ethic of virtue can free us from uncritically accepting the "necessities" and "givens" that often influence our moral decisions.[67] By considering the hypothetical question, "What would you do if an armed attacker threatened you and your family?" Yoder sets up the terms differently so that we are able to consider options that do not readily seem possible. The first option is that the attacker would be able to succeed; the second is the possibility of martyrdom for the victim or me; the third could involve a "providential" opening or looking for a way out that could involve a caring gesture that might emotionally disarm the attacker. Last, there is the option of attempting to kill the attacker, which also includes the possibility of failing to do so. By reframing the scenario, Yoder shows us that we no longer have to "choose" violence as the lesser of two evils because a set of options is open to us. "Our convictions, then, are much like the skills of artists, forming us to be the kind of people capable of corresponding to the way the world ought to be but is not."[68]

Not to be confused with naive wishfulness, moral imagination flows from the type of discipline and training that we associate with good artists and provides the agent with skills that can capitalize upon the unpredictable. Moreover, the exercise of it is often quite costly, as reflected in the lives of those who embody it. While Martin Luther King, Jr., "dreamed" of a world where his children would not be judged by virtue of their race (a speech we tend to remember),[69] he placed children on the front lines of the Civil Rights movement to ensure the dream's reality (a history we tend to forget).[70] For King and countless witnesses, the cost of moral imagination was the laying down of their lives and the willingness to allow apprentices, even children, to sacrifice their lives *before* they had mastered all the lessons of virtue theory. Children pursued the goods internal to the practice of nonviolence in the face of hoses, attack dogs, and weapons. The virtue of courage was required not only to sustain the ability to think creatively but to conquer the fear of death.

Our conviction that Christ has invited us to be part of his kingdom, a kingdom that is a present reality, has made us "capable of the unimaginable: forgiveness of enemies unto death, loving service knowing no boundaries . . . trust in

65. This section is dependent upon Stanley Hauerwas, *Against the Nations: War and Survival in a Liberal Society* (Minneapolis: Winston Press, 1985), 51–59.

66. Ibid., 55.

67. Hauerwas, *The Peaceable Kingdom,* 123–27.

68. Hauerwas, *Against the Nations,* 57.

69. James Melvin Washington, ed., *A Testament of Hope: The Essential Writings of Martin Luther King, Jr.* (San Francisco: Harper and Row, 1986), 219.

70. For a powerful account of the 1963 "D-Day" Children's March in Birmingham, see Taylor Branch, *Parting the Waters: America in the King Years, 1954–63* (New York: Simon and Schuster, 1988), 751–68.

the surpassing power of God's peace."[71] Moral imagination is therefore required if we are to challenge the "conventional wisdom" and givens of racism, that is, "It's always going to be around; 'they're' never going to change." Such wisdom is, in fact, vulnerable to the power of costly imagination.

The Narrative Quality of a Virtuous Life

Any theory of the virtues must insist upon an account of personhood inasmuch as the moral self is the bearer of the virtues. In delineating the concept of the "narrative self" in contradistinction to liberalism's "detachable self," MacIntyre rejects modernity's understanding of morality as a matter of choosing or deciding by the individual: "I am what I myself choose to be,"[72] a self without a history, one that detaches itself from social roles. The narrative characterization of the self, in contrast, views human life as more than a sequence of discrete actions and episodes, as a life that can be conceived and evaluated as a whole. This unity of the self resides in the "unity of a narrative which links birth to life to death as narrative beginning to middle to end."[73] Put differently, when we characterize human actions in terms of intentions and the social settings that render the intentions intelligible, we are engaged in narrative description and can speak of human actions as enacted narratives because of the historical character of such activity.

The narrative concept of selfhood insists that the narrative of my life is part of an interrelated set of narratives; I am not only the subject of my story but part of the stories of others.[74] Therefore, understanding who I am in relation to others and the implications of my connectedness is morally prerequisite to deliberating about what I must do. "To ask 'What is the good for me?' is to ask how I might live out the unity of the narrative embodied in my life and bring it to realization. To ask 'What is the good for man?' is to ask what all answers to the former question must have in common."[75] By drawing upon the metaphor of a quest, MacIntyre underscores the teleological and unpredictable nature of human existence in which the moral life is better thought of as a journey than a series of decisions. The role of the virtues in this journey is to sustain us in our quest for the good. The good life for human beings is then to be defined as the life spent in seeking the good life for human beings.

An Overview of the Virtues and Practices in the Life of John Perkins

I have chosen to highlight the life of John Perkins for a variety of reasons. As a Christian leader of national stature, he offers us insight into how reconciliation — as a costly response to racism — can be lived out in a unified life within

71. Hauerwas, *Against the Nations,* 58.
72. MacIntyre, *After Virtue,* 220.
73. Ibid., 205.
74. Ibid., 217–18.
75. Ibid., 218–19.

the backdrop of multiple racisms embedded in a variety of practices, both institutional and informal. Although historically the institutional black churches embraced reconciliation from within their separate institutions, Perkins offers another perspective on how the practice of reconciliation can be actualized; how it often emerges from rage rather than reticence. His life is also instructive as the journey of a "racialized self" with impeded agency to a self whose life is its own. His story, which reveals constraints by way of limited choices, also reflects the ability to "create" options by exercise of the moral imagination, coupled with the willingness to sacrifice. Finally, Perkins's story complements our emphasis on contemporary forms of racism by providing an account of "old-fashioned" racism — a form of racism that, however modified, is still alive and well.[76]

Born in 1930 to a family of poor sharecroppers in rural Mississippi, John Perkins began his life story in *Let Justice Roll Down*[77] not with his birth but with the death of his unarmed brother at the hands of a white deputy marshal. This incident, which provoked bitterness, was a fundamental reason that Perkins eventually "chose" to move to California at the age of seventeen. "You see, back then blacks . . . had three choices: we could stay, accept the system and become dehumanized niggers; we could go to jail or get killed; or we could leave for the big city."[78] After serving in the Korean War, getting married, and starting a family, Perkins was introduced to Christianity by observing the transformation in the life of his young son, who was attending a community Bible club. He surrendered his own life to Jesus Christ shortly after attending church with his family and engaging in personal Bible study.

While being mentored by both black and white Christians, Perkins became involved with various ministries. In addition to Child Evangelism Fellowship, Perkins also participated in the Christian Businessmen's Committee, through which he shared his testimony at youth detention camps. Observing how many of the young men shared his southern, poverty-stricken background and had never resolved many of the conflicts that had led them to leave the South, Perkins felt a "call" to return to Mississippi to do ministry among the black rural poor.

Arriving in Simpson County, Mississippi, in 1960 with his family, Perkins and his wife began to work with youth by organizing Bible classes in public schools. Because "Mendenhall was overrun with the very kinds of needs the church was so strategically positioned to meet,"[79] within the next four to six years, the Voice of Calvary (VOC) ministries included a Bible institute, church, day care center, and Head Start program as evidence of Perkins's conviction that a holistic gospel that responded to social needs as well as spiritual ills should be incarnated in the community. This same biblical conviction led

76. Omi and Winant, *Racial Formation,* 157.

77. John Perkins, *Let Justice Roll Down: John Perkins Tells His Own Story* (Glendale, Calif.: Regal Books, 1976).

78. John Perkins, *With Justice for All* (Ventura, Calif.: Regal Books, 1982), 17.

79. Ibid., 35.

VOC to become involved in voter registration and two of Perkins's children to be among the first blacks to integrate the local high school. By investing in the long-term cultivation of moral agents, VOC focused on leadership development, which in later years culminated in the founding of the John M. Perkins International Study Center.[80] "First, we had to keep the kids in school until they graduated. Second, some . . . had to go to college to be trained — outside of Mississippi where they could get a new vision. Third, some of them had to bring their skills back . . . to provide the needed leadership."[81] These community-based efforts were later supplemented by economic ventures such as a housing cooperative, a farmers' cooperative, a cooperative store owned and operated by blacks in the community, and a medical clinic.

Just as his brother's violent confrontation with the authorities signaled a turn of events in Perkins's life, so does his own encounter with the police. While being arrested along with a white co-worker and a large group of VOC members who had accompanied him to the local jail to inquire about the arrests of two black men earlier that day, Perkins, cognizant of the growing anger of his supporters gathered outside the jail, extemporaneously launched into a "speech" which began by exhorting the crowd to respond nonviolently and ended by calling for the group to organize a boycott. After being released days later, Perkins and three colleagues were arrested within several weeks by highway patrol officers during a "set-up." This time Perkins and his colleagues were unmercifully beaten. Perkins was beaten and tortured — almost to the point of death. Yet miraculously he walked away alive — armed with a new call to extend the gospel to whites who, he realized, were just as damaged by racism as blacks.

Two years later while Perkins was recovering from major surgery, he relived the rage and pain of the past during a time of crisis as he reflected upon his return to do ministry in Mississippi.[82] He recounted how the Klan and intimidation stopped some white teachers from becoming involved in the work; how his family had been threatened because of his involvement in voters' registration; how he had yet to see the gospel make an impact in the churches — especially in the churches. Yet as he responded to the care he received from his doctors, one of whom was white, Perkins was flooded by images of hope:

> Our first converts were now away at college, getting trained so they could return to teach others.
>
> My own son, Spencer, had been one of the first to integrate Mendenhall's high school, one of a few blacks among 500 whites. He spent two terribly lonely years in that school. But he'd survived. In this family, in the VOC community, he had

80. Ibid., 82.
81. Ibid., 67.
82. Perkins's experience of bitterness raises the issue of how the church as a community must recognize and address racial anger and define the role of virtue development in this process. Indeed it has been suggested that one reason for the relative absence of men in black churches, in particular, is the churches' inability to deal with the rage of black males.

> found the strength to survive. And already scores of others were now integrating schools — and surviving.
>
> Slowly but surely, change was coming. The gospel was bringing changes. And I was a part of the change.[83]

Another image formed in Perkins's mind — the image of the cross bearing a crucified Christ, who also was arrested, falsely accused, and beaten. As Perkins prayed and "saw" the faces of each white police officer, he was able to forgive each one. Faces of other whites from the past appeared, and he was able to forgive them also. God had now healed the wounds and memories that had barred him from forgiving.

In 1973 he and a white co-worker set out to begin a new *ministry of reconciliation* in Jackson, Mississippi, envisioning the Jackson VOC as "a reconciled community, a fellowship of blacks and whites ministering to blacks and whites, drawing into its fellowship both blacks and whites."[84]

Varieties of Christian Responses to Racism

Perkins's narrative provides us with an opportunity to recognize the working of multifaceted racisms upon the life of a community and allows us a glimpse of how racism often precludes and undermines the conception of the good for the individual and the community. Although racism in the form of *exclusion* predominated, primarily by means of segregation, and was embedded in educational, medical, ecclesial, and economic institutions, racism as *domination* or *control* was also prevalent in certain economic practices, in law enforcement, and the judiciary. While instances of structural racism abounded, racism was also incorporated in the form of *personal prejudice* through intimidation and threats or by means of silence, as in the shunning of Perkins's two children while they attended a white high school. Underlying all of these forms was *racism as common sense* in which stereotypical understandings of black intelligence, ability, and dignity were accepted as givens and transmitted and learned generationally in most instances.

Less evident than the various manifestations of racism was its impact upon identity, whereby the racialized narrative self was no longer the subject of its own story because of the negative role it played in the stories of others. "You see, who I was in those days was described only in terms of a dependent relationship to a white man," Perkins wrote. "Because I wasn't anybody all by myself . . . I wasn't important in their eyes; only the person [landowner] I was connected to. And it meant that my own name, John Perkins, had no significance. . . ."[85] In light of this, many of the responses were directed not only toward racism itself but toward healing a damaged self and cultivating a positive sense of identity.

83. Perkins, *Let Justice Roll Down,* 204.
84. Perkins, *With Justice for All,* 103.
85. Perkins, *Let Justice Roll Down,* 26.

Inasmuch as there is no singular strategy of the church that applies equally to all communities, let us examine the varieties of virtue-centered, church-based responses to racism as embodied in Perkins's story.

Anti-Racist Responses to Counter Exclusion. The VOC responded with *courage* and *hope* in heading the county's voter registration campaign when harassment was discouraging blacks from voting. In response to exclusion of blacks from ownership and production, the VOC formed a series of economic cooperatives to foster entrepreneurship and self-sufficiency among local blacks; such economic stability provided a means of supporting the practice of sustaining families. To counter exclusion in education, some VOC members incarnated the virtue of *forbearance* as they helped to integrate the local high school; at the same time, VOC organized its own community-based educational programs such as a preschool, a Bible institute, and leadership education. VOC helped to foster the creative skills of its younger members by placing them in settings where they could experience the community's needs and in time respond innovatively. For many members, the initial creative response was to return to the community after college to live. Such training also gave younger leaders the responsibility to inculcate virtue in other community members, a task that by necessity stirred the improvisational abilities of would-be leaders. In contrast to the exclusion of blacks from white churches, the VOC engaged in multiracial ministry by inviting local white teachers to join its staff, by hosting white interns, and by having Perkins take the initiative to meet with white evangelical leaders. Years later in the Jackson branch of the VOC, the practices of sharing meals, playing, praying, and studying converged in community formation.

Anti-Racist Responses to Counter Domination. When Perkins instructed his supporters to channel their anger over the arrests into a nonviolent boycott, he demonstrated his own *forbearance* in the face of police oppression and displayed both *courage* and *creativity.* In heeding the call, local blacks and others displayed their willingness to sacrifice for a common purpose by forfeiting purchases and traveling long distances to other stores. The virtue of *beneficence* was displayed by those who owned property and were willing to post it as bond for Perkins and his colleagues despite threats from the authorities.

Perkins's Response to Injustice. It is Perkins's own response to a near-fatal beating and his subsequent journey that allows us to judge him as "virtuous" — not only in the popular sense of the term as "exemplary" — but in a particularly Christian sense as embodying virtues, such as forgiveness, that would be absent from Aristotle's list, though prominent in the New Testament. Not only did his response change the direction of his own story; it also rewrote the narrative of his community. That Perkins identified the officers as being filled with hatred requires no moral insight; yet his honed ability to "see" the impact of their hatred and perceive that racism provided them with the means of establishing their own self-worth allowed him to respond with a desire to see them healed, rather than with hatred.

But it is not until much later, when Perkins confronted his own bitterness and anger, that he was faced with the temptation to deny his new call to inclusive ministry: "And I began to think that maybe there was only one way to go — to give up on whites and white Christians and just work for me and mine."[86] Perhaps our greatest temptation in encountering racism as Christians is not that we may abuse or disrespect or even exclude one another, but simply that we may leave one another behind — and go our own separate ways.

Perkins was able to resist the temptation to choose the good that is not the best and accept what he was called to do by first remembering *all* the lives in Mendenhall that had intersected his own, by recalling "*all* the stories he was a part of," both black and white. By remembering those whites, however few, who were anti-racist and displayed courage and constancy in their practices and in their commitments to blacks, Perkins realized that it was this intertwined narrative that he had to bear witness to in his new ministry. He was again able to hope — to forgive — and to love by means of the cross. Through the embodiment of the virtue of love in the practice of reconciliation, the conception of the good for Perkins and his community was *redefined* as was the community itself. The boundaries of Perkins's community had been *redrawn* to encompass both blacks and whites.

After Racism

The efficacy of any theory of racism should be evaluated in terms of how it renders *resistance* to racism possible.[87] Yet there have been too few attempts in academia to provide a clear analytical structure for examining ideas and practices associated with anti-racism.[88] This lopsided emphasis on racism rather than resistance, evident in popular literature, the media, and many of our own lives, no doubt speaks of our own lack of moral creativity. Perhaps our inability to envision a world where children will not be judged by the color of their skin is more reflective of the content of our own character *than the actual state of racism in this society.* To counter racism is to engage in a sacrificial, imaginative search for ways to oppose it that are faithful to the Christian story and resonate with our own. Anti-racism, therefore, requires people of virtue who have the audacity to construe the world differently, perhaps, from their parents, children, neighbors, pastors — and enemies — and see what others may never see: opportunities to *end racism.*

Killing Rage: Ending Racism.[89] Ending racism? The title of the book arrested me in the form of a blinding accusation, for the thought *had never occurred to me.* Besides, after exporting memories of months of painful discussions about race from England to South Africa, and importing a greater number of race-based memories back to the States, where I am constantly provided with

86. Perkins, *With Justice for All,* 100.
87. Goldberg, *Racist Culture,* 41.
88. Solomos and Back, *Racism and Society,* 105–6.
89. bell hooks, *Killing Rage: Ending Racism* (New York: Henry Holt, 1995).

unsolicited evidentiary narratives on racism, I understand all too well why so few commentators and too few Christians speak on that level.

Clearly, many Christians are as pessimistic about the future of "race relations" as MacIntyre is about the future of modern morality (I'm thinking here of the conclusion of *After Virtue*). Yet if we conceive of the eradication of racism as a *telos* for which we must aim, then "tolerance" or "improving" race relations falls short of this end. The church's journey from slavery to abolition and from segregation to integration will never be completed if we do not move toward ending racism — the *telos* toward which the historic practices of abolition and integration (versions of the older practices of hospitality and reconciliation) were directed. The dismantling of racism can be a working option if we move beyond racial reasoning and the abridged moral vocabulary of partisan politics. Both alternatives appear to be heavily invested in the belief that racism will never end. To move forward to terminate racism requires that we as Christians place as much faith in repentance and conversion, in the ability of racists to be transformed, as we have in policies. The virtues of courage and hope are essential in this journey if we are to survive the debilitating hopelessness that engulfs many of our communities as policies continue to be dismantled while racism remains intact. Though readily admitting that we have a long way to go, cultural critic bell hooks offers a stinging rebuke to such hopelessness by stating, "[h]ow any of us can continue to hold those feelings when we study the history of racism in this society and see how much has changed makes no logical sense."[90]

When Perkins had no visible, contemporary examples of a multiracial incarnational ministry of reconciliation in Mississippi, convinced by the truthfulness of the Acts narrative, he "created" his own model, a form of ministry that was composed of and opposed by both black and white Christians. Perkins underscores that racism also damages its participants and, therefore, they too stand to gain by ensuring that racism is ended. Indeed, the formation of, and participation in, multiracial structures and partnerships by all groups highlights the interdependence of our social existence and underscores our collective responsibility as Christians from all backgrounds to help one another in the task of terminating racial oppression. Just as our histories are inextricably intertwined, so too are our destinies.

Only our collective imaginations supplemented by hope can generate the moral creativity needed to envisage a society transformed not by our own efforts but by the in-breaking of God's reign. The cultivation of hope can grant us the incentive to continue a practice profoundly damaged by racism: that of sustaining community life. Courage can enable us to have and raise children *in the world-as-it-is* and equip them to live and play and worship *as if the world-as-it-ought-to-be is already a reality.* Hope can empower us to conceive of the unimaginable: a world *after racism.*

90. Ibid., 271.

Suggestions for Further Reading

Garrow, David J. *Bearing the Cross: Martin Luther King, Jr., and the Southern Christian Leadership Conference.* New York: William Morrow, 1986.

Harrington, Walt. *Crossings: A White Man's Journey into Black America.* New York: HarperPerennial, 1994.

Lincoln, C. Eric, and Lawrence H. Mamiya. *The Black Church in the African American Experience.* Durham, N.C.: Duke University Press, 1990.

Omi, Michael, and Howard Winant. *Racial Formation in the United States: From the 1960s to the 1990s.* 2d ed. New York: Routledge, 1994.

Perkins, John. *Let Justice Roll Down: John Perkins Tells His Own Story.* Glendale, Calif.: Regal Books, 1976.

Perkins, Spencer, and Chris Rice. *More than Equals: Racial Healing for the Sake of the Gospel.* Downers Grove, Ill.: InterVarsity Press, 1993.

Sanders, Cheryl J. *Saints in Exile: The Holiness-Pentecostal Experience in African American Religion and Culture.* New York: Oxford University Press, 1996.

West, Cornel. "Critique and Mercy in the Cross of Christ." *The Other Side* 22 (July–August 1993): 8–14.

———. *Prophesy Deliverance!* Philadelphia: Westminster Press, 1982.

Chapter 13

Feminism, Political Philosophy, and the Narrative Ethics of Jean Bethke Elshtain

Mark Thiessen Nation

Editor's Introduction

One purpose of Nation's essay is to commend to Christians the work of feminist ethicist and political theorist Jean Bethke Elshtain. A second purpose is to show how Elshtain's position could be strengthened by greater attention to the church as a community and an institution. Nation's essay nicely serves the purposes of the present volume in that both his analysis of Elshtain's work and his recommendation to her manifest the value of a MacIntyrean understanding of ethics.

Nation points out that Elshtain rightly takes MacIntyre's point that a social ethic can be understood only in light of sociology – an account of its actual or potential social embodiment. Thus, her work is replete with richly textured historical or sociological detail when she addresses herself to questions of politics or ethics. For example, Elshtain rejects blanket accounts of women's lives as powerless victimization, and in their place tells stories of the everyday lives of women, reflecting both power and powerlessness.

Nation highlights Elshtain's claim that Christianity represented a revolution in ancient concepts of the public and the private and in what it meant to lead a virtuous life. Not only were women welcomed into the new social and political entity called the church, but the virtues and qualities once associated with women's roles – gentleness, concern for the helpless – were celebrated as ideals for the whole community in both public and private spheres.

Elshtain agrees with MacIntyre in criticizing the hyperindividualism of modern political liberalism. She calls for attention to the "mediating institutions" of civil society – families, communities, voluntary associations and movements. Why, then, Nation asks, does she pay so little attention to the church? It would make sense to tie her concern for mediating institutions to her recognition of the revolutionary role of Christianity and argue for the church's potential for transforming the current social order.

Elshtain's reason seems to be her judgment that the church has failed to promote the revolution it began in the early centuries. Nation uses Elshtain's own strategy of storytelling — recounting incidents from organized Christian resistance to the Nazis — to show the church's ongoing potential for social transformation.

MacIntyre himself is wary of institutions, believing that they inevitably corrupt practices. Nation's focus on the church as *community* (rather than institution) is quite helpful here. We could add that it is only when a community is truly embodying its own narrative that it avoids the corruption against which MacIntyre warns.

NANCEY MURPHY

Introduction: On Living between Heaven and Hell

Jean Bethke Elshtain, a longtime feminist, has written six books, edited several others, and written more than two hundred articles. For most of her writing and teaching career she has focused on political philosophy. Her first book dealt with the way in which the public and private realms have defined men's and women's lives throughout the history of politics in the Western world.[1] But it was in the wake of her 1995 book, *Democracy on Trial,* that she was invited to the White House to be a consultant on the challenges to contemporary American democracy, was dubbed a "public intellectual," and joined the *Utne Reader* magazine's list of 100 visionaries for the next century.[2]

Jean Bethke Elshtain has much to teach us, on many subjects. However, in this essay I want to focus on what her writings in political philosophy have to teach us about Christian social ethics. Christian ethics is not a subject on which she has written much directly. Only fairly recently has she switched from teaching political philosophy and become the first Laura Spelman Rockefeller Professor of Social and Political Ethics in the Divinity School at the University of Chicago. Likewise only recently has she become a member of the American Academy of Religion.[3] At this transitional point in her career I would like to suggest ways in which her writings have implications for Christian social ethics.

Because this essay is intended to focus on some constructive insights from Elshtain's work, it is important to put those insights into a context. This is im-

1. Jean Bethke Elshtain, *Public Man, Private Woman: Women in Social and Political Thought* (Princeton: Princeton University Press, 1981).

2. Jean Bethke Elshtain, *Democracy on Trial* (New York: Basic Books, 1995). For a brief biographical sketch of Elshtain see Debra Shore, "The Trials of a Public Intellectual," *University of Chicago Magazine* 88 (June 1996).

3. I gave a very different version of this essay as a lecture at a symposium on Elshtain's work at the American Academy of Religion meeting, New Orleans, November 1996. I appreciated her gracious response. Another version, closer to the present one, was presented at a political theology seminar at Oxford University. Both Elshtain's comments and the comments of the seminar participants clarified ways in which I needed to alter and expand the present essay.

portant for at least two reasons. First, Elshtain is often accused of being too easy on patriarchy; she often finds herself at odds with many other feminists.[4] Second, it is important that we have before us the reminders of abuses within society and the church before looking at constructive proposals based on Elshtain's writings.

Elshtain would be the last person to want us to ignore the realities of suffering perpetrated throughout the history of the West. She believes that "the task of the political imagination must be to serve as witness for the victims, all those the final solutions, ends-of-history, and politics-as-usual either eliminate, manipulate, degrade, or deny."[5] Having read widely in the literature of politics and war, Elshtain is quite conscious of the fact that, within history, "there is much that is unconscionable and cries out for relief. There is much that is ugly, sordid, and violent; tragic, pathetic, and heartbreaking. There are events that arouse horror, outrage, and disbelief."[6]

Elshtain also knows that such abuses are not only history. She raises critical questions in her reflections on contemporary issues as well.[7] Take one example. Elshtain is known as one who praises the call for civic virtue. However, when she was asked to offer her reflections on the work of Robert Bellah and his colleagues in the influential *Habits of the Heart,* precisely about civic virtue, she insisted that "a hard look" was required at "what might be called the dark underside of evocations of civic virtue and the common good — something the authors of *Habits* fail to do."[8] She indicates her nervousness when "the lan-

---

4. See Jean Bethke Elshtain, "Judge Not?" *First Things* 46 (October 1994): 37; and Debra Shore, "The Trials of a Public Intellectual," *University of Chicago Magazine* 88 (June 1996). The present essay is based on the writings of a feminist writer and, therefore, in that sense is on feminism. However, I am well aware that Elshtain's approach is only one among a variety of feminist approaches to the various disciplines within which her writings fall. For some sense of the variety among feminists within the field of Christian ethics see Lois K. Daly, ed., *Feminist Theological Ethics: A Reader* (Louisville: Westminster John Knox Press, 1994); Kathryn Tanner, "The Care That Does Justice: Recent Writings in Feminist Ethics and Theology," *Journal of Religious Ethics* 24 (spring 1996): 171–91; and Susan F. Parsons, *Feminism and Christian Ethics* (Cambridge: Cambridge University Press, 1996).

5. Elshtain, *Public Man, Private Woman,* 300.

6. Ibid., 299.

7. One discovers in following Elshtain's work that she not only is incredibly prolific but also writes on a wide range of topics. Some of the range is represented by these works of Elshtain: "The New Eugenics and Feminist Quandaries: Philosophical and Political Reflections," in *Guaranteeing the Good Life: Medicine and the Return of Eugenics,* ed. Richard John Neuhaus (Grand Rapids, Mich.: Wm B. Eerdmans, 1990), 68–88; "Just War as Politics: What the Gulf War Told Us about Contemporary American Life," in *But Was It Just?: Reflections on the Morality of the Persian Gulf War,* ed. David E. Decosse (New York: Doubleday, 1992), 43–60; "Trial by Fury" [review of *The Real Anita Hill* by David Brock], *New Republic* 209 (6 September 1993): 32–36; "The Screwtape Files: Sources and Conditions of Anti-Virtue," in *Seedbeds of Virtue,* ed. Mary Ann Glendon and David Blankenhorn (New York: Madison Books, 1995), 253–69; "Why End 'Welfare as We Know It'?" in *Welfare in America: Christian Perspectives on a Policy in Crisis* (Grand Rapids, Mich.: Wm. B. Eerdmans, 1996), 3–19; and "The Lost Children" [review of *Dubious Conceptions* by Kristin Luker], *New Republic* 215 (21 October 1996): 30–36.

8. Jean Bethke Elshtain, "Citizenship and Armed Civic Virtue: Some Critical Questions on the Commitment to Public Life," *Soundings* 69 (spring/summer 1986): 100.

guage of *the* public interest, or *the* common good takes over."[9] Preoccupation with *the* common good can lead to conquest. Elshtain knows from her study of the history of politics and war that far too often "the notion of virtue itself got assimilated to the glory of conquest."[10] And the glory of conquest has often been joined to the creation of nation-states, the creation of which "rests on mounds of bodies."[11] "The problem with the tradition of civic virtue can be stated succinctly: that virtue is *armed*."[12] No, Jean Elshtain is not one to ignore abuses against women or other victims. Quite the contrary, her writings are filled with critiques of ideas and actions that lead to abuses.

Elshtain also does not spare the church her critiques. She is quite aware that "Christianity, like *any* powerful doctrine infused with a set of images, symbols, and ideas from which an awesome edifice of thought as well as diverse social practices and institutional forms have arisen contains its share of caprice, villainy, and dogmatism."[13]

But with her consciousness of all the failings and abuses, Elshtain believes that "the presumption that some universally true, ubiquitous, and pervasive misogynistic urge explains everything is simplistic and wrong." "I have no heaven to offer," says Elshtain, "perhaps because I have not discovered in ordinary reality the irredeemable hell many feminists have seen in present social arrangements and experiences."[14] Or, again, she says: "I have a long-standing animus against philosophers and political model builders who disdain our ordinary humanity and who, in their quest for a comprehensive, universal standpoint, wind up, in Martha Nussbaum's words, making 'the humanly possible work look boring and cheap.' "[15]

As an alternative to any heavens or hells, to simplistic and reductionistic accounts of reality, Elshtain offers careful, nuanced discussions of the ambiguities of the political and violent pasts we have inherited and then asks how a critical appropriation of these pasts might help us navigate the hazardous waters of the present and future. I cannot attempt here to give more than a glimpse of the richness of Elshtain's textured writings about both politics and the redeeming of everyday life. But whether in book-length treatments of political philosophy or war, individual essays on political philosophers or on women with remarkable lives — whether well-known or unknown — Elshtain refuses to reduce complicated ideas, communities, or individuals to simple, unambiguous good or evil.[16]

9. Ibid., 102, emphasis in original.
10. Ibid.
11. Ibid., 104.
12. Ibid., 102, emphasis in original.
13. Elshtain, *Public Man, Private Woman*, 55, emphasis mine.
14. Ibid., xv, 299.
15. Jean Bethke Elshtain, *Power Trips and Other Journeys: Essays in Feminism as Civic Discourse* (Madison: University of Wisconsin Press, 1990), xvii.
16. See Jean Bethke Elshtain, *Women and War*, rev. ed. (Chicago: University of Chicago Press,

What I hope to offer in this brief essay are suggestions for how some of Elshtain's reflections may help us in thinking about Christian social ethics. I do this by looking at three elements of Elshtain's thought. The first, and most central, is Elshtain's claim about the way in which early Christianity represented a transformation, in the context of the ancient world, regarding the realms of public and private and what it means to live a virtuous life. A second, and related, element is Elshtain's concern to redeem everyday life. This effort on Elshtain's part is connected to the desire both to appreciate more fully the lives of those whose existence is relatively private and mundane and to value the virtues connected to such existence. A third element is a focus on the significance of "mediating institutions." In the final section of this essay I focus on one of those "mediating institutions," namely the church.

A Moral Revolution

Two things struck me almost immediately when I began to read Elshtain. First, given that her writings were not theological, Christian claims — especially as embodied in the origins of the Christian Church — figured prominently in some of her writings. Second, her normative judgments often appear to be rooted in sensibilities that are shaped by these Christian claims. Let us look at this where it is most obviously displayed — in her book *Public Man, Private Woman.*

Elshtain, not surprisingly, began her study of the history of politics by looking at the ancient Greeks.

> If one goes back to the Greeks, one discovers that war from the beginning was construed as something of a natural condition for mankind. The Greek city-state was a community of warriors whose political rights were determined in large part by the fundamental privilege of the soldier to decide his own fate. . . . Civic identity was restricted to those who bore arms. . . . It need hardly be added that the civically heroic ethic enshrined in these institutions diminished the world of everyday production and reproduction — the business of metics, women and slaves. Not having the bodies of protectors, of men constituted as warrior-citizens, women were those who had to be defended, whose role in the household, the *oikos,* was a necessary precondition for, but not an integral part of, the structure of the dominant political warrioring world. . . . This should help us to see the many ways in which political philosophy has construed its mission in heroic or quasi-heroic terms — bringing order, curing the universe of its ills and woes — at odds with [an] insistent embrace of the dignity of the ordinary and everyday.[17]

Indeed Elshtain knows that this ancient Greek version of political theorizing became the norm for defining the roles of public and private and for defining the

1995), and Jean Bethke Elshtain, *Meditations on Modern Political Thought: Masculine/Feminine Themes from Luther to Arendt* (University Park: Pennsylvania State University Press, 1992).

17. Elshtain, "The Risks and Responsibilities of Affirming Ordinary Life," in *Philosophy in an Age of Pluralism: The Philosophy of Charles Taylor in Question,* ed. James Tulley (Cambridge: Cambridge University Press, 1994), 69–70. For a longer narrative describing this reality see Elshtain, *Public Man, Private Woman,* 19–54.

world of the *polis*. Because of the stark contrast, therefore, when she reaches the beginning of Christianity she declares: "Christianity ushered a moral revolution into the world which dramatically, and for the better, transformed the prevailing images of male and female, public and private."[18] Specifically she claims that Christianity "ushered in a dramatic transformation in our way of seeing the world, created a new vocabulary of basic notions with performative requirements, and posed answers to the question Socrates earlier asked: How might a human being live a just life?"[19]

> Welcomed into that new community, the *res publica Christiana,* women shared in the norms, activities, and ideals that were its living tissue. She found (try to suspend time and place yourself as a woman of the first century after Christ in Judea hearing *this* message!) that qualities most often associated with her activities as mother — giving birth to and sustaining human life; an ethic of responsibility for the helpless, the vulnerable, the weak; gentleness, mercy, and compassion — were celebrated. The realm of necessity generated its own sanctity. Women, like men, might be called upon to die for a cause, not as Homeric heroes wielding great swords, but as witnesses to the strength of their inner conviction and living sacrifices to the evil that absolute political power trails in its wake. (61)

In other words, Elshtain is claiming that in the early Christian community the virtues that had often been assigned only to the private sphere of life in the ancient world were being upheld for the whole community in both their private and public lives. On the one hand, this change grants dignity to roles usually assigned to women. On the other, it calls on men to live in the same way. Within the context of both the ancient world and the subsequent development of political philosophy, this reorientation was revolutionary.

One of the worries of our contemporaries regarding this new ethic is that it was "sectarian." Many would agree that it affirmed virtues formerly considered private. The worry, then, is that these virtues were intended only for the "private" world of the church. Elshtain addresses such worries: "Christianity challenged the primacy of politics. It did not relegate secular power to silence and shadows as secular power had formerly relegated the private, but the claims of the public-political world no longer went unchallenged" (59). But what of the "common good"? asks our contemporary critic. Did the early Christians care about it? Elshtain replies: "How could one possibly speak of a 'common good'

---

18. *Public Man, Private Woman,* 56. This statement is repeated in her "Christianity and Patriarchy: The Odd Alliance," *Modern Theology* 9 (April 1993): 110. In making this claim about a "moral revolution" Elshtain does not make it clear whether she means to refer only to the world of early Christianity as it is reported in the Christian canon of Scriptures or means also to include some period beyond the biblical one. Either way, there is hardly a consensus on the "moral revolution" she describes. However, there is clearly solid scholarship to substantiate the thrust of her claims. Two such books regarding the New Testament materials are John Howard Yoder, *The Politics of Jesus,* rev. ed. (Grand Rapids, Mich.: Wm. B. Eerdmans, 1994), and Richard B. Hays, *The Moral Vision of the New Testament* (New York: HarperCollins, 1996). In this brief essay I cannot, however, enter into the complicated debate regarding her claim about a "moral revolution."

19. *Public Man, Private Woman,* 57. The page numbers in parentheses in the following text refer to this volume.

in a world composed of masters and slaves, victors and victims, imperialists and colonialists?" (60). No, the church had goods of its own.

> If the old politics of the *polis* was exclusionary and that of the Roman Empire a deadly imperialism, the new Christian community, though not political, was available to any who, like Socrates, had a hunger and thirst for righteousness. How different the Christian band of men, women, children, the infirm, the "possessed," the crippled, even the criminal from the participants in Plato's symposium! (63–64)

In the world of the early church it is a mistake to see them as sectarian, if what one means by that is a withdrawal from the world. For as Elshtain says, "The Christian version of 'withdrawal' from the world, as one option open to the faithful, was not a retreat into solipsism but a vocation that required contemplation and purification of the self, ideally in a life lived among others" (61). This sort of withdrawal was necessary in a world so powerfully dominated and defined by Caesar. For Christians knew that "what was not under the purview of Caesar was how one chose to see oneself and the world and to live, breathe, and die within it" (60). No, the defining of the world and their life was only under the purview of Jesus the Christ. And they knew that "Christ himself never counseled a retreat into private virtuousness" (62).

Of course, Elshtain is quite aware that this revolution underwent transformation in subsequent centuries. She observes:

> That Christianity failed to live up to the promise of its early mission surprises no one in a skeptical and cynical time. . . . But that Christianity secured a moral revolution and established a set of claims which must be faced and answered today . . . is a feature essential to any exploration of human identity, especially that of woman. (64)

Women as Fools: Toward the Redemption of Everyday Life

One of the reasons Elshtain so celebrates the moral revolution of early Christianity is that she knows there was generally disdain in the ancient world for the private world of women. Wisdom was associated with the powerful and worldly, foolishness with the private realm of women. Elshtain asks us to reflect more critically on this "foolishness." "Perhaps women are the 'fools' in Western political thought and practice whose official powerlessness [nonetheless] grants them a paradoxical freedom from full assimilation into the dominant public identity whose aims, in our day, are efficiency and control."[20] This "freedom" can, understandably, invite despair. It certainly forecloses certain possibilities. "Nevertheless, if at least partial exclusion from wholesale absorption into terms

20. Elshtain, "The Power and Powerlessness of Women," in *Power Trips and Other Journeys,* 144. Elshtain does not accidentally choose the word *fool* to refer to typical political views of women. In the writings of Plato and Aristotle the word for a private person (such as a woman) was *idiot* (*Public Man, Private Woman,* 22).

of institutional power is maintained, space for critical reflection and challenge to that power is more likely to be sustained."[21]

With this move, Elshtain is able both to appreciate the contributions of the everyday lives of women and to acknowledge the power, real power, they wielded within their own contexts. As she expresses it:

> women are and have been powerful; women are and have been powerless. There is no contradiction here. Instead we find a resonant paradox, an ambiguity that seeps through all reflective attempts to confront "the powerlessness of women." In recent decades, to be sure, important commentators reflecting various feminist positions often ignored or denied associations of women with images of authority, potency, and power, concentrating instead on women's historic oppression, "second-class citizenship," and, in the view of some, universal victimization.... But in telling only one side of the story the commentators ... sometimes wound up portraying women as so uniformly and universally downtrodden, demeaned, infantilized, and coerced that men came to seem invincible, individually and collectively terrifying in their power and their intent to oppress.... The "oppressed group model," as Kathleen Jones has described it, "tended to present a one-dimensional view of women's experiences that denies categorically that there was anything redemptive, or politically valuable about them. Ironically, this view incorporated the devaluation of women's experiences, and accepted the patriarchal reading of the significance of women's lives it claimed to be criticizing." ... We know that our foremothers deeded to us much more than a sustained tale of woe. We contemporary women are the heirs of centuries of women's stories and strengths, all the many narratives of perseverance and survival, of determination to go on through tragedies and defeats. We know that our mothers and grandmothers often had laughter in their hearts, songs on their lips, and pride in their identities. Knowing this we cannot accept any account that demeans women in the name of taking measure of our powerlessness.[22]

Elshtain cannot tolerate the demeaning of everyday life, whether it be the life of women or men. She has been attempting to follow a summons to participate in "the redemption of everyday life," even while granting that "it has never been crystal clear ... what the full implications of such a summons might be."[23] That is why she so appreciated the work of the populist historian Christopher Lasch, whose life and work she celebrated in a number of articles upon his death.[24] And that is why she repeatedly evokes the lives of "ordinary" people, including her own mother and grandmother, when writing about matters of great importance.[25] She has repeatedly focused on the efforts of the Argentinean "mothers of the disappeared" to save lives.[26] And she has written fine essays on three in-

21. "The Power and Powerlessness of Women," 144–45.
22. Ibid., 134–35.
23. "The Risks and Responsibilities of Affirming Ordinary Life," 67.
24. Two such articles are "Eulogy for Christopher Lasch," *New Oxford Review* 61 (May 1994): 25–27, and "The Life and Work of Christopher Lasch: An American Story," *Salmagundi* 106–7 (spring-summer 1995): 146–61.
25. See, for instance, the evocation of the life of her mother in "The Life and Work of Christopher Lasch," 157–59, and of her grandmother in "Judge Not?" 36.
26. Most recently she told this story in *Democracy on Trial,* 126–33.

fluential women—Jane Addams, Simone Weil, and Eleanor Roosevelt—whose lives were lived somewhere between the private and public.[27]

There are undoubtedly a number of reasons that Elshtain chose to write on these three women. Intriguingly, however, the self-understanding of each of the three centrally involves the Christian faith (though in different ways). For example,

> "Jenny" Addams viewed her world through the prism of Christian symbols and injunctions, purposes and meanings. These gave her world its shape—a narrative form involving the use of instructive parables in the conviction that the moral life consists in "the imitation of Christ," not in abstract obedience to a formal model of moral conduct.... Life, she declares, is a quest, and a life of virtue lies within reach if one emulates exemplary individuals.[28]

This reminds me of the claims of James Wm. McClendon, Jr.: "Christianity turns upon the character of Christ. But that character must continually find fresh exemplars if it is not to be consigned to the realm of mere antiquarian lore."[29] Which brings me to my concluding section.

Fools for Christ, Redeeming Everyday Life, and Disarming Civic Virtue

Jean Elshtain's writings have many marvelous qualities. One, as mentioned earlier, is her evocation of the life of ordinary people while dealing with important matters. Undoubtedly I enjoy these evocations both because I become present to the people she describes and because her pictures also conjure images from my own life. As I read her essay "Suffer the Little Children," I can almost smell the breath and see the wrinkled clothes of Pete Morton, the town drunk, and hear the piety and friendliness in the voice of Mrs. Bates who "would give [us children] hot fresh raised doughnuts," but only after we had sung "Jesus Loves Me" and "What a Friend We Have in Jesus."[30] I almost see Jean Bethke's little village of Timnath. And I remember Hank Mormon, our town drunk when I was a child. I always enjoyed Hank. He was a bit eccentric, always very tense, and he occasionally published odd poetry in the local newspaper. We were always told Hank "got this way" from being unable to cope with being a soldier during World War II. These are real people from a real village.

And I know exactly what Elshtain is talking about when she writes:

> Ah, the neighbors. Always a mixed blessing. A blessing without a doubt, but mixed. They helped and they meddled. They would without hesitation grab a child

27. See chaps. 1, 2, and 3 of *Power Trips and Other Journeys.*

28. Elshtain, "A Return to Hull House: Reflections on Jane Addams," in *Power Trips and Other Journeys,* 5.

29. James Wm. McClendon, Jr., *Biography as Theology,* new ed. (Philadelphia: Trinity Press International, 1990), 23.

30. Jean Bethke Elshtain, "Suffer the Little Children," *New Republic* 214 (4 March 1996): 33.

> poised treacherously on the edge of the irrigation ditch; but they also condemned hair styles, clothing that "showed too much," poor housekeeping and loose ways in general. They rallied and they ostracized. That is what real neighbors do. You can't have it both ways. If they care enough to help, they also have the power—indeed, they would say, the responsibility—to chasten, to correct, to chastise.[31]

That Elshtain evokes the life of the village in which she grew up is not incidental to the point of her essay. Quite the contrary. Her point is precisely to evoke images of real life in an actual village. This is to avoid what she sometimes refers to as "the unbearable lightness of liberalism" that leads to the hollow use of terms like *village,* such that they refer to no particular place and a very loose configuration of relationships.[32]

It is Elshtain's connectedness to real, everyday life that enriches her writings and helps her to avoid the "unbearable lightness of liberalism." It is this connectedness that causes her to applaud those who challenge what she labels "hyperindividualism" and affirm, with some reservations, what often goes by the label "communitarianism."[33]

Given her commitment to particularity, I want to suggest one crucial, yet undeveloped, element of Elshtain's thought. The suggestion is really quite simple: she should add the church as a substantive component of both her conception of political philosophy and her future contributions to a Christian social ethic.[34] This will simultaneously draw on her insights about the moral revolution of early Christianity, redeem the everyday life of Christians, avoid hyperindividualism, and tie into some suggestions she has made in passing. But let me emphasize: this is an undeveloped element of Elshtain's thought, not an absent one.

Elshtain has made several passing suggestions about the value of the church. In a recent essay Elshtain put forward "a third option" for approaching the social problems we face, one that focuses on "the mediating institutions of civil society."[35] Instead of relying "either on the market or the state 'to organize their

31. Ibid., 33.

32. The essay "Suffer the Little Children," mentioned above, is largely a critique of Hillary Rodham Clinton's book *It Takes a Village,* in which, Elshtain believes, Clinton "extends the metaphor of the village to the breaking point—no, beyond it" (33).

33. See, e.g., Jean Bethke Elshtain, "Slaying Straw Dragons," *Commonweal* 120 (5 November 1993): 30–32, and "The Communitarian Individual," in *New Communitarian Thinking: Persons, Virtues, Institutions, and Communities,* ed. Amitai Etzioni (Charlottesville: University Press of Virginia, 1995), 99–109.

34. I should make it clear that I see these two conceptions as being significantly different. The conceptions potentially overlap in that both see the church as a social institution that shapes the behavior and convictions of those who are substantially part of it. However, a political philosopher sees something like "mediating institutions" as instrumental to the purpose of the larger culture. For Christians, on the other hand, the church does not primarily exist to serve the larger society; it exists for the purposes of serving God and all that that entails. As is indicated by the stories of André Trocmé and Dietrich Bonhoeffer, below, sometimes the church will understand itself as needing to be primarily against the larger culture. But, as the brief narrative from Charles Fish, below, shows, the church will also be about inculcating virtues valuable to the larger society. These two differing views—one political and one theological—should not be confused.

35. Jean Bethke Elshtain, "Catholic Social Thought, the City, and Liberal America," in *Cathol-*

codes of moral obligation'... what they [that is, both liberals and conservatives] really need is 'civil society — families, communities, friendship networks, solidaristic workplace ties, voluntarism, spontaneous groups and movements.'"[36] Elshtain would surely include the church as one of the communities, or mediating institutions, that is needed for the organizing of "codes of moral obligation." In fact, elsewhere she comments, "Often, religious communities aim explicitly to counter ultraindividualism and provide an institutional framework which nourishes alternatives."[37] Or again, she observes, "a resonant motif in Christian theory and practice emerged from the conviction, sanctified by the Eucharist, that the faithful could achieve a good life only in the fellowship of others."[38] At the end of her essay on Catholic social thought, she quotes Peter Brown's preface to his well-known book *The Cult of the Saints:* "Above all, by slow degrees the thoughts of our forefathers [and foremothers!], their common thought about common things, will have become thinkable once more. There are discoveries to be made; but also there are habits to be formed."[39] Elshtain believes it matters what habits are formed in us. In one work she speculates on what Augustine would think about a group of sexologists who are displaying, on cable television, various sex paraphernalia. She concludes,

> Somehow I doubted whether the folks fingering all those "sex tools" and displaying them to the world spent much time thinking about what it means to be a neighbor or tending to the delights of thinking itself. I could be wrong, of course; perhaps they are sexologists by night and Brothers and Sisters of Charity by day, but I doubt it. For these habituating distractions make knowledge of self harder to come by: one hasn't the time or the occasion to pay attention. This would be Augustine's worry, that and what sort of community of mutual predation such people presuppose and require. As he would say, look at what people love, for that is how the self tends.[40]

What sort of community do such people presuppose and require? Yes, it is true, isn't it, that habituation requires and presupposes community. The primary community that provides habituation and norms for habituation for Christians

---

icism and Liberalism: Contributions to American Public Philosophy, ed. R. Bruce Douglass and David Hollenbach (Cambridge: Cambridge University Press, 1994), 151–71. For some helpful comments on the value of mediating institutions or structures see Peter L. Berger, "In Praise of Particularity: The Concept of Mediating Structures," in *Facing Up to Modernity: Excursions in Society, Politics, and Religion* (New York: Basic Books, 1977), 130–41.

36. Elshtain, "Catholic Social Thought, the City, and Liberal America," 157. Internal quotation is from Alan Wolfe, *Whose Keeper? Social Science and Moral Obligation* (Berkeley: University of California Press, 1989), 20.

37. Elshtain, "The Communitarian Individual," 108.

38. Elshtain, "The Risks and Responsibilities of Affirming Ordinary Life," 73. Quoting from Peter Brown, *The Cult of the Saints* (Chicago: University of Chicago Press, 1982), xv.

39. Elshtain, "Catholic Social Thought, the City, and Liberal America," 169. For an essay that moves in a direction that is helpful, in relation to Brown's suggestive comment, see Robert L. Wilken, "The Lives of the Saints and the Pursuit of Virtue," in his *Remembering the Christian Past* (Grand Rapids, Mich.: Wm. B. Eerdmans, 1995), 121–44.

40. Jean Bethke Elshtain, *Augustine and the Limits of Politics* (Notre Dame: University of Notre Dame Press, 1995), 65.

is the church.[41] And the love that is central for the church is God revealed in Jesus Christ, connected closely with love for neighbors.

Elshtain is quite right that "Christianity ushered a moral revolution into the world." But despite her belief that this revolution "established a set of claims which must be faced and answered today,"[42] she has not given a thick account of what this "moral revolution" means. Or, to put it differently, she has not reckoned seriously enough with Alasdair MacIntyre's notion that "a moral philosophy... characteristically presupposes a sociology."[43]

Elshtain is, justifiably, not happy with Hillary Rodham Clinton's overextended use of the metaphor "village." In much the same way I am not happy with Elshtain's loose use of "our" in the phrase "*our* way of seeing the world." Who is this "our"? I would certainly be prepared to argue that the church has influenced, in substantial ways, the societies in which it has existed. Similarly, Marian Wright Edelman has influenced the lives of many children, but as Elshtain observes,

> You cannot mother a country the way you mother your own children. To convince herself of the romantic continuity of her own life, Edelman must downgrade the special, ongoing responsibility that parents have to their concrete, particular children. Indeed, she decries our unfortunate tendency to "distinguish between our own and other people's children." But how can any human being not do precisely that? We would be monsters if we made no such distinction, if our children simply oozed into some puree called "the child."[44]

Elshtain is right. Real parents have concrete, particular children. And just as Elshtain does not want some generic puree called "the child," so I do not want some puree called "our" or "mediating institution" or even "community." One problem of many discussions within the communitarian debates is the abstract way in which community is discussed. In general this is not true of Elshtain, but it is true in relation to her references to the church. It need not be. She and I would probably agree on the need to support family structures, because they are so vital for nurturing children and habituating them into living certain ways, for the acquisition of appropriate virtues.[45] And Elshtain and I would probably agree

41. I refer throughout this paper to "the church." By *church* I mean nothing arcane. I mean primarily what many of us experience as church week in and week out—that is to say, our local church or parish. Of course, I realize these local bodies are connected to regional, national, and international bodies as well and that that is a part of what is entailed by *church.*

I should also say, in case it is not obvious, that, in a formal way, what I say about the church is true for a mosque, synagogue, or other place of worship. But this essay and this book are about Christian ethics.

42. Elshtain, *Public Man, Private Woman,* 64, 56.

43. Alasdair MacIntyre, *After Virtue,* 2d ed. (Notre Dame: University of Notre Dame Press, 1984), 23.

44. Elshtain, "Suffer the Little Children," 37.

45. For two very different accounts of why and how family structures are important see David Popenoe, *Life without Father* (New York: Free Press, 1996); and John R. Gillis, *A World of Their Own Making: Myth, Ritual, and the Quest for Family Values* (New York: Basic Books, 1996). For a wonderful theological account of the family see Rodney Clapp, *Families at the Crossroads: Beyond*

on the need to pay attention to the destruction of various mediating structures in our society, while wanting to avoid wallowing in nostalgia.[46] But if her account of the moral revolution of Christianity is not to devolve into "the unbearable lightness of liberalism," it needs a thicker description of what the "our" in "our way of seeing" refers to. This "thicker description" is usually called the church.

Let me repeat her statement: the moral revolution of Christianity entailed "a dramatic transformation in our way of seeing the world" and "created a new vocabulary of basic notions with performative requirements."[47] What does this mean for the actual life of the church? Let me hint at a response by telling some brief stories.

One of the most remarkable is the story of the parish in Le Chambon, in southern France, during World War II.[48] André and Magda Trocmé led this parish of 3,000 people in the saving of the lives of between 2,000 and 6,000 Jews by their willingness to offer hospitality to those who had come to be labeled their enemies. These acts did not happen in a vacuum. Their Huguenot heritage (for most of them) and understanding of persecution; their regular Bible teaching and sermons on hospitality and other acts of love; their understanding of the mandate to love neighbors and enemies; the spiritual vitality they had come to experience through the pastoral leadership of André Trocmé — all of these nourished their alternative perspective on the Jewish refugees who began entering their village in the winter of 1940–41.

Another instance is Dietrich Bonhoeffer. Elshtain appreciates, along with many of us, the life of Bonhoeffer.[49] What is often not emphasized enough, however, in many writings about Bonhoeffer is the importance of the church for his life and thought.[50] As Bonhoeffer put it:

> The member of the Body of Christ has been delivered from the world and called out of it. He must give the world a visible proof of his calling, not only by sharing

Traditional and Modern Options (Downers Grove, Ill.: InterVarsity Press, 1993), and his essay "From Family Values to Family Virtues" in this volume.

46. One brilliant instance of the kind of analysis I find helpful is Alan Ehrenhalt, *The Lost City: Discovering the Forgotten Virtues of Community in the Chicago of the 1950s* (New York: Basic Books, 1995).

47. Elshtain, *Public Man, Private Woman,* 57.

48. For a longer version of this story see Mark Nation, "Living in Another World as One Response to Relativism," in *Theology without Foundations: Religious Practice and the Future of Theological Truth,* ed. Stanley Hauerwas, Nancey Murphy, and Mark Nation (Nashville: Abingdon Press, 1994), 238–41. See also Philip Hallie, *Lest Innocent Blood Be Shed: The Story of the Village of Le Chambon and How Goodness Happened There* (New York: Harper and Row, 1979).

49. Of course the indispensable work on Bonhoeffer's life is Eberhard Bethge, *Dietrich Bonhoeffer,* trans. Erich Mosbacher et al. (New York: Harper and Row, 1970). For one of her several essays on Bonhoeffer see Jean Bethke Elshtain, "Bonhoeffer and the Sovereign State," *First Things* 65 (August/September 1996): 27–30.

50. I have developed this notion at some length in an unpublished essay, "*Nachfolge:* A Legacy of Dietrich Bonhoeffer for Social Ethics." I published a much abbreviated version of an earlier essay on Bonhoeffer's "pacifism": "'Pacifist and Enemy of the State': Bonhoeffer's 'Straight and Unbroken Course' from Costly Discipleship to Conspiracy," *Journal of Theology for Southern Africa* 77 (December 1991): 61–77.

> in the Church's worship and discipline, but also through the new fellowship of brotherly [and sisterly] living.[51]

Or again:

> Let [the Christian] remain in the world to engage in frontal assault on it, and let him live the life of his secular calling in order to show himself as a stranger in this world all the more. But that is only possible if we are visible members of the Church. The antithesis between the world and the Church must be borne out in the world.[52]

Because Bonhoeffer was concerned about the actual life of the church in his day, because he believed it was mostly embracing what he termed "cheap grace," and because he believed that, within German Protestantism, the only hope lay in the Confessing Church movement, he issued the following infamous statement: "Whoever knowingly separates himself from the Confessing Church in Germany separates himself from salvation."[53] He wanted the church to embrace what he believed to be the costly grace of Christ. This included, among other things, renouncing revenge, loving enemies, being meek, pursuing mercy, raising up the oppressed, bearing testimony to the truth, living with few material possessions, and having a willingness to suffer persecution and rejection for the sake of righteousness.[54] When he was given the opportunity to train pastors for the church, he specifically attempted to train them in convictions and practices that would shape people who could live in this manner and shape those whom they would pastor likewise.[55]

Again, because people often suspect that a focus on the church entails some kind of sectarian withdrawal, it is important to remember Bonhoeffer's declaration that Christians must "remain in the world." But if Elshtain saw the distinction between Aristotle and the early church as stark enough to deserve the term "moral revolution," Bonhoeffer even more, in the midst of Nazi Germany, could not help noting the "antithesis between the world and the church" — at least the church as he envisioned it and sought to call it forth at the Finkenwalde seminary.

Of course these last two stories are set in a crisis situation. The contrast between Christian behavior and typical behavior was stark. But that does not mean that the principles do not apply elsewhere. Bonhoeffer began working out his views about the church before Germany was obviously in a crisis, and André Trocmé before refugees came to Le Chambon. Neither Bonhoeffer nor Trocmé

51. Dietrich Bonhoeffer, *The Cost of Discipleship*, rev. ed., trans. R. H. Fuller and Irmgard Booth (New York: Macmillan, 1959), 289.

52. Ibid., 297.

53. Quoted in Bethge, *Dietrich Bonhoeffer*, 430.

54. Bonhoeffer, *Cost of Discipleship*, 133, 156–71, 192–201, 289.

55. See Bethge, *Dietrich Bonhoeffer*, 409ff. Also see the wonderful account of Bonhoeffer's understanding of forgiveness within the life of the church in L. Gregory Jones, *Embodying Forgiveness: A Theological Analysis* (Grand Rapids, Mich.: Wm. B. Eerdmans, 1995), 3–33.

would have imagined that the ethic they were committed to was only for a time of crisis.

We should not make the mistake of thinking that the extraordinary ethic of Bonhoeffer or the parish of Le Chambon is removed from everyday life. But, nonetheless, before we move on, it may be fitting to look at some reflections on a life not lived in a period of special crisis. Charles Fish gives an account of the simple faith of his grandmother, Pauline Williams. The narrative has the limitations of being a grandson's reminiscence, but it is delightful and instructive.

> Grandmother read her Bible every day. Abraham and Isaac were as familiar to her as the next-door neighbors. . . . There was no gap for her between daily life on a Vermont farm in the mid-twentieth century and the life of the Jews or the early Christians two thousand years ago. . . . She did not send me to Sunday school, she went with me, and when she did so she was thinking not only of the boy I was but of the man she wanted me to become. . . . That a boy should be free to choose opinions and principles like a shopper at a flea market would have struck her as preposterous. It would have appalled her that a family could be so lacking in self-confidence or casual about the roots of its being that it could leave so fundamental a matter to the vagaries of chance or the corruptibility of human nature. . . . And so she paid attention. She seldom preached, but by reminder and example she taught the importance of honesty, duty, charity, compassion, sexual restraint, clean speech, frugality, faith . . . and hard work. She was not theoretical, she did not categorize, she did not puzzle over the unity or separability of the virtues. She thought she knew what made a human being good and she wanted it for those she loved.[56]

Of course this brief recollection is about one person (and it tells us something about her grandson as well). But it is the church, its Scriptures, and its practices that shaped her soul, her life, her virtues, and her desires for those she loved.

For Bonhoeffer, for the parish of Le Chambon, for Pauline Williams, the church was not an abstraction. It was a place where people gathered for worship, baptism, the Eucharist, sermons, education, relationships, and much more. It was a community of memory that invoked the presence of the God they were called to worship; it reminded them of how they were to see the world and what behaviors were appropriate and inappropriate for the worship they were engaged in.[57]

The ethic they taught and embodied is really "the moral revolution" Elshtain has so powerfully articulated.[58] It may be that this revolution has given a new

56. Charles Fish, *In Good Hands: The Keeping of a Family Farm* (New York: Farrar, Straus and Giroux, 1995), 22–24.

57. For much more adequate discussions of the church see, among other writings, Rodney Clapp, *A Peculiar People: The Church as Culture in a Post-Christian Society* (Downers Grove, Ill.: Inter-Varsity Press, 1996); James Wm. McClendon, Jr., *Doctrine: Systematic Theology, Volume II* (Nashville: Abingdon Press, 1994); John Howard Yoder, *The Priestly Kingdom* (Notre Dame: University of Notre Dame Press, 1984); and John Howard Yoder, *The Royal Priesthood: Essays Ecclesiological and Ecumenical* (Grand Rapids, Mich.: Wm. B. Eerdmans, 1994).

58. Elshtain, *Public Man, Private Woman,* 57.

vocabulary and new possibilities for the world in general. But before we move too quickly to the "world in general" or "society as a whole," let us reflect on the church, one of those "mediating institutions" that is so vital for the health of our society. And let us realize that for the church, this "moral revolution" is normative as a part of its ongoing story if it is to be the church.

It may be, as Elshtain has said, that "the early Christian man or woman was a 'fool' to the received 'wisdom' of the powerful and worldly" and that "women are the 'fools' in Western political thought and practice."[59] There are fools and there are fools. Many of us believe, with the apostle Paul, that the foolishness of the cross is true wisdom (1 Cor. 1:18). If this is foolishness, let us be fools for Christ, redeeming everyday life.

Let us also realize that as Christians we enter the world of the *civitas* disarmed; we seek to embody the virtues of Christ, hoping, with Elshtain, that "if at least partial exclusion from wholesale absorption into terms of institutional power is maintained, space for critical reflection and challenge to that power is more likely to be sustained."[60] What this means in detail cannot be worked out here. These matters are quite complicated and, in fact, always need to be worked out contextually. It would be a mistake, however, for anyone to imagine that the approach suggested in the last section of this essay entails some form of sectarianism.[61] The lives of Bonhoeffer, Trocmé, and others with similar convictions suggest otherwise. It is imperative that we not forget that we as Christians are called to be "fools" for Christ, joining a moral revolution that involves a transformation in our way of seeing, and that the Christian vocation is a "vocation that required [and requires] contemplation and purification of the self, . . . in a life lived among others," those "others" being those who name Jesus as Christ and Lord, namely the church.[62]

59. Elshtain, "The Power and Powerlessness of Women," 144.

60. Ibid., 144–45.

61. If I were to work at the detail it would involve centrally, though certainly not exclusively, the employment of the writings of John Howard Yoder and Stanley Hauerwas. By Yoder see especially "The Christian Case for Democracy," in *The Priestly Kingdom* (Notre Dame: University of Notre Dame Press), 151–71; the first four essays in *The Royal Priesthood,* 53–140; *For the Nations: Essays Public and Evangelical* (Grand Rapids, Mich.: Wm. B. Eerdmans, 1997); and his old book, *The Christian Witness to the State* (Newton, Kan.: Faith and Life Press, 1964). For guidance in reading more deeply and broadly in Yoder see Mark Thiessen Nation, "A Comprehensive Bibliography of the Writings of John Howard Yoder," *Mennonite Quarterly Review* 71 (January 1997): 93–145. For a fine overview of Hauerwas (and, secondarily, Yoder) see Arne Rasmusson, *The Church as Polis* (Notre Dame: University of Notre Dame Press, 1995). By Hauerwas see *The Peaceable Kingdom* (Notre Dame: University of Notre Dame Press, 1983); *Christian Existence Today: Essays on Church, World, and Living in Between* (Durham, N.C.: Labyrinth Press, 1988); and, with William Willimon, *Resident Aliens* (Nashville: Abingdon Press, 1989).

62. Elshtain, *Public Man, Private Woman,* 61.

Suggestions for Further Reading

Elshtain, Jean Bethke. *Augustine and the Limits of Politics.* Notre Dame: University of Notre Dame Press, 1995.

———. "Christianity and Patriarchy: The Odd Alliance." *Modern Theology* 9 (April 1993): 109–22.

———. *Public Man, Private Woman: Women in Social and Political Thought.* 2d ed. Princeton: Princeton University Press, 1993.

Fox-Genovese, Elizabeth. *Feminism without Illusions: A Critique of Individualism.* Chapel Hill: University of North Carolina Press, 1991.

Fulkerson, Mary McClintock. *Changing the Subject: Women's Discourses and Feminist Theology.* Minneapolis: Fortress Press, 1994.

Martin, Francis. *The Feminist Question: Feminist Theology in the Light of Christian Tradition.* Grand Rapids, Mich.: Wm. B. Eerdmans, 1994.

Chapter 14

Business Ethics: Kindred Spirit or Idolatry?

Michael Goldberg

Editor's Introduction

One of the perennial problems for Christian ethicists has been that of finding an adequate basis for speaking to the business world. One typical approach relies on the assumption that unethical business practice can be corrected by the presence of a suitable number of morally upright *individuals* holding strategic positions of corporate power. This view treats moral obligations as though they are first determined in the religious sphere and only subsequently carried by individuals into the morally unstructured marketplace.

Rabbi Michael Goldberg wonders whether the business world is, in fact, as amoral as we imagine it to be. If corporations have the same shape as moral communities – unified in the pursuit of a common *telos,* constituted by members standing in interdependent and mutually embedded relationships, driven by a common master story, evaluated by a set of virtues which are exemplified in the lives of its paradigmatic heroes – then MacIntyre's approach to ethics can be applied directly within the business world. For example, a corporation *can* determine what sort of character it *ought* to be, by simply reflecting on its master story or "creed." Further, if corporations have become surrogate communities in an otherwise fractured and individualistic age, then it is conceivable that, by virtue of the fact that they share with religious communities a basic communal shape, corporations have ears to hear what religious communities have to say about moral obligation in communal life. If Goldberg is correct in this, then Christian ethics has the hope of going beyond moral instruction for individuals to tutelage of corporations themselves.

Goldberg's essay compares the biblical nation of Israel with General Electric in order to show the way master stories (the Exodus; the biography of Edison) impart moral vision and propagate certain practices (remembering; inventing), and esteem in the performance of these practices particular virtues (faithfulness; persistence). However, Goldberg's job of teasing out similarities between corporations and religious communities is made difficult by MacIntyre's own explicit claim that corporations have contributed determinatively to the fracturing of moral life. Westerners in the corporate age struggle to inhabit two incommensurable roles: that of *employee,* and that of *family member/citizen.* Yet Goldberg asks whether corporations, rather than contributing to the *demise* of community, might not represent the *last bastion* of community in the secular world. The middle section of his essay systematically dismantles four objections MacIntyre might raise against this thesis.

However, just when it seems as though Goldberg has sewn up the case for similarity, he turns the tables. If there are reasons for thinking MacIntyrean ethics applies directly within corporate culture, there are limitations to this similarity which, from the religious perspective, are not merely unfortunate but downright evil. Granted, modern corporations, for the most part, emerged in an era after Western civilization had already lost sight of the common good. Therefore, it is not surprising that corporations overlook what virtually everyone misses. What is surprising are examples of companies that offer a creedal version of the "common" (that is, corporate) good and tenaciously abide by the creed even at great cost. That we readily recognize such companies as "excellent" shows MacIntyre's claim that all business ethics is merely utilitarian to be wide of the mark. Nevertheless, there is a demonic side to excellence. Goldberg notes that no story to which corporate culture demands "religious" fidelity is, in fact, genuinely *biblical.* Neither is the moral vision that corporations cultivate any wider than the boundaries of their financial market. Nor are the goods that corporations seek anything but partial and conflicting ones. Under these conditions, the corporation that demands total allegiance is *idolatrous.*

Goldberg applies MacIntyre's analysis of the moral life to draw attention to the tension that Christian ethicists face when addressing the business world. On the one hand, there is enough similarity for Christian ethicists to hope that our moral prescriptions can be heard and understood by the quasi-communal corporation. Yet, on the other hand, that the comparison can be made at all means that the business "community" is a distinct species, and therefore in competition for that devotion which we insist ought to be rendered to God alone.

BRAD J. KALLENBERG

Corporations as Community

As American business enters the last decade of this century, its corporate watchword might well be: *"The era of 'human capital' is upon us."*[1] The structural barriers of the past that protected companies — geography, regulation, technology, and scale — are all breaking down. The strategic question of the eighties was "Where best to compete?" The question for the nineties will be *"Who* can

1. Robert A. Irvin and Edward G. Michaels III, "Core Skills: Doing the Right Things Right," *McKinsey Quarterly* 25 (summer 1989): 10.

compete best?"[2] The previous agenda was dominated by such financial matters as economic forecasts and stock values; business strategies in the coming decade will be governed more and more by such matters of corporate culture as corporate vision and corporate values.

This nineties phenomenon may well imply another: at the end of the twentieth century some American corporations may constitute the closest thing our society has to community. Such companies form communities of their members by providing them with common goals, common procedures for attaining those goals, and common standards for marking success and failure. Unlike most other associations in contemporary American life, ranging from men's clubs to marriages, the corporate community's existence depends on neither mutual admiration nor a spirit of volunteerism; businesspeople who find themselves in a corporate setting are not necessarily nor even primarily together because they like each other. Instead, such people are bonded by "a sense of reliance on one another toward a common cause. . . ."[3]

Such talk of joint reliance in pursuit of a common cause may call to mind medieval sagas of sacred quests for holy grails. No wonder. For some corporations hold out to their members a community of a particular kind: in fundamental ways, the community they present is a *religious* one.

Although speaking of a corporation as a religious community may at first sound shocking, we find among the earliest manifestations of corporations just that: namely, such corporate bodies as monasteries and bishoprics. St. Benedict, for example, wished to form a religious institution that was virtually self-contained, a kind of miniature society. Indeed, the very word *corporation* springs from the root *corpus*, signifying a "body sharing a common purpose in a common name."[4]

Closer to our own time, several observers have noted the key role that corporate cultures play in shaping the attitudes and actions of those who inhabit them. But few—if any—have noticed a concept closely related to culture: *cult*. Both cult and culture trace their roots to a common etymological ancestor, *colere*, meaning "to cultivate or cherish." Indeed, for many late-twentieth-century Americans, the corporate cultus is more cherished, more venerated, than any other institution, including their churches and synagogues. Not only do the corporation and its cult help construct the basic reality of their lives, à la Geertz, but, à la Tillich, they also furnish those lives with the "ultimate concerns" of meaning, vision, and values. Consequently, for Americans such as these (that is, people living in an increasingly atomistic, fragmented society), some

2. Ibid., 8.

3. Warren Bennis and Burt Nanus, *Leaders* (New York: Harper and Row, 1985), 83.

4. Alan Trachtenberg and Eric Foner, *The Incorporation of America: Culture and Society in the Gilded Age* (New York: Hill and Wang, 1982), 5. As for St. Benedict, his Rule gives "directions for the formation, government, and administration of a monastery and for the spiritual and daily life of its monks. . . . The Rule provides for an autonomous, self-contained community. . . . The monastery of the Rule is a microcosm containing inmates of every age and condition . . ." *(The New Catholic Encyclopedia,* s.v. "Benedictine Rule," by B. Colgrave).

corporations truly do create some overarching meaning. Moreover, "through their rituals, [such corporations] teach people how to behave, not just in their corridors of power but in the world at large."[5]

Whatever rituals, visions, or values have blossomed in the traditions of such corporations *cum* religious communities, the ground from which they have sprouted is the same as that for any other human community, whether religious or otherwise: a *story* of a corporate past arcing toward some future. For those who remain faithful to their story line, the risk of faith is that the future will be one of blessing rather than of curse, of good fortune and not of doom.

The Centrality of Narratives

In *After Virtue,* Alasdair MacIntyre calls attention to the centrality of stories for human life by reminding us that "I can only answer the question 'What am I to do?' if I can answer the prior question 'Of what story... do I find myself a part?' "[6] In other words, larger communal stories frame our individual life stories, thereby framing our identities as well. Often cast as histories, such communal narratives, by requiring that we look back at significant persons and events in the past, implicitly suggest characters and occurrences for us to look for in the future. In short, such stories impart to us a *vision.* That vision shows us a future in which, according to MacIntyre,

> certain possibilities beckon us forward and others repel us, some seem already foreclosed and others perhaps inevitable.... If the narrative of our [life] is to continue intelligibly... it is always both the case that there are constraints on how the story can continue and that within those constraints there are indefinitely many ways it can continue.[7]

Such classical communal stories therefore invite their hearers to think of themselves as participants in an embodied narrative quest toward some future goal or end.[8] As a consequence, these selfsame stories will also provide their hearers guidance in what will be "counted as harm and danger and... how success and failure, progress and its opposite, are understood and evaluated."[9] Thus,

5. Terrence E. Deal and Allen A. Kennedy, *Corporate Cultures* (Reading, Mass.: Addison-Wesley, 1982), 83. Though subtitled *The Rites and Rituals of Corporate Life,* the book contains precious little that approaches corporate life from the vantage point of religious life, or for that matter, religious studies. Instead, the volume and its bibliography are top-heavy with the standard fare of business organization.

Let me be clear here. My point is *not* that corporate life can be understood *only* from the perspective of religion; obviously, it can be analyzed from other standpoints as well—economics, sociology, social psychology, and the like. However, I am suggesting that various forms of religious life may offer rather fruitful ways for thinking about certain instances of corporate life, together with their visions and their values. In that respect, my primary task in this essay is more descriptive than prescriptive.

6. Alasdair MacIntyre, *After Virtue: A Study in Moral Theory* (Notre Dame: University of Notre Dame Press, 1981), 201.

7. Ibid., 200–201.

8. Ibid., 203.

9. Ibid., 135.

prominently depicted in these stories will be certain *recurring kinds of performances,* that is, *practices;* also strikingly displayed will be certain *habitual ways of performing those practices,* that is, *virtues.* For those who would embark on the quests recounted in the narrated traditions of story-based communities, practices and virtues are indispensable moral resources, because they have the power to "sustain us in the relevant kind of quest for the good by enabling us to overcome the harms, dangers, temptations and distractions which we encounter, and which will furnish us with increasing self-knowledge and increasing knowledge of the good [desired]."[10] Stories, by giving us a vision of communal quests toward some end accompanied by the requisite practices and virtues, thereby give us our "values."[11]

Israel's exodus from Egypt is just such a story.[12] It is a narrative about a quest embarked upon by a community-in-formation toward a common goal — the fulfillment of a promise:

> The Lord said to Abram, "Go forth from your native land and from your father's house to the land that I will show you. I will make of you a great nation and I will bless you; I will make your name great, and you shall be a blessing. I will bless those who bless you and curse him who curses you. All the families of the earth shall bless themselves by you." (Gen. 12:1–3)

It is the dynamic of that promise's fulfillment that drives the narrative forward. No matter how many twists and turns the story line may take — a Hebrew baby raised by the daughter of the Hebrews' genocidal enemy, a speech-impeded man called to be spokesman par excellence, a forty-year wilderness trek to kill off the generation just rescued! — certain outcomes are nevertheless precluded: Israel may turn back to Egypt no more than she may worship a golden calf.[13] Instead, an altogether different destiny is envisaged:

> Now then, if you will obey Me faithfully and keep My covenant, you shall be My treasured possession among all the peoples. Indeed, all the earth is Mine, but you shall be to Me a kingdom of priests and a holy nation. (Exod. 19:5–6)

But the narrated keeping of the promise does more than power the story forward. It also calls into being a practice and a virtue absolutely essential for

---

10. Ibid., 204.

11. I have set the word *values* in quotation marks to call attention to the fact that for ethics, that notion reflects a particularly modern understanding — namely, that there are finally no moral goods or standards apart from individual preferences, desires, and wants. For powerful critiques of this position, see MacIntyre, *After Virtue,* chap. 2, "The Nature of Moral Disagreement Today and the Claims of Emotivism"; and Allan Bloom, *The Closing of the American Mind* (New York: Simon and Schuster, 1987), 60–61.

The fact that American business as a whole tends to use *values* as synonymous for — and to the virtual exclusion of — other terms such as *ethics, goods,* and *standards* indicates that even for the corporation, an institution whose premodern motifs can still be heard, the trope of modernity is nevertheless inescapable.

12. See my *Jews and Christians: Getting Our Stories Straight* (Philadelphia: Trinity Press International, 1991).

13. See, e.g., Exod. 16:3, 17:3, and 32:25–35.

the existence of the community of Israel; the practice is *remembering,* the virtue *faithfulness.* In the Exodus narrative, it is an act of remembering that triggers the chain of events leading to Israel's eventual deliverance:

> The Israelites were groaning under the bondage and cried out; and their cry for help from the bondage rose up to God. God heard their moaning, and God remembered his covenant with Abraham and Isaac and Jacob. (Exod. 2:23–24)

Later, another act of remembering preserves Israel when, though recently delivered from Egyptian servitude and pledged to serve the Lord, she renders him false service instead:

> The Lord spoke to Moses, "Your people... have acted basely. They have been quick to turn aside from the way that I enjoined upon them. They have made themselves a molten calf and bowed low to it.... Now, let me be, that my anger may blaze forth against them, and that I may destroy them...."
>
> But Moses implored the Lord his God, saying, "Let not your anger, O Lord, blaze forth against your people.... Turn from your blazing anger and renounce the plan to punish your people. Remember your servants, Abraham, Isaac, and Jacob, how you swore to them..., 'I will make your offspring as numerous as the stars of heaven, and I will give to your offspring this whole land of which I spoke, to possess forever.'" And the Lord renounced the punishment he had planned to bring upon his people. (Exod. 32:7–8, 10–14)

For the community of Israel, remembering past promises is indispensable for realizing whatever promise the future may hold.

But remembering the past, like keeping a promise, requires one virtue above all others: faithfulness. In the Hebrew Bible, the word that typically expresses that virtue is *chesed.* The term, appearing in one form or another over two hundred times in Scripture, has at bottom a specific, quasi-technical meaning: "covenantal loyalty."[14] In the Exodus narrative the paradigmatic exemplar of that virtue is God. Thus, in an act of covenant renewal following Israel's transgression with the calf, God reveals to Moses his hallmark character trait, his chief virtue, which enables him to renew the covenant in the first place: "The Lord! A God compassionate and gracious, slow to anger, rich in covenantal loyalty [*chesed*], showing faithfulness [*chesed*] to thousands..." (Exod. 34:6–7). Just as important, Moses has whatever authority and leadership he possesses precisely because in many ways he, too, displays that singular virtue. As depicted in the Exodus narrative, neither God nor Moses is particularly charismatic, or particularly eloquent, or particularly good at "managing" people.[15] And yet both excel at steadfastly persevering to realize the ends they seek. Since Israel's continued existence depends on just such steadfast devotion, God and Moses are,

14. See Nelson Glueck, *[Ch]esed in the Bible,* trans. A. Gottschalk (Cincinnati: Hebrew Union College Press, 1967). Even if one prefers a less technical rendering of *chesed,* such as the RSV's "steadfast love," the term's basic thrust remains the same: faithful devotion.

15. See MacIntyre's description on pp. 29–31 of *After Virtue* of the manager and therapist as embodying quintessentially modern roles that enable them to manipulate people to achieve certain ends, without regard for any moral concerns about such manipulation or such ends.

not surprisingly, the heroes of the story that Israel tells from generation to generation.

Are there similar stories to be told—and heard—in corporate America?

The Narratives of Corporate America

> For those who hold them, shared values define the fundamental character of their organization . . . that distinguishes [it] from all others. . . . [Such values] create a special sense of identity . . . , giving meaning to work as something more than . . . earning a living. . . . Sometimes managers refer explicitly to . . . these values in [guiding] subordinates. . . . New people may be told stories about the company's past that underline the importance of these values to the company.[16]

As in any corporate cult, General Electric's employees are deeply devoted to its values, and in any recitation of those values, the company's motto stands as the central tenet of its corporate creed: "Progress Is Our Most Important Product." Yet even more fundamental than that corporate article of faith are General Electric's stories about the GE heroes, the GE *saints,* who gave rise to that creed by *embodying it.*

One of their corporate saints is Thomas Edison, a figure revered not only in GE's pantheon of heroes but in the larger American society. Virtually every American schoolchild knows the story of Edison conducting experiment after experiment to find the right filament for the electric light. And virtually every GE employee knows the story of Edison developing the vehicle for simultaneous two-way telegraphic communication: after spending twenty-two consecutive nights testing twenty-three different duplexes, he finally invented one that worked.[17]

Another GE saint is Charles Steinmetz, a man whose life coincided with Edison's in many ways. He worked in Edison's lab, which he ran after Edison left.[18] Like Edison, Steinmetz suffered from a physical disability.[19] Like Edison, Steinmetz also played a large part in GE's growth as a company, for he "brought alternating current into electrical systems of the world."[20] And as with Edison, stories about his work at GE germinated values which, along with their corporate exemplar, are revered to this day, as the following episode reported by one of the authors of *Corporate Cultures* makes clear:

> We drove by the General Electric Research Lab where — in an earlier era and building — Charles Steinmetz had conducted his experiments. The driver of the car motioned to the building and said, "Sometimes I get the feeling I can still see

16. Julien R. Phillips and Allen A. Kennedy, "Shaping and Managing Shared Values," *McKinsey Staff Paper* (December 1980), 4; emphasis added.

17. Ibid., 11.

18. Deal and Kennedy, *Corporate Cultures,* 45.

19. Steinmetz was crippled, and Edison, having had his ears "boxed" as a child, suffered from a serious hearing loss.

20. Deal and Kennedy, *Corporate Cultures,* 8.

> the lights on in there and Steinmetz working away." For the driver, and for other employees of GE *who never knew Steinmetz,* he still was a strong influence....[21]

Not for nothing is *inventing* GE's cardinal practice,[22] and *persistence*[23] its cardinal virtue.

But Steinmetz also plays a saintly role in GE's lore in another way. He is responsible for creating the vision that stands at the heart of the company's story-based self-understanding as a community of inventive engineers and scientists with *close personal ties* to one another:

> Whenever young engineers joined GE, Steinmetz would invite them home for the weekend in order to learn, sincerely and without political intent, what kind of people they were. Once he adopted one of GE's leading engineers as his own son — and the man's whole family. They all moved into Steinmetz's house and lived with him for twenty years.[24]

With this bit of hagiography as background, General Electric nurtures a corporate cult that emulates the saintliness of Steinmetz through fostering supportiveness, loyalty, and respect among peer-group members.

Thus, like vibrant religious communities, some corporations have stories in which a venerated past bears promise for the future. In fact, many writers have suggested that companies displaying high financial performance and potential are precisely those with powerful narrative traditions.[25]

But is this account of the implications of story-based values for corporations, like some medieval morality play, a story too good to be true?

Corporate Community or Moral Fragmentation?

MacIntyre would almost certainly answer yes. For him, while classical societies tended to reflect a single unified — and unifying — core narrative, modern cul-

21. Ibid., 47.

22. For a discussion of the relationship between practices and goods, see MacIntyre, *After Virtue,* 175, and my discussion below.

23. In fact, much of the current literature on leadership points to persistence as the outstanding character trait — that is, virtue — of those considered leaders. See Deal and Kennedy, *Corporate Cultures,* 46; Bennis and Nanus, *Leaders,* 45, 47, 187–88; Phillips and Kennedy, "Shaping and Managing Shared Values," 18, 19; and Nigel Williams, "Managing Values on Wall Street," keynote speech to the Securities Industry Association Conference, 29 October 1987, 9.

Perhaps a necessary though not sufficient condition for any leader is a single-minded willingness to act out a vision and live out a story. Tom Peters, referring to the work of Bennis and Nanus, points out that leaders have clear visions, which are "lived with almost frightening consistency..." (*Thriving on Chaos: Handbook for a Management Revolution* [New York: Perennial Library, 1987], 631). That observation may help to remind us that corporate communities, particularly in their early days, are often like religious cults — that is, they are tightly organized around a central person, the *cult figure.* If that person is a cult figure like Jesus of Nazareth, well and good; if, however, that person is a cult figure like Jim Jones...

24. Deal and Kennedy, *Corporate Cultures,* 45.

25. Ibid., 7, 30. See also Williams, "Managing Values on Wall Street," 5; Phillips and Kennedy, "Shaping and Managing Shared Values," 2, 12; and Alan Wilkins, "Organizational Stories as an Expression of Management Philosophy" (Ph.D. diss., Stanford University, 1978).

ture reflects many different story fragments, thereby shattering our moral vision. Corporate life, for its part, fragments the moral life even more:

> Within any one large formal organization not only variety, but incoherence is to be found [since] corporate structures fragment consciousness and more especially moral consciousness.[26]
>
> Corporate existence . . . presupposes a separation of spheres of existence, a moral distancing of each social role from each of the others.[27]

In MacIntyre's view, corporate life splits the moral life into (at least) two distinct and incompatible realms: that of the individual corporate employee governed by utilitarian considerations, and that of the family member or citizen whose moral considerations are anything but utilitarian.[28] Consequently, for MacIntyre, the corporation, far from providing the closest thing our society has to community, is rather the institutional embodiment of a modern, individualistic ethos — the very antithesis of any genuine notion of community.

And yet MacIntyre may well have gotten his labels reversed. For it could also be that in contemporary American society, the corporation in its basic structure and daily operation is the last bastion of any truly functioning community, while modern politics and the modern family run on little more than fleeting individual preferences and fickle personal desires.[29] As MacIntyre himself admits, corporate

> organization [must] be conceived in terms of roles and not of persons. Any role, any position, will be filled from time to time by different persons. . . . Correspondence for example is conducted with this or that office of the organization and not — except accidentally — with individuals. Hence the formal character of bureaucratic correspondence; hence the importance of files. Each file has a history [that is, *a narrative*] which outlives that of the individuals who contribute to it.[30]

Indeed, many observers have taken note of the role that so-called excellent companies play in creating an entire reality for those working in them; even more than that, for many corporate employees, the reality thus created catches them up in something transcendent, even bordering on the religious. As Tom Peters has remarked in his best-selling book, *In Search of Excellence,*

26. Alasdair MacIntyre, "Corporate Modernity and Moral Judgment: Are They Mutually Exclusive?" in *Ethics and Problems of the 21st Century,* ed. K. E. Goodpaster and K. M. Sayre (Notre Dame: University of Notre Dame Press, 1979), 122.

27. Ibid., 126.

28. Ibid., 126–27.

29. Regarding contemporary politics, MacIntyre himself has written, "Modern politics is civil war carried on by other means" *(After Virtue,* 236). As for modern family, see Robert N. Bellah, Richard Madsen, William Sullivan, Ann Swidler, and Steven M. Tipton, *Habits of the Heart: Individualism and Commitment in American Life* (New York: Harper and Row, 1985), chap. 4, "Love and Marriage." See also Christopher Lasch's *Haven in a Heartless World: The Family Besieged* (New York: Basic Books, 1977); for many Americans, the family might be likened to an emotional gas station, where they drop by to tank up on affection before pulling out into social traffic once more.

30. MacIntyre, "Corporate Modernity and Moral Judgment," 124.

> By offering *meaning* as well as money, [the excellent companies] give their employees a *mission* as well as a sense of feeling great. Every man becomes a pioneer, an experimenter, a leader. The institution provides *guiding belief* and creates a sense of excitement, *a sense of being part of the best*....[31]

In fact, at a time when the general culture provides little or no stability regarding values, corporations may play an especially crucial role by providing "structure and standards and a value system in which to operate."[32] In just that way, "corporations may be among the last institutions in America that can effectively take on the role of shaping values."[33]

Nevertheless, MacIntyre might still object that within the corporation values are not shaped but shattered as mixed signals are sent regarding them, so that the workplace is pervaded by the same moral chaos as any other place in contemporary American society:

> Unfortunately the very same quality is often presented in one guise as a virtue, in another as a vice. The same executive is characteristically required to be meticulous in adhering to routines... *and* to show initiative.... Especially perhaps among upwardly mobile middle management, contemporaries in the organization are presented at one and the same time as those with whom he or she is expected to cooperate and against whom he or she is expected to compete.[34]

Such conflicting imperatives, however, need not *necessarily* indicate moral anarchy. On the contrary, their conflict may arise in the first place precisely because both spring from a moral outlook more fundamentally shared than shattered. In *Antigone,* for instance, the protagonist is faced with the dilemma of two apparently incommensurate moral claims: those calling her to honor her familial and religious obligations to bury her dead brother and those calling her to keep her political obligations to deny burial to a traitor to the state. As a consequence, no matter how Antigone acts, her act can and will appear at one and the same time both a display of virtue — loyalty — and of vice — betrayal. Yet we must not miss the fact that this conflict between moral obligations in *Antigone* grows out of a unified, coherent moral vision in which life, its values, and its goods are understood principally in terms of concrete relationships, roles, and duties rather than abstract principles, rights, and "oughts."[35]

Similarly, the underlying tension between cooperation and competition in corporate life may stem from a deeper shared commitment to a common goal or good. We can think, for example, of a high school basketball team in which competition between team members exists side by side with cooperation for the sake of realizing a common purpose. In the context of practice, for instance,

31. Thomas J. Peters and Robert H. Waterman, Jr., *In Search of Excellence: Lessons from America's Best-Run Companies* (New York: Warner Books, 1982), 323; emphasis added.

32. Deal and Kennedy, *Corporate Cultures,* 16.

33. Ibid.

34. MacIntyre, "Corporate Modernity and Moral Judgment," 123.

35. See Alasdair MacIntyre, *Against the Self-Images of the Age* (New York: Schocken Books, 1971; 1978), 123–24, 168–69 (page references are to first ed.).

team skills such as the fast break and the zone defense, which demand cooperation among team members, coexist with competition between individuals to increase their respective amounts of playing time or to crack the starting lineup. What must not be overlooked is that *both* cooperation *and* competition must be employed if the team itself is to achieve excellence, especially the excellence needed to be a champion prevailing over all opponents. So, too, if a company wants to achieve preeminence over other companies, its members must learn cooperation as well as competition.

But MacIntyre, undaunted, might still object that where achievement of excellence is equated with achievement of victory, any notion of virtue is summarily defeated, along with any claims to moral seriousness made on behalf of the corporation. For excellence and victory, though closely related, are nevertheless distinct concepts: after all, it is possible *to be excellent yet lose.* To see the difference between being excellent and being victorious, just look, says MacIntyre, at "the Spartan sacrifice at Thermopylae."[36]

But witness, too, the fact that even the excellent high school basketball team can lose if poor officiating costs it a crucial free-throw opportunity or if a player's poor grades cost the team the services of its star. Likewise, an excellent corporation may incur or even choose to court loss(es) in order to maintain certain standards of excellence: just witness the case of Johnson & Johnson during the Tylenol scare.

In the fall of 1982, seven people died when they swallowed Extra-Strength Tylenol capsules laced with cyanide. At the time, Tylenol was the top-selling product in the United States in the health and beauty aid category.[37] Its corporate parent, Johnson & Johnson, from the time of its founding as an innovator in supplying sterile surgical dressings, had built the company's reputation on trust and responsibility. Now J&J was faced with the very real possibility that if it acted in a trustworthy and responsible fashion, it might well lose not only its premier product in the marketplace but a significant slice of its total corporate revenues.

Nevertheless, within the first few days following the poisonings, the company, under the leadership of its chairman, James Burke, withdrew virtually its whole Tylenol line from market shelves and ceased all Tylenol advertising. Within a week, J&J stock had dropped about 20 percent, amounting to a paper loss of $2 billion. But said Burke, "It's important that we demonstrate that we've taken every single step possible to protect the public. . . ."[38] Hardly, it would seem, the words of someone blind to the difference between excellence and winning.

As events wore on, Burke stayed the course he had set. The consensus of his advertising consultants was that the Tylenol name was dead, and many, in-

36. Alasdair MacIntyre, *Whose Justice? Which Rationality?* (Notre Dame: University of Notre Dame Press, 1988), 27–28.

37. Thomas J. C. Raymond with Elisabeth Ament Lipton, "Tylenol," *Harvard Business School Case* (Boston: President and Fellows of Harvard College, 1984), 1.

38. Ibid., 2–3.

cluding media maven Jerry Della Femina, were adamant that the Tylenol name had to be changed before the product could be reintroduced. But Burke and J&J held firm. Wayne Nelson, J&J Company Group chairman, remarked, "It would almost be an admission of guilt ... to walk away from that name."[39] Echoing Nelson, Burke said on the *Donahue* show,

> It seems to me that there is a certain not-playing-it-straight with the consumers on that one. If you are going to sell Tylenol, to sell it under a name other than its own name is kind of asking you to change your name after you've had a serious disease....[40]

Throughout the whole affair, Burke and J&J stuck to their conviction that informing and protecting the nation would eventually result in "an eminently fair decision about the future of Tylenol."[41] In the end, the company saw its commitment to excellence in providing reliable health care vindicated. Within a year of the crisis, Tylenol had regained over 90 percent of the market it had enjoyed prior to the tragedies.[42] And in a *Fortune* magazine poll for America's most admired companies, J&J won top honors for its commitment to community and environmental responsibility.[43]

Even so, however, MacIntyre might once more mount a protest: the corporate practices of even a company like J&J have no real moral power or depth to them, because none of the goods pursued through those practices is *internal* to them. That is, in the course of pursuing the standards of excellence appropriate to and definitive of J&J's business activities, no good intrinsically related to such activities is realized; nor, for that matter, is any human power to achieve excellence or any human conception of the good involved systematically extended.[44] At best, only certain external or contingent goods are realized, such as money or power.

But the matter is not so easily settled. If we recall for a moment the key practice at General Electric — inventing — we discover that the chief good internal to the practice is the very one named in the company's motto: progress. And as GE's corporate story makes clear, progress is a good that would be difficult if not impossible to achieve without invention and the virtue necessary to sustain that practice, namely, persistence. As for J&J, it is a company at whose heart stands a Credo, a corporate catechism of convictions concerning its responsibilities to its customers, its employees, its community, and its shareholders — in just that order. To provide products and services in pursuit of health — an internal good

39. Ibid., 4.
40. Ibid., 11.
41. Ibid., 10.
42. James E. Burke, "The Leverage of Goodwill" (speech to the Advertising Council, 16 November 1983), 4.
43. "Leadership of the Most Admired," *Fortune*, 29 January 1990, 50.
44. MacIntyre, *After Virtue*, 175.

if ever there was one — J&J must cultivate exactly those virtues it demonstrated during the Tylenol crisis: trustworthiness, practical wisdom, and courage.[45]

MacIntyre has pointed out that "in the ancient and medieval worlds the creation and sustaining of human communities — of households, cities, and nations — is generally taken to be a practice...."[46] And so, too, ought we to take the creation and sustaining of certain corporate communities in the modern world. Hence, all moral misgivings regarding the corporation in its modern form would seem to be unwarranted.

Or are they? Before answering, we would be wise to hear the whole story of the rise of the modern American corporation.

Corporate Credos

"Are the vultures still out there?" — [Former] Drexel staffer, sneering at reporters as she walked out the door [following the firm's announcement of bankruptcy]. "Vultures? Look who's talking." — Security guard. (*Time,* 26 February 1990, 46)

Earlier we spoke of monastic communities as among the first corporations, as bodies of persons joined to pursue a common enterprise.[47] Such bodies, however, were interested in benefiting not only their own members but others as well. As Trachtenberg and Foner have reminded us, "It was assumed, as it is still in non-profit corporations, that the incorporated body earned its charter by serving the public good."[48] Similarly, the authors of *Habits of the Heart* have pointed out that "incorporation [was] a concession of public authority to a private group *in return* for service to the public good...."[49] Again, from the time of the earliest monastic orders, these corporate communities sought to contribute to the common good beyond the monastery walls. For example, because of "the paramount obligations of charity toward one's fellow man," St. Basil sought to establish his fourth-century monasteries "in towns instead of in desert wastes," while his forerunner, Pachomius, gathered his *koinonia* or monastic community a century earlier out of a broader commitment to "the service of humankind."[50]

45. Cf. Jeffrey Stout, *Ethics after Babel* (Boston: Beacon Press, 1988), 269. Speaking of medical practice in his article in *Against the Grain: New Approaches to Professional Ethics,* ed. Michael Goldberg (Valley Forge, Pa.: Trinity Press International, 1993), 37–54, titled "We Are All Pragmatists Now: The Limits of Modern Medical Ethics in American Medical Education," Richard Vance has insightfully pointed out that *contra* Stout (and thus MacIntyre as well), there is not so wide or clear a gap between internal and external goods as we have been led to believe: "Yet medicine as a craft has always, even in Hippocratic times, considered remuneration to be closely connected to the quality of care. Money and prestige are not, of course, direct goals of medical practice, but they are not merely external attachments either. One need not be a cynical critic of medicine to note that financial issues are more complexly related to medical practice than Stout's analysis admits" (50). Vance's observation concerning medical practice obviously has implications for other kinds of practices as well.

46. MacIntyre, *After Virtue,* 175.

47. See above, note 4.

48. Trachtenberg and Foner, *Incorporation of America,* 5–6.

49. Bellah et al., 290.

50. St. Basil, *Ascetical Works,* trans. Monica M. Wagner, C.S.C. (New York: Fathers of the Church, 1950), xi; Armand Veilleux, trans. and introduction, *The Life of Saint Pachomius and His*

Clearly, such corporate models presupposed a model of society in which it made sense to speak of "the common good." But as American society became more and more industrialized following the Civil War, notions of the common good became less and less coherent. The bonds among Americans, both political and economic, grew increasingly attenuated. In the earlier life of the Republic, the dominant social metaphor was the town meeting, where all joined in an effort to reach consensus to pursue a common good. After the Civil War, the regnant image became the marketplace, where each pursued his or her own good. Indifferent or even hostile to the goods pursued by others, individuals were bound to others only by a few thin procedures meant to ensure that competition was — at least minimally — "fair."

Such was the social climate that spawned the modern business corporation. As Lawrence Friedman has noted, in the late nineteenth century "the overriding need was for an efficient, trouble-free device to aggregate capital and manage it in business, with limited liability and transferable shares."[51] Here the idea of "limited liability" is crucial, for the novel legal fiction giving the corporation the status of a "person" meshed perfectly with the social fabric of the times. In an age celebrating laissez-faire competition among rugged individuals, concocting a "super-individual" to join the fray was a master stroke. Better still, if the fray proved too hot and the adversaries too strong, then even though the corporation's legal person might be bested, its human persons, still shielded by the doctrine of limited liability, could withdraw unscathed with their own resources intact. As a result, incorporation, which once had been a rare privilege granted only by special charter for the sake of the common good, became an ever-present right, routinely available by application to any private enterprise — which could remain oblivious to any good but its own.[52]

Accordingly, in a society where the notion of a common good has long since died, to find corporations acting without any regard for such a good is hardly surprising. Why, for instance, should anyone be surprised to find R. J. Reynolds attempting to regain lost cigarette sales by targeting blacks and young women in its advertising for new brands? In the fragmented, atomistic America of the late twentieth century, the burden of making a *coherent* moral argument is heavier for RJR's critics than it is for the company.

In its earlier days, of course, the company at least displayed commitment to those who fell within the orbit of its own corporate community. It provided adequate day care for workers' children, it offered RJR stock and liberal loans to its employees, and it gave generously to its hometown of Winston-Salem, North Carolina. And yet, as it continued to flourish in a culture that had increasingly lost sight of any *shared* good, RJR's commitments to share even with

Disciples, foreword by Adalbert de Vogue, vol. 1, Cistercian Studies Series, no. 45 (Kalamazoo, Mich.: Cistercian Publications, 1980), xvii.

51. Lawrence M. Friedman, *A History of American Law,* 2d ed. (New York: Simon and Schuster, 1985), 201.

52. Trachtenberg and Foner, *Incorporation of America,* 6.

those in its own purview weakened. Thus, in connection with the RJR Nabisco takeover, over five thousand employees were eventually thrown out of work as the company virtually pulled out of Winston-Salem. In the leveraged buyout's aftermath, former RJR employees in Winston-Salem were besieged by brokers offering to buy their now highly valuable stock. In response, the townspeople asked incredulously, "You want to buy *stock?*" Explained Nabley Armfield, a local stockbroker, "You have to understand. Reynolds wasn't a stock. It was a *religion.*"[53]

But to the extent that American culture makes corporations like RJR Nabisco unsurprising, to just that extent, the corporate culture of a company like Johnson & Johnson is truly astonishing for binding the company to some larger, shared notion of the good. Like some religious order formed in another time and place, the Johnson & Johnson community lives by a Credo:

> We are responsible to the communities in which we live and work and to the world community as well. We must be good citizens — support good works and charities and bear our fair share of taxes. We must encourage civic improvements and better health and education. We must maintain in good order the property we are privileged to use, protecting the environment and natural resources.

For J&J, these words are not part of a dead doxology intoned as an ancient, fossilized rite. Instead, it is a living text that is revised periodically to keep J&J's corporate vision alive and vital. Hence, looking back on the "Tylenol nightmare" in which "literally dozens of people [had] to make hundreds of decisions in painfully short periods of time," James Burke could say with wholehearted conviction, "All of us . . . truly believe that the guidance of the Credo played *the* most important role in our decision-making."[54]

J&J and Burke are not alone in witnessing to a corporate life with striking similarities to certain aspects of religious life; they are joined by Herman Miller, Inc., and its chairman, Max De Pree. In the previously mentioned *Fortune* listing of the nation's most admired companies, Herman Miller ranked ninth overall, while taking sixth place for management excellence. In a newspaper interview, De Pree expressed his belief that one reason for America's lack of leadership "is that people have felt it was OK to put themselves ahead of the common good." He further noted that leadership is not a question "of techniques . . . but of what is in the heart," and that "corporations can and should have a redemptive purpose. . . . " De Pree's convictions about the corporation are nothing if not religious — especially this one: "Being faithful to a set of beliefs is more important than being successful."[55]

That claim, perhaps more than any other, raises the question whether some forms of corporate life can genuinely be considered as instances of the religious

53. Bryan Burrough and John Helyar, *Barbarians at the Gate: The Fall of RJR Nabisco* (New York: Harper and Row, 1990), 45, 49, 91, 511; emphasis added.

54. Burke, "Leverage of Goodwill," 3–4.

55. *Atlanta Journal-Constitution,* 11 December 1989, B6.

life. Would any corporation be willing to remain faithful to its values *even unto death?* If doing good and doing well do not necessarily go hand in hand, then corporations may need to weigh carefully the stories they live out: not all of them will have happy endings.

Testing Corporate Stories against the Biblical Story

Stories and values are not only sources of corporate performance but also constraints against it:

> Although [shared values] provide a source of clear common understanding in a business, they also constitute a constraint. When a company with strongly held values finds that [it has] lost marketplace or economic relevance, it generally has great difficulty adjusting successfully.[56]

A storied past thus not only *informs* us but, displaying a vision to guide our present and future, also *forms* us in the way we envisage our world and our options for acting in it. There is a reason that some 70 percent of corporate mergers fail, as companies find themselves unable to merge their separate and often incompatible story lines into a new ongoing narrative.[57] In such circumstances, corporate stories may spell death instead of life.

The most basic test of any story, whether corporate or religious, is finally the kind of life that it produces — indeed, if it produces any life at all. Stories die when their communal embodiments do — which is only fitting justice. Hence, without Zeus worshippers, what are the stories of Zeus *but* stories? Granted, it may take a relatively long time for a community and its culture to see whether the story they have been living out may actually be leading to their dying out. Corporate cultures, however, may come by such knowledge more quickly with the rapid feedback provided by the marketplace. That feedback may carry with it possible correctives to prevent the company's story from having reached its final chapter. Thus, at the height of the Tylenol crisis, Burke told a press conference:

> We consider it a moral imperative, as well as good business, to restore Tylenol to its preeminent position in the marketplace. It is ironic that the job of rebuilding Tylenol is made more difficult because we all . . . did our job of informing and protecting the nation so efficiently. In the final analysis, we believe that the American consumer . . . will make an eminently fair decision about the future of Tylenol.[58]

Burke had faith that J&J's willingness to continue to live out its traditional story line would be matched by the marketplace's willingness to let the company live on. J&J's willingness to act on that article of faith was what made its Credo credible.

Consequently, to dismiss business ethics such as J&J's as "*merely* utilitarian" is unwarranted. When executives like Burke "bet the company," they take nothing

56. Phillips and Kennedy, "Shaping and Managing Shared Values," 5.
57. Peters and Waterman, *In Search of Excellence,* 292–93, and McKinsey and Co. research.
58. Raymond with Lipton, "Tylenol," 10.

less than a risk of faith. In that regard, faith such as theirs may well resemble that of some religious communities during times of persecution, as reflected, for example, by this teaching from Jewish tradition: "At a time of persecution when . . . decrees are issued against Israel aimed at abolishing their religious practice . . . , then let [a Jew] suffer death and not breach even one of . . . the commandments."[59]

Jewish tradition here makes sense precisely to the extent that there is a truly steadfast King of Kings to come to Israel's rescue before the life of the last Jewish man or woman is given up. If Jews act on this teaching, and the whole Jewish people subsequently perishes, then though the teaching may have been foolish, it will most assuredly *not* have been utilitarian. And the same could have been said about the Credo's teaching had J&J perished during the Tylenol crisis.

And yet, for all the virtues and all the faith that a company like Johnson & Johnson has shown, the virtues and the faith displayed, though in certain key ways religious, are in no way *biblical.*[60] For neither their "structurings of reality" nor their ultimate concerns are finally unified with the One, who according to the Bible's story has made all of life *one corpus,* sustained it, and, for Christians at least, redeemed it. In contrast, for many contemporary corporate communities, the horizons of their moral vision typically extend no farther than the boundaries of their market. By comparison, a community whose vision has been expanded by the lenses provided by biblical narrative may be able to see *the world as a corporate whole* with the blessing of life offered as a common good above any individual partial goods.

Yet modern corporations tussling in the marketplace have no goods to offer but partial — and often conflicting — ones. In the pursuit of such limited goods, companies may ask unlimited commitment from their employees; indeed, it may be precisely the most conscientious companies that ask for the most commitment, whether an Edison-like dedication to round-the-clock inventing or a Credo-like fidelity to putting one's customers above all else. And yet, such commitment, even in the best of contemporary corporate communities and even with all the attendant piety, still falls short of being single-minded, wholehearted devotion to God.

One last reference to Johnson & Johnson may prove illuminative. During one of the company's periodic reviews of its Credo, Burke wanted to include an explicit reference and commitment to God. Others in the company, however, talked him out of it, warning against the possibility of a consumer backlash, and the idea was dropped. Burke and J&J, it would seem, made their choice of Mammon over God. Hence, whatever practices commitments such as J&J's may engender, those whose corporate vision has been shaped by biblical narrative —

59. Maimonides, Mishneh Torah, Hilchot Yesodei HaTorah 5:3.

60. A failure to see this difference can result in the kind of business apologia written by Michael Novak; see his *Toward a Theology of the Corporation* (Washington, D.C.: American Enterprise Institute, 1981), and *The Spirit of Democratic Capitalism* (New York: Simon and Schuster, 1982).

Jews, Christians, Muslims — may recognize such practices by another name: idolatry.

At present, such a biblical vision may be particularly difficult to attain, not merely because the biblical notion of idolatry seems so hopelessly anachronistic, but more fundamentally because the very corporations engaged in idol worship appear in many other ways to be so virtuous, so admirable, so noble. But, after all, that is the way it is with *noble pagans.* For them, religious practice does not consist of child sacrifice, nor do their values find expression in drunken orgies. Instead, virtue for such noble ones as these lies in a kind of honorable polytheism; that is, in paying due homage to the many gods, the many powers, and the many roles at work in the agora and the forum.

Thus, as America's corporate communities move into the first century of the next millennium, they may well carry with them religious values reminiscent of the first century of the first millennium. Those values, of course, stem from a story that in fundamental ways differs from one called biblical. Consequently, no matter the millennium, no matter the community, the bottom-line issue remains the same: In which story and in which values ought we to invest our lives?

Suggestions for Further Reading

Berry, Wendell. "Economy and Pleasure." In *What Are People For?* 129–44. New York: North Point Press, 1990.

———. *Sex, Economy, Freedom, and Community.* New York: Pantheon Books, 1993.

———. "Two Economies." In *On Moral Business: Classical and Contemporary Resources for Ethics in Economic Life,* ed. Max L. Stackhouse et al., 827–36. Grand Rapids, Mich.: Wm. B. Eerdmans, 1995.

May, William F. "The Virtues of the Business Leader." In *On Moral Business: Classical and Contemporary Resources for Ethics in Economic Life,* ed. Max L. Stackhouse et al., 692–700. Grand Rapids, Mich.: Wm. B. Eerdmans, 1995.

Chapter 15

Images of the Healer

William F. May

Editor's Introduction

In this essay on medical ethics, William F. May distinguishes a code (which governs practitioners' style of performance and technique, with little or no regard to ongoing personal relations) from a covenant (which focuses on the ongoing relationship and mutual obligation between covenant partners). Modern medical practice has opted for code as the ruling ideal in relation to patients. However, the Hippocratic oath contains two sets of obligations: not only to patients but also to benefactors who provided for the physician's training, the benefactors' progeny, and the physician's own students. These are covenant relations in that they are historically particular and involve an element of gratuitousness. May argues that relations with patients could better be conceived in covenantal terms, recognizing that the physician owes a debt of gratitude to society as a whole for education and for public support of the practice of medicine.

The ideal of a covenant relation is also preferable to that of a contract, since the latter notion also suppresses the element of gift in human relations. However, the proper balance between duty and gift cannot be struck in a covenantal relation without reference to the original use of the term to describe the relationship between God and Israel. "For the biblical tradition this transcendent was the secret root of every gift between human beings, of which the human order of giving and receiving could only be a sign."

Although May's essay (first published in the *Hastings Center Report* in 1975) predates the publication of MacIntyre's *After Virtue,* the language MacIntyre develops there can usefully be employed to redescribe May's arguments. Medicine is a practice; as such there must be rules setting boundaries within which the practice is possible (contracts), and technical skill (governed by codes) will be an important virtue. However, attention to these rules and techniques is not sufficient for the flourishing of the practice. There is a virtue — the mean between a condescending philanthropy and a tit-for-tat orientation — that needs for its cultivation an awareness of how the practice of medicine fits into the physician's own life story (a sense of her or his indebtedness to teachers and to society as a whole). But even more important for the development of this virtue is situating the physician's life and the practice of medicine itself within the story of God and God's gratuitous blessings of life, well-being, and forgiveness.

NANCEY MURPHY

Code, Covenant, Contract, or Philanthropy

Questions in medical ethics cannot be resolved apart from the professional matrix in which most decisions are made. What is the nature of the relationship between physicians and their patients? How best can we conceptualize professional ethics and understand its binding power? The times press these questions, while tradition offers us several starting points, alternative ways of interpreting professional obligations: the concepts of code and covenant, and the allied notions of philanthropy and contract.

The Hippocratic oath, as Ludwig Edelstein notes in his unsurpassed study of that document,[1] contains two distinct sets of obligations — those that pertain to the doctor's treatment of his patients and those that are owed his teacher and his teacher's progeny. Edelstein characterizes the first set of obligations, those owed patients, as an ethical code and the second set, those toward the professional guild, as a covenant.

This distinction between code and covenant is extremely revealing and useful. Code itself, furthermore, may be divided into the unwritten codes of practical behavior, transmitted chiefly in a clinical setting from generation to generation of physicians, and into the written codes, beginning with the Hippocratic oath and concluding with the various revisions of the American Medical Association (AMA) codes that have had wide currency in this country. Technical proficiency is the prized ideal in the unwritten and informal codes of behavior passed on from doctor to doctor; the ideal of philanthropy (that is, the notion of gratuitous service to humankind) looms large in the more official engraved tablets of the profession. Then, the notion of covenant stands in contrast not only with the ideals of technical proficiency and philanthropy but also with the legal instrument of a contract to which, at first glance, a covenant seems so similar. With these distinctions, then, let us begin.

The Hippocratic Oath

As elaborated in the Hippocratic oath, the duties of physicians toward their patients include a series of absolute prohibitions: against performing surgery, against assisting patients in attempts at suicide or abortion, against breaches in confidentiality, and against acts of injustice or mischief toward the patient and their patient's household, including sexual misconduct. More positively, the

1. Ludwig Edelstein, *Ancient Medicine* (Baltimore: Johns Hopkins University Press, 1967).

physician must act always for the benefit of the sick — the chief illustration of which is to apply dietetic measures according to the physician's best judgment and ability — and, more generally, to keep them from harm and injustice. These various professional obligations to the patient have a religious reference, as the physician declares, "In purity and holiness I will guard my life and art," and petitions, "If I fulfill this oath and do not violate it, may it be granted to me to enjoy life and art . . . ; if I transgress it and swear falsely, may the opposite of all this be my lot."

The second set of obligations, directed to the physician's teacher, his teacher's children, and his own children, require him to accept full filial responsibilities for his adopted father's personal and financial welfare and to transmit without fee his art and knowledge to the teacher's progeny, to his own, and to other pupils, but only those others who take the oath according to medical law.

It is the contention of this essay that the development of the practice of modern medicine, for understandable reasons, has tended to reinforce the ancient distinction between these two obligations, that is, between code and covenant; and that it has opted for code as the ruling ideal in relations to patients. The choice has not had altogether favorable consequences for the moral health of the profession.

The Characteristics of a Code

For the purposes of this essay, it can be said, a code shapes human behavior in a fashion somewhat similar to habits and rules. A habit, as Peter Winch has pointed out,[2] is a matter of doing the same thing on the same kind of occasion in the same way. A moral rule is distinct from a habit in that the agent in this instance *understands what is meant* by doing the same thing on the same kind of occasion in the same way. Both habits and rules are categorical, universal, and to this degree ahistorical: they do not receive their authority from particular events by which they are authorized or legitimated. They remain operative categorically on all similar occasions: *never* assist patients in attempts at suicide or abortion; never break a confidence except under certain specified circumstances.

A code is usually categorical and universal in the aforementioned senses, but not in the sense that it is binding on any and all groups. Hammurabi's code is obligatory only for particular peoples. Moreover, inner circles within certain societies — whether professional or social groups — develop their special codes of behavior. We think of code words or special behaviors among friends, workers in the same company, or professionals within a guild. These codes offer directives not only for the content of action but also for its form. In its concern with appropriate form, a code moves in the direction of the aesthetic. It is concerned not only with what is done but with how it is done; it touches on matters of

2. Peter Winch, *The Idea of a Social Science and Its Relation to Philosophy* (New York: Humanities Press, 1958).

style and decorum. Thus medical codes include directives not only on the content of therapeutic action but also on the fitting style for professional behavior including such matters as suitable dress, discretion in the household, appropriate behavior in the hospital, and prohibitions on self-advertisement.

This tendency to move ethics in the direction of aesthetics is best illustrated in the work of the modern novelist most associated with the ideal of a code. The ritual killing of a bull in the short stories and novels of Ernest Hemingway symbolizes an ethic in which stylish performance is everything.

> ...the bull charged and Villalta charged and just for a moment they became one. Villalta became one with the bull and then it was over. (Hemingway, *In Our Time)*

For the Hemingway hero, there is no question of permanent commitments to particular persons, causes, or places. Robert Jordan of *For Whom the Bell Tolls* does not even remember the "cause" for which he came to Spain to fight. Once he is absorbed in the ordeal of war, the test of a man is not a cause to which he is committed but his conduct from moment to moment. Life is a matter of eating, drinking, loving, hunting, and dying well. Hemingway writes about lovers but rarely about marriage or the family. Catherine in *A Farewell to Arms* and Robert Jordan in *For Whom the Bell Tolls* inevitably must die. Just for a moment, lovers become one and then it is over.

The bullfighter, the wartime lover, the doctor — all alike — must live by a code that eschews involvement; for each there comes a time when the thing is over; matters are terminated by death. But this does not mean that one cannot live beautifully, stylishly, fittingly. Discipline is all. There is a right and a wrong way to do things. And the wrong way usually results from a deficiency in technique or from an excessive preoccupation with one's ego. The bad bullfighter either lacks technique or lets his ego — through fear or vanity — get in the way of his performance. The conditions of beauty are technical proficiency and a style wholly purified of disruptive preoccupation with oneself. Literally, however, when the critical moment is consummated, it is over; it cannot shape the future. Partners must fall away; only the code remains.

For several reasons, the medical profession has been attracted to the ideal of code for its interpretation of its ethics. First, a code requires one to subordinate the ego to the more technical question of how a thing is done and done well. At its best, the discipline of a code has an aesthetic value. It encourages a proficiency that is quietly eloquent. It conjoins the good with the beautiful. Since the technical demands of medicine have become so great, the standards of the guild are transmitted largely by apprenticeship to those whose preeminent skills define the real meaning of the profession without significant remainder. All the rest is a question of disciplining the ego to the point that nervousness, fatigue, faintheartedness, and temptations to self-display (including gross efforts at self-advertisement) have been smoothed away.

A code is additionally attractive in that it does not, in and of itself, encourage personal involvement with the patient; and it helps free the physician of the destructive consequences of that personal involvement. Compassion, in the strictest sense of the term — "suffering with" — has its disadvantages in the professional relationship. It will not do to pretend that one is the second person of the Trinity, prepared to make with every patient the sympathetic descent into her suffering, pain, particular form of crucifixion, and hell. It is enough to offer whatever help one can through finely honed services. It is important to remain emotionally free so as to be able to withdraw the self when those services are no longer pertinent, when as Hemingway says, "it is over."

Finally, a code provides the modern doctor with a basic style of operation that shapes not only her professional but her free time, not only her vocation but her avocations. The selfsame pleasure she derives from proficiency in her professional life, she transposes now to her recreational life — flying, skiing, traveling, or sailing. Since her obligations have placed her daily in the precincts of suffering and death, she learns that life is available only from moment to moment. As a hard-pressed professional, she knows that both her life and free time are limited — like the soldier's furlough. It makes sense to live by a code that operates from moment to moment, savoring pleasure in stylish action. Thus her code not only frees her from some of the awkwardness and distress that sentient beings are prey to in the midst of agony; but, when she is momentarily free of the battle, it provides her with a style and allows her to live, like most warriors who have tasted death, by the canons of hedonism, which money places specially within her reach.

The Ideal of a Covenant

A covenant, as opposed to a code, has its roots in specific historical events. Like a code, it may give inclusive shape to subsequent behavior, but it always has reference to specific historical exchange between partners leading to a promissory event. Edelstein is quite right in distinguishing code from covenant in the Hippocratic oath. Rules governing behavior toward patients have a different ring to them from that fealty which a physician owes to his teacher. Loyalty to one's instructor is founded in a specific historical event — that original transaction in which the student received his knowledge and art. He accepts, in effect, a specific gift from his teacher which deserves his lifelong loyalty, a gift that he perpetuates in his own right and turn as he offers his art without fee to his teacher's children and to his own progeny. Covenant ethics is responsive in character.

In its ancient and most influential form, a covenant usually included the following elements: (1) an original experience of gift between the soon-to-be covenanted partners; (2) a covenant promise based on this original or anticipated exchange of gifts, labors, or services; and (3) the shaping of subsequent life for each partner by the promissory event. The Scriptures of ancient Israel are littered with such covenants between people and controlled throughout by that singular covenant which embraces all others. The covenant between God and Israel includes the aforementioned elements: (1) a gift — the deliverance of the people from Egypt; (2) an exchange of promises — at Mount Sinai; and (3) the shaping of all subsequent life by the promissory event. God "marks the forehead" of the Jews forever, as they respond by accepting an inclusive set of ritual and moral commandments by which they will live. These commands are both specific enough (for example, the dietary laws) to make the future duties of Israel concrete, yet summary enough (for example, love the Lord thy God with all thy heart . . .) to require a fidelity that exceeds any specification.

The most striking contemporary restatement of an ethic based on covenant is offered by Hemingway's great competitor and contemporary as a novelist — William Faulkner. While the Hemingway hero lives from moment to moment, Faulkner's characters take their bearings from a covenant event. Like Hemingway, Faulkner also writes about a ritual slaying, but with a difference. In "Delta Autumn," a young boy, Isaac McCaslin, "comes of age" in the course of a hunt:

> And the gun levelled rapidly without haste and crashed and he walked to the buck still intact and still in the shape of that magnificent speed and bled it with Sam Father's knife and Sam dipped his hands in the hot blood and marked his face forever. . . . (Faulkner, "Delta Autumn")

The Hemingway hero slays his bull and then it is over; but young Isaac McCaslin binds the whole of his future in the instant.

> I slew you; my bearing must not shame your quitting of life. My conduct forever onward must become your death.

From then on, just as the marked Jew, the errant, harassed, and estranged Jew, recovers the covenant of Mt. Sinai through ritual renewal, Isaac returns to the delta every autumn to renew the hunt and to suffer his own renewal despite the alienation and pain and defeat which he has subsequently known across a lifetime. This covenant moreover looms over all else — his relationship to the land, to women, to blacks, to all of which and whom he is bound.

For some of the reasons already mentioned, the bond of covenant, in the classical period, tended to define and bind together medical colleagues to one another, but it did not figure large in interpreting the relations between the doctor and his patients. The doctor receives his professional life from his teacher; this gift establishes a bond between them and prompts him to assume certain lifetime duties not only toward the teacher (and his financial welfare) but toward his children. This symbolic bond with one's teacher acknowledged in the Hippocratic oath is strengthened in modern professional life by all those exchanges between colleagues — referrals, favors, personal confidences, and collaborative work on cases. Thus loyalty to colleagues is a responsive act for gifts already, and to be, received.

Duties to patients are not similarly interpreted in the medical codes as a responsive act for gifts or services received. This is the essential feature of covenant that is conspicuously missing in the interpretation of professional duties from the Hippocratic oath to the modern codes of the AMA.

The Code Ideal of Philanthropy vs. Covenantal Indebtedness

The medical profession includes in its written codes an ideal that Hemingway never shared and that seldom looms large in the ethic of any self-selected inner group — the ideal of philanthropy. The medical profession proclaims its dedication to the service of humankind. This ideal is implicitly at work in the Hippocratic oath and the culture out of which it emerged;[3] it continues in the Code of Medical Ethics originally adopted by the American Medical Association at its national convention in 1847, and it is elaborated in contemporary statements of that code.

This ideal of service, in my judgment, succumbs to what might be called the conceit of philanthropy when it is assumed that the professional's commitment to others is a gratuitous, rather than a responsive or reciprocal, act. Statements of medical ethics that obscure the doctor's prior indebtedness to the community are tainted with the odor of condescension. The point is obvious if one contrasts the way in which the code of 1847 interprets the obligations of patients and the public to the physician, as opposed to the obligations of the physician to the patient and the public. On this particular question, I see no fundamental change from 1847 to 1957.

Clearly the duties of patients are founded on what they have received from the doctor:

> The members of the medical profession, upon whom is enjoined the performance of so many important and arduous duties toward the community, and who are required to make so many sacrifices of comfort, ease, and health, for the welfare of those who avail themselves of their services, certainly have a right to expect a just sense of the duties which they owe to their medical attendants.[4]

In like manner, the section on the obligations of the public to physicians emphasizes those many gifts and services which the public has received from the medical profession and which are the basis for its indebtedness to the profession.

> The benefits accruing to the public, directly and indirectly, from the active and unwearied beneficence of the profession, are so numerous and important, that physicians are justly entitled to the utmost consideration and respect from the community.[5]

But turning to the preamble for the physician's duties to the patient and the public, we find no corresponding section in the code of 1847 (or 1957) which founds the doctor's obligations on those gifts and services that she has received from the community. Thus we are presented with the picture of a relatively

3. See P. Lain Entralgo, *Doctor and Patient* (New York: McGraw-Hill, 1969), for his analysis of the classic fusion of *techne* with *philanthropia;* skill in the art of healing combined with a love of humankind defines the good physician.

4. Chapter 1, Article 2, "Obligations of Patients to Their Physicians," *Code of Medical Ethics,* American Medical Association, May 1847 (Chicago: A.M.A. Press, 1897).

5. Ibid., Chapter 3, Article 2.

self-sufficient monad, who, out of the nobility and generosity of her disposition and the gratuitously accepted conscience of her profession, has taken upon herself the noble life of service. The false posture in all this cries out in one of the opening sections of the 1847 code. Physicians "should study, also, in their deportment so as to unite tenderness with firmness, and condescension with authority, so as to inspire the minds of their patients with gratitude, respect and confidence."

I do not intend to demean the specific content of those duties which the codes set forth in their statement of the duties of physicians to their patients, but I am critical of the setting or context in which they are placed. Significantly the code refers to the *Duties* of physicians to their patients but to the *Obligations* of patients to their physicians. The shift from "duties" to "obligations" may seem slight, but, in fact, I believe it is a revealing adjustment in language. The AMA thought of the patient and public as *indebted* to the profession for its services, but the profession has accepted its *duties* to the patients and public out of noble conscience rather than a reciprocal sense of indebtedness.

Put another way, the medical profession imitates God not so much because it exercises power of life and death over others but because it does not really think itself beholden, even partially, to anyone for those duties to patients which it lays upon itself. Like God, the profession draws its life from itself alone. Its action is wholly gratuitous.

Now, in fact, the physician is in very considerable debt to the community. The first of these debts is already adumbrated in the original Hippocratic oath. He is obliged to someone or some group for his education. In ancient times, this led to a special sense of covenant obligation to one's teacher. Under the conditions of modern medical education, this indebtedness is both substantial (far exceeding the social investment in the training of any other professional) and widely distributed (including not only one's teachers but those public monies on the basis of which the medical school, the teaching hospital, and research into disease are funded).

In view of the fact that many more qualified candidates apply for medical school than can be admitted and many more doctors are needed than the schools can train, the doctor-to-be has a second order of indebtedness for privileges that have almost arbitrarily fallen her way. While the 1847 code refers to the "privileges" of being a doctor, it does not specify the social origins of those privileges. Third, and not surprisingly, the codes do not make reference to that extraordinary social largesse that befalls the physician, in payment for services, in a society where need abounds and available personnel is limited. Further, the codes do not concede the indebtedness of the physician to those patients who have offered themselves as subjects for experimentation or as teaching material (either in teaching hospitals or in the early years of practice). Early practice includes, after all, the element of increased risk for patients who lay their bodies on the line as the doctor "practices" on them. The pun in the word but reflects the inevitable social price of training. This indebtedness to the patient was most recently and eloquently acknowledged by Judah Folkman, M.D., of Harvard Medical School in a Class Day Address.

> In the long run, it is better if we come to terms with the uncertainty of medical practice. Once we recognize that all our efforts to relieve suffering might on occasion cause suffering, we are in a position to learn from our mistakes and appreciate the debt we owe our patients for our education. It is a debt which we must repay—it is like tithing.
>
> I doubt that the debt we accumulate can be repaid our patients by trying to reduce the practice of medicine to a forty-hour week or by dissolving the quality of our residency programs just because certain groups of residents in the country have refused, through legal tactics, to be on duty more than every fourth or fifth night or any nights at all.
>
> And it can't be repaid by refusing to see Medicaid patients when the state can't afford to pay for them temporarily.
>
> But we can repay the debt in many ways. We can attend postgraduate courses and seminars, be available to patients at all hours, teach, take recertification examinations; maybe in the future even volunteer for national service, or, most difficult of all, carry out investigation or research.[6]

The physician, finally, is indebted to his patients not only for a start in his career. He remains unceasingly in their debt in its full course. This continuing reciprocity of need is somewhat obscured, for we think of the mature professional as powerful and authoritative rather than needy. He seems to be a self-sufficient virtuoso whose life is derived from his competence while others appear before him in their neediness, exposing their illness, their crimes, or their ignorance, for which the professional—doctor, lawyer, or teacher—offers remedy.

In fact, however, a reciprocity of giving and receiving is at work in the professional relationship that needs to be acknowledged. In the profession of teaching, for example, the student needs the teacher to assist her in learning, but so also the professor needs her students. They provide her with regular occasion and forum in which to work out what she has to say and to rediscover her subject afresh through the discipline of sharing it with others. Likewise, the doctor needs her patients. No one can watch a physician nervously approach retirement without realizing how much she has needed her patients to be herself.

A covenantal ethics helps acknowledge this full context of need and indebtedness in which professional duties are undertaken and discharged. It also relieves the professional of the temptation and pressure to pretend that he is a demigod exempt from human exigency.

Contract or Covenant

While criticizing the ideal of philanthropy, I have emphasized the elements of exchange, agreement, and reciprocity that mark the professional relationship.

6. *New York Times,* editorial and comment, 6 June 1975.

This leaves us with the question whether the element of the gratuitous should be suppressed altogether in professional ethics. Does the physician merely respond to the social investment in his training, the fees paid for his services, and the terms of an agreement drawn up between himself and his patients, or does some element of the gratuitous remain?

To put this question another way: is covenant simply another name for a contract in which two parties calculate their own best interests and agree upon some joint project in which both derive roughly equivalent benefits for goods contributed by each? If so, this essay would appear to move in the direction of those who interpret the doctor-patient relationship as a legal agreement and who want, on the whole, to see medical ethics draw closer to medical law.

The notion of the physician as contractor has certain obvious attractions. First, it represents a deliberate break with more authoritarian models (such as priest or parent) for interpreting the role. At the heart of a contract is informed consent rather than blind trust; a contractual understanding of the therapeutic relationship encourages full respect for the dignity of the patient, who has not, through illness, forfeited his sovereignty as a human being. The notion of a contract includes an exchange of information on the basis of which an agreement is reached and a subsequent exchange of goods (money for services); it also allows for a specification of rights, duties, conditions, and qualifications limiting the agreement. The net effect is to establish some symmetry and mutuality in the relationship between the doctor and patient.

Second, a contract provides for the legal enforcement of its terms — on both parties — and thus offers both parties some protection and recourse under the law for making the other accountable for the agreement.

Finally, a contract does not rely on the pose of philanthropy, the condescension of charity. It presupposes that people are primarily governed by self-interest. When two people enter into a contract, they do so because each sees it to his own advantage. This is true not only of private contracts but also of that primordial social contract in and through which the state came into being. So argued the theorists of the eighteenth century. The state was not established by some heroic act of sacrifice on the part of the gods or people. Rather people entered into the social contract because each found it to her individual advantage. It is better to surrender some liberty and property to the state than to suffer the evils that would befall except for its protection. Subsequent enthusiasts about the social instrument of contracts[7] have tended to measure human progress by the degree to which a society is based on contracts rather than status. In the ancient world, the Romans made the most striking advances in extending the areas in which contract rather than custom determined commerce between people. In the modern world, the bourgeoisie extended the instrumentality of contracts farthest into the sphere of economics; the free churches, into the arena of religion. Some educationists today have extended the device into the classroom (as

7. Sir Henry Sumner Maine, *Ancient Law* (London: Oxford University Press, 1931).

students are encouraged to contract units of work for levels of grade); more recently some women's liberationists would extend it into marriage; and still others would prefer to see it define the professional relationship. The movement, on the whole, has the intention of laicizing authority, legalizing relationships, activating self-interest, and encouraging collaboration.

In my judgment, some of these aims of the contractualists are desirable, but it would be unfortunate if professional ethics were reduced to a commercial contract without significant remainder. First, the notion of contract suppresses the element of gift in human relationships. Earlier I verged on denying the importance of this ingredient in professional relations, when I criticized the medical profession for its conceit of philanthropy, for its self-interpretation as the great giver. In fact, this earlier objection should be limited to the failure of the medical profession to acknowledge those gifts and goods it has itself received. It is unbecoming to adopt the pose of spontaneous generosity when the profession has received so much from the community and from patients, past and present.

But the contractualist approach to professional behavior falls into the opposite error of minimalism. It reduces everything to tit for tat: do no more for your patients than what the contract calls for; perform specified services for certain fees and no more. The commercial contract is fitting instrument in the purchase of an appliance, a house, or certain services that can be specified fully in advance of delivery. The existence of a legally enforceable agreement in professional transactions may also be useful to protect the patient or client against the physician or lawyer whose services fall below a minimal standard. But it would be wrong to reduce professional obligation to the specifics of a contract alone.

Professional services in the so-called helping professions are directed to subjects who are in the nature of the case rather unpredictable. One deals with the sickness, ills, crimes, needs, and tragedies of humankind. These needs cannot be exhaustively specified in advance for each patient or client. The professions must be ready to cope with the contingent, the unexpected. Calls upon services may be required that exceed those anticipated in a contract or for which compensation may be available in a given case. These services, moreover, are more likely to be effective in achieving the desired therapeutic result if they are delivered in the context of a fiduciary relationship that the patient or client can really trust.

The Limitations of Contract

Contract and covenant, materially considered, seem like first cousins; they both include an exchange and an agreement between parties. But, in spirit, contract and covenant are quite different. Contracts are external; covenants are internal to the parties involved. Contracts are signed to be expediently discharged. Covenants have a gratuitous, growing edge to them that nourishes rather than limits relationships. To the best of my knowledge, no one has put quite so effectively the difference between the two as the novelist already cited in the earlier discussion of covenant.

At the outset of Faulkner's *Intruder in the Dust,* a white boy, hunting with young blacks, falls into a creek on a cold winter's day. After the boy clambers out of the river, Lucas Beauchamp, a proud, commanding black man, brings him, shivering, to his house, where Mrs. Beauchamp takes care of him. She takes off his wet clothes and wraps him in Negro blankets, feeds him Negro food, and warms him by the fire.

When his clothes dry off, the boy dresses to go, but, uneasy about his debt to the other, he reaches into his pocket for some coins and offers seventy cents compensation for Beauchamp's help. Lucas rejects the money firmly and commands the two black boys to pick up the coins from the floor where they have fallen and return them to the white boy.

Shortly thereafter, still uneasy about the episode at the river and his frustrated effort to pay off Lucas for his help, the boy buys some imitation silk for Lucas's wife and gets his Negro friend to deliver it. But a few days later, the white boy goes to his own backdoor stoop only to find a jug of molasses left there for him by Lucas. So he is back where he started, beholden to the black man again.

Several months later, the boy passes Lucas on the street and scans his face closely, wondering if the black man remembers the incident between them. He can't be sure. Four years pass, and Lucas is accused of murdering a white man. He is scheduled to be taken to the jail. The boy goes early before the crowd gathers and ponders whether the old man remembers their past encounter. Just as Lucas is about to enter the jailhouse, he wheels and points his long arm in the direction of the boy and says, "Boy, I want to see you." The boy obeys and visits Lucas in the jailhouse, and eventually he and his aunt are instrumental in proving Lucas's innocence.

Faulkner's story is a parable for the relationship of the white man to the black in the South. The black man has labored in the white man's fields, built and cared for his houses, fed, clothed, and nurtured his children. In accepting these labors, the white man has received his life and substance from the black man over and over again. But he resists this involvement and tries to pay off the black with a few coins. He pretends that their relationship is transient and external, to be managed at arm's length.

For better or for worse, blacks and whites in this country are bound up in a common life and destiny together. The problem between them will not be resolved until they accept the covenant between them which is entailed in the original acceptance of labor.

There is a donative element in the nourishing of covenant — whether it is the covenant of marriage, friendship, or professional relationship. Tit for tat characterizes a commercial transaction, but it does not exhaustively define the vitality of that relationship in which one must serve and draw upon the deeper reserves of another.

This donative element is important not only in the doctor's care of the patient but in other aspects of health care. In his fascinating study *The Gift Relationship,* the late Richard M. Titmuss compares the British system of obtaining blood by donations with the American partial reliance on the commercial purchase and sale of blood.[8] The British system obtains more and better blood, without the exploitation of the indigent, which the American system has condoned and which our courts have encouraged when they refused to exempt nonprofit blood banks from the antitrust laws. By court definition, blood exchange becomes a commercial transaction in the United States. Titmuss expanded his theme from human blood to social policy by offering a sober criticism of the increased commercialism of American medicine and society at large. Recent court decisions have tended to shift more and more of what had previously been considered services into the category of commodity transactions, with negative consequences he believes for the health of health delivery systems.[9] Hans Jonas has had to reckon with the importance of voluntary sacrifice to the social order in a somewhat comparable essay titled "Human Experimentation." Others have done so on the subject of organ transplants.

The kind of minimalism encouraged by a contractualist understanding of the professional relationship produces a professional too grudging, too calculating, too lacking in spontaneity, too quickly exhausted to go the second mile with his patients along the road of their distress.

Not only does contract medicine encourage minimalism, it also provokes a peculiar kind of maximalism, the name for which is "defensive medicine." Especially under the pressure of malpractice suits, doctors are tempted, for reasons of self-protection, to order too many examinations and procedures. Paradoxically, contractualism simultaneously tempts the doctor to do too little and too much for the patient: too little in that one extends oneself only to the limits of what is specified in the contract; yet, at the same time, too much in that one orders procedures useful in protecting oneself as the contractor even though they are not fully indicated by the condition of the patient. The link between these apparently contradictory strategies of too little and too much is the emphasis in contractual decisions grounded in self-interest.

Three concluding objections to contractualism can be stated summarily. Parties to a contract are better able to protect their self-interest insofar as they are informed about the goods bought and sold. Insofar as contract medicine encourages increased knowledge on the part of the patient, well and good. Nevertheless the physician's knowledge so exceeds that of the patient that the patient's knowledgeability alone is not a satisfactory constraint on the physician's behavior. One must, at least in part, depend upon some internal fiduciary checks which the professional and the guild take on.

Another self-regulating mechanism in the traditional contractual relationship is the consumer's freedom to shop and choose among various vendors of services. Certainly this freedom of choice needs to be expanded for the patient by an

---

8. Richard M. Titmuss, *The Gift Relationship: From Human Blood to Social Policy* (New York: Pantheon, 1971).

9. Titmuss does not observe that physicians in the United States had already prepared for this commercialization of medicine by their substantial fees for services (as opposed to salaried professors in the teaching field or salaried health professionals in other countries).

increase in the number of physicians and paramedical personnel. However, the crisis circumstances under which medical services are often needed and delivered does not always provide the consumer with the kind of leisure or calm required for discretionary judgment. Thus normal marketplace controls cannot be fully relied upon to protect the consumer in dealings with the physician.

For a final reason, medical ethics should not be reduced to the contractual relationship alone. Normally conceived, ethics establishes certain rights and duties that transcend the particulars of a given agreement. The justice of any specific contract may then be measured by these standards. If, however, such rights and duties adhere only to the contract, then a patient might legitimately be persuaded to waive her rights. The contract would solely determine what is required and permissible. An ethical principle should not be waivable (except to give way to a higher ethical principle). Professional ethics should not be so defined as to permit a physician to persuade a patient to waive rights that transcend the particulars of their agreement.

Transcendence and Covenant

This essay has developed two characteristics of covenantal ethics in the course of contrasting it with the ideal of philanthropy and the legal instrument of contracts. As opposed to the ideal of philanthropy that pretends to wholly gratuitous altruism, covenantal ethics places the service of the professional within the full context of goods, gifts, and services received; thus covenantal ethics is responsive. As opposed to the instrument of contract that presupposes agreement reached on the basis of self-interest, covenantal ethics may require one to be available to the covenant partner above and beyond the measure of self-interest; thus covenantal ethics has an element of the gratuitous in it.

We have to reckon now with the potential conflict between these characteristics. Have we developed our notion of covenant too reactively to alternatives without paying attention to the inner consistency of the concept itself? On the one hand, we had cause for suspicion of those idealists who founded professional duties on a philanthropic impulse, without so much as acknowledging the sacrifice of others by which their own lives have been nourished. Then we had reasons for drawing back from those legal realists and positivists who would circumscribe professional life entirely within the calculus of commodities bought and sold. But now, brought face to face, these characteristics conflict. Response to debt and gratuitous service seem opposed principles of action.

Perhaps our difficulty results from the fact that we have abstracted the concept of covenant from its original context within the transcendent. The indebtedness of a human being that makes his life — however sacrificial — inescapably responsive cannot be fully appreciated by totaling up the varying sacrifices and investments made by others in his favor. Such sacrifices are there; and it is lacking in honesty not to acknowledge them. But the sense that one is inexhaustibly the object of gift presupposes a more transcendent source of donative activity than the sum of gifts received from others. For the biblical tradition this transcendent was the secret root of every gift between human beings, of which the human order of giving and receiving could only be a sign. Thus the Jewish Scriptures enjoin: when you harvest your crops, do not pick your fields too clean. Leave something for the sojourner, for you were once sojourners in Egypt. Farmers obedient to this injunction were responsive but not simply mathematically responsive to gifts received from the Egyptians or from strangers now drifting through their own land. At the same time, their actions could not be construed as wholly gratuitous. Their ethic of service to the needy flowed from Israel's original and continuing state of neediness and indebtedness before God. Thus action which at a human level appears gratuitous, in that it is not provoked by a specific gratuity from another human being, is at its deepest level but gift answering to gift. This responsivity is theologically expressed in the New Testament as follows: "In this is love, not that we loved God, but that he loved us.... since God loved us so much, we also ought to love one another" (1 John 4:10–11). In some such way, covenant ethics shies back from the idealist assumption that professional action is and ought to be wholly gratuitous, and from the contractualist assumption that it be carefully governed by quotidian self-interest in every exchange.

A transcendent reference may also be important not only in setting forth the proper context in which human service takes place but also in laying out the specific standards by which it is measured. Earlier we noted some dangers in reducing rights and duties to the terms of a particular contract. We observed the need for a transcendent norm by which contracts are measured (and limited). By the same token, rights and duties cannot be wholly derived from the particulars of a given covenant. What limits ought to be placed on the demands of an excessively dependent patient? At what point does the keeping of one covenant do an injustice to obligations entailed in others? These are questions that warn against a covenantal ethics that sentimentalizes any and all involvements, without reference to a transcendent by which they are both justified and measured.

Further Reflections on Covenant

So far we have discussed those features of a covenant that affect the doctor's conduct toward his patient. The concept of covenant has further consequences for the patient's self-interpretation, for the accountability of health institutions, for the placement of institutional priorities within other national commitments, and, finally, for such collateral problems as truth-telling.

Every model for the doctor-patient relationship establishes not only a certain image of the doctor but also a specific concept of the self. The image of the doctor as priest or parent encourages dependency in the patient. The image of the doctor as skillful technician prompts the patient to think less in terms of his personal dependence, but still it encourages a somewhat impersonal passivity, with the doctor and her technical procedures the only serious agent in the relationship. The image of the doctor as covenantor or contractor bids the patient to become a more active participant in both the prevention and the healing of the disease. He must bring to the partnership a will to life and a will to health.

Differing views of disease are involved in these differing patterns of relationship to the doctor. Disease today is usually interpreted by the layperson as an extra-ordinary state, discrete and episodic, disjunct from the ordinary condition of health. Illness is a special time when the doctor is in charge and the layperson renounces authority over his life. This view, while psychologically understandable, ignores the growth during apparent periods of health of those pathological conditions that invite the dramatic breakdown when the doctor "takes over."

The cardiovascular accident is a case in point. Horacio Fabrega[10] has urged an interpretation of disease and health that respects more fully the processive rather than episodic character of both disease and health. This interpretation, I assume, would encourage the doctor to monitor more continuously health and disease than ordinarily occurs today, to share with the patient more fully the information so obtained, and to engage the layperson in a more active collaboration with the doctor in health maintenance.

The concept of covenant has two further advantages for defining the professional relationship, not enjoyed by models such as parent, friend, or technician. First, covenant is not so restrictively personal a term as parent or friend. It reminds the professional community that it is not good enough for the individual doctor to be a good friend or parent to the patient; that it is important also for whole institutions — the hospital, the clinic, the professional group — to keep covenant with those who seek their assistance and sanctuary. Thus the concept permits a certain broadening of accountability beyond personal agency.

At the same time, however, the notion of covenant also permits one to set professional responsibility for this one human good (health) within social limits. The professional covenant concerning health should be situated within a larger set of covenant obligations that both the doctor and patient have toward other institutions and priorities within the society at large. The traditional models for the doctor-patient relationship (parent, friend) tend to establish an exclusivity of relationship that obscures those larger responsibilities. At a time when health needs command a substantial portion of the national budget, one must think about the place held by the obligation to the limited human good of health among a whole range of social and personal goods for which people are compacted together as a society.

A covenantal ethic has implications for other collateral problems in biomedical ethics, some of which have been explored in the searching work of Paul Ramsey, *The Patient as Person.*[11] I will restrict myself simply to one issue that has not been viewed from the perspective of covenant: the question of truth-telling.

---

10. Horacio Fabrega, Jr., "Concepts of Disease: Logical Features and Social Implications," *Perspectives in Biology and Medicine* 15 (summer 1972).

11. Paul Ramsey, *The Patient as Person: Explorations in Medical Ethics* (New Haven: Yale University Press, 1970).

Key ingredients in the notion of covenant are promise and fidelity to promise. The philosopher J. L. Austin drew the distinction, now famous, between two kinds of speech: descriptive and performative utterances. In ordinary declarative or descriptive sentences, one describes a given item within the world. (It is raining. The tumor is malignant. The crisis is past.) In performative utterances, one does not merely describe a world; in effect, one alters the world by introducing an ingredient that would not be there apart from the utterance. Promises are such performative utterances. (I, John, take thee, Mary. We will defend your country in case of attack. I will not abandon you.) To make or to go back on a promise is a very solemn matter precisely because a promise is world-altering.

In the field of medical ethics, the question of truth-telling has tended to be discussed entirely as a question of descriptive speech. Should the doctor, as technician, tell the patient he has a malignancy or not? If not, may he lie or must he merely withhold the truth?

The distinction between descriptive and performative speech expands the question of the truth in professional life. The doctor, after all, not only tells descriptive truths, he also makes or implies promises. (I will see you next Tuesday; or, Despite the fact that I cannot cure you, I will not abandon you.) In brief, the moral question for the doctor is not simply a question of telling truths but of being true to her promises. Conversely, the total situation for the patient includes not only the disease he's got but also whether others ditch him or stand by him in his extremity. The fidelity of others will not eliminate the disease, but it affects mightily the human context in which the disease runs its course. What the doctor has to offer her patient is not simply proficiency but fidelity.

Perhaps more patients could accept the descriptive truth if they experienced the performative truth. Perhaps also they would be more inclined to believe in the doctor's performative utterances if they were not handed false diagnoses or false promises. That is why a cautiously wise medieval physician once advised his colleagues: "Promise only fidelity!"

The Problem of Discipline

The conclusion of this essay is not that covenantal ethics should be preferred to the exclusion of some of those values best symbolized by code and contract. If we turn now to the problem of professional discipline, we can see that both alternatives have resources for self-criticism.

Those who live by a code of technical proficiency have a standard on the basis of which to discipline their peers. The Hemingway novel, especially *The Sun Also Rises,* is quite clear about this. Those who live by a code know how to ostracize deficient peers. Indeed, any "in-group," professional or otherwise, can be quite ruthless about sorting out those who are "quality" and those who do not have the "goods." Medicine is no exception. Ostracism, in the form of discreetly refusing to refer patients to a doctor whose competence is suspected, is probably the commonest and most effective form of discipline in the profession today.

Defenders of an ethic based on code might argue further that deficiencies in enforcement today result largely from too strongly developed a sense of covenantal obligations to colleagues and too weakly developed a sense of code. From this perspective, then, covenant is the source of the problem in the profession rather than the basis for its amendment. Covenantal obligation to colleagues inhibits the enforcement of code.

A code alone, however, will not in and of itself solve the problem of professional discipline. It provides a basis for excluding from one's own inner circle an incompetent physician. But, as Eliot Freidson has pointed out in *Professional Dominance,*[12] under the present system the incompetent professional, when he is excluded from a given hospital, group practice, or informal circle of referrals, simply moves his practice and finds another circle of people of equal incompetence in which he can function. It will take a much stronger, more active and internal sense of covenant obligation to patients on the part of the profession to enforce standards within the guild beyond local informal patterns of ostracism. In a mobile society with a scarcity of doctors, local ostracism simply hands on problem physicians to other patients elsewhere. It does not address them.

Code patterns of discipline not only fall short of adequate protection for the patient; they may also fail in collegial responsibility to the troubled physician. To ostracize may be the lazy way of handling a colleague when it fails altogether to make a first attempt at remedy and to address the physician himself in his difficulty.

At the same time, it would be unfortunate if the indispensable interest and pride of the medical profession in technical proficiency were allowed to lapse out of an expressed preference for a professional ethic based on covenant. Covenant fidelity to the patient remains unrealized if it does not include proficiency. A rather sentimental existentialism unfortunately assumes that it is enough for human beings to be "present" to one another. But in crisis, the ill person needs not simply presence but skill, not just personal concern but highly disciplined services targeted on specific needs. Code behavior, handed down from doctor to doctor, is largely concerned with the transmission of technical skills. Covenant ethics, then, must include rather than exclude the interests of the codes.

Neither does this essay conclude with a preference for covenant to the total exclusion of the interests of enforceable contract. While the reduction of medical ethics to contract alone incurs the danger of minimalism, patients ought to have recourse against those physicians who fail to meet minimal standards. One ought not to be dependent entirely upon disciplinary measures undertaken within the profession. There ought to be appeal to the law in cases of malpractice and for breach of contract explicit or implied.

On the other hand, in the case of an injustice a legal appeal cannot be sustained without assistance and testimony from physicians who take their obli-

12. Eliot Freidson, *Professional Dominance: The Social Structure of Medical Care* (Chicago: Aldine, 1970).

gations to patients seriously. If, in such cases, fellow physicians simply herd around and protect their colleague like a wounded elephant, the patient with just cause is not likely to get far. Thus the instrument of contract and other avenues of legal redress can be sustained only by a professional sense of obligation to the patient. Needless to say, it would be better for all concerned if professional discipline and continuing education were so vigorously pursued within the profession as to cut down drastically on the number of cases that needed to reach the courts.

The author inclines to accept covenant as the most inclusive and satisfying model for framing questions of professional obligation. Covenant fidelity includes the code obligation to become technically proficient; it reenforces the legal duty to meet the minimal terms of contract; but it also requires much more. This surplus of obligation moreover may redound not only to the benefit of patients but also to the advantage of troubled colleagues and their welfare.

Suggestions for Further Reading

Hauerwas, Stanley. *God, Medicine, and the Problem of Suffering.* Grand Rapids, Mich.: Wm. B. Eerdmans, 1990.

———. *Suffering Presence: Theological Reflections on Medicine, the Mentally Handicapped, and the Church.* Notre Dame: University of Notre Dame Press, 1986.

May, William F. *The Physician's Covenant: Images of the Healer in Medical Ethics.* Philadelphia: Westminster Press, 1983.

———. *Testing the Medical Covenant: Active Euthanasia and Health Care Reform.* Grand Rapids, Mich.: Wm. B. Eerdmans, 1996.

Meilaender, Gilbert. *Bioethics: A Primer for Christians.* Grand Rapids, Mich.: Wm. B. Eerdmans, 1996.

Verhey, Allen, and Stephen E. Lammers, eds. *Theological Voices in Medical Ethics.* Grand Rapids, Mich.: Wm. B. Eerdmans, 1993 (especially chapters on Paul Ramsey, Stanley Hauerwas, and William F. May).

Chapter 16

Christian Economy

D. Stephen Long

Editor's Introduction

Long points out that for Aristotle, *economy* referred to the structuring of the household according to the virtue of justice. Thomas Aquinas provided an important transformation of this view by arguing that justice was subject to charity, the latter a virtue infused by grace. Thus, economics could not be understood or properly regulated apart from theology—apart from participation in the life and love of God himself.

Modern economic theory severs the relations between economics and theology. It is this modern move that Long sets out to challenge in his chapter. He argues that Christians' inevitable participation in the external goods of the current market system should be qualified by goods intrinsic to the Christian life itself. Here, *economy* signifies how God orders creation. That order is one of charity, and it should render Christians' practices of production, consumption, and distribution intelligible.

In his chapter, Long first summarizes MacIntyre's argument concerning why capitalist society makes the achievement of goods internal to traditions difficult, if not impossible.

Long's second step is constructive: to explain how Christians can reorder their participation in capitalist economic practices in such a way that they serve the ultimate ends of the Christian tradition. The central resource for Christians is Christ himself, who makes possible our participation in the life of God. Baptism, the Eucharist, and repentance and reconciliation make possible the reception of the infused virtue of charity. Christian economic rules (prohibition of stealing and coveting, the command to lend without expectation of return) arise within the context of the Christian narrative.

These three sources—baptism; Eucharist, with its entailed practice of repentance, forgiveness, and reconciliation; and the narrative of God's self-revelation in the life of Jesus—all assume the centrality of Jesus' presence to us, and also the development of certain social institutions: the church and the neighborhood.

Thus, Long employs MacIntyre's own analysis of the way in which the capitalist system strips economic practices of any relation to any ongoing traditions, while at the same time it severs the relation between workers' characters and the products of their labor, thus making virtue in the workplace nearly impossible.

Long's own constructive account of Christian transformation of economic activity involves the use of MacIntyre's concepts of tradition, narrative, and goods internal to practices. Because of Long's recognition of relations between economic activity and the subpractices involved in Christian community formation, his analysis grows out of much of what is said in Part II of the present volume.

NANCEY MURPHY

Introduction

The term *economy* has an ancient lineage. Aristotle used it to signify how someone should structure a household so that its members share in meeting the needs of daily life. Households then combine into cities for the purpose not only of living but of living well.[1] A household economy served the greater interest of political well-being; economics and politics were intrinsically related, and the virtue of justice regulated both.[2]

The thirteenth-century Christian theologian Thomas Aquinas gave this ancient tradition a theological twist. He still considered economic matters under the virtue of justice; regulations on buying, selling, loaning, and stealing required some measure for ordering exchanges equitably. To fulfill that measure was to establish justice, but to rightly know that measure, justice required charity. Charity is a power infused in us by the Holy Spirit that orders all our activities, including those activities falling within the virtue of justice, to their true end — the love of God and neighbor. The centrality of charity utterly transformed the ancient tradition because charity is an infused virtue; it is not an achievement but a gift of God. Thus economics served political interests, but theology gave both activities their proper order.

The rise of modern economics severs any intrinsic theoretical relationship between economics, politics, and theology. This resulted from the transformation elicited by the 1776 publication of Adam Smith's *Wealth of Nations.* However, the early generation of economists maintained residual elements of the ancient tradition by designating their works *The Principles of Political Economy.*[3] Economics was severed from Christian theology, particularly in the economists' reaction against the tradition of the usury prohibition, but it was not yet severed from politics. Yet by the end of the nineteenth century, economists also freed economics from any intrinsic relationship to political philosophy. Many, if

1. See *The Politics,* 1252b5–30.
2. See *Nicomachean Ethics,* 1131a–1134b.
3. James Stuart, David Ricardo, and John Stuart Mill, among others, published works titled *The Principles of Political Economy.*

not most, economists now claim that their economic analysis is valid irrespective of the theological or philosophical "values" someone holds.[4] If this is true, it demonstrates that theology's relevance for economics can be at most indirect. Then language such as *Christian economy* makes little sense. Theology might influence the cultural values within which an economic system operates, but the economic facts themselves are true irrespective of the theological or political "values" someone holds.

If *economics* is used in this modern sense, then this essay can only be read as nonsensical. But this modern usage of *economy* is precisely what I intend to challenge. By employing the term *Christian economy* I do not intend to imply a separate economic system only for Christians. Nor shall I argue that a Christian economy requires a countercultural posture. Instead, I intend to argue that Christians' inevitable participation in the external goods of the current market system should be qualified by goods intrinsic to the Christian life itself. The term *economy* signifies how God orders creation. That order is one of charity, and it should render our practices of production, consumption, and distribution intelligible. The phrase *Christian economy* assumes that the external goods provided by the market should be in service to the goods internal to the Christian tradition itself. But this is not easily accomplished, for as Alasdair MacIntyre has shown, capitalist society makes the achievement of goods internal to traditions difficult if not impossible.

The first step in this essay will be to follow MacIntyre's argument in order to explain why finding space to pursue goods internal to the Christian tradition is so difficult. We must first see what we are up against. The next step is constructive. If we are to use the term *Christian economy* intelligibly, then we must order production, consumption, and distribution so that these activities serve the centrality of the life of Christ. Of course, such an ordering is not ours to produce *de novo.* Both Scripture and tradition provide us with the necessary resources.

The central resource is Christ himself, who makes possible our participation in the life of God. This participation occurs through the practice of conversion and baptism. It is then celebrated and strengthened through our communion in the Eucharist. But the integrity of our movement from baptism to the celebrations of the Eucharist also requires repentance and reconciliation. The result of this entire movement should be the reception of the virtue of charity. Through charity we are oriented to both God and neighbor. Thus internal to charity is the natural virtue of justice, which regulates our exchanges with one another. Traditional Christian economic regulations — do not steal, do not covet your

4. For instance, in his *Principles of Macroeconomics,* 7th ed. (New York: W. W. Norton, 1992), Edwin Mansfield suggests that "the economic organization of a prisoner of war camp is an elementary form of economic system that illustrates certain important economic principles simply and well" (53). I could not imagine either Aristotle or Aquinas allowing economic principles to be illustrated in this way because they were not autonomous but rendered intelligible by political or theological considerations. However, for Mansfield this demonstrates the universal and objective nature of these principles.

neighbors' goods, do not take interest on your loans but lend expecting nothing in return — find their purpose and have their significance constituted within this broader understanding of a charitable justice. The meaning of these rules is not self-evident; it arises only in the context of a theological narrative that holds forth the aim of a Christian's economic activities as life with God, which is charity.

Charity: A Difficult Virtue in a Capitalist Society

Alasdair MacIntyre criticizes capitalism for destroying the possibility of a virtuous life. This has been a consistent theme throughout his work, and it is central to his discovery of the failure of liberalism. In his 1995 introduction to his 1953 work, *Christianity and Marxism,* MacIntyre honors those Christian laity and clergy "who recognized relatively early the systematic injustices generated by nascent and developed commercial and industrial capitalism."[5] Then he explains that systematic injustice, giving us insight into how capitalism destroys virtue:

> The relationship of capital to labour is such that it inescapably involves an entirely one-sided dependence, except insofar as labour rebels against its conditions of work. The more effective the employment of capital, the more labour becomes no more than an instrument of capital's purposes and an instrument whose treatment is a function of the needs of long-term profit maximization and capital formation. The relationships that result are the impersonal relationships imposed by capitalist markets upon all those who participate in them. What is necessarily absent in such markets is any justice of deserts. Concepts of a just wage and a just price necessarily have no application to transactions within those markets.... It becomes impossible for workers to understand their work as a contribution to the common good of a society which at the economic level no longer has a common good, because of the different and conflicting interests of different classes.[6]

Because workers' labor is unintelligible in terms of a "contribution to the common good," the possibility of labor's exercise as a training in virtue is rendered difficult if not altogether impossible in capitalist societies.

Capitalist modes of production separate a person's labor from her just rewards and from her contribution to a community's good. A worker who is a faithful and conscientious employee of a company for the majority of her life is not viewed as contributing to that company such that she has produced its goods with her labor and her labor marks that corporation with her identity. Instead, the goods of that company are owned by owners and consumers. No intrinsic connection exists between a laborer's identity, even over a complete lifetime, and the good of the corporation. In fact, the goods of the owners and owner-consumers actually conflict with the goods of the laborers. Any increase in a laborer's real wages will be viewed as a threat to the owners' profit. Thus, the

5. Alasdair MacIntyre, *Marxism and Christianity* (Notre Dame: University of Notre Dame Press, 1995), viii.

6. Ibid., x.

relationship between a worker and that which is proper to him or her (including both virtue and property) excludes a proper exercise of the latter. One's property is a function not of one's work but of one's consumption; what someone does is not rewarded, but what someone buys is. A proper exercise of one's property would assume some intrinsic connection between one's character and one's labor. Without this connection, virtue is seldom possible.[7]

Virtue assumes "goods internal" to certain "forms of activity" which can be "realized" through one's participation in those forms of activity.[8] Internal goods cannot be scarce. Any person's possession of such goods contributes to the good of all the participants in a particular community.[9] These internal goods differ from external goods because the latter do not achieve the good of the whole community; they are achieved at the expense of others. Yet for internal goods to flourish, some connection must exist between them and external goods. This is where capitalist societies create problems for the cultivation of virtue. Because the success and advancement of capitalist societies do not depend (or depend very little) on an intrinsic relationship between the internal goods of the participants in those societies and their achievement of external goods, such societies make the exercise of virtue difficult.[10] External goods are widely available, but the efficient production of these external goods lacks connection with internal goods.

Internal goods depend on an acknowledgment that our lives are embedded in histories and traditions that give us the resources to be moral agents. Without historical traditions, there are no internal goods. Without acknowledging that my life comes as a gift already embedded in a narrative, I cannot adequately be a moral agent. I lose the practices that make possible a virtuous life. But capitalism denies this sense of embeddedness. Neither the pursuit nor the production of goods is "intelligible in terms of the larger and longer history of the tradition through which the practice in its present form was conveyed to us."[11] Instead, the production of goods is viewed as a unique process that subverts and destroys the old by introducing a new element hitherto unknown into the process of

---

7. MacIntyre's definition of a virtue is "an acquired human quality the possession and exercise of which tends to enable us to achieve those goods which are internal to practices and the lack of which effectively prevents us from achieving any such goods" *(After Virtue,* 2d ed. [Notre Dame: University of Notre Dame Press, 1984], 191). MacIntyre also states that this account of virtue "requires for its application the acceptance for some prior account of certain features of social and moral life in terms of which it has to be defined and explained" (186).

8. This draws on MacIntyre's account of a practice (*After Virtue,* 187).

9. Ibid., 190.

10. Examples of this truth are the profitability of corporate downsizing and the inverse relationship between approaching full employment and a "healthy" economy, as well as the inverse relationship between workers' wages and salaries and the profitability and desirability of investments.

11. *After Virtue,* 222. MacIntyre also states, "The virtues find their point and purpose not only in sustaining those relationships necessary if the variety of goods internal to practices are to be achieved and not only in sustaining the form of an individual life in which that individual may seek out his or her good as the good of his or her whole life, but also in sustaining those traditions which provide both practices and individual lives with their necessary historical context" (223).

production.[12] Capitalist societies deny that laborers' identities are embedded in the histories of its own corporations. The practice of work lacks tradition.

By recovering the "narrative phenomenon of embedding," MacIntyre calls us to account for those inheritances that contribute to the narrative unity of our lives in their possibilities for both vice and virtue.[13] This recovery of the narrative unity of life should include an acknowledgment of the embeddedness of a laborer's work in the common good of a corporate community. But this is precisely what is not recognized when wealth is supposedly produced either by introducing a completely new idea (new growth theory) or by managing class antagonisms to favor the employment of capital (classical liberalism).

Once the narrative phenomenon of embedding is lost, traditional moral rules about economics either become unintelligible or are transmuted to serve new interests. This is precisely what has occurred within the Christian tradition; rules such as the just wage, prohibition of usury, and specific forms of the admonition not to steal no longer are viable for us. All we have are the fragments of these rules, but we lack the narrative context within which they could be intelligible. For these rules to make sense, we must recover the theological narrative out of which they arise.

MacIntyre's virtue ethic sets him at odds with capitalism because capitalism is a form of "traditioning" that refuses to acknowledge its history. For a similar reason his virtue ethic sets him at odds with the poststructuralists. Their efforts to subvert, disrupt, expose, and interrupt the inherited totalities do not fundamentally challenge modern economic configurations. The denial of any continuity to personal identity lodges no objection to the dis-acknowledgment of the narrative phenomenon of embedding.[14] Creative destruction poses no threat to a capitalist economy.

An alternative to capitalism's inability to produce virtue could be embodied in a community capable of recognizing its inheritances, both virtuous and vicious.

---

12. See Joseph Schumpeter's discussion in "Creative Destruction," in *Capitalism, Socialism, and Democracy* (New York: Harper Torchbooks, 1976), or its contemporary manifestation in Paul Michael Romer's "new growth theory," where new and original ideas are viewed as the sources of wealth production ("Dynamic Competitive Equilibria with Externalities, Increasing Returns, and Unbounded Growth," Ph.D. diss., University of Chicago, 1983). Of course, what actually produces wealth remains a mystery to economists; perhaps it must remain such a mystery since it is viewed as nonhistorical.

13. MacIntyre writes that "from the standpoint of individualism I am what I myself choose to be. I can always, if I wish to, put in question what are taken to be the merely contingent social features of my existence.... Such individualism is expressed by those modern Americans who deny any responsibility for the effects of slavery upon black Americans, saying 'I never owned any slaves.'... And of course there is nothing peculiar to modern Americans in this attitude: the Englishman who says, 'I never did any wrong to Ireland; why bring up that old history as though it had something to do with me?' or the young German who believes that being born after 1945 means that what the Nazis did to Jews has no moral relevance to his relationship to his Jewish contemporaries, exhibits the same attitude...." And I would submit, so does the corporate executive who lays off workers because the market demands it, denying that the workers' daily contribution to the good of that corporate community in any way constitutes the identity of that good.

14. See MacIntyre, *Three Rival Versions of Moral Enquiry: Encyclopaedia, Genealogy, and Tradition* (Notre Dame: University of Notre Dame Press, 1990), 212–18. MacIntyre writes, "What I am

Such an alternative can be found in the rationality of traditions. A tradition is by definition an acknowledgment of an inheritance. The logic of a tradition eschews both the illusion of modernist self-made individuals (especially the entrepreneur) and the postmodernist linguistic revolutionaries' exploitation of fissures in the totalities. As a participant in a tradition I need not destroy to create, but I need to discover, confess, repent, and constantly seek the unity of reconciliation that may give my life integrity. Social practices that produce this life of integrity can be found in the Christian tradition and could provide the sources for a Christian economy.

The Divine Economy: The Order of Charity

The sources for a Christian economy are the virtues of charity and justice, the practices of repentance and reconciliation embedded in the sacraments of baptism and Eucharist, and the narrative of God's self-revelation in Jesus and his continual presence in the life of the church. These three sources are not fundamentally different, for they all assume the centrality of Jesus' presence to us. These three sources also assume the presence of certain social institutions for our sense of moral agency, primarily the church and the neighborhood.

The Centrality of Jesus

For Christians, a good human life is discovered in the blessedness pronounced by Jesus in the Sermon on the Mount. All of our actions are to be directed toward such beatitude. For only a blessed life can ultimately be a happy life. Jesus' blessings are eschatological verifications of forms of life pleasing to God.[15] One of the best articulations of this vision is found in the work of Thomas Aquinas, who took these blessings as the heart of a Christian social ethic. He wrote,

> ...the discourse given by the Lord on the Mount contains all that a Christian needs to conduct his life. In it man's interior motions are perfectly regulated. For after announcing blessedness as the end, and recommending the dignity of the Apostles by whom the gospel teaching was to be promulgated, he regulated man's interior motions, firstly in regard to himself and secondly in regard to his neighbor.[16]

---

suggesting, then, is that the genealogist faces grave difficulties in constructing a narrative of his or her past which would allow any acknowledgment in that past of a failure, let alone a guilty failure, which is also the failure of the same still-present self..." (213). Notice the similarity between MacIntyre's claim here against the genealogists and their loss of identity and the "individualist" identity of liberalism which also dis-acknowledges the narrative phenomenon of embeddedness *(After Virtue,* 220). In fact, both positions seem to fall under the category of the damnable as MacIntyre, drawing upon Aquinas, explains it: "hell is persistence in defection from the integrity both of a self and of its communities" (*Three Rival Versions,* 144).

15. By "eschatological verification" I mean that Jesus' blessings are final pronouncements of vindication on persons and forms of activity that God judges as constituting God's rule.

16. *Summa Theologica* IaIIae, q. 108, 3.

The Lord of the Sermon on the Mount pronouncing blessedness is the central image of the moral life. This vision properly orders nature.

For Thomas, we cannot fully embody perfect moral virtue without the gift of grace which is the new law of the gospel. This new law is the life of Jesus present to the community of faith through his ongoing presence mediated by the Holy Spirit. The significance of Jesus for economics is not merely that he gives rules but that he himself rules. He orders a person's actions so that she is directed toward her proper, and ultimate, end — the love of God. Contained within this proper end is an ordering of one's life to one's neighbor. Thus a properly oriented moral action will be congruent with the order of charity.

The Virtues of Charity and Justice

Charity is not a formal principle; it names the relationship between the Father and the Son through the Holy Spirit which we can participate in by grace. Charity is the life of God, and it is the structure upon which creation rests. Because of this we should not be surprised that Thomas explains the order of charity before he discusses the natural virtue of justice. This is significant because under the virtue of justice Thomas develops rules for ordering economic relations. However, these rules cannot be explained by the virtue of justice alone; they also require the virtue of charity. This fundamentally qualifies the ancients' political economy.[17]

Thomas's discussion of justice begins with the traditional Roman definition as articulated by the jurist Ulpian, where justice is rendering to each person his or her due. Consistent with this classical definition, Thomas defines justice as "some work adequate to another according to some mode of equality."[18] Justice then is a right ordering based on some rule for recognizing the equality between people and things. However, Thomas drastically alters this order by finding the ultimate good to which all things are to be ordered to exist outside human nature, in God. This poses a serious problem for the traditional rendering of justice. As MacIntyre notes, Thomas does not find our ultimate good to be related to any "state available in this created world." Instead, Thomas draws upon Scripture to argue that the *summum bonum* is God. This could leave the soul finding itself "directed beyond all finite goods, unsatisfiable by those goods, and yet able to find nothing beyond them to satisfy it," and thus in a state of "permanent dissatisfaction."[19] This permanent dissatisfaction was exacerbated in Thomas's understanding of the moral life because of "a rooted tendency to disobedience in the will and distraction by passion which causes obscuring of

17. For a discussion of how Christian tradition "challenges the primacy of the political" see Jean Bethke Elshtain's *Public Man, Private Woman: Women in Social and Political Thought* (Princeton: Princeton University Press: 1981), 55–99. See also John Milbank's "The Other City: Theology as a Social Science," in *Theology and Social Theory: Beyond Secular Reason* (Oxford: Basil Blackwell, 1990), 380–434.

18. *Summa Theologica* IIaIIae, q. 57, art. 1.

19. MacIntyre, *Three Rival Versions,* 137–38.

the reason and on occasion systematic cultural deformation." However, suggests MacIntyre, rather than leading to despair or the loss of any intelligible conception of human nature,

> . . . it is in fact this discovery of willful evil which makes the achievement of the human end possible. How so? The acknowledgment by oneself of radical defect is a necessary condition for one's reception of the virtues of faith, hope and charity. It is only the kind of knowledge which faith provides, the kind of expectation which hope provides, and the capacity for friendship with other human beings and with God which is the outcome of charity which can provide the other virtues with what they need to become genuine excellences, informing a way of life in and through which the good and the best can be achieved. The self-revelation of God in the events of the scriptural history and the gratuitous grace through which that revelation is appropriated, so that an individual can come to recognize his or her place within that same history, enable such individuals to recognize also that prudence, justice, temperateness and courage are genuine virtues, that the apprehension of the natural law was not illusory, and that the moral life up to this point requires to be corrected in order to be completed but not displaced.[20]

Repentance gives our lives integrity because in repenting we acknowledge the ruptures in our lives and are prepared to receive the virtues of faith, hope, and charity. These virtues come to us as a gift and not as an achievement. They do not arise from our own integrity but through confession of the lack of continuity our lives possess. Faith gives knowledge that our lives can be recognized within God's life. Hope expects continuity, constancy, and permanence. Charity establishes friendship with God and our neighbor. Once our lives are founded on these grace-infused virtues, then we can properly order the natural virtues. Natural virtues alone, such as justice or prudence, cannot establish a Christian economic ethic. The natural virtues assume the narrative of God's self-revelation of which our knowledge implies the infusion of faith, hope, and charity. This is God's economy, and it is present in the material practices of the sacraments.

Baptism, Repentance, and Communion-Reconciliation

In baptism we receive faith and recognize our place in God's economy. This recognition is sealed, strengthened, and renewed in the celebration of the Eucharist. The blessed meal is our participation in the life of God. Such a meal makes us holy and cultivates in us the practice of *koinōnia,* which is both our communion around the table and our communion with God.

Koinōnia can be translated as participation, fellowship, or communion. The narrative contexts for this practice are found in the Acts of the Apostles 2:43–47 and 4:32–37 and in 2 Peter 1:4. These passages convey the double movement of a Christian economy: our life with our neighbors is a participation in the life of God, and our life with God is a participation in the life of our neighbors. In the passages in Acts people are converted as a response to Peter's preaching of

20. Ibid., 140.

the gospel. The result is "they held all things *koina*" (2:44). This is not surprising because we were already told that these new believers devoted themselves to "*koinōnia.*" Precisely what this devotion to *koinōnia* is we do not know. However, a description of it is found in Acts 4:32, where it is related to the believer's relationship with her or his property: "Now the whole group of those who believed were of one heart and soul, and no one claimed private ownership of any possessions, but everything they owned was held in common." The contrast here is between holding our property "*idiōn*" — as our own — and holding all things "*koina*" — in common. The first possibility speaks of one's property as one's own. The second sees one's property as a participation within the community of faith.[21]

The term *koinōnia* refers not only to one's participation in the community of faith but also to one's participation in the life of God. For when 2 Peter informs us that all things that we need for life and godliness have been given to us, we are reminded that all that is given to us is so that we might be "*koinōnia*" of the divine nature. This participation in the life of God includes not only what is needed for a pious, spiritual life (*eusebeia*) but also what is needed for life itself (*zōē*). The things necessary here are not only spiritual; otherwise there would be no need to include the *zōē* with the *eusebeia.* Instead, a pious life with God implies participation in the material processes of life itself, concrete, material participation in the life of one's neighbor. This double movement of the life of charity finds its ultimate expression in the sacrament of the Eucharist.

The virtue of a charitable justice should find its measure of equality in the communion practiced at the Eucharist. The reconciliation embedded in the Eucharist is a meta-practice that renders intelligible a Christian's daily activities of producing and consuming. What we discover embedded in the Eucharist is a glimpse and foretaste of the ultimate good for God's creation. Resources are not scarce or subject to competition, but everyone can be satisfied and each person's satisfaction only increases that of her neighbor. Distribution is made subject only to the condition of one's baptism and willingness to repent and seek reconciliation.

A Christian economy assumes a life of charity ordered toward God and one's neighbor. Such a discovery will also entail a broader conception of the moral life; we then recognize the natural law is not illusory. The natural law is the cre-

---

21. The extent to which these passages should be viewed as common ownership has been challenged by Luke Timothy Johnson in his *Sharing Possessions: Mandate and Symbol of Faith* (Philadelphia: Fortress Press, 1981), and his *Acts of the Apostles,* Sacra Pagina Series, vol. 5 (Collegeville, Minn.: Liturgical Press, 1992). He sees in these passages a rhetorical strategy by Luke to portray the early Christians as exhibiting the ideal of Greek friendship, which has misled Christian theologians to be fascinated with common ownership. Johnson seeks to recover the tradition of almsgiving as practiced by Judaism in place of the ideal of common ownership. Justo González has subjected Johnson's position to criticism in his *Faith and Wealth: A History of Early Christian Ideas on the Origin, Significance, and Use of Money* (San Francisco: Harper and Row, 1990), 80–86. He believes the early Christian practice of *koinōnia* involved relinquishing one's possessions not merely for the sake of a common bond of elitist philosophers but to meet the needs of the poor. The difference between Johnson and González seems to be more a matter of emphasis than of discontinuity.

ation's inevitable participation in God's economy in varying degrees. Christians should not be surprised that such participation is discovered even outside faith in such virtues as prudence, justice, courage, and temperance. But even these natural virtues have their rightful place within the order of charity. The Ten Commandments themselves give us this order, for the first table directs our lives toward God and the virtues of faith, hope, and charity, while the second table directs us to our neighbor, and such a direction produces "natural" virtues. But these natural virtues are not separate from the theological particularities implied by the first table. In fact the negative commands of the second table assume the virtues implicit in the first table; otherwise the negative commands become "arbitrary prohibitions."[22] This means that commands such as "do not steal" and "do not covet your neighbor's possessions" cannot in and of themselves be the condition for an economic ethic. Instead, they require the virtues of faith, hope, and especially charity for their intelligibility.[23] And these virtues assume a particular narrative, the narrative of God's revelation in Jesus.

A just ordering of economic life assumes the ordering of charity. This assumption entails the specifics of Christian theology, for charity is not natural to us. As Thomas put it, "charity, since it greatly exceeds proportion to human nature, does not depend on any natural virtues, but only on the grace of the Holy Spirit infusing it."[24] This statement of Thomas's poses a problem for moral agency because it could be misconstrued to suggest that the human will is either forced to be charitable or reduced to the status of a mere instrument for the Spirit's activity. Thomas rejects both of these positions and suggests instead that "[i]t is chiefly necessary for charitable action to exist in us that some habitual form be superadded to potential nature inclining itself to charitable action and to do it with ease and pleasure."[25] This requires then that charity be a virtue and a virtue that is both outside of us — we cannot achieve it through our natural powers — and at the same time within us, our interior action.

Because the virtue of charity is both *extra nos* and *intra nos,* it has a motion similar to that of the biblical practice of *koinōnia.* In fact, Thomas defines charity as the divine essence and gives it a Trinitarian determination. "Charity can be in us neither naturally, nor through acquisition by the natural powers but by the infusion of the Holy Spirit who is the love of the Father and the Son and the participation of whom in us is created charity."[26] As the natural law is our participation in the divine reasons for creation, the life of charity is our participation in the divine life itself. Perfect justice cannot be had without the life of charity.

22. MacIntyre, *Three Rival Versions,* 139. See also *After Virtue,* 119.

23. This point has also been made persuasively by Servais Pinckaers in his *Sources of Christian Ethics* (Washington, D.C.: Catholic University of America Press, 1995), where he challenges the ethics of obligation that has come to characterize Catholic moral theology. It is also found in John Paul II's reading of the rich young ruler in part 1 of *Veritatis Splendor,* in *Origins, CNS Documentary Source* 23, no. 18 (1993): 297–334.

24. *Summa Theologica* IIaIIae, q. 24, art. 3.

25. Ibid., q. 23, art. 2.

26. Ibid., q. 24, art. 3.

Thomas does not explicitly state that justice requires charity for its completion when he develops the natural virtue of justice in the *secunda secundae*. This could mislead someone into thinking that Thomas argues for a justice separate from charity. Then we could develop an economic ethic based on the natural moral virtues alone such that justice orders relations within political and economic society and charity orders relations among Christians within the Church. But this two-tiered interpretation of Thomas cannot make sense of his discussion either of charity or of injustice. For Thomas has already explicitly stated in the *Summa Theologica* that charity is necessary for all the moral virtues.[27] And we see implicitly how charity is necessary for justice in his discussion of injustice. He defines injustice as a person wanting to have "more of goods, namely wealth and honor, and less of evils, namely labor and toil."[28] This particular vice requires restitution not only for the good of the political or economic order but for salvation itself.[29] To seek to accumulate external goods without labor jeopardizes one's salvation. The virtue of justice is obviously not merely a matter of natural morality but central to salvation itself.

The Just Ordering of Commands

Having established the narrative context within which the virtues of charity and justice reside, we can now better understand some of Christianity's traditional rules about economics.

Do Not Steal or Covet Your Neighbor's Property

The Ten Commandments occupy a significant place in any Christian economy. Their meaning, however, is not self-evident. These commandments are unique in that they are both "revealed" and "natural." The sequence of the ten reveals the order of charity, which should be natural to us even though it often seems otherwise. Our first motion should be toward God. Thus the first three commandments remind us to have no strange gods, not to take the name of God in vain, and to remember to keep holy the Lord's day. Only when the virtues of faith and hope are established as we direct our lives toward God can we then turn toward our neighbors in charity. This leads us to the second table of the Ten Commandments. Because this order of charity establishes a narrative context that makes the commandments intelligible, a premodern Christian interpretation of the command not to steal is startling in comparison to property laws in a capitalist society. Thomas argued that "by natural law whatever people have in abundance should sustain the poor." Therefore if a clear urgent necessity

27. Ibid., IaIIae, q. 65, art. 2: "all the infused moral virtues also depend on charity." He states this in the context of a discussion of "infused prudence" where he argues that even the moral virtue of prudence requires the grace of the Holy Spirit for its completion. Thus, even the acquired virtues require "infusion" if they are to be properly ordered to our ultimate end.

28. Ibid., IIaIIae, q. 59, art. 1.

29. Ibid., q. 62, art. 1–4.

arises, someone can take the property of another even secretly and such taking does not have the nature of theft.[30] The basis for such an understanding of "do not steal" resides in the order of charity.

Our property, like our virtue, finds its purpose in the life of charity. Thus, any right to our property is directed by charity. We are to use our property in service to ourselves, our family, and our immediate neighbors. If we have a neighbor in need and we do not share our goods with her, our neighbor does not steal by taking our surplus property to meet her basic needs. No violation of the seventh commandment occurs. However, any neighbor who is unwilling to share from his surplus with his neighbor has violated the tenth commandment. God has given him his property not as an inalienable right but as a means for him to participate in a life of charity. By refusing to share his goods with others in need, he covets what actually belongs to them.

For a similar reason, Christian tradition forged rules about a just wage. A just wage was what an employer owed an employee. Since the just wage regulated exchanges between people, it obviously fell under the description of the virtue of justice. But the mode of equality by which such exchanges were regulated was also normed by the demands of charity. Because a worker's labor contributes to the common good, he should be rewarded for his labor with a wage sufficient for the basic necessities of life and enough surplus that he can use his property to contribute to the common good of both his family and neighborhood. An employer who does not pay such a wage commits intrinsically evil acts. They are intrinsically evil because they are deprived of any possibility of being ordered toward the life of charity. Even though the laborer's skills may command a lesser wage on the basis of a market analysis, this alone cannot determine just reimbursement. A wage that does not allow a laborer's work to be directed toward the good of her family or neighbors does not allow her to participate in the life of charity. It would be better for her not to work and live from the gratuity of others than to work under such circumstances where her actions are made intelligible by another's intrinsically evil actions. Her refusal to work under these conditions would increase the possibility of the internal good of charity, whereas her work in an unjust environment would lose all connection with the possibility of any internal goods.

Lend, Expecting Nothing in Return (Luke 6:35)

Central to the life of charity for premodern theologians was the ancient philosophic and biblical admonition to lend without expectation of gain. The usury prohibition was the dominant economic regulation put forth by the church until the rise of modern economics. In fact, modern economists freed the market from the theological and political interference that the usury prohibition represented. Adam Smith objected to the usury prohibition, arguing that a fee should be paid

30. Ibid., q. 66, art. 7.

for the use of money since gain could be made from it.[31] Jeremy Bentham developed his economic ideas opposing the church's traditional stance against usury when he argued in "Defence of Usury" that only a person's will to enter into contracts should limit contracts.[32] The influential economists Eugen von Böhm-Bawerk, Ludwig von Mises, and the early Joseph Schumpeter all argued that the medieval church's effort to regulate economic matters based on the usury principle revealed the irrationality of theological or political interference in the market.[33] Of the modern economists, only John Maynard Keynes seems to find anything good to say about the ancient rule proscribing usury.[34] The resounding judgment by the economists on the church's traditional teaching was that it was irrational and was based on the false assumption that economics involved a zero-sum game where any loan was by nature exploitative of the one who received it. Thus, the economists suggested, the theologians were incapable of recognizing that loans could be productive.

This, however, is a false reading of the theologians' efforts to integrate the ancient philosophic prohibition of usury into Luke 6:35. Thomas Aquinas clearly recognized that both the lender and the borrower could benefit from the arrangement. Thus he wrote,

> He that entrusts his money to a merchant or craftsman so as to form a kind of society does not transfer the ownership of his money to them, for it remains his so that at his risk the merchant speculates with it, or the craftsman uses it for his craft and consequently he may lawfully demand as something belonging to him part of the profits derived from his money.[35]

Thomas did not argue that profit could not be made by employing one's money in enterprising activities. What the ancient prohibition sought to insure was a connection between one's labor and one's compensation. As Albert the Great, Thomas's teacher, stated it, "Usury is a sin of avarice; it is against charity because the usurer without labor, suffering or fear gathers riches from the labor, suffering and vicissitudes of his neighbor."[36] And Thomas notes that usury is intrinsically evil because "we ought to treat every man as our neighbor and brother, especially in the State of the Gospel whereunto we are called."[37]

---

31. *Wealth of Nations* (New York: Modern Library, 1965), 52.

32. Letter 13, "Defence of Usury," in *Jeremy Bentham's Economic Writings,* ed. W. Stark (London: Blackfriars, 1952).

33. Böhm-Bawerk, *Capital and Interest,* trans. George D. Huncke and Hans F. Sennholz (South Holland, Ill.: Libertarian, 1959), 16–36. Ludwig von Mises, *The Theory of Money and Credit* (Indianapolis: Liberty Fund, 1980), 84. Joseph Schumpeter, *Theory of Economic Development,* trans. Redivers Opie (Cambridge: Harvard University Press, 1949), 178.

34. *General Theory of Employment, Interest, and Money* (San Diego: Harcourt Brace, 1964), 351–52. For a fuller discussion of the usury prohibition and the modern economists see D. Stephen Long, "Bernard Dempsey's Theological Economics: Usury, Profit, and Human Fulfillment," *Theological Studies* 57 (1996).

35. *Summa Theologica* IIaIIae, q. 78, art. 1, rep. obj. 5.

36. Quoted in Albert R. Jonsen and Stephen Toulmin, *The Abuse of Casuistry* (Berkeley and Los Angeles: University of California Press, 1988), 183.

37. *Summa Theologica* IIaIIae, q. 78, art. 1.

The principle behind the ancient prohibition is not as absurd as the modern economists tell us it is. The principle is quite simple; money does no work, people do. So when we assume that our money is working for us to make more money, we are not describing accurately God's economy. We lose the ability to describe how our lives are embedded in the narratives of others. The food that we eat, the clothes we wear, the transportation available to us, clean restrooms, floors, and so on — all these things are provided for us without any awareness on our part of other people's practices which make such external goods possible. We cannot name our debts. Thus we cannot pray well. We lose the possibility of cultivating internal goods.

The usury prohibition did not deny the legitimacy of profit. To use one's money to assist another in a joint venture could be an act of charity. But to use one's money only to make money, especially when it is made through layoffs, exploitation, and the production of unjust things, is intrinsically evil because it cannot be ordered to that which should become natural to us — a life of charity.

Buying and Selling

The same narrative that prompted the Christian tradition's odd notion of stealing and the usury prohibition also seeks to order our buying and selling. According to the early church father Tertullian, how a person earned his or her living was a matter that required examination before baptism. Not only were Christians to refrain from the production of idolatrous commodities, they were also to refrain from trades that would require mendacity or covetousness.[38]

St. Thomas sought to regulate buying and selling with the virtue of justice by emphasizing the importance of truth-telling in exchanges. He also guarded against greed by prohibiting trading merely for the sake of gain.

> Trading, considered in itself, has a certain debasement attaching thereto, in so far as, by its very nature, it does not imply a virtuous or necessary end. Nevertheless gain which is the end of trading, though not implying by its nature anything virtuous or necessary, does not, in itself, connote anything sinful or contrary to virtue: wherefore nothing prevents gain from being directed to some necessary or even virtuous end and thus trading becomes lawful.[39]

This regulation on selling and buying reveals the role of charity in exchanges. Trading can never be an end in itself. It is a means and thus gets its moral species from the end it serves. While a number of legitimate ends are present to make trading moral, such as "payment for labor" and the desire to serve the common good, all such legitimate ends will also point to humanity's ultimate end — blessedness. And this cannot be attained without charity. Such is God's economy.

38. Tertullian, *On Idolatry,* chap. 11.
39. *Summa Theologica* IIaIIae, q. 77, art. 4.

Conclusion

The first task of any Christian reflection on the economy is not to speculate whether Christianity sides with capitalism or socialism but to seek to interpret our "economic activity," that is, our producing, buying, selling, and consuming, within the larger narrative of God's economy. Too much ink has been spilt by theologians' deciding for or against capitalism, for or against socialism as if the politicians and corporate executives were waiting for the theologians' pronouncements. Such is obviously not the case. Theologians lose their sense of purpose when they find their task to be nothing but announcing the death of socialism or the triumph of capitalism. The first question Christian theologians should ask is, Given God's economy toward us, how does our inevitable participation in the material goods of this world reflect that economy?[40] God's economy does not imply a blueprint for how Christians should organize the world economically. It does not give us any specific public policy easily translatable into terms either Capitol Hill or Wall Street will find useful. This is not surprising because God's economy is ultimately not about the profitability of things but about their proper enjoyment.

The first task of a Christian economics is to narrate the order of charity, which is to move our will and intellect toward Christ. It is to orient our life toward beatitude, toward living out of and into the grace that Jesus gave his disciples. This ordering of creation is the life of charity that lives, moves, and has its being from the Triune life. Our lives are to participate in God's as God communicates God's life to us. A condensed version of this story is found in the practical wisdom that we are to love God and our neighbor as ourselves.

Such practical wisdom assumes certain social structures.[41] The church contains the necessary means to orient our lives toward God and thus to fulfill the basic command to love God found in the first three commandments of the Decalogue. We should not expect the state to enforce the virtue of charity; love of God and neighbor is a gift, never an achievement of our will in its own strength. But we should expect the church to demand this order of charity from its members. That is our politics. The first social institution that bears the practices of a charitable justice is the church.

Apart from the church, the family, and a limited role for the state, the Ten Commandments assume a central role for neighborhoods. God does not direct us toward citizens or comrades, but God orders relations with our neighbors. Jesus' summary of the law — love God and love your neighbor as yourself — assumes first an institution that will assist us in charity toward God, which

40. Such a question obviously shows my indebtedness to M. Douglas Meeks, *God the Economist: The Doctrine of God and Political Economy* (Minneapolis: Fortress Press, 1989).

41. My reflections here are indebted to James Wm. McClendon, Jr., "The Community of the Ten Commandments," in his *Ethics: Systematic Theology, Volume I* (Nashville: Abingdon Press, 1986), 177–86.

can only be the church, and then charity toward our neighbors, which assumes neighborhoods.

Neighborhoods have been vastly diminished because of the hegemonic power of the nation-state and the global market in all our lives. Michael Ignatieff has made this argument in his compelling critique of the welfare state, *The Needs of Strangers*. Ignatieff describes how the welfare state mediates goods to the needy and turns "relationships" into contractual transactions among strangers. He writes,

> The mediated quality of our relationship seems necessary to both of us. [The needy] are dependent upon the state, not upon me, and we are both glad of it. Yet I am also aware of how this mediation walls us off from each other. We are responsible for each other, but we are not responsible to each other. My responsibilities towards them are mediated through a vast division of labour. In my name a social worker climbs the stairs to their rooms and makes sure they are as warm and as clean as they can be persuaded to be.... It is this solidarity among strangers, this transformation through the division of labour of needs into rights and rights into care that gives us whatever fragile basis we have for saying that we live in a moral community.[42]

Citizens as strangers is indeed a fragile basis for moral community. It may be preferable to citizens as strangers competing for basic goods that the so-called free-market state seeks to produce. However, to imagine that the disorder created by the welfare state is the only alternative to the greater disorder of a state-instituted deregulated market is merely to accept one state of disorder in place of a greater one.

Both the welfare state and the free-market state destroy neighborhoods. In both political configurations corporations are the central actors. Malls can be built, incinerators established, educational institutions closed or consolidated, and neighbors have little recourse. "Public" education seeks parents' participation in the school system only through bake sales and fund-raisers. We are constantly alienated and isolated from the tasks of everyday life, which are given over to the professionals and experts. The only control remaining is the occasional vote for those who will rule us. How can we fulfill the command to love our neighbors when we are no longer neighbors but strangers?

In such a world, not only does a Christian economy make sense but its implementation has an urgent necessity. Neither through the necessary violence of the wage contract of classical liberalism,[43] nor through an inevitable and bloody

42. Michael Ignatieff, *The Needs of Strangers: An Essay on Privacy, Solidarity, and the Politics of Being Human* (New York: Penguin Books, 1986). 10.

43. See for instance Adam Smith's *Wealth of Nations*, where he argues that owners and laborers are locked in conflict, with the advantage given to the owners ([New York: Modern Library, 1965], 66–67). Likewise David Ricardo suggests, in his essay "On Wages," that overpopulation remains the key problem with workers and is only exacerbated by policies that unnaturally support more poor than the market can care for (such as the Poor Laws). Thus he argues for their abolition "with the least violence" afflicted upon the poor as is possible (*Principles of Political Economy* [Cambridge: Cambridge University Press, 1990], 107).

revolution based on the contradiction between the mode of production and the mode of exchange, can such an economy occur. It occurs through the charitable justice found in baptism and Eucharist actually lived by the church and extended beyond its borders when it is given away.

Suggestions for Further Reading

Clapp, Rodney. "Why the Devil Takes Visa: A Christian Response to the Triumph of Consumerism." *Christianity Today* 40 (7 October 1996): 19–33.

Gnuse, Robert. *You Shall Not Steal: Community and Property in the Biblical Tradition.* Maryknoll, N.Y.: Orbis Books, 1985.

Johnson, Luke T. *Sharing Possessions: Mandate and Symbol of Faith.* Philadelphia: Fortress Press, 1981.

Martin, Mike W. *Virtuous Giving: Philanthropy, Voluntary Service, and Caring.* Bloomington: Indiana University Press, 1994.

Mullin, Redmond. *The Wealth of Christians.* Maryknoll, N.Y.: Orbis Books, 1984.

Pilgrim, Walter E. *Good News to the Poor: Wealth and Poverty in Luke-Acts.* Minneapolis: Augsburg, 1981.

Wheeler, Sondra Ely. *Wealth as Peril and Obligation: The New Testament on Possessions.* Grand Rapids, Mich.: Wm. B. Eerdmans, 1995.

Wuthnow, Robert. *Poor Richard's Principle: Rediscovering the American Dream through the Moral Dimension of Work, Business, and Money.* Princeton: Princeton University Press, 1996.

Retrospect

On Cultivating Moral Taste

Brad J. Kallenberg

Suppose that I wanted to convince you that Rembrandt was the world's greatest painter. How might I go about accomplishing this? I might begin by teaching you a theory of aesthetics. Once you had mastered this theory you would be capable of following my "proof" of Rembrandt's superiority. Of course, if you were a bright student, you might ask what makes this theory of aesthetics preferable to others. In that case, I would be forced to retrace my steps, teach you *many* theories of aesthetics, prove the superiority of *my* theory of aesthetics, and only then get on with the business of demonstrating what makes Rembrandt history's premier painter. Undaunted, you might challenge the very grounds on which I built my case for my particular theory of aesthetics which supports secondarily my conclusion that Rembrandt is the greatest painter. And so on.

This strategy doesn't look very promising, does it? The scenario could be made all the more ridiculous if we supposed that I just happen to be a world-class art critic who has made the study of Rembrandt my life's work and you . . . well, let's just say that you are "culturally challenged" — along the lines of someone who hankers after Elvis on black velvet. Now the case of theorizing about great art is quite beside the point; you simply have poor taste. Before we can discuss "greatness" in art, you must first cultivate your sensibilities. This requires a very different strategy.

Suppose that, instead of teaching you a theory of aesthetics, I begin by taking you to the Hermitage in St. Petersburg where you confront, firsthand, Rembrandt's enormous (eight feet by six feet) painting "The Return of the Prodigal Son." When I ask you what you like about *this* painting, you say (pointing) that you're quite taken by the color of that individual's eye and think you will paint your walls back home just that shade. In response, I simply raise the question of whether a color might be what it is because of its relation to the rest of a painting. Not waiting for you to finish processing this suggestion, I go on to describe the details of the painting — ranging from the obvious (one of the prodigal's sandals is off) to the more subtle (the face of the prodigal has the shape and texture of a just-born infant) — which, save for my pointing them out, would have been lost on you. Perhaps then I begin to draw your attention to the artistic conventions (such as the play of light and shadows) that distinguish paintings from photographs. I proceed to describe details of Rembrandt's own life that may have influenced which character he identified with or the manner in which he read the biblical text behind the painting.

Now suppose, after all this, I then asked you for an evaluation of Rembrandt and you say: "Well, I know what I like when I see it, and, to be frank, this just doesn't do anything for me." My next move would be to place you in front of another Rembrandt, and while I make similar descriptions as I did with the first painting, I ask *you* to make comparisons between the two paintings for me. After repeating this exercise with several (many?) Rembrandt pieces I finally stand you before a work by an artist of an entirely different sort, say Monet, and ask your opinion of *it.* It is not inconceivable that at this point you might say, "I don't know if Rembrandt is great art, but *that* (pointing to the Monet) is plainly *bad* art. Just look at how washed out the colors are! I prefer Rembrandt."

At that moment, I've scored a minor victory. For I would have succeeded in moving you from ambivalence with respect to Rembrandt to using Rembrandt as the benchmark against which you measure all other paintings. Your artistic sensibilities may still be primitive (after all, you are disgusted by Monet!), yet you have begun to develop a taste for Rembrandt — albeit not without a price. The hours we have spent together in museums have been an expenditure of energy, as well as time, in your struggle to see what I see.

I want to suggest that the practice of moral reasoning, or ethics, requires the same sort of tutored struggle as one's induction into the practice of art appreciation. All of us require our moral taste to be cultivated and our moral eyesight sharpened. Thus, a course in ethics ought to aim at changing precisely these aspects of our character. But, be forewarned, there are no shortcuts on this journey.

In 1846 Søren Kierkegaard wrote that his mission was not to make difficult matters easier for the sake of his reader's comprehension but to make simple matters more difficult for the sake of his reader's character.[1] Nearly a century later another philosopher, Ludwig Wittgenstein, insisted that his conceptual forays into human life and language (published posthumously as *Philosophical Investigations*) were purposefully written in a style that would not spare readers the trouble of thinking but leave them much to struggle with, because a "present-day teacher of philosophy doesn't select food for his pupil with the aim of flattering his taste, but with the aim of changing it."[2] One senior Cambridge philosopher who admired the junior scholar enough to attend his lectures reported,

> He went on to say that, though philosophy had now been "reduced to a matter of skill," yet this skill, like other skills, is very difficult to acquire. One difficulty

1. Søren Kierkegaard, *Concluding Unscientific Postscript,* with intro. and notes by Walter Lowrie, trans. David F. Swenson (Princeton: Princeton University Press, 1968), 165–66.

2. Ludwig Wittgenstein, *Culture and Value,* ed. G. H. von Wright and Heikki Nyman, trans. Peter Winch, English translation of the amended 2d ed. (Oxford: Basil Blackwell, 1980), 17. See also 76, 77; and *Philosophical Investigations,* ed. G. E. M. Anscombe and Rush Rhees, trans. G. E. M. Anscombe (New York: Macmillan, 1953), x.

> was that it required a "sort of thinking" to which we are not accustomed and to which we have not been trained — a sort of thinking very different from what is required in the sciences. And he said that the required skill could not be acquired by merely hearing the lectures: discussion was essential. As regards his own work, he said it did not matter whether his results [concerning some particular grammatical investigation] were true or not: what mattered was that "a method had been found."[3]

The "method" in philosophy that Wittgenstein exemplified illustrates the close link between ethics and art appreciation.

Wittgenstein explained his method by drawing his readers' attention to the way the word *game* defies general definition:

> Consider for example the proceedings that we call "games." I mean board-games, card-games, ball-games, Olympic games, and so on. What is common to them all? — Don't say: "There *must* be something in common, or they would not be called 'games' " — but *look and see* whether there is anything common to all. — For if you look at them you will not see something that is common to *all,* but similarities, relationships, and a whole series of them at that. To repeat: don't think, but look! — Look for example at board-games, with their multifarious relationships. Now pass to card-games; here you find many correspondences with the first group, but many common features drop out, and others appear. When we pass next to ball-games, much that is common is retained, but much is lost. — Are they all "amusing"? Compare chess with noughts and crosses [tic-tac-toe]. Or is there always winning and losing, or competition between players? Think of patience [solitaire]. In ball games there is winning and losing; but when a child throws his ball at the wall and catches it again, this feature has disappeared. Look at the parts played by skill and luck; and at the difference between skill in chess and skill in tennis. Think now of games like ring-a-ring-a-roses; here is the element of amusement, but how many other characteristic features have disappeared! And we can go through the many, many other groups of games in the same way; can see how similarities crop up and disappear.
>
> And the result of this examination is: we see a complicated network of similarities overlapping and criss-crossing: sometimes overall similarities, sometimes similarities of detail.
>
> I can think of no better expression to characterize these similarities than "family resemblances"; for the various resemblances between members of a family: build, features, color of eyes, gait, temperament, etc. etc. overlap and criss-cross in the same way. — And I shall say: "games" form a family.[4]

Despite the fact that no one thing is common to all games, we are still able to recognize a game when we see one. How do we do this? Here is the important point: *our ability to recognize a family resemblance is more of a tacit skill than an exercise of theoretical reasoning.*

---

3. G. E. Moore, "Wittgenstein's Lectures in 1930–33," in *Philosophical Occasions, 1912–1952,* ed. James C. Klagge and Alfred Normann (Indianapolis and Cambridge: Hackett Publishing, 1993), 113.

4. Wittgenstein, *Philosophical Investigations* §§66, 67.

As we have seen, this is the same sort of skill required by aesthetic judgment. What makes art "good" cannot be explained by any theory of aesthetics. Rather, the word *good* in reference to works of art names a family resemblance. And only to the extent that one's skills have been trained can one use the term *good* authoritatively among those who know art well. What matters most in the case of aesthetic judgment is simply, "Have I been trained to see the family resemblance between this piece of art and other examples of good art?"

Things stand in much the same way for ethics. Ethical judgment does not rely as heavily on theoretical reasoning as once thought. On the contrary (and *pace* Kant, Kohlberg, and so on), both children and mentally handicapped individuals are generally capable of learning right from wrong because recognizing family resemblances such as "cheating" or "lying" or "being cruel" is a skill that doesn't require heavy cognitive horsepower. But it *does* require the formation of a habitual way of seeing. Just as the keenness of one's eye for "good" art is sharpened by exposure to more and more good art, so, too, ethical perspicacity requires prolonged and repeated exposure to examples (usually in the form of stories) of moral truthfulness selected in advance by a moral guide for the express purpose of sharpening our moral vision.

To put matters this way highlights our conviction, as authors of this volume, that moral reasoning itself is very much a communal practice. The canonical voice of our tradition gives the practice of moral reasoning its direction: human life is for living in resonance with our community's stockpile of stories about moral heroes. These stories exemplify the very same sorts of roles in which *we* find ourselves embedded. And in our struggle to "get it right" we are aided by those expert practitioners living in our midst who have struggled longer and more excellently than we.

Your ability to understand the previous paragraph is evidence that you, having worked through the exercises we have assembled, now have what it takes to see what we as authors have been up to all along.

It would have been silly for us to provide a *theory* of ethics when what we were really after in this volume was changing your way of seeing. Granted, providing a theory would have been a much simpler task. But theorizing runs against the grain of what ethics is shown to be after MacIntyre. There is no moral calculus into which we can plug ethical variables and crank out full descriptions of moral obligations. Nor are there any theoretical explanations which anyone (and therefore everyone) is bound to understand. As *After Virtue* has shown, these approaches to ethics are fruitless because "Which variables are germane to such-and-such a case?" and "What constitutes a valid explanation?" are questions that are answered differently by different moral communities. But be very careful not to mistake our appropriation of MacIntyre's work for yet another theoretical attempt to transcend the hubbub. Rather, we have utilized MacIntyre's analysis in three *nontheoretical* ways.

First, we learn from MacIntyre a language or vocabulary by which moral reasoning can be conducted. Since post-Enlightenment ethics has been mired by terms (such as *good* and *justice*) whose histories have been lost or obscured, the learning of an unfamiliar language—one whose terms (for example, *virtue*) are at once very old and very new—by studied attention to the history of ethics once again gives us dry ground upon which to travel. Not surprisingly, since moral reasoning is itself a practice, the central terms of MacIntyre's description (virtue, practice, *telos,* narrative, tradition) name family resemblances that characterize the writings of our own tradition's expert moral practitioners.

The second application we have made of MacIntyre's analysis has been to take seriously the moral voices of our own *particular* (in this case, *Christian*) community. We have tried to show what Christian ethics might look like after MacIntyre by parading the artistry of a number of Christian ethicists before the eyes of you, our reader, in order to help you see in what ways *Christian* and *ethics* fit together.

Third, we take MacIntyre to be correct on one final point: by identifying ourselves as *Christian* thinkers we assume (together with the rest of our community) the responsibility for extending our tradition, practices, and narratives. Our contribution to this corporate task in this case has been to extend our tradition by offering to assist the development of *your* moral virtues by engaging you in the practice of Christian moral reasoning by means of exposure to the form of the Christian narrative embodied in Chapters 4–16.

Cultivating moral taste, like gaining an eye for fine art, requires that we struggle. Having grappled with the collection of "masterpieces" we've assembled for you, we trust that you have gained something of an eye for recognizing virtue as well as a will for cultivating it. In addition, we hope that you will have also gained something of an appreciation for the struggle itself. Although our moral odysseys have just begun, the destination of the journey is the journey itself! For only as we struggle regularly and repeatedly will we come to be at home with the truth.

> No one *can* speak the truth if he has still not mastered himself. He *cannot* speak it—but not because he is not clever enough yet.
>
> The truth can be spoken only by someone who is already *at home* in it; not by someone who still lives in falsehood and reaches out from falsehood toward truth on just one occasion.[5]

5. Wittgenstein, *Culture and Value,* p. 35e.

A Selected Bibliography of the Works of Alasdair MacIntyre

MacIntyre, Alasdair. "Analogy in Metaphysics." *Downside Review* 69 (winter 1950): 45–61.

———. "Notes from the Moral Wilderness I." *New Reasoner* 7 (winter 1958–59): 90–100.

———. *Difficulties in Christian Belief.* London: SCM Press, 1959.

———. "Notes from the Moral Wilderness II." *New Reasoner* 8 (spring 1959): 89–98.

———. "Purpose and Intelligent Action." *Aristotelian Society,* suppl. vol. 34 (1960): 79–96.

———. "A Mistake about Causality in Social Science." In *Philosophy, Politics, and Society,* 2d series, ed. Peter Laslett and W. G. Runciman, 48–70. Oxford: Blackwell, 1962.

———. "Against Utilitarianism." In *Aims in Education: The Philosophical Approach,* ed. T. H. B. Hollins, 1–23. Manchester, England: Manchester University Press, 1964.

———. *A Short History of Ethics.* New York: Collier Books, 1966.

———. "The Fate of Theism." In *The Religious Significance of Atheism,* ed. Alasdair MacIntyre and Paul Ricoeur, 3–29. New York: Columbia University Press, 1969.

———. "Ideology, Social Science, and Revolution." *Comparative Politics* 5, no. 3 (1972): 321–42.

———. "Praxis and Action." *Review of Metaphysics* 25 (June 1972): 737–44.

———. "Predictability and Explanation in the Social Sciences." *Philosophic Exchange* 1, no. 3 (1972): 5–13.

———. "Causality and History." In *Essays on Explanation and Understanding: Studies in the Foundations of Humanities and Social Sciences,* ed. J. Manninen and R. Tuomela, 137–58. Dordrecht and Boston: Reidel, 1976.

———. "Epistemological Crises, Dramatic Narrative, and the Philosophy of Science." *The Monist* 60 (1977): 453–72.

———. "Utilitarianism and the Presuppositions of Cost-Benefit Analysis." In *Values in the Electric Power Industry,* ed. Kenneth Sayre, 217–37. Notre Dame: University of Notre Dame Press, 1977.

———. *Against the Self-Images of the Age.* Notre Dame: University of Notre Dame Press, 1978.

———. "How to Identify Ethical Principles." *The Belmont Report: Ethical Principles and Guidelines for the Protection of Human Subjects of Research I.* U.S. Department of Health, Education, and Welfare. (OS) 78–0013 (1978).

———. "Objectivity in Morality and Objectivity in Science." In *Morals, Science, and Sociality,* ed. H. T. Engelhardt and D. Callahan, 21–29. Hastings-on-Hudson, N.Y.: Hastings Center, 1978.

———. "Corporate Modernity and Moral Judgment: Are They Mutually Exclusive?" In *Ethics and Problems of the 21st Century,* ed. K. E. Goodpaster and K. M. Sayre, 122–35. Notre Dame: University of Notre Dame Press, 1979.

———. "Social Science Methodology as the Ideology of Bureaucratic Authority." In *Through the Looking Glass: Epistemology and the Conduct of Enquiry: An Anthology,* ed. M. S. Falco, 42–58. Washington, D.C.: University Press of America, 1979.

———. "Why Is the Search for the Foundations of Ethics So Frustrating?" *Hastings Center Report* 9 (August 1979): 16–22.

———. "A Crisis in Moral Philosophy." In *Knowing and Valuing the Search for Common Roots,* ed. H. Tristram Engelhardt, 18–35. Hastings-on-Hudson, N.Y.: Hastings Center, 1980.

———. *After Virtue: A Study in Moral Theory.* Notre Dame: University of Notre Dame Press, 1981.

———. "The Magic in the Pronoun 'My.'" *Ethics* 94 (October 1983): 113–25.

———. "Moral Arguments and Social Contexts." *Journal of Philosophy* 80 (1983): 813–17.

———. "Moral Rationality, Tradition, and Aristotle: A Reply to Onora O'Neill, Raimond Gaita, and Stephen R. L. Clark." *Inquiry* 26 (1983): 447–66.

———. *After Virtue.* 2d ed. Notre Dame: University of Notre Dame Press, 1984.

———. "Bernstein's Distorting Mirrors: A Rejoinder." *Soundings* 67 (1984): 30–41.

———. "The Claims of *After Virtue.*" *Analyse und Kritik* 6 (1984): 3–7.

———. "The Relationship of Philosophy to Its Past." In *Philosophy in History: Essays on the Historiography of Philosophy,* ed. Richard Rorty, J. B. Schneewind, and Quentin Skinner. Cambridge: Cambridge University Press, 1984.

———. "The Intelligibility of Action." In *Rationality, Relativism, and the Human Sciences,* ed. J. Margolis, M. Krausz, and R. M. Burian, 63–80. Dordrecht: Martinus Nijhoff, 1986.

———. "Positivism, Sociology, and Practical Reasoning: Notes on Durkheim's *Suicide.*" In *Human Nature and Natural Knowledge,* ed. A. Donogan, Jr., A. N. Perovich, and M. V. Wedin. Dordrecht and Boston: Reidel, 1986.

———. "Which God Ought We to Obey and Why?" *Faith and Philosophy* 3, no. 4 (October 1986): 359–71.

———. "Practical Rationalities as Forms of Social Structure." *Irish Philosophical Journal* 4 (1987): 3–19.

———. "Rival Justices, Competing Rationalities." *This World* 21 (spring 1988): 78–87.

———. "Sophrosune: How a Virtue Can Become Socially Disruptive." *Midwest Studies in Philosophy* 13 (1988): 1–11.

———. *Whose Justice? Which Rationality?* Notre Dame: University of Notre Dame Press, 1988.

———. *First Principles, Final Ends, and Contemporary Philosophy.* Milwaukee: Marquette University Press, 1990.

———. "The Form of the Good, Tradition, and Enquiry." In *Value and Understanding: Essays for Peter Winch,* ed. Raimond Gaita, 242–62. London and New York: Routledge, 1990.

———. "Individual and Social Morality in Japan and the United States: Rival Conceptions of the Self." *Philosophy East and West* 40 (October 1990): 489–97.

———. "Rejoinder to My Critics, Especially Solomon." *Review of Politics* 52 (1990): 375–77.

———. "The Return to Virtue Ethics." In *The Twenty-Fifth Anniversary of Vatican II: A Look Back and a Look Ahead: Proceedings of the Ninth Bishops' Workshop, Dallas, Texas,* ed. Russell E. Smith, 239–49. Braintree, Mass.: Pope John Centre, 1990.

———. *Three Rival Versions of Moral Enquiry: Encyclopaedia, Genealogy, and Tradition.* Notre Dame: University of Notre Dame Press, 1990.

———. *How to Seem Virtuous without Actually Being So,* Occasional Paper Series No. 1 of the Centre for the Study of Cultural Values. Lancaster, England: Lancaster University, 1991.

———. "I'm Not a Communitarian, But . . ." *The Responsive Community* 1, no. 3 (summer 1991): 91–92.

———. "Précis of *Whose Justice? Which Rationality?*" *Philosophy and Phenomenological Research* 51 (1991–92): 149–52.

———. "Plain Persons and Moral Philosophy: Rules, Virtues, and Goods." *American Catholic Philosophical Quarterly* 66 (1992): 3–20.

———. "What Has *Not* Happened in Moral Philosophy." *Yale Journal of Criticism* 5 (1992): 193–99.

———. "How Can We Learn What *Veritatis Splendor* Has to Teach?" *The Thomist* 58, no. 2 (April 1994): 171–95.

Hauerwas, Stanley, and Alasdair MacIntyre, eds. *Revisions: Changing Perspectives in Moral Philosophy.* Notre Dame: University of Notre Dame Press, 1983.

MacIntyre, Alasdair, and Paul Ricoeur, eds. *The Religious Significance of Atheism.* New York: Columbia University Press, 1969.

Toulmin, Stephen, Ronald Hepburn, and Alasdair C. MacIntyre. "The Logical Status of Religious Belief." In *Metaphysical Beliefs: Three Essays,* with a preface by Alasdair MacIntyre, 157–201. London: SCM Press, 1957.

Contributors

Rodney Clapp is editorial director of Brazos Press. His work on theology, ethics, and culture has appeared in more than forty journals and books. His most recent books are *A Peculiar People: The Church as Culture in a Post-Christian Society* and *Border Crossings: Christian Trespasses on Popular Culture and Public Affairs.*

Grady Scott Davis holds the Lewis T. Booker Chair in Religion and Ethics at the University of Richmond in Virginia, where he also chairs the Religion Department. He is the author of *Warcraft and the Fragility of Virtue: An Essay in Aristotelian Ethics* and editor of *Religion and Justice in the War over Bosnia.* He has published numerous articles on the just war theory, the history of ethics, and contemporary moral theory.

Craig Dykstra is vice president for religion at Lilly Endowment Inc. and a minister in the Presbyterian Church (U.S.A.). He previously served as professor of Christian education at Princeton Theological Seminary and at Louisville Presbyterian Theological Seminary. He has contributed to *Practicing Our Faith: A Way of Life for a Searching People*, edited by Dorothy C. Bass, and *Practicing Theology: Beliefs and Practices in Christian Life*, edited by Miroslav Volf and Dorothy C. Bass.

Stephen E. Fowl is professor of theology and departmental chair at Loyola College in Baltimore, Maryland. His scholarly work concentrates on relationships between biblical interpretation and Christian theology and ethics. He has edited *The Theological Interpretation of Scripture: Classic and Contemporary Readings* and is the author of several works, including, most recently, *Engaging Scripture: A Model for Theological Interpretation.* He has served as editor of *Modern Theology* and currently is on the editorial board of the *Journal for the Study of the New Testament* supplements series.

Michael Goldberg is a published author and speaker in the field of ethics and has held two endowed chairs at major universities. He has served Fortune 500 clients as an organizational change consultant with the firm of McKinsey and Company. As special consultant to the Georgia Supreme Court and State Bar, he launched an ABA-recognized professional ethics program for lawyers. In a pastoral capacity, he has been a congregational rabbi and hospice chaplain. His publications include *Theology and Narrative; Jews and Christians: Getting Our Stories Straight; Why Should Jews Survive?;* and *Against the Grain: New Approaches to Professional Ethics.*

Stanley Hauerwas is the Gilbert T. Rowe Professor of Theological Ethics in the Divinity School at Duke University, Durham, North Carolina. His most recent book is *With the Grain of the Universe: The Church's Witness and Natural Theology.*

Richard B. Hays is George Washington Ivey Professor of New Testament at the Divinity School, Duke University, Durham, North Carolina. His books include *The Faith of Jesus Christ; Echoes of Scripture in the Letters of Paul; The Moral Visions of the New Testament: Community, Cross, New Creation; First Corinthians* (Interpretation Commentaries); and *the Letter to the Galatians* (New Interpreter's Bible). He is also the author of numerous articles and reviews in scholarly journals. He was formerly chair of the Pauline Epistles Section of the Society of Biblical Literature, and he has served on the editorial boards of the *Journal of Biblical Literature* and *New Testament Studies.*

Luke Timothy Johnson is the Robert W. Woodruff Professor of New Testament and Christian Origins at Candler School of Theology, Emory University, Atlanta, Georgia. His books include *The Writings of the New Testament: An Interpretation* and *Faith's Freedom: A Classic Spirituality for Contemporary Christians*, as well as commentaries on Luke, Acts, Romans, the Pastoral Letters, and the Letter of James. A version of the essay included here is part of *Scripture and Discernment: Decision Making in the Church.*

L. Gregory Jones is professor of theology and dean of the Divinity School, Duke University, Durham, North Carolina. A noted scholar, teacher, and church leader, he is the author or editor of eleven books, including the acclaimed *Embodying Forgiveness.*

Brad J. Kallenberg is assistant professor of religious studies at the University of Dayton in Ohio. He has published articles in the *Scottish Journal of Theology* and the *Evangelical Quarterly* and is the author of *Ethics as Grammar: Changing the Postmodern Subject.*

D. Stephen Long is associate professor of systematic theology at Garrett-Evangelical Theological Seminary, Evanston, Illinois. He is a United Methodist minister and the author of several works, including, most recently, *The Divine Economy: Theology and the Market* and *The Goodness of God: Theology, Church, and Social Order.*

William F. May is the Cary M. Maguire University Professor of Ethics emeritus, Southern Methodist University, Dallas, Texas, where he also served as founding director of the Cary M. Maguire Center for Ethics and Public Responsibility. He is the author of *The Physician's Covenants*, *The Patient's Ordeals*, and, most recently, *Beleaguered Rulers: The Public Obligation of the Professional.* He serves on the President's Council on Bioethics.

James Wm. McClendon, Jr., was Distinguished Scholar-in-Residence at Fuller Theological Seminary, Pasadena, California. He taught in a seminary of his own Baptist denomination, at the (Episcopal) Church Divinity School in Berkeley, California, and in secular and Catholic universities as well. His books include *Biography as Theology*; *Convictions: Defusing Religious Relativism* (with James. M. Smith); and his three-volume *Systematic Theology*: *Ethics, Doctrine,* and *Witness.*

Nancey Murphy is professor of Christian philosophy at Fuller Theological Seminary, Pasadena, California. She is an ordained minister in the Church of the Brethren. Her research and writing have been on the contributions of contemporary Anglo-American philosophy to theology and on the relations between theology and science. Her books include *Theology in the Ages of Scientific Reasoning*; *Reasoning and Rhetoric in Religion*; *On the Moral Nature of the Universe* (with G. F. R. Ellis); *Beyond Liberalism and Fundamentalism*; *Anglo-American Postmodernity*; and *Reconciling Theology and Science: A Radical Reformation Perspective*. She is co-editor of *Neuroscience and the Person.*

Mark Thiessen Nation is associate professor of theology at Eastern Mennonite Seminary, Harrisonburg, Virginia. He was the founder and director of an ecumenical peace and justice organization, has pastored several churches, and was the director of the London Mennonite Centre, London, England. He is the author of numerous articles and co-editor of four books, most recently, *The Wisdom of the Cross: Essays in Honor of John Howard Yoder* and *Faithfulness and Fortitude: In Conversation with the Theological Ethics of Stanley Hauerwas.*

Tammy Williams is a doctoral candidate in systematic theology at Fuller Theological Seminary, Pasadena, California, where she has also served as an adjunct instructor in the Preaching Department. Her academic interests include ecclesiology and homiletics. She is a licensed preacher with the American Baptist Churches USA, and has preached in seminaries and churches in England and South Africa as a Parish Pulpit Fellow. She recently contributed to *Practicing Theology: Beliefs and Practices in Christian Life,* edited by Miroslav Volf and Dorothy C. Bass.

John Howard Yoder was professor of theology at the University of Notre Dame and a fellow of Notre Dame's Joan B. Kroc Institute for International Peace Studies. He taught at Goshen Biblical Seminary and was its president from 1970 to 1973. His research and writing have been in the fields of Reformation history, ecumenism and church renewal, and Christian social ethics. He served the Mennonite denomination in overseas relief and mission administration. His best-known books are *The Politics of Jesus; The Original Revolution; When War is Unjust; The Priestly Kingdom; Body Politics;* and *The Royal Priesthood.*

Scripture Index

General Index